MADE IN ABYSS 03

Presented by Akihito Tsukushi

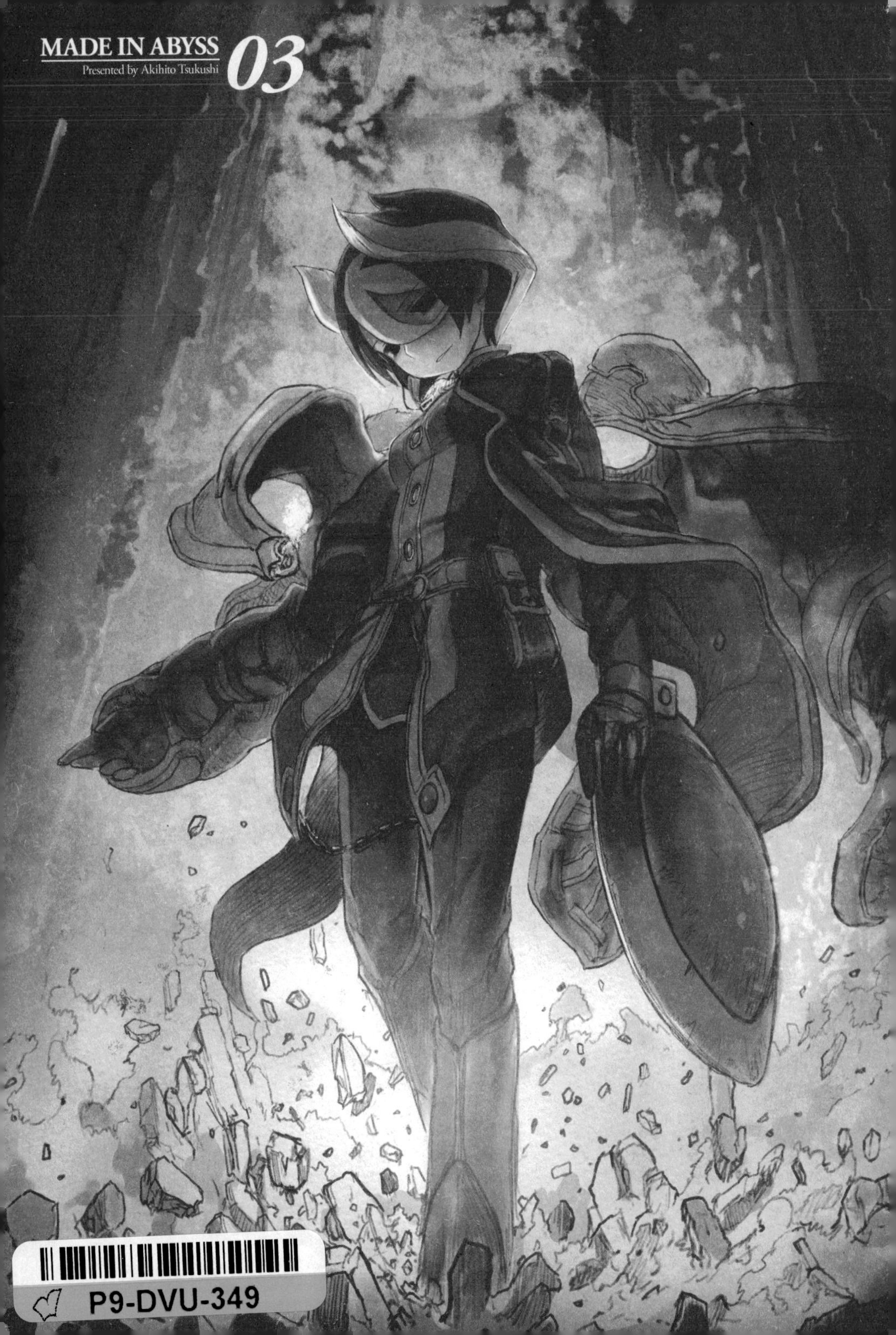

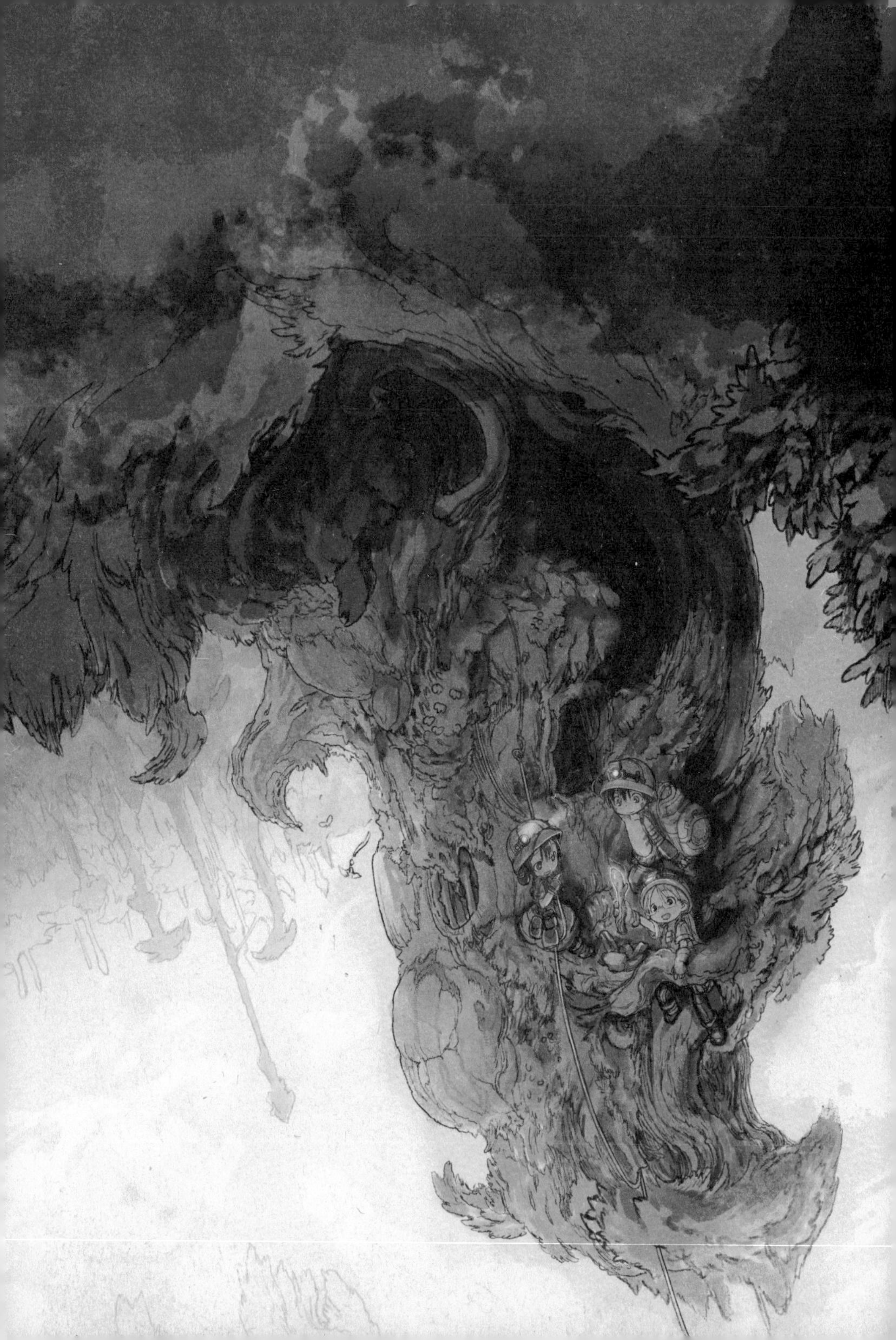

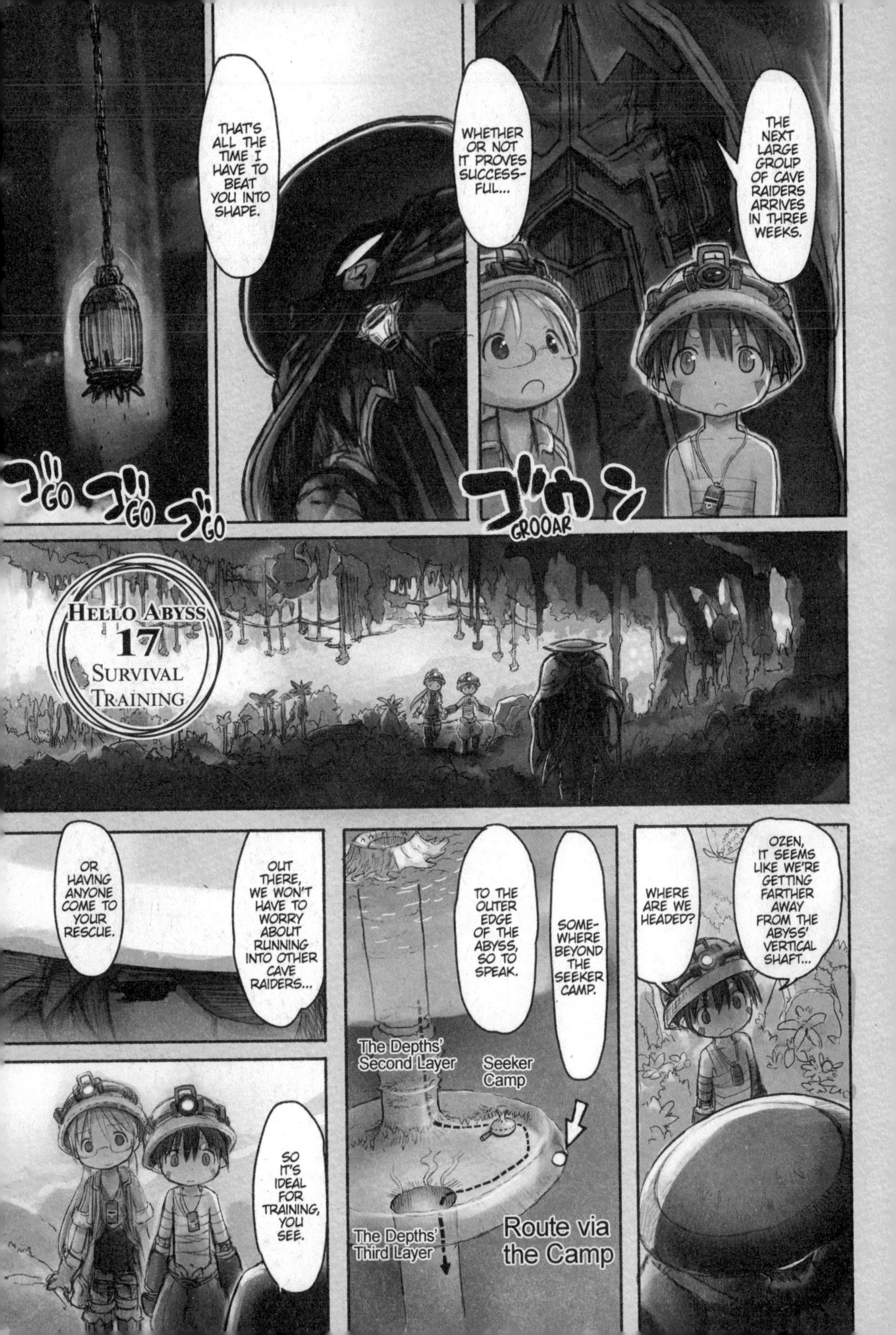
THE NEXT LARGE GROUP OF CAVE RAIDERS ARRIVES IN THREE WEEKS.
WHETHER OR NOT IT PROVES SUCCESS-FUL...
ゴウン GROOAR
THAT'S ALL THE TIME I HAVE TO BEAT YOU INTO SHAPE.
ゴ GO ゴ GO ゴ GO
HELLO ABYSS 17 SURVIVAL TRAINING
OZEN, IT SEEMS LIKE WE'RE GETTING FARTHER AWAY FROM THE ABYSS' VERTICAL SHAFT...
WHERE ARE WE HEADED?
SOME-WHERE BEYOND THE SEEKER CAMP.
TO THE OUTER EDGE OF THE ABYSS, SO TO SPEAK.
The Depths' Second Layer
Seeker Camp
The Depths' Third Layer
Route via the Camp
OUT THERE, WE WON'T HAVE TO WORRY ABOUT RUNNING INTO OTHER CAVE RAIDERS...
OR HAVING ANYONE COME TO YOUR RESCUE.
SO IT'S IDEAL FOR TRAINING, YOU SEE.

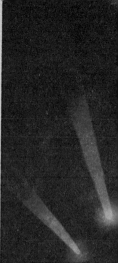

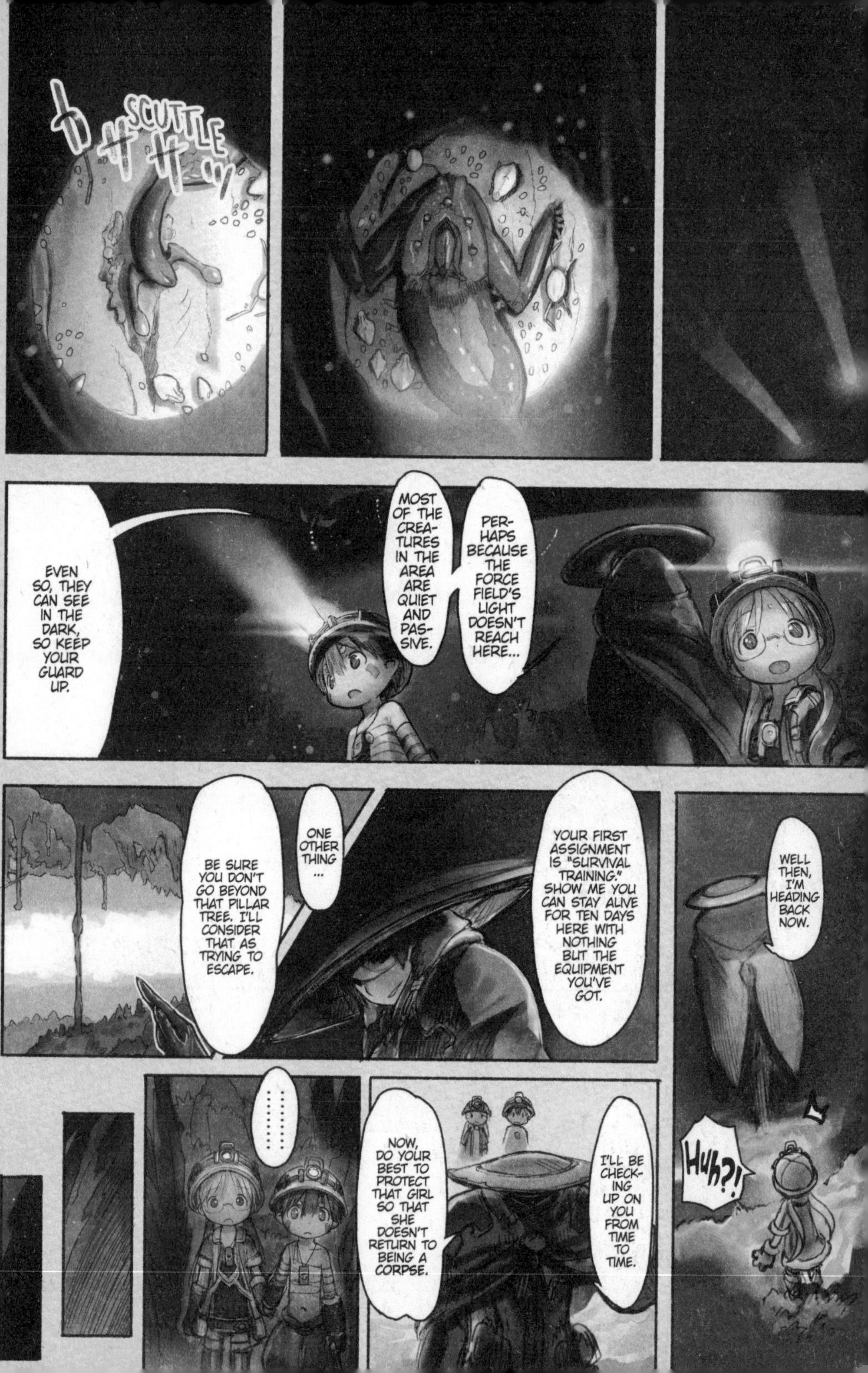
SCUTTLE
PERHAPS BECAUSE THE FORCE FIELD'S LIGHT DOESN'T REACH HERE...
MOST OF THE CREATURES IN THE AREA ARE QUIET AND PASSIVE.
EVEN SO, THEY CAN SEE IN THE DARK, SO KEEP YOUR GUARD UP.
WELL THEN, I'M HEADING BACK NOW.
Huh?!
YOUR FIRST ASSIGNMENT IS "SURVIVAL TRAINING." SHOW ME YOU CAN STAY ALIVE FOR TEN DAYS HERE WITH NOTHING BUT THE EQUIPMENT YOU'VE GOT.
ONE OTHER THING...
BE SURE YOU DON'T GO BEYOND THAT PILLAR TREE. I'LL CONSIDER THAT AS TRYING TO ESCAPE.
I'LL BE CHECKING UP ON YOU FROM TIME TO TIME.
NOW, DO YOUR BEST TO PROTECT THAT GIRL SO THAT SHE DOESN'T RETURN TO BEING A CORPSE.
......

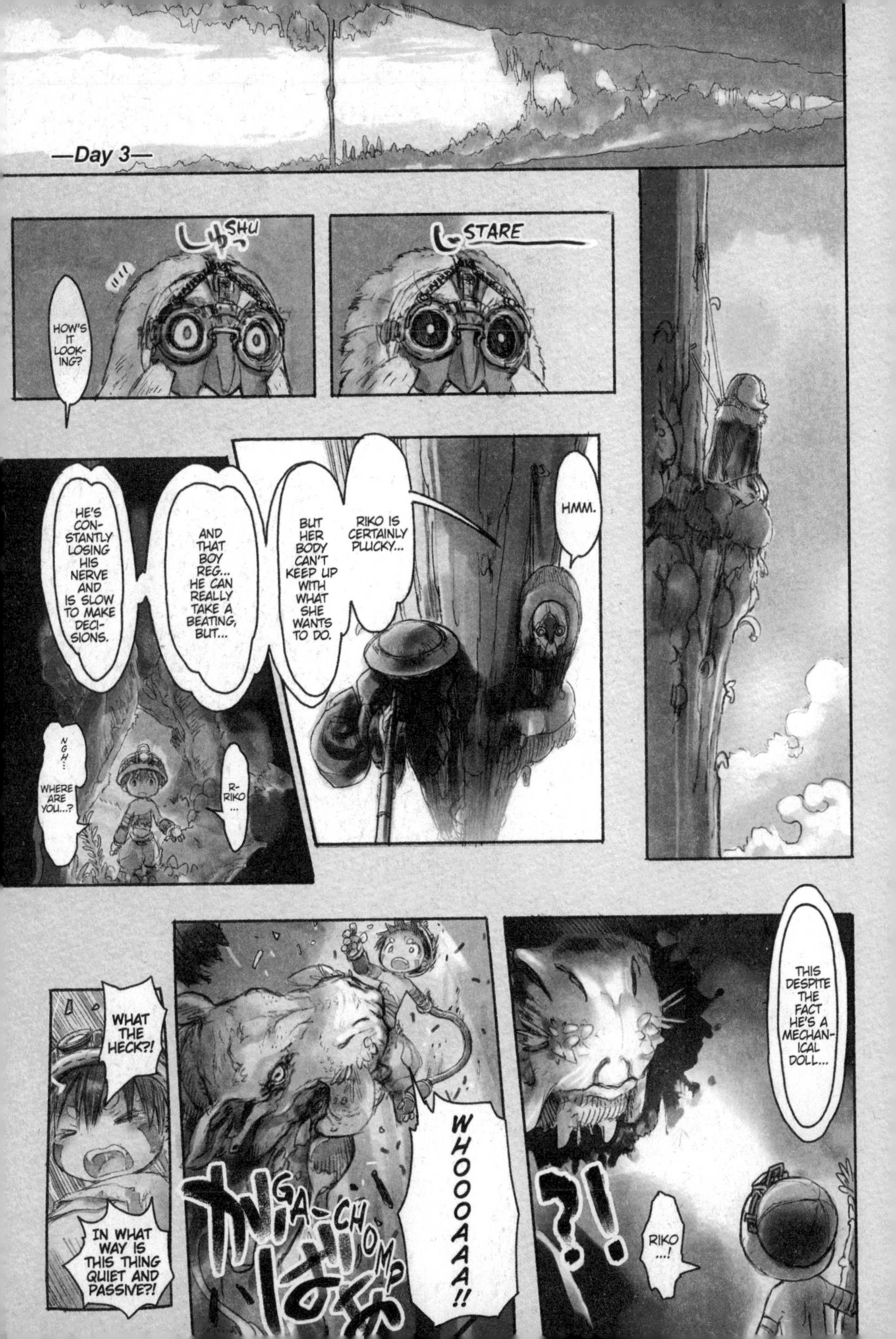
—Day 3—
STARE
SHU
!!!
HOW'S IT LOOKING?
HMM.
RIKO IS CERTAINLY PLUCKY...
BUT HER BODY CAN'T KEEP UP WITH WHAT SHE WANTS TO DO.
AND THAT BOY REG... HE CAN REALLY TAKE A BEATING, BUT...
HE'S CONSTANTLY LOSING HIS NERVE AND IS SLOW TO MAKE DECISIONS.
R-RIKO...
NGH... WHERE ARE YOU...?
THIS DESPITE THE FACT HE'S A MECHANICAL DOLL...
?!
RIKO...!
WHOOOAAA!!
GA-CHOMP
WHAT THE HECK?!
IN WHAT WAY IS THIS THING QUIET AND PASSIVE?!

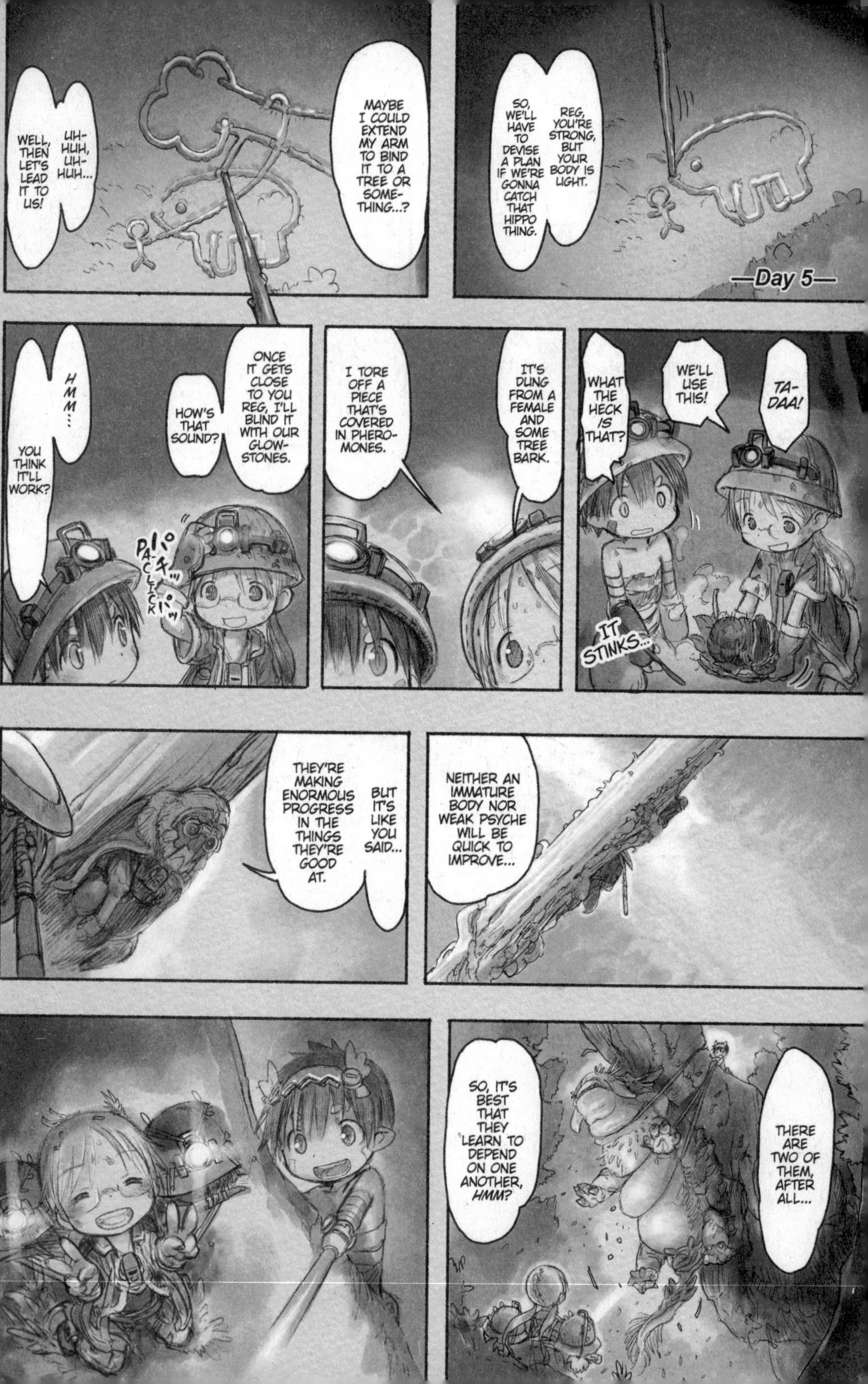
—Day 5—
REG, YOU'RE STRONG, BUT YOUR BODY IS LIGHT.
SO, WE'LL HAVE TO DEVISE A PLAN IF WE'RE GONNA CATCH THAT HIPPO THING.
MAYBE I COULD EXTEND MY ARM TO BIND IT TO A TREE OR SOMETHING...?
UH-HUH, UH-HUH, UH-HUH...
WELL, THEN LET'S LEAD IT TO US!
TA-DAA!
WE'LL USE THIS!
WHAT THE HECK *IS* THAT?
IT STINKS...
IT'S DUNG FROM A FEMALE AND SOME TREE BARK.
I TORE OFF A PIECE THAT'S COVERED IN PHEROMONES.
ONCE IT GETS CLOSE TO YOU REG, I'LL BLIND IT WITH OUR GLOW-STONES.
HOW'S THAT SOUND?
PA-CLICK
HMM...
YOU THINK IT'LL WORK?
NEITHER AN IMMATURE BODY NOR WEAK PSYCHE WILL BE QUICK TO IMPROVE...
BUT IT'S LIKE YOU SAID...
THEY'RE MAKING ENORMOUS PROGRESS IN THE THINGS THEY'RE GOOD AT.
THERE ARE TWO OF THEM, AFTER ALL...
SO, IT'S BEST THAT THEY LEARN TO DEPEND ON ONE ANOTHER, *HMM*?

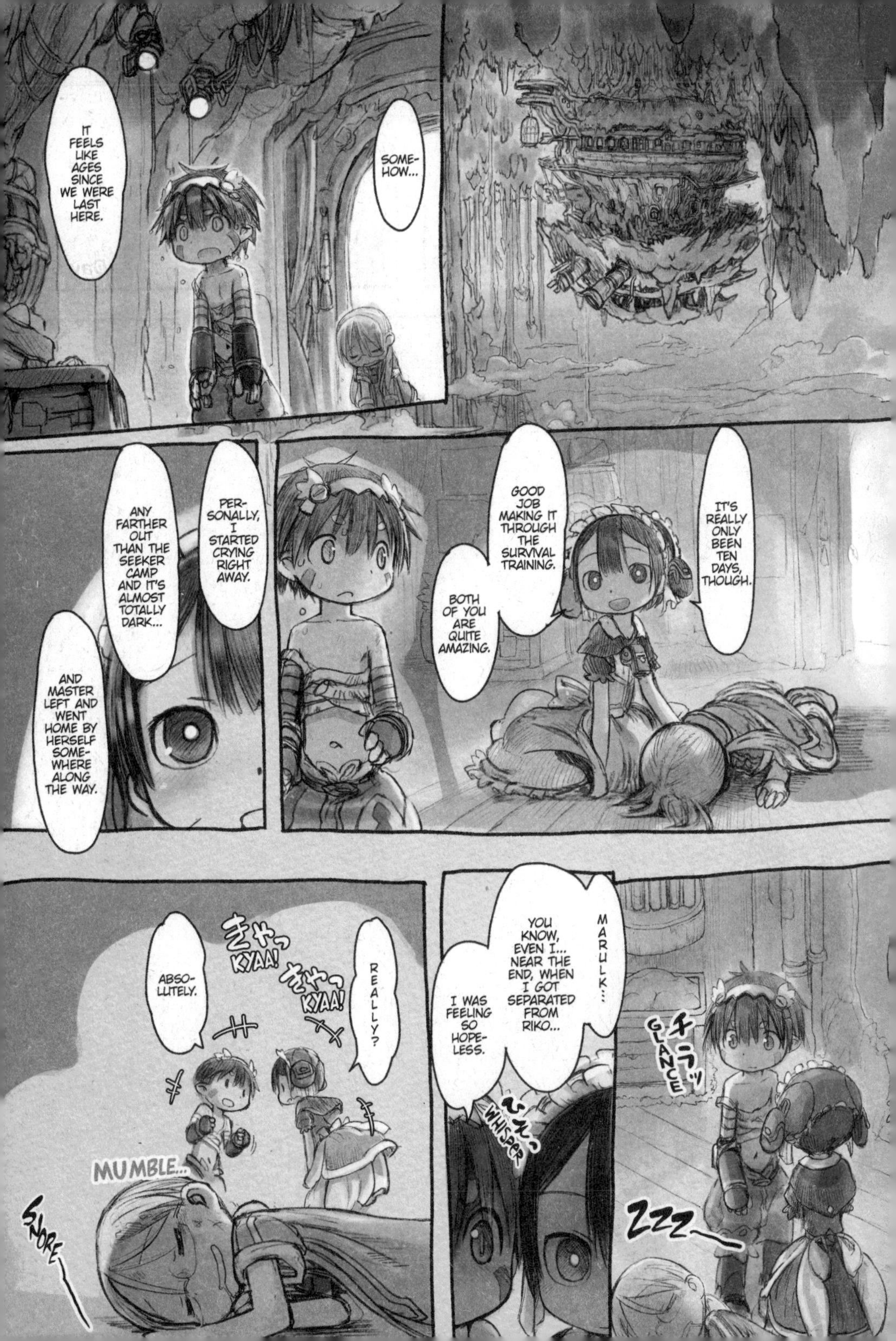
SOME-HOW...
IT FEELS LIKE AGES SINCE WE WERE LAST HERE.
IT'S REALLY ONLY BEEN TEN DAYS, THOUGH.
GOOD JOB MAKING IT THROUGH THE SURVIVAL TRAINING.
BOTH OF YOU ARE QUITE AMAZING.
PER-SONALLY, I STARTED CRYING RIGHT AWAY.
ANY FARTHER OUT THAN THE SEEKER CAMP AND IT'S ALMOST TOTALLY DARK...
AND MASTER LEFT AND WENT HOME BY HERSELF SOME-WHERE ALONG THE WAY.
MARULK...
YOU KNOW, EVEN I... NEAR THE END, WHEN I GOT SEPARATED FROM RIKO...
I WAS FEELING SO HOPELESS.
GLANCE
WHISPER
ZZZ
REALLY?
ABSO-LUTELY.
KYAA!
KYAA!
MUMBLE...
SNORE

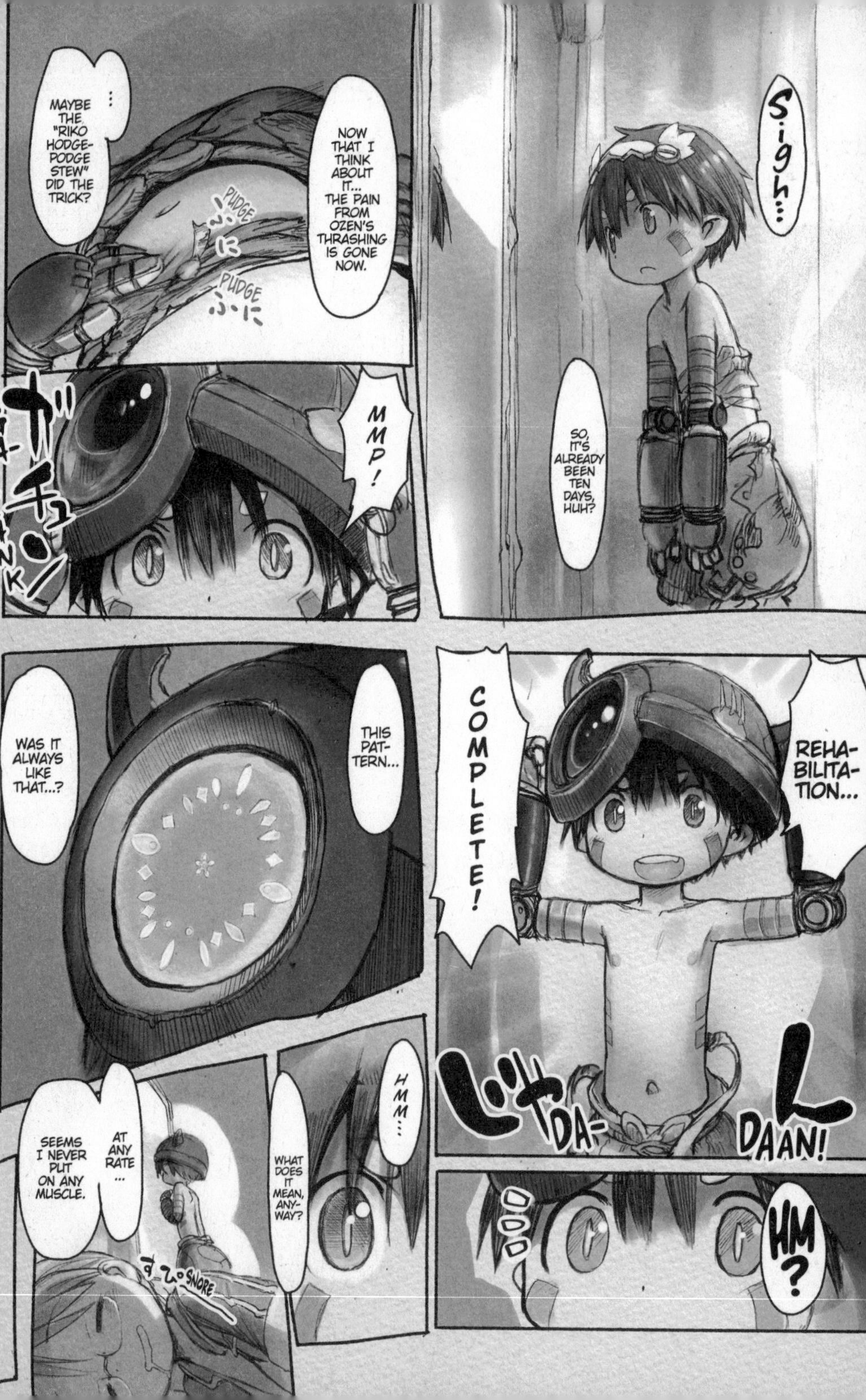
Sigh...
SO, IT'S ALREADY BEEN TEN DAYS, HUH?
NOW THAT I THINK ABOUT IT... THE PAIN FROM OZEN'S THRASHING IS GONE NOW.
...
MAYBE THE "RIKO HODGE-PODGE STEW" DID THE TRICK?
PUDGE
PUDGE
MMP!
GA-CHNK!
REHABILITATION...
COMPLETE!
DA-DAAN!
THIS PATTERN...
WAS IT ALWAYS LIKE THAT...?
HM?
HMM...
WHAT DOES IT MEAN, ANYWAY?
AT ANY RATE...
SEEMS I NEVER PUT ON ANY MUSCLE.
SNORE

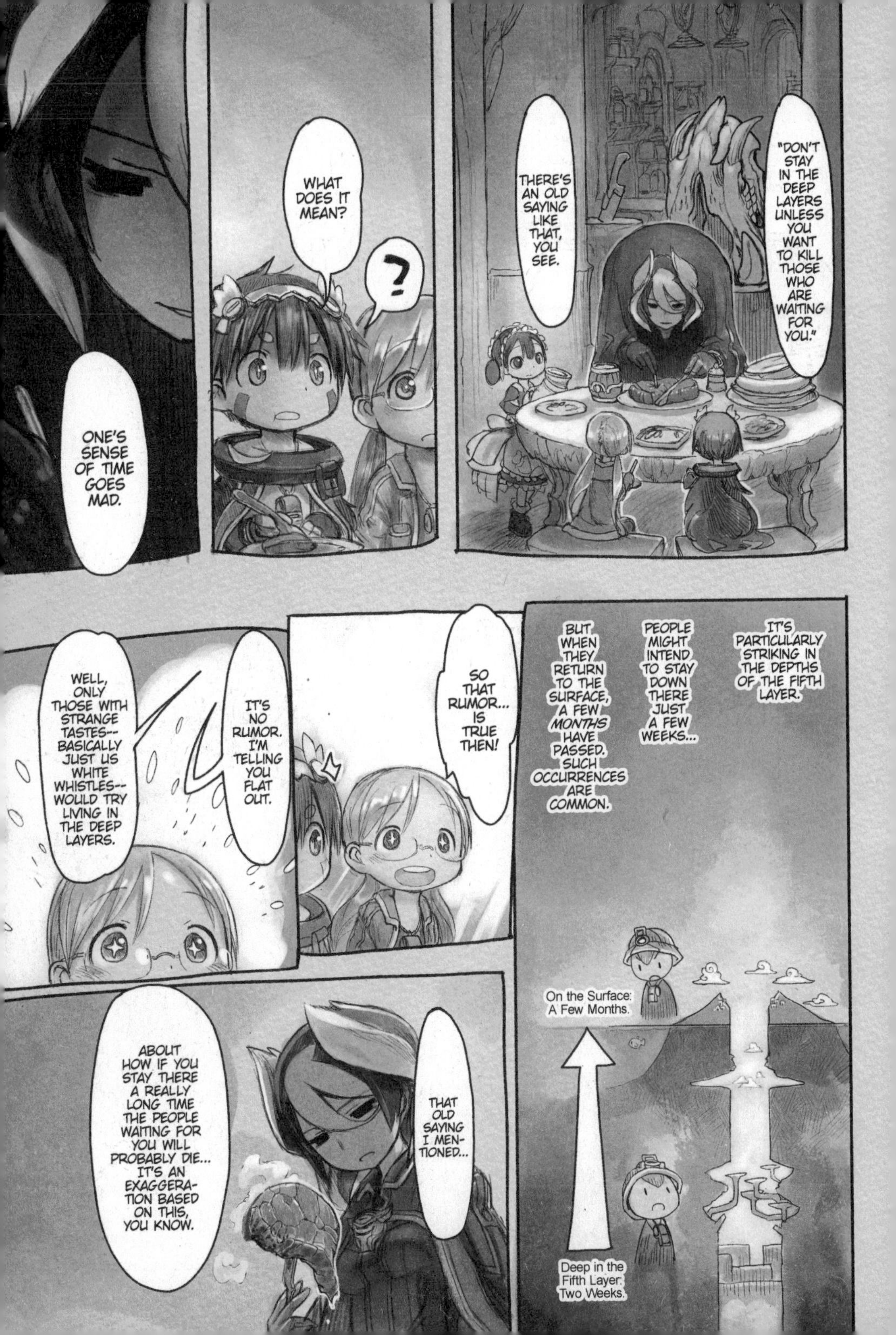
"DON'T STAY IN THE DEEP LAYERS UNLESS YOU WANT TO KILL THOSE WHO ARE WAITING FOR YOU."
THERE'S AN OLD SAYING LIKE THAT, YOU SEE.
WHAT DOES IT MEAN?
?
ONE'S SENSE OF TIME GOES MAD.
IT'S PARTICULARLY STRIKING IN THE DEPTHS OF THE FIFTH LAYER.
PEOPLE MIGHT INTEND TO STAY DOWN THERE JUST A FEW WEEKS...
BUT WHEN THEY RETURN TO THE SURFACE, A FEW *MONTHS* HAVE PASSED. SUCH OCCURRENCES ARE COMMON.
On the Surface: A Few Months.
Deep in the Fifth Layer: Two Weeks.
SO THAT RUMOR... IS TRUE THEN!
IT'S NO RUMOR. I'M TELLING YOU FLAT OUT.
WELL, ONLY THOSE WITH STRANGE TASTES--BASICALLY JUST US WHITE WHISTLES--WOULD TRY LIVING IN THE DEEP LAYERS.
THAT OLD SAYING I MENTIONED...
ABOUT HOW IF YOU STAY THERE A REALLY LONG TIME THE PEOPLE WAITING FOR YOU WILL PROBABLY DIE... IT'S AN EXAGGERATION BASED ON THIS, YOU KNOW.

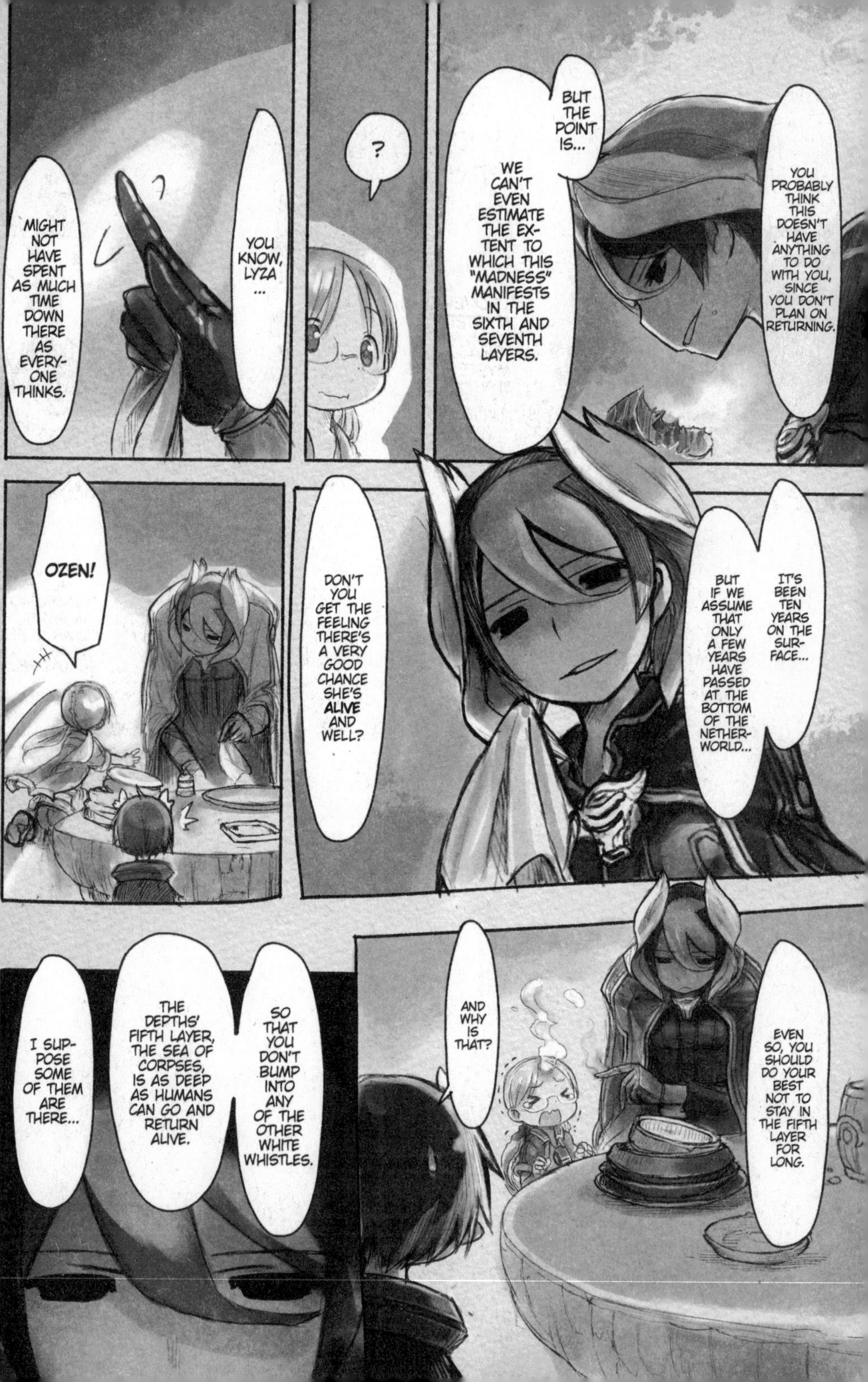
YOU PROBABLY THINK THIS DOESN'T HAVE ANYTHING TO DO WITH YOU, SINCE YOU DON'T PLAN ON RETURNING.
BUT THE POINT IS...
WE CAN'T EVEN ESTIMATE THE EXTENT TO WHICH THIS "MADNESS" MANIFESTS IN THE SIXTH AND SEVENTH LAYERS.
?
YOU KNOW, LYZA...
MIGHT NOT HAVE SPENT AS MUCH TIME DOWN THERE AS EVERYONE THINKS.
IT'S BEEN TEN YEARS ON THE SURFACE...
BUT IF WE ASSUME THAT ONLY A FEW YEARS HAVE PASSED AT THE BOTTOM OF THE NETHERWORLD...
DON'T YOU GET THE FEELING THERE'S A VERY GOOD CHANCE SHE'S **ALIVE** AND WELL?
OZEN!
EVEN SO, YOU SHOULD DO YOUR BEST NOT TO STAY IN THE FIFTH LAYER FOR LONG.
AND WHY IS THAT?
SO THAT YOU DON'T BUMP INTO ANY OF THE OTHER WHITE WHISTLES.
THE DEPTHS' FIFTH LAYER, THE SEA OF CORPSES, IS AS DEEP AS HUMANS CAN GO AND RETURN ALIVE.
I SUPPOSE SOME OF THEM ARE THERE...

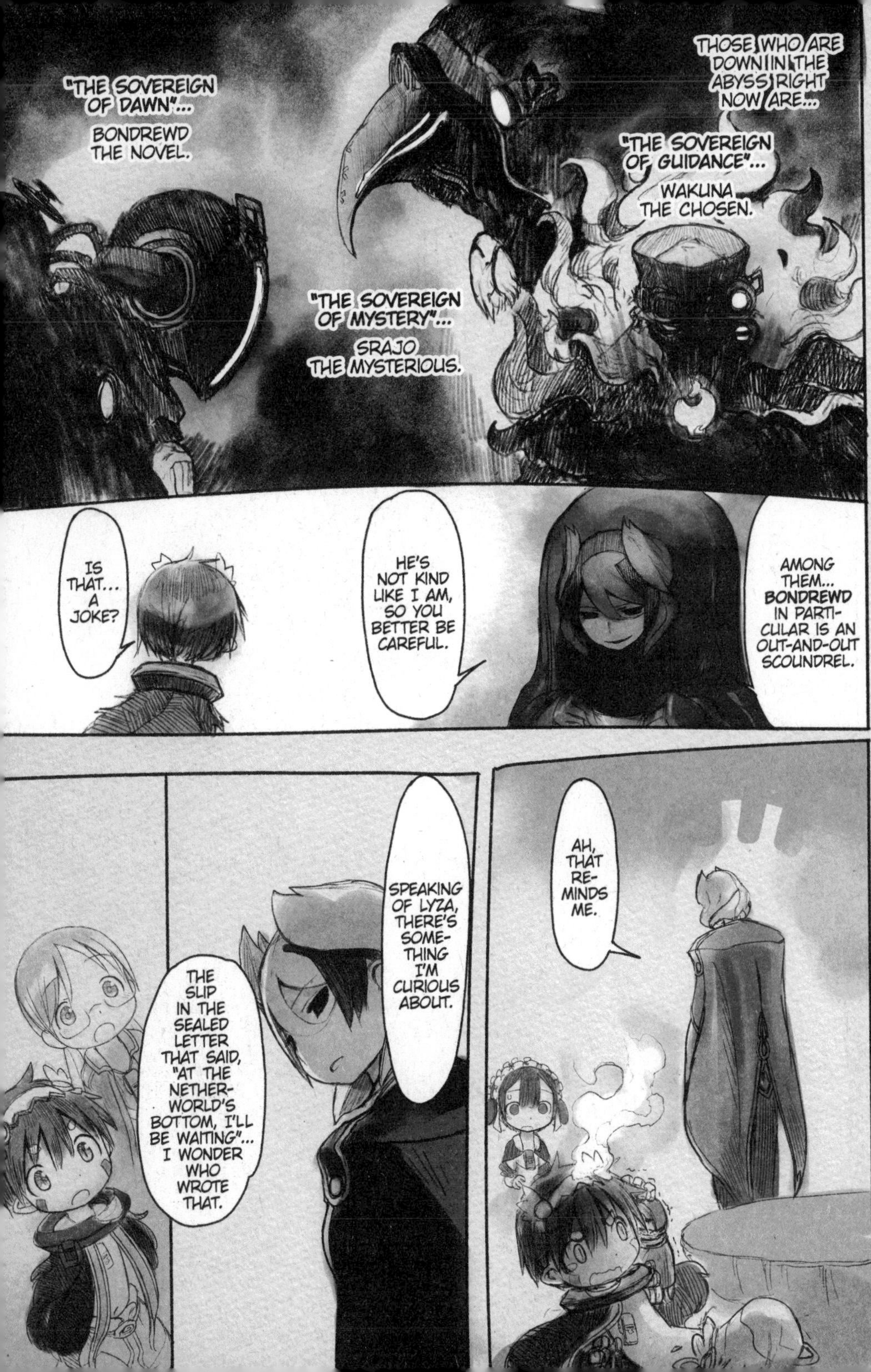
THOSE WHO ARE DOWN IN THE ABYSS RIGHT NOW ARE...
"THE SOVEREIGN OF GUIDANCE"...
WAKUNA THE CHOSEN.
"THE SOVEREIGN OF DAWN"...
BONDREWD THE NOVEL.
"THE SOVEREIGN OF MYSTERY"...
SRAJO THE MYSTERIOUS.
AMONG THEM... BONDREWD IN PARTICULAR IS AN OUT-AND-OUT SCOUNDREL.
HE'S NOT KIND LIKE I AM, SO YOU BETTER BE CAREFUL.
IS THAT... A JOKE?
AH, THAT REMINDS ME.
SPEAKING OF LYZA, THERE'S SOMETHING I'M CURIOUS ABOUT.
THE SLIP IN THE SEALED LETTER THAT SAID, "AT THE NETHERWORLD'S BOTTOM, I'LL BE WAITING"... I WONDER WHO WROTE THAT.

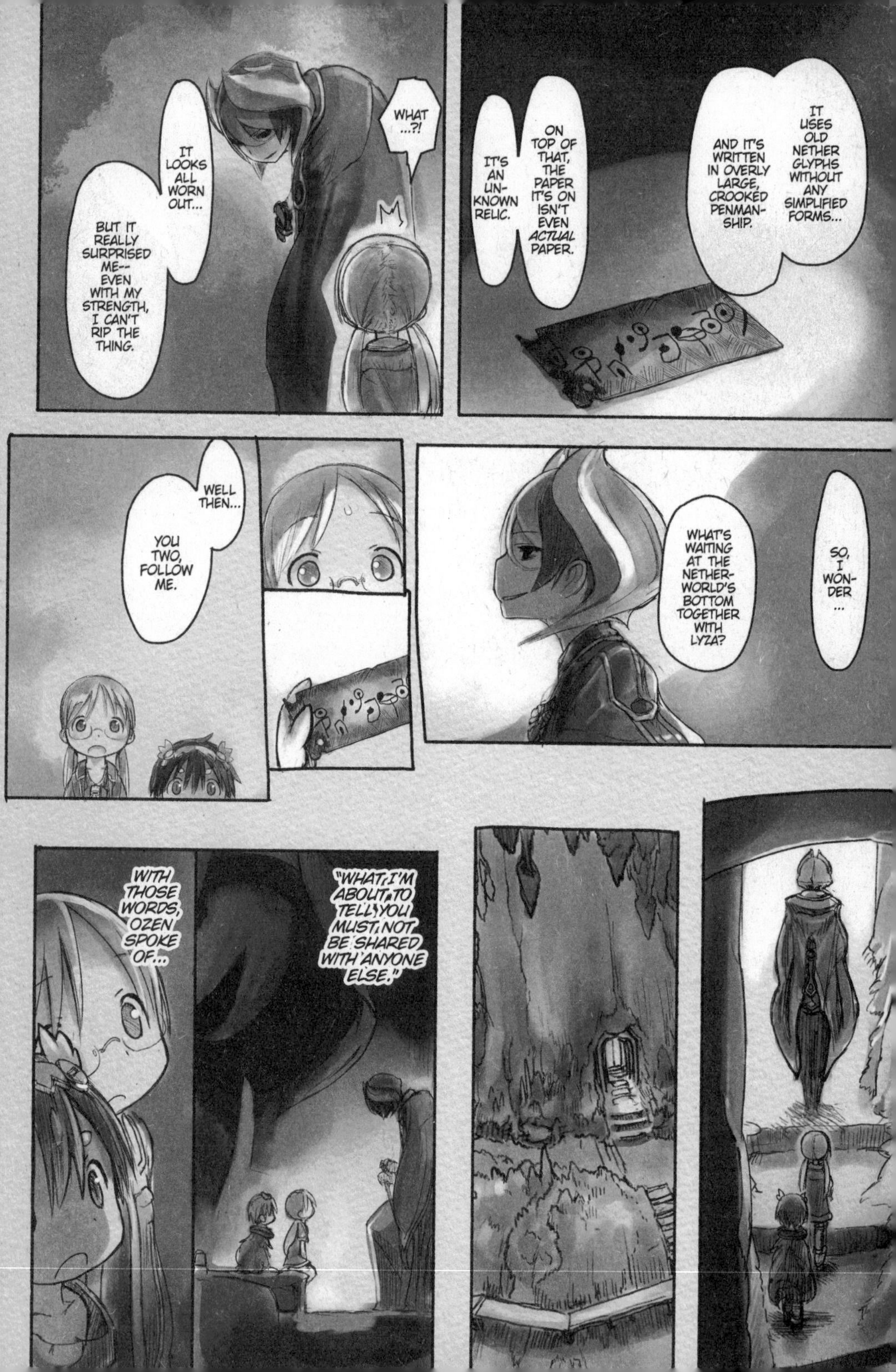
IT USES OLD NETHER GLYPHS WITHOUT ANY SIMPLIFIED FORMS...
AND IT'S WRITTEN IN OVERLY LARGE, CROOKED PENMANSHIP.
ON TOP OF THAT, THE PAPER IT'S ON ISN'T EVEN ACTUAL PAPER.
IT'S AN UNKNOWN RELIC.
WHAT ...?!
IT LOOKS ALL WORN OUT...
BUT IT REALLY SURPRISED ME-- EVEN WITH MY STRENGTH, I CAN'T RIP THE THING.
SO, I WONDER...
WHAT'S WAITING AT THE NETHERWORLD'S BOTTOM TOGETHER WITH LYZA?
WELL THEN...
YOU TWO, FOLLOW ME.
"WHAT I'M ABOUT TO TELL YOU MUST NOT BE SHARED WITH ANYONE ELSE."
WITH THOSE WORDS, OZEN SPOKE OF...

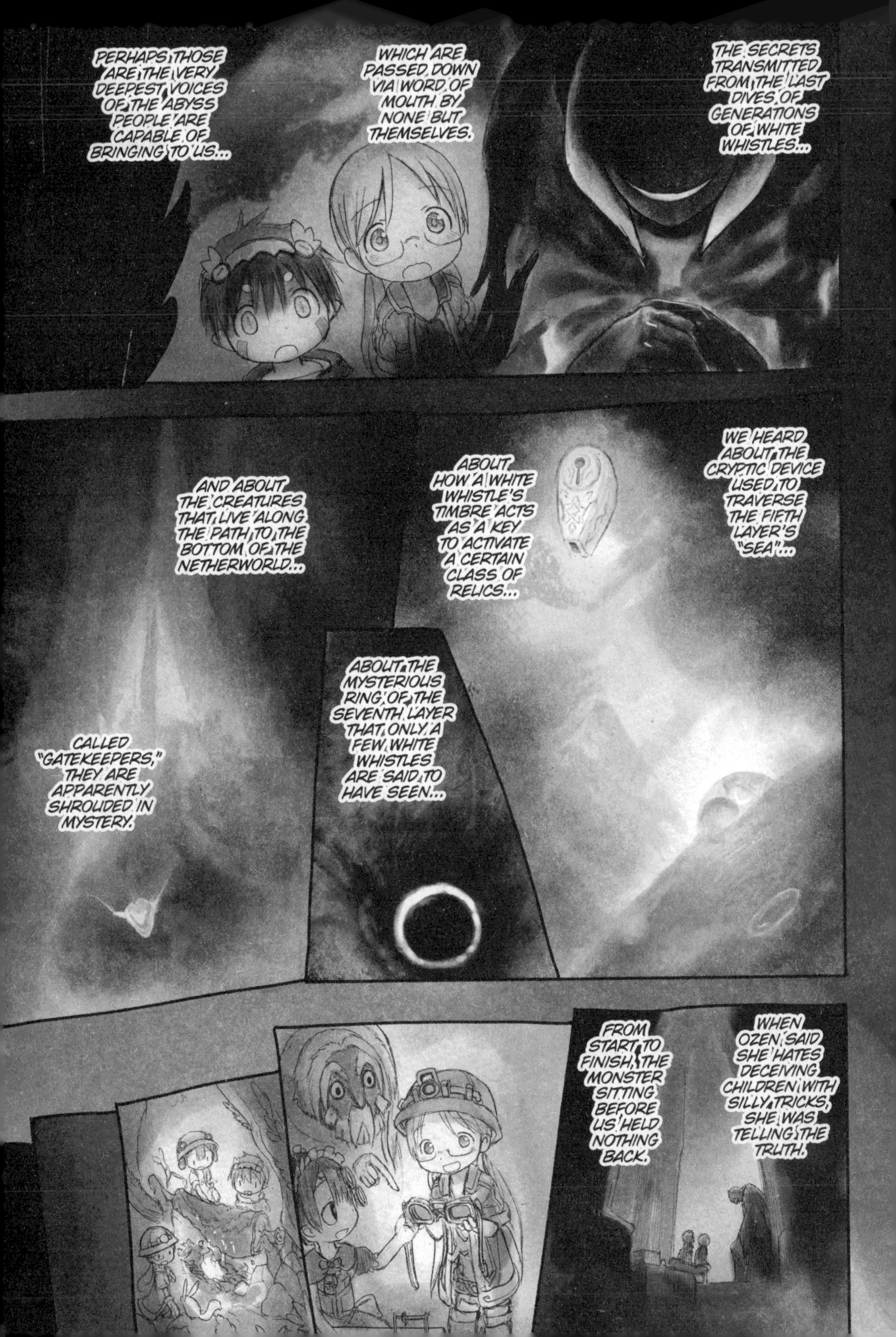
THE SECRETS TRANSMITTED FROM THE LAST DIVES OF GENERATIONS OF WHITE WHISTLES...
WHICH ARE PASSED DOWN VIA WORD OF MOUTH BY NONE BUT THEMSELVES.
PERHAPS THOSE ARE THE VERY DEEPEST VOICES OF THE ABYSS PEOPLE ARE CAPABLE OF BRINGING TO US...
WE HEARD ABOUT THE CRYPTIC DEVICE USED TO TRAVERSE THE FIFTH LAYER'S "SEA"...
ABOUT HOW A WHITE WHISTLE'S TIMBRE ACTS AS A KEY TO ACTIVATE A CERTAIN CLASS OF RELICS...
ABOUT THE MYSTERIOUS RING OF THE SEVENTH LAYER THAT ONLY A FEW WHITE WHISTLES ARE SAID TO HAVE SEEN...
AND ABOUT THE CREATURES THAT LIVE ALONG THE PATH TO THE BOTTOM OF THE NETHERWORLD...
CALLED "GATEKEEPERS," THEY ARE APPARENTLY SHROUDED IN MYSTERY.
WHEN OZEN SAID SHE HATES DECEIVING CHILDREN WITH SILLY TRICKS, SHE WAS TELLING THE TRUTH.
FROM START TO FINISH, THE MONSTER SITTING BEFORE US HELD NOTHING BACK.

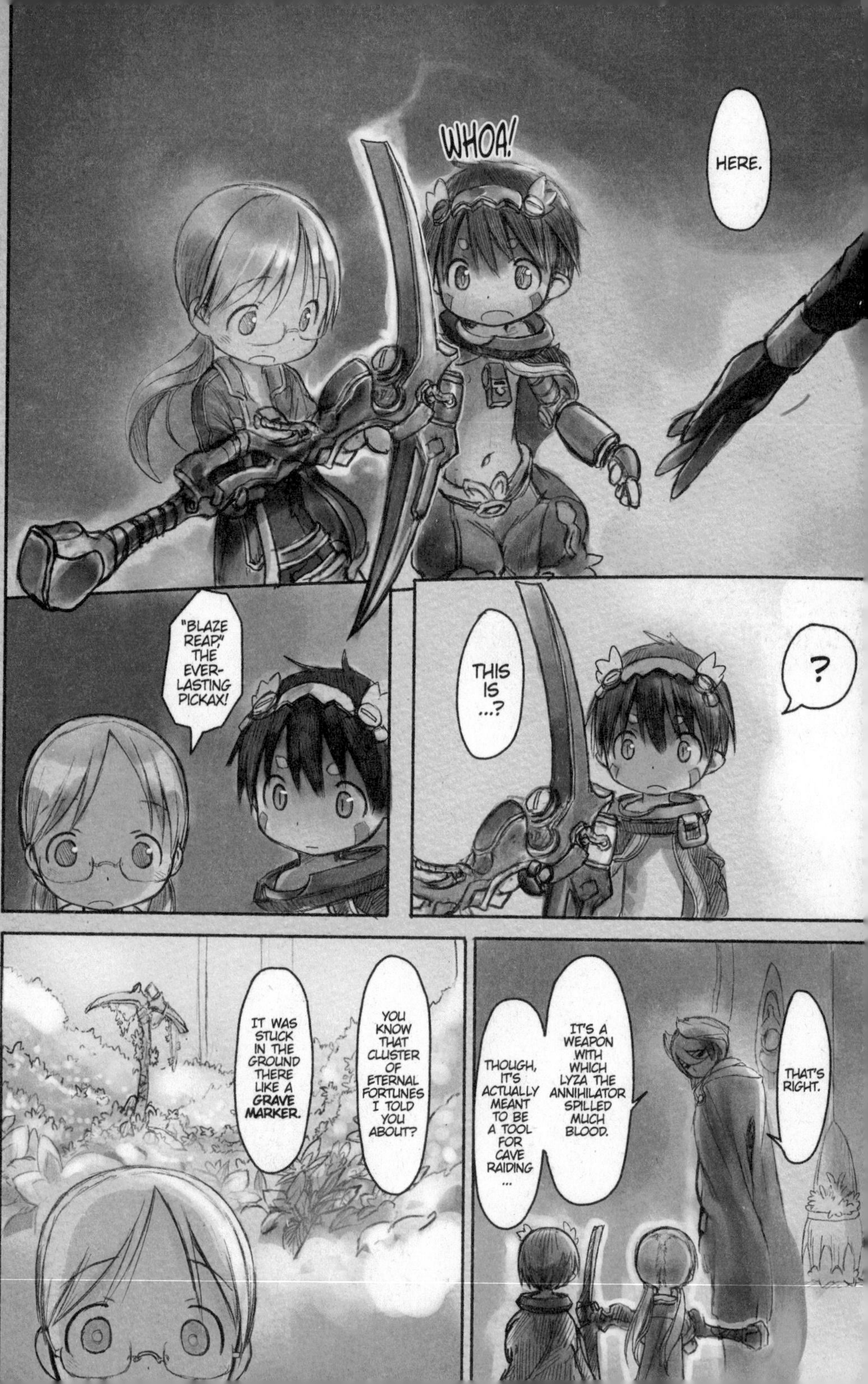
HERE.
WHOA!
?
THIS IS ...?
"BLAZE REAP," THE EVER-LASTING PICKAX!
THAT'S RIGHT.
IT'S A WEAPON WITH WHICH LYZA THE ANNIHILATOR SPILLED MUCH BLOOD.
THOUGH, IT'S ACTUALLY MEANT TO BE A TOOL FOR CAVE RAIDING ...
YOU KNOW THAT CLUSTER OF ETERNAL FORTUNES I TOLD YOU ABOUT?
IT WAS STUCK IN THE GROUND THERE LIKE A **GRAVE MARKER.**

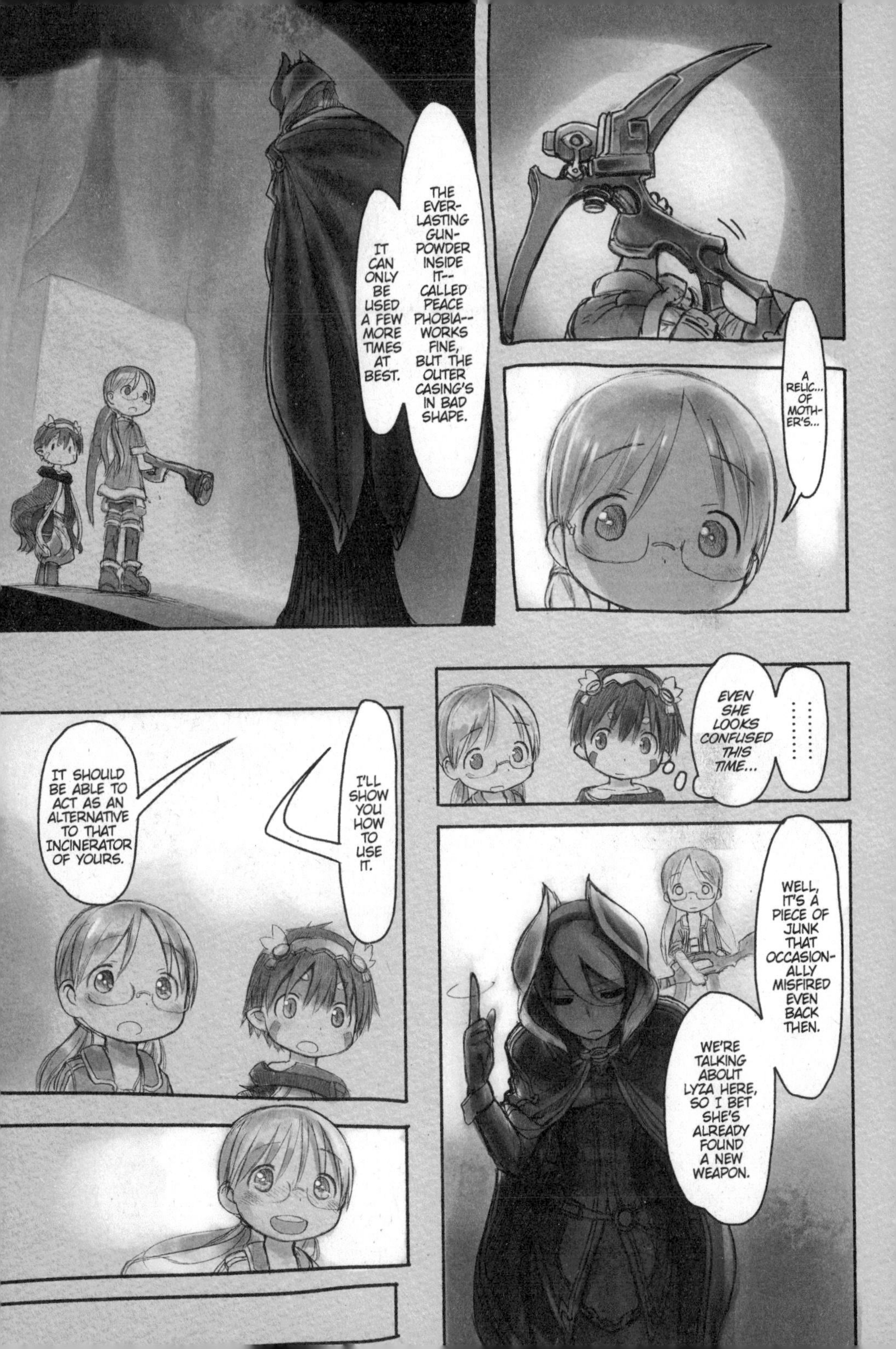
A RELIC... OF MOTHER'S...
THE EVER-LASTING GUN-POWDER INSIDE IT-- CALLED PEACE PHOBIA-- WORKS FINE, BUT THE OUTER CASING'S IN BAD SHAPE.
IT CAN ONLY BE USED A FEW MORE TIMES AT BEST.
......
EVEN SHE LOOKS CONFUSED THIS TIME...
WELL, IT'S A PIECE OF JUNK THAT OCCASION-ALLY MISFIRED EVEN BACK THEN.
WE'RE TALKING ABOUT LYZA HERE, SO I BET SHE'S ALREADY FOUND A NEW WEAPON.
I'LL SHOW YOU HOW TO USE IT.
IT SHOULD BE ABLE TO ACT AS AN ALTERNATIVE TO THAT INCINERATOR OF YOURS.

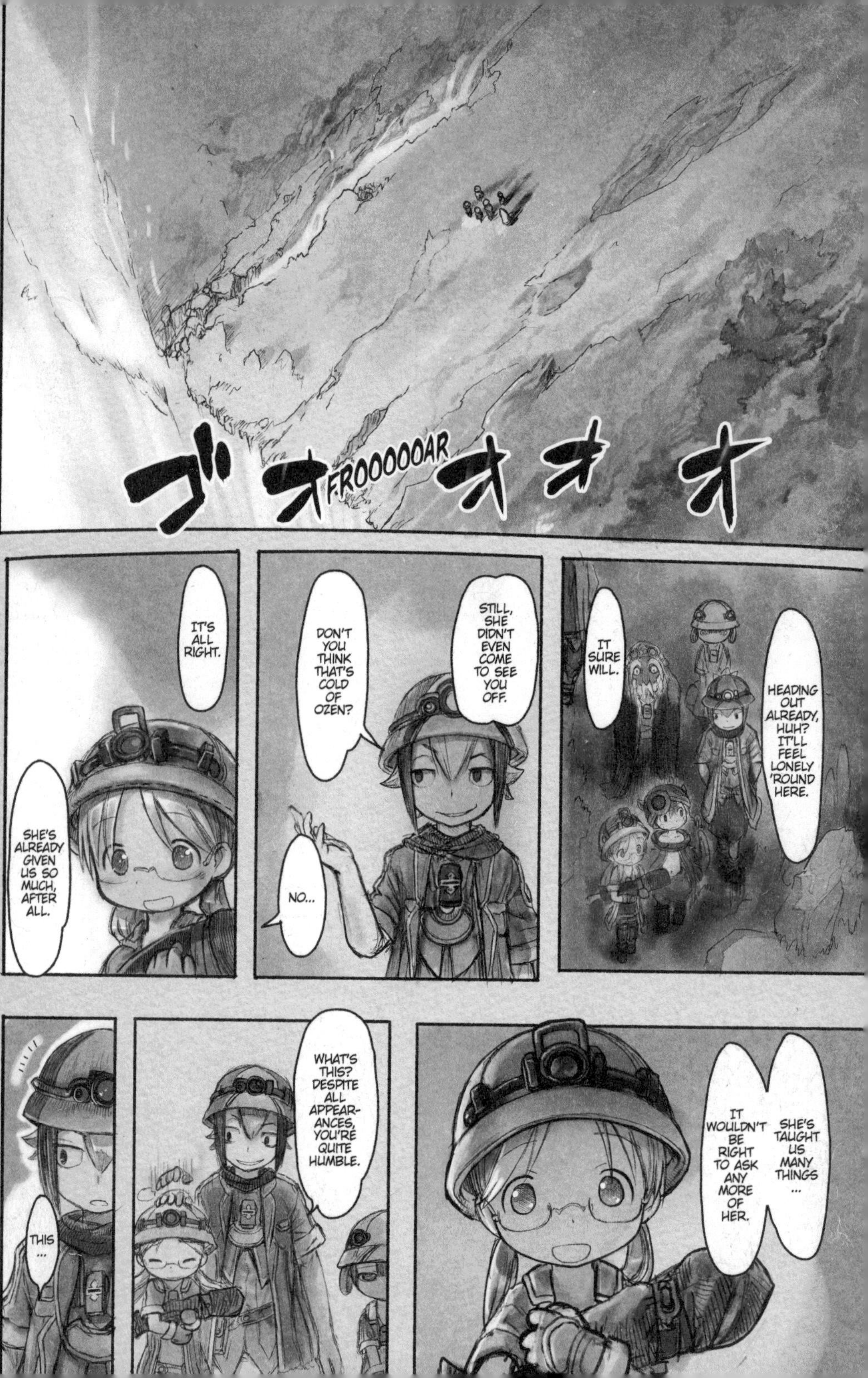
ゴオFROOOOOARオオオ
HEADING OUT ALREADY, HUH? IT'LL FEEL LONELY 'ROUND HERE.
IT SURE WILL.
STILL, SHE DIDN'T EVEN COME TO SEE YOU OFF.
DON'T YOU THINK THAT'S COLD OF OZEN?
NO...
IT'S ALL RIGHT.
SHE'S ALREADY GIVEN US SO MUCH, AFTER ALL.
SHE'S TAUGHT US MANY THINGS...
IT WOULDN'T BE RIGHT TO ASK ANY MORE OF HER.
WHAT'S THIS? DESPITE ALL APPEARANCES, YOU'RE QUITE HUMBLE.
THIS...

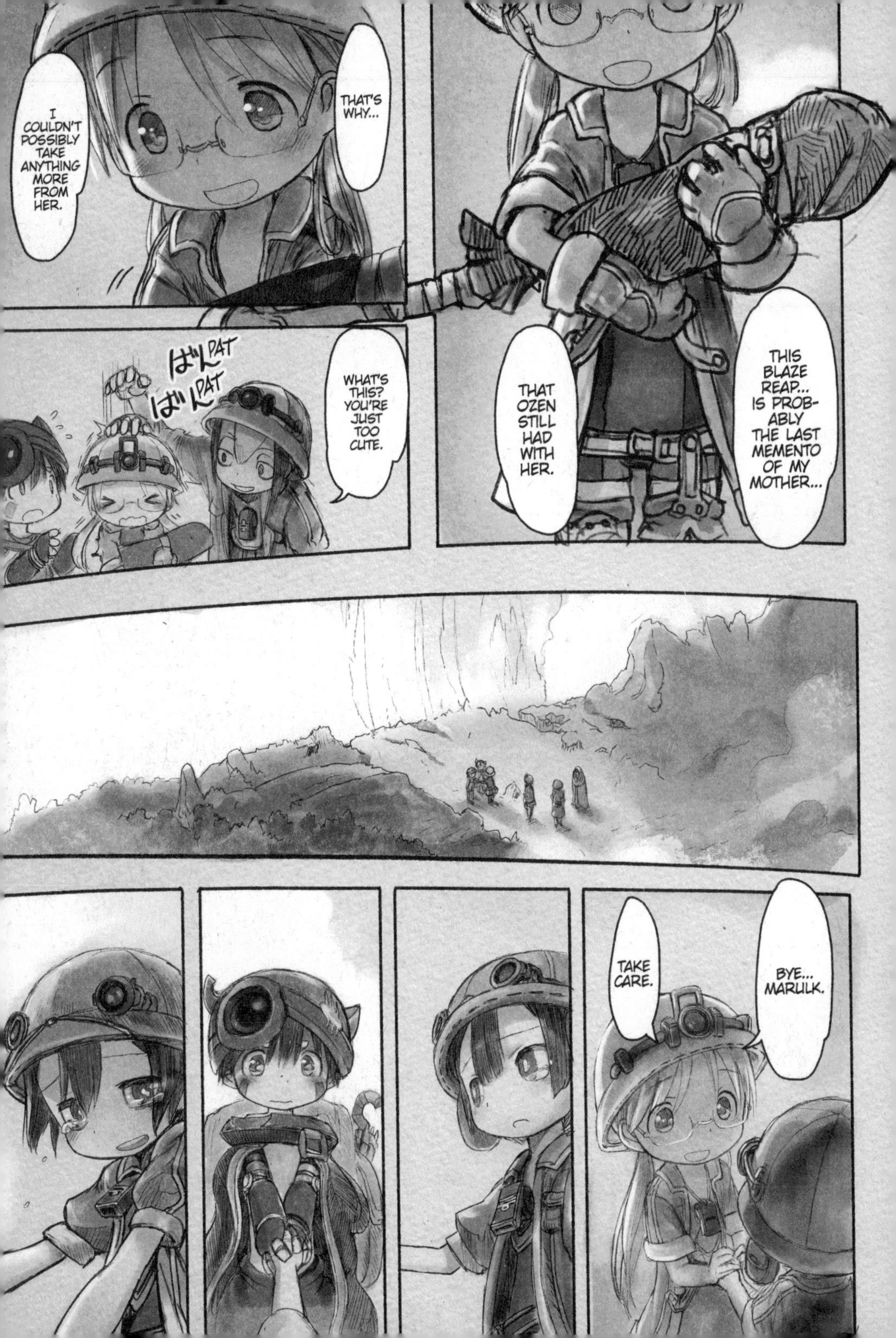
THIS BLAZE REAP... IS PROBABLY THE LAST MEMENTO OF MY MOTHER...
THAT OZEN STILL HAD WITH HER.
THAT'S WHY...
I COULDN'T POSSIBLY TAKE ANYTHING MORE FROM HER.
WHAT'S THIS? YOU'RE JUST TOO CUTE.
ばんPAT
ばんPAT
BYE... MARULK.
TAKE CARE.

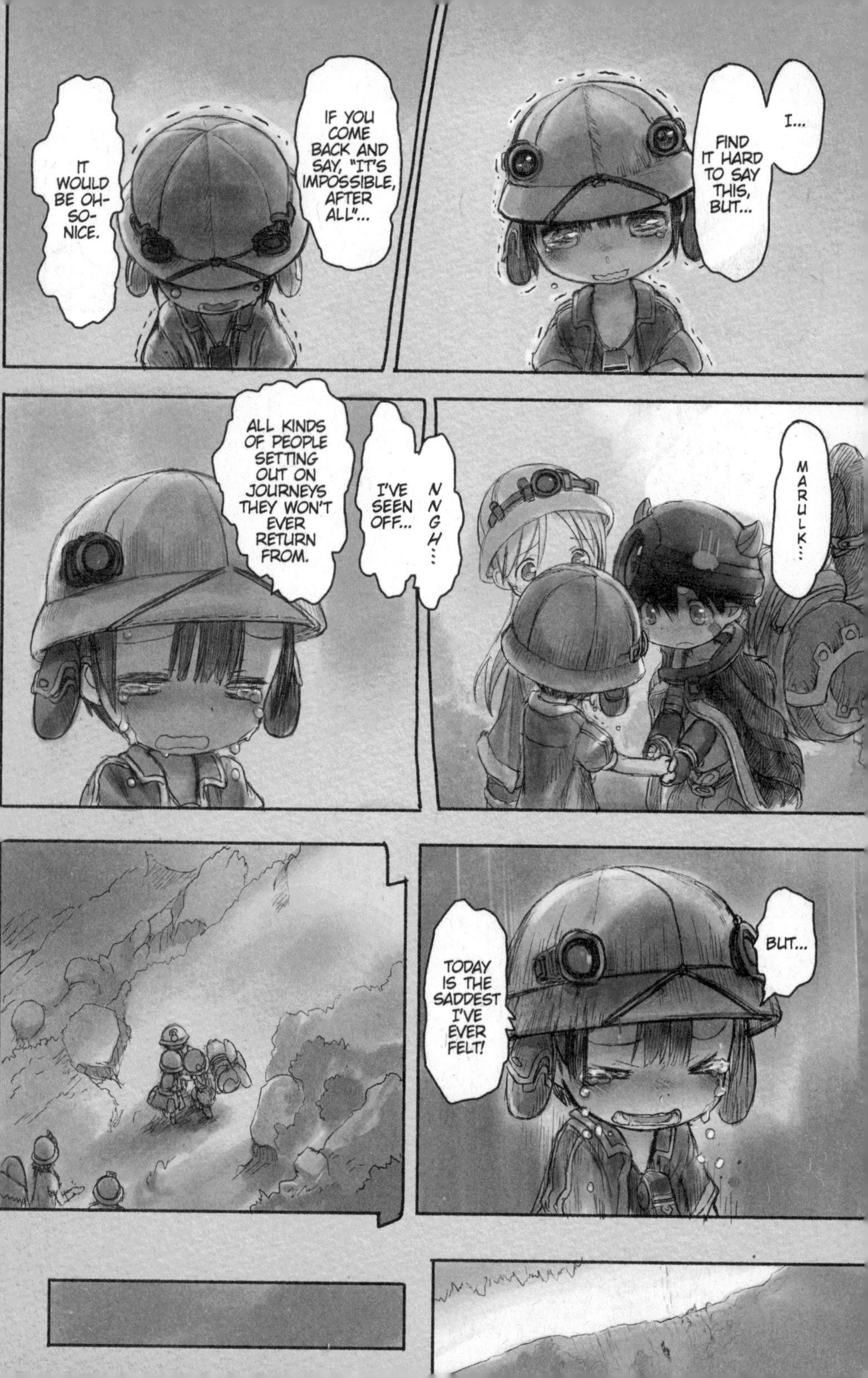
I...
FIND IT HARD TO SAY THIS, BUT...
IF YOU COME BACK AND SAY, "IT'S IMPOSSIBLE, AFTER ALL"...
IT WOULD BE OH-SO-NICE.
MARULK...
NNGH...
I'VE SEEN OFF...
ALL KINDS OF PEOPLE SETTING OUT ON JOURNEYS THEY WON'T EVER RETURN FROM.
BUT...
TODAY IS THE SADDEST I'VE EVER FELT!

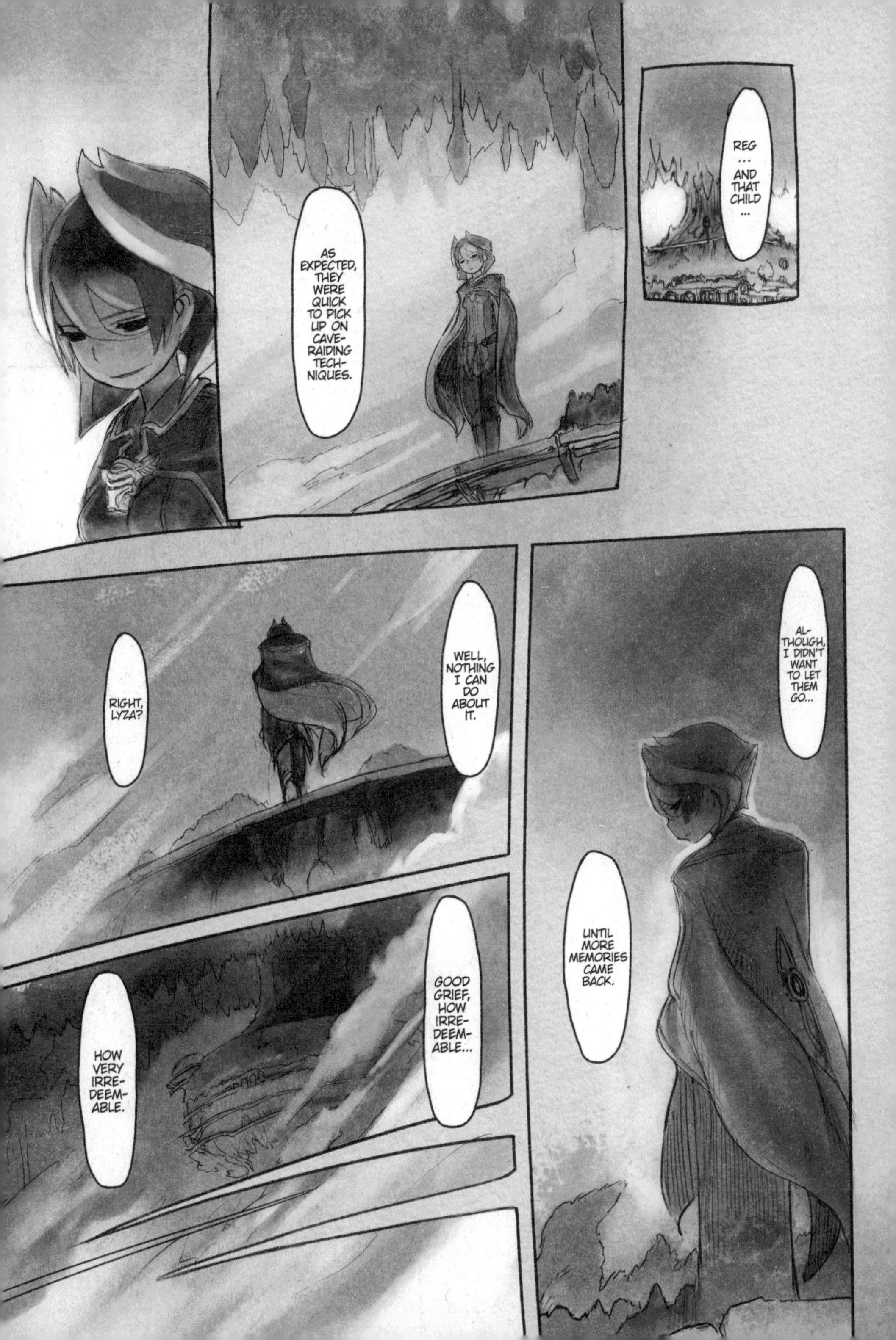
REG... AND THAT CHILD...
AS EXPECTED, THEY WERE QUICK TO PICK UP ON CAVE-RAIDING TECHNIQUES.
ALTHOUGH, I DIDN'T WANT TO LET THEM GO...
UNTIL MORE MEMORIES CAME BACK.
WELL, NOTHING I CAN DO ABOUT IT.
RIGHT, LYZA?
GOOD GRIEF, HOW IRREDEEMABLE...
HOW VERY IRREDEEMABLE.

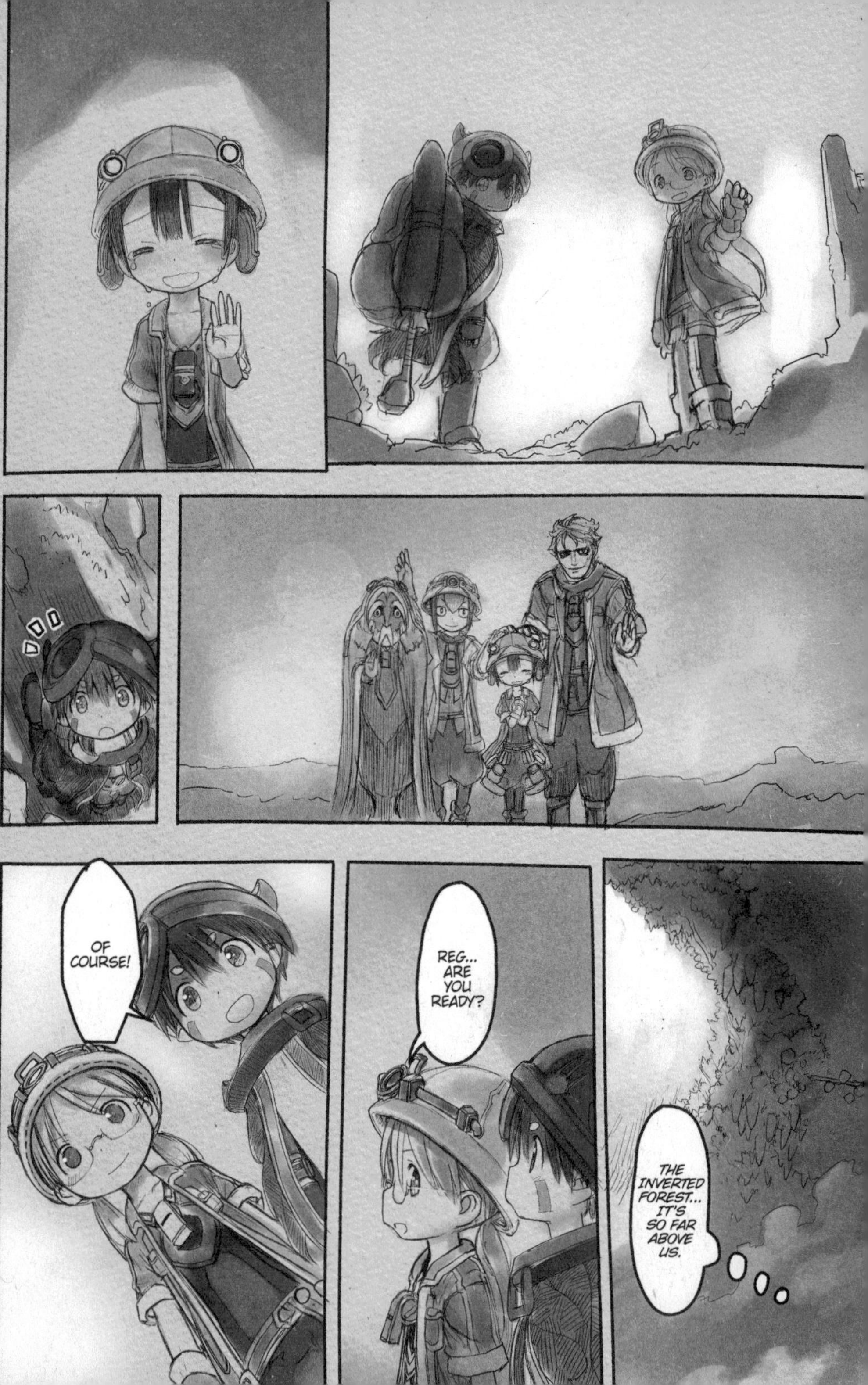
THE INVERTED FOREST... IT'S SO FAR ABOVE US.
REG... ARE YOU READY?
OF COURSE!

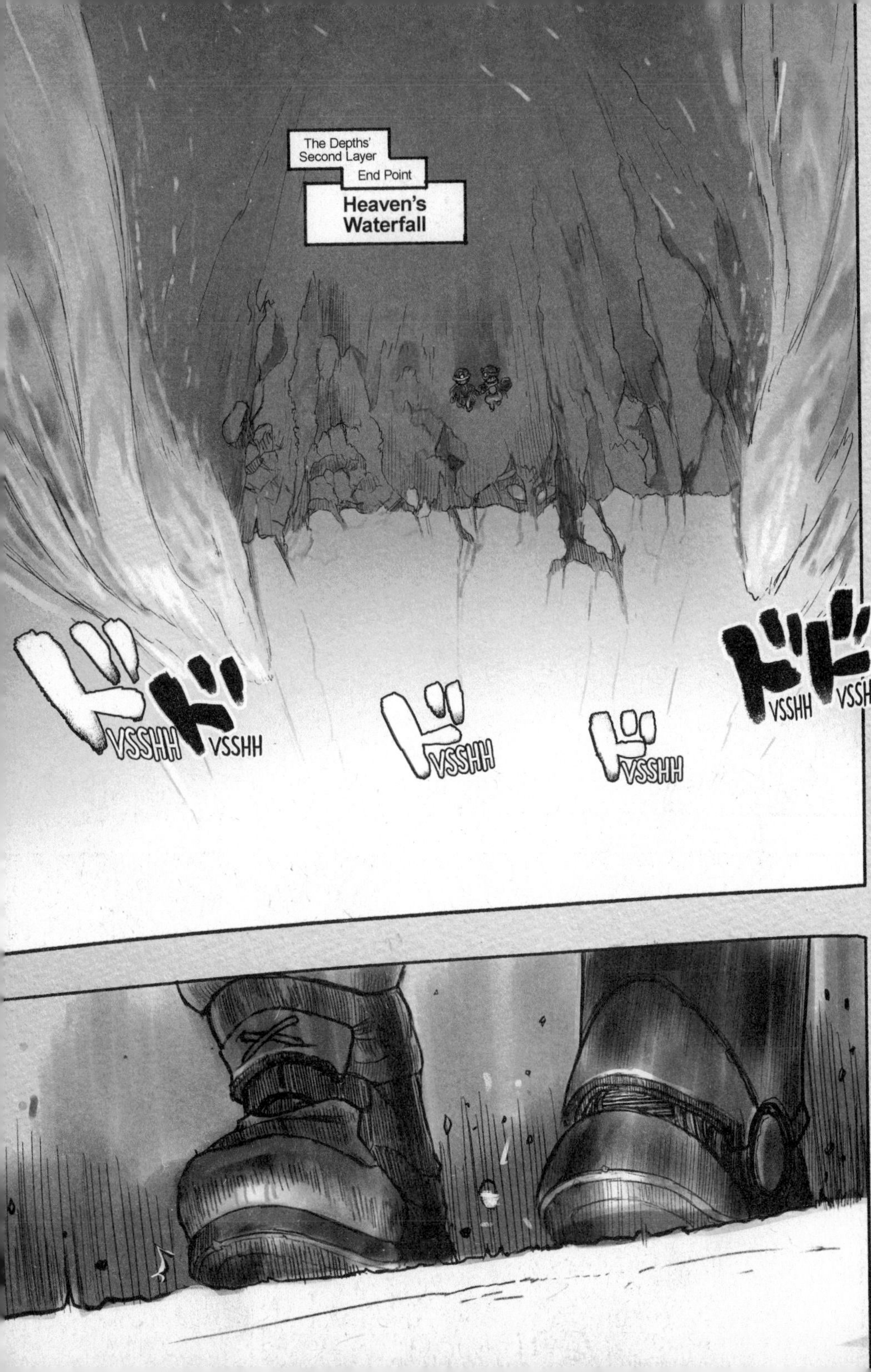
The Depths' Second Layer
End Point
Heaven's Waterfall
ドド VSSHH VSSHH
ド VSSHH
ド VSSHH
ドド VSSHH VSSHH

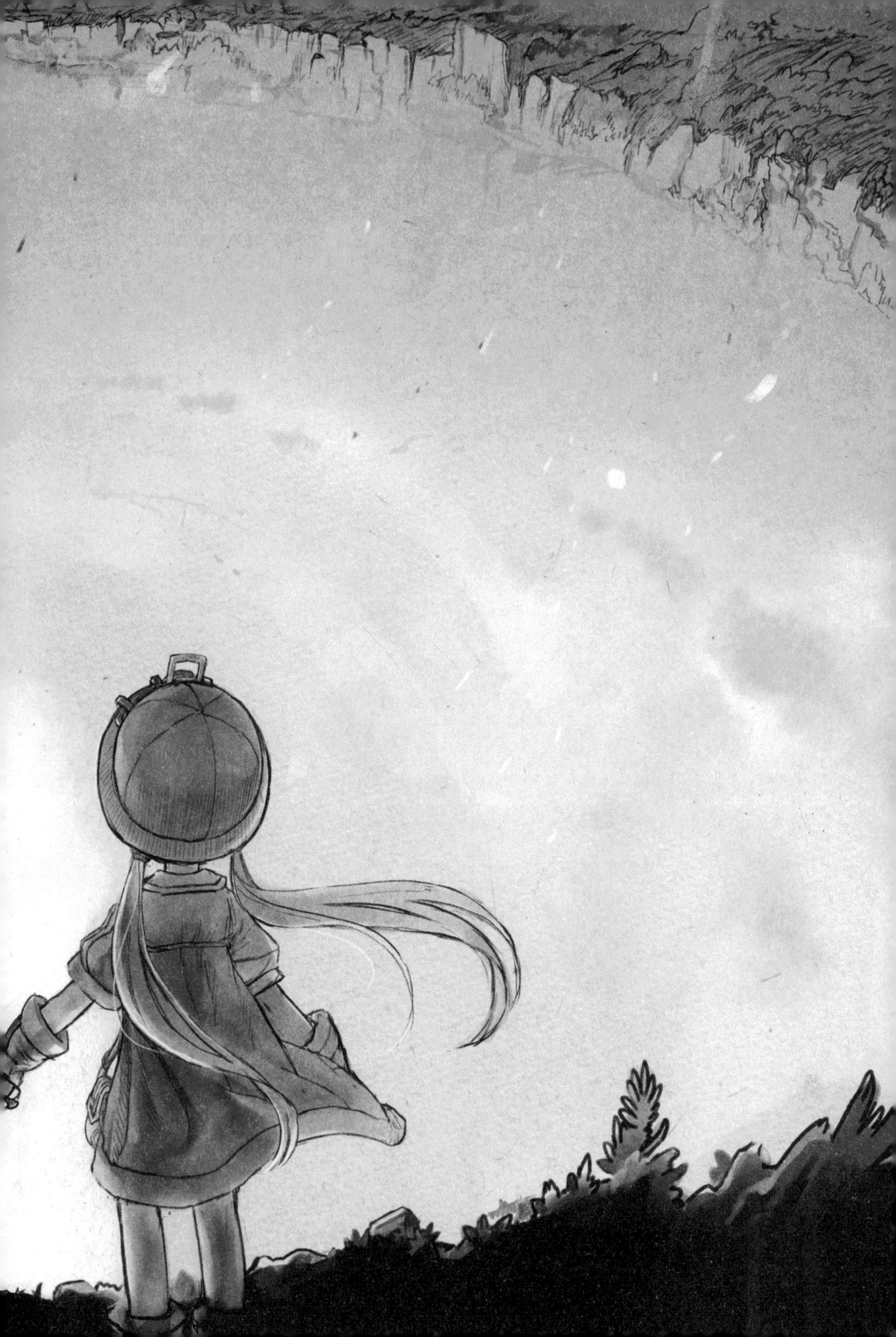

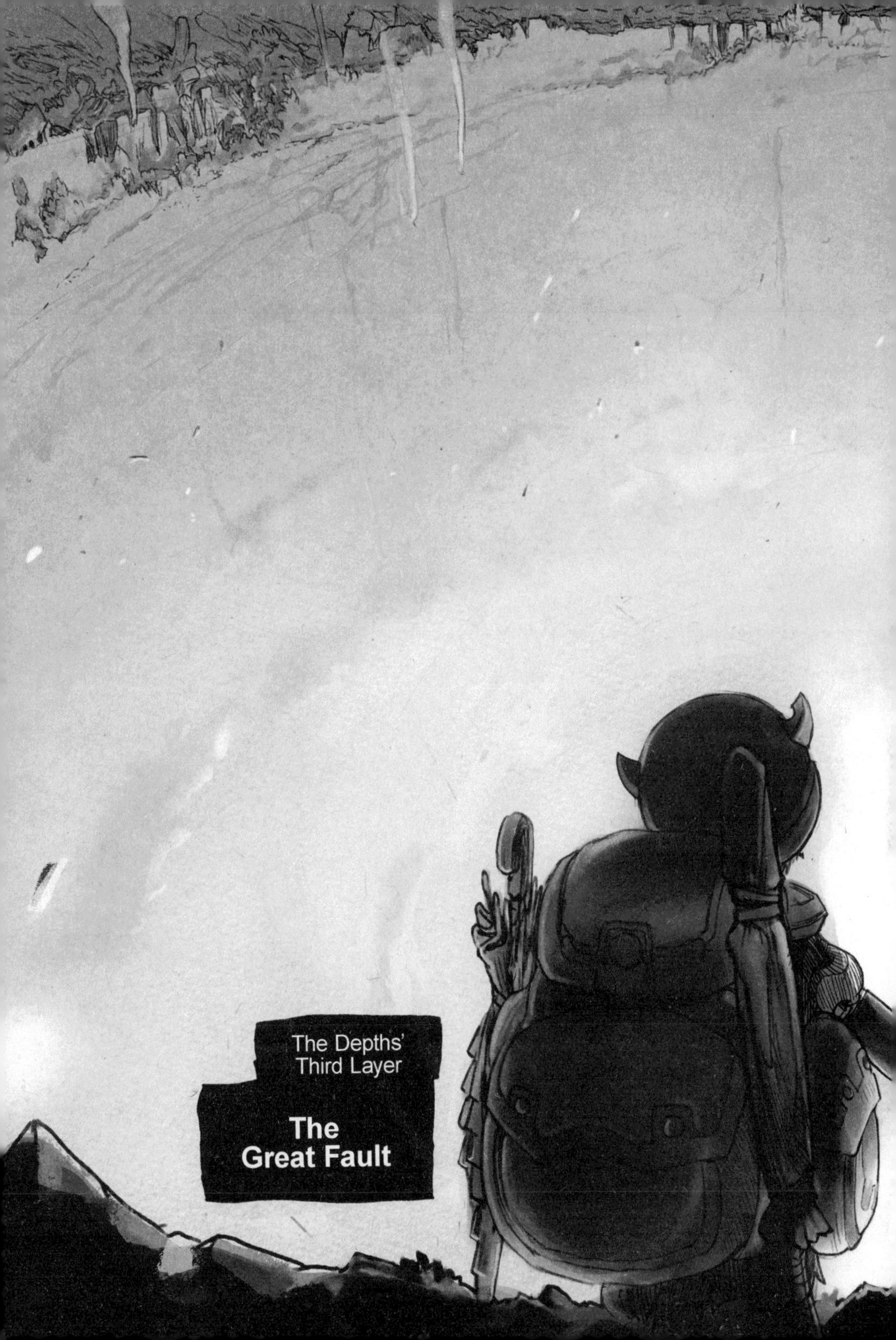
The Depths' Third Layer
The Great Fault

OTTOBAS

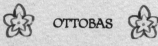

THIS LARGE AQUATIC ANIMAL LIVES IN THE OUTSKIRTS OF THE INVERTED FOREST,
LOCATED IN THE LOWER REACHES OF THE DEPTHS' SECOND LAYER.

THEY HAVE MIRACULOUSLY BECOME ESTABLISHED IN THE ABYSS DESPITE BEING
A NON-NATIVE SPECIES THAT WAS BROUGHT FROM OVERSEAS. IN THEIR COUNTRY
OF ORIGIN, THEY WERE CONSIDERED KINGS OF THE JUNGLE'S WATERFRONT AREAS.

HOWEVER, AS THEY WERE UNABLE TO RIVAL THE PREDATORS THAT
DOMINATE THE AREA SURROUNDING THE ABYSS' VERTICAL SHAFT,
THEY WERE DRIVEN TO THE FARTHEST REACHES OF THE INVERTED FOREST
WHERE THE FORCE FIELD IS EXTREMELY WEAK.

THEIR IMPOSING APPEARANCE HELPED THEM BLEND INTO THEIR NATIVE HABITAT TO SOME DEGREE.

ALTHOUGH THEY WERE DRIVEN FROM THE CENTRAL SHAFT, THEY HAVE
ADAPTED TO GROW MUCH BIGGER THAN THE ONES FOUND IN THEIR ORIGINAL
LOCALE. FURTHERMORE, THEY CAN SWALLOW SOMETHING THE SIZE
OF A HUMAN IN ONE GULP (THEY'RE OMNIVOROUS).
TAKE CARE TO NOT INADVERTENTLY APPROACH ONE.

THEY HAVE A THICK LAYER OF FAT AND SKIN,
SO THEY ARE GENERALLY NOT FIT FOR CONSUMPTION.
HOWEVER, IF THE MEANS TO PROPERLY BUTCHER AND
PREPARE ONE ARE AVAILABLE, THEIR MEAT IS DELICIOUS
AND A SINGLE INDIVIDUAL CAN PROVIDE AROUND
TWO HUNDRED PEOPLE WITH A GOOD MEAL.

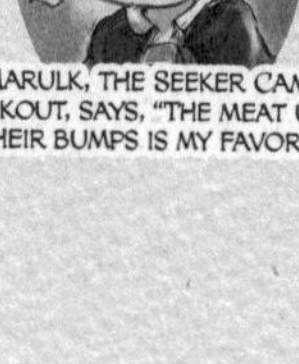

MARULK, THE SEEKER CAMP'S
LOOKOUT, SAYS, "THE MEAT UNDER
THEIR BUMPS IS MY FAVORITE."

DANGER LEVEL: ★★★ (SERIOUS)

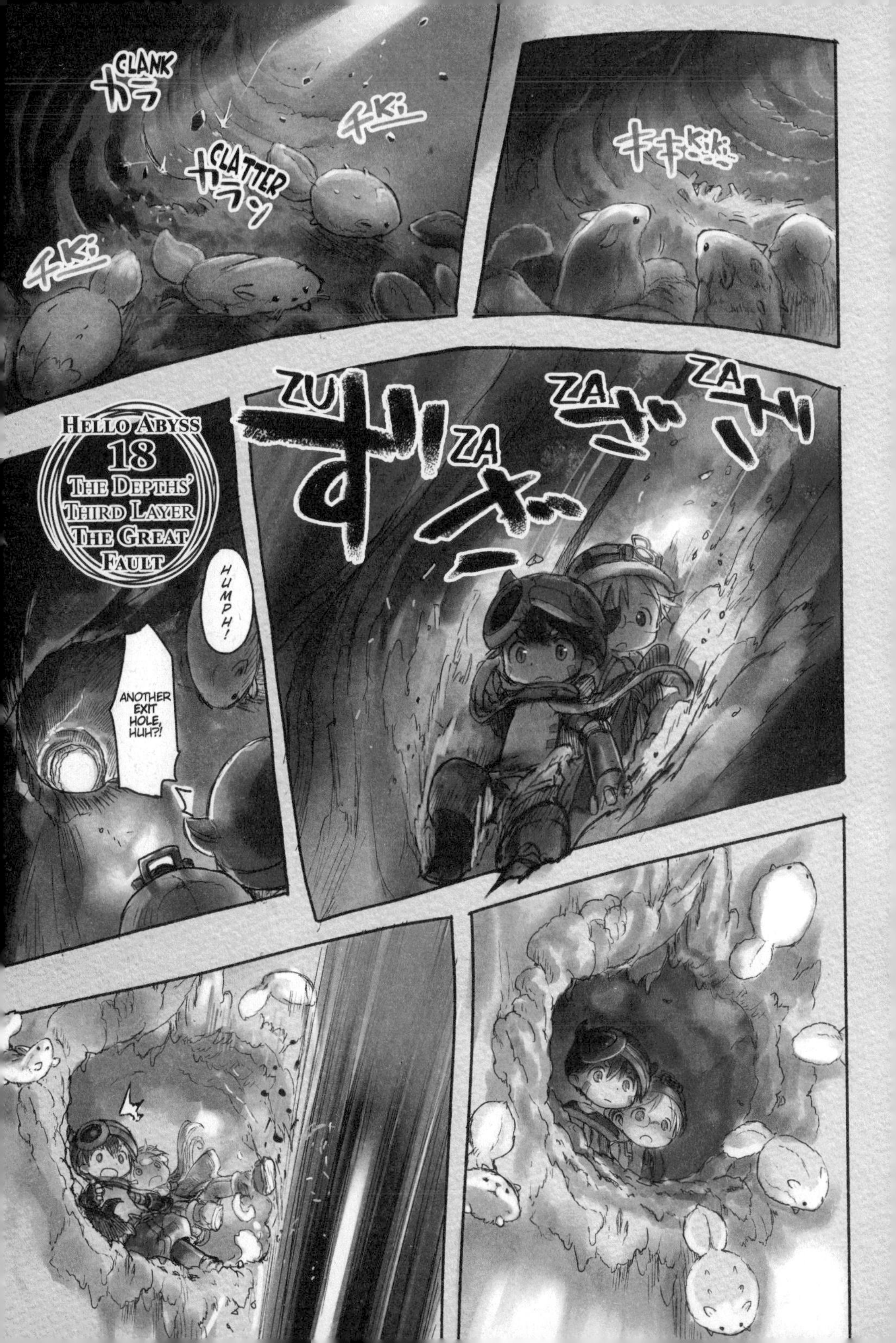
キキ KiKi
キ Ki
CLANK カラ
CLATTER カラッ
キ Ki
ZA ざ
ZA ざ
ZU ずり
ZA ざ
HELLO ABYSS 18 THE DEPTHS' THIRD LAYER THE GREAT FAULT
HUMPH!
ANOTHER EXIT HOLE, HUH?!

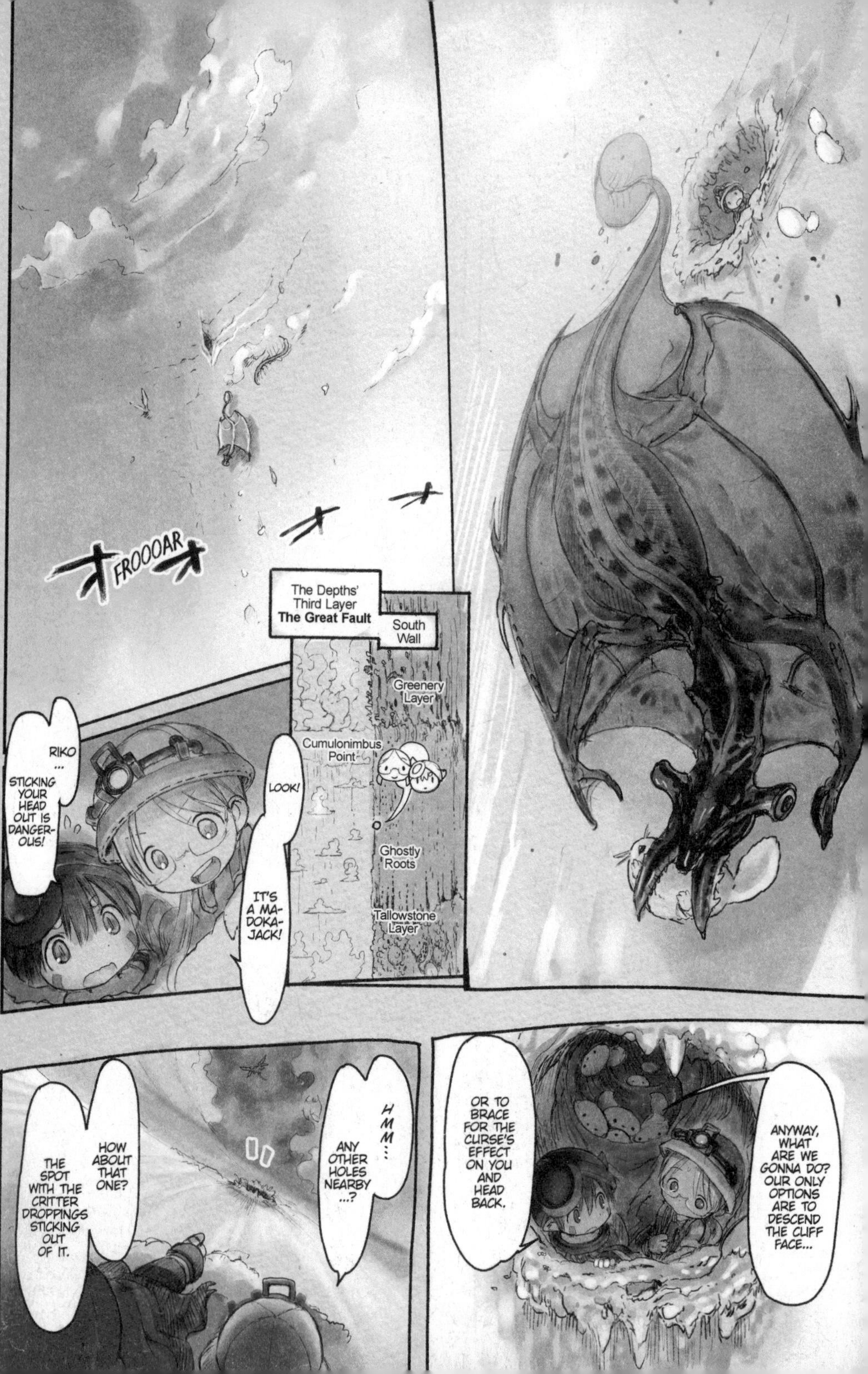
FROOOAR
The Depths' Third Layer
The Great Fault
South Wall
Greenery Layer
Cumulonimbus Point
Ghostly Roots
Tallowstone Layer
LOOK!
IT'S A MADOKAJACK!
RIKO... STICKING YOUR HEAD OUT IS DANGEROUS!
ANYWAY, WHAT ARE WE GONNA DO? OUR ONLY OPTIONS ARE TO DESCEND THE CLIFF FACE...
OR TO BRACE FOR THE CURSE'S EFFECT ON YOU AND HEAD BACK.
HMM...
ANY OTHER HOLES NEARBY...?
HOW ABOUT THAT ONE?
THE SPOT WITH THE CRITTER DROPPINGS STICKING OUT OF IT.

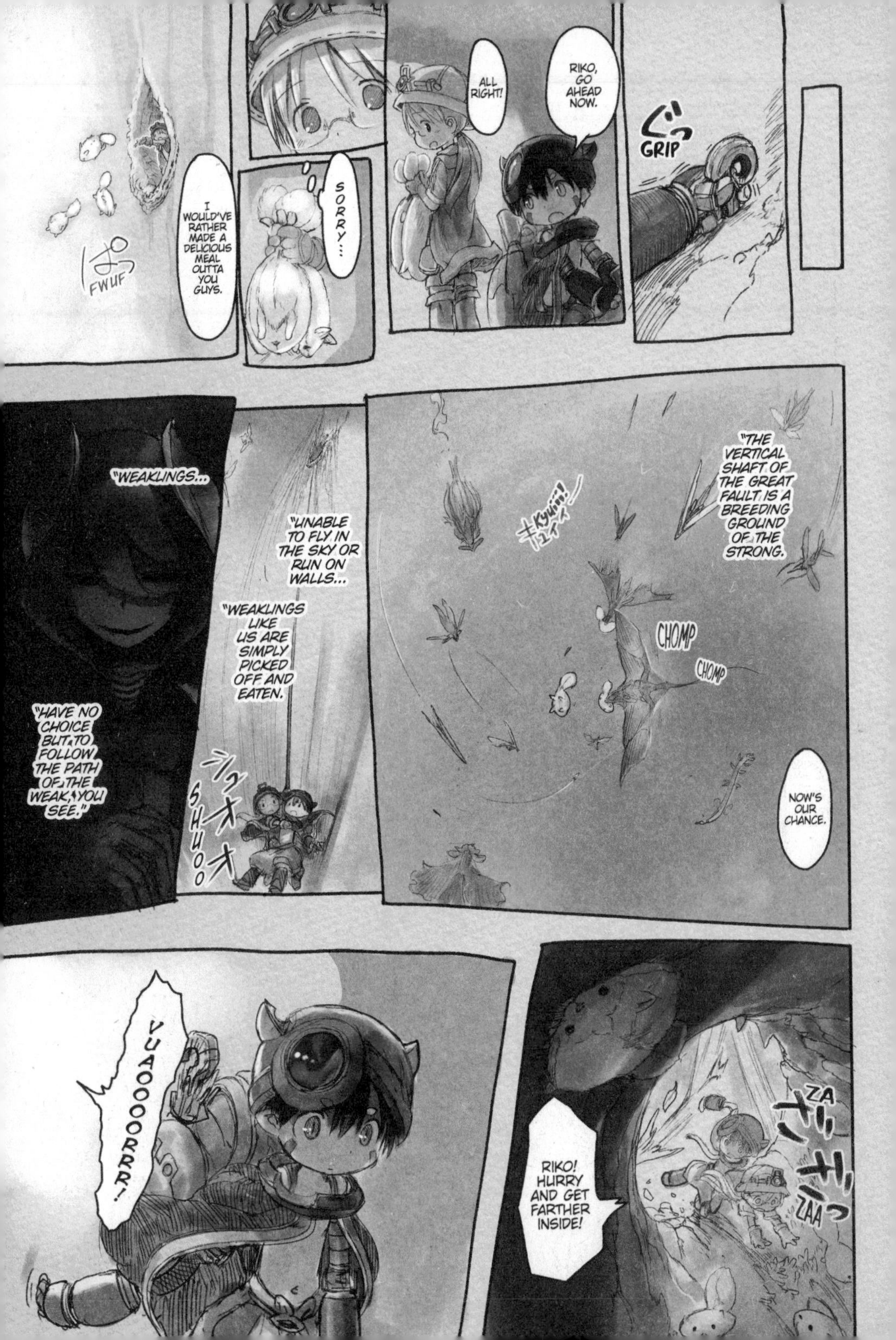
GRIP
RIKO, GO AHEAD NOW.
ALL RIGHT!
SORRY...
I WOULD'VE RATHER MADE A DELICIOUS MEAL OUTTA YOU GUYS.
FWUF
"THE VERTICAL SHAFT OF THE GREAT FAULT IS A BREEDING GROUND OF THE STRONG.
Kyuiii!
CHOMP
CHOMP
NOW'S OUR CHANCE.
"UNABLE TO FLY IN THE SKY OR RUN ON WALLS...
"WEAKLINGS LIKE US ARE SIMPLY PICKED OFF AND EATEN.
SHUOO
"WEAKLINGS...
"HAVE NO CHOICE BUT TO FOLLOW THE PATH OF THE WEAK, YOU SEE."
ZA
ZAA
RIKO! HURRY AND GET FARTHER INSIDE!
VUAOOOOORRR!

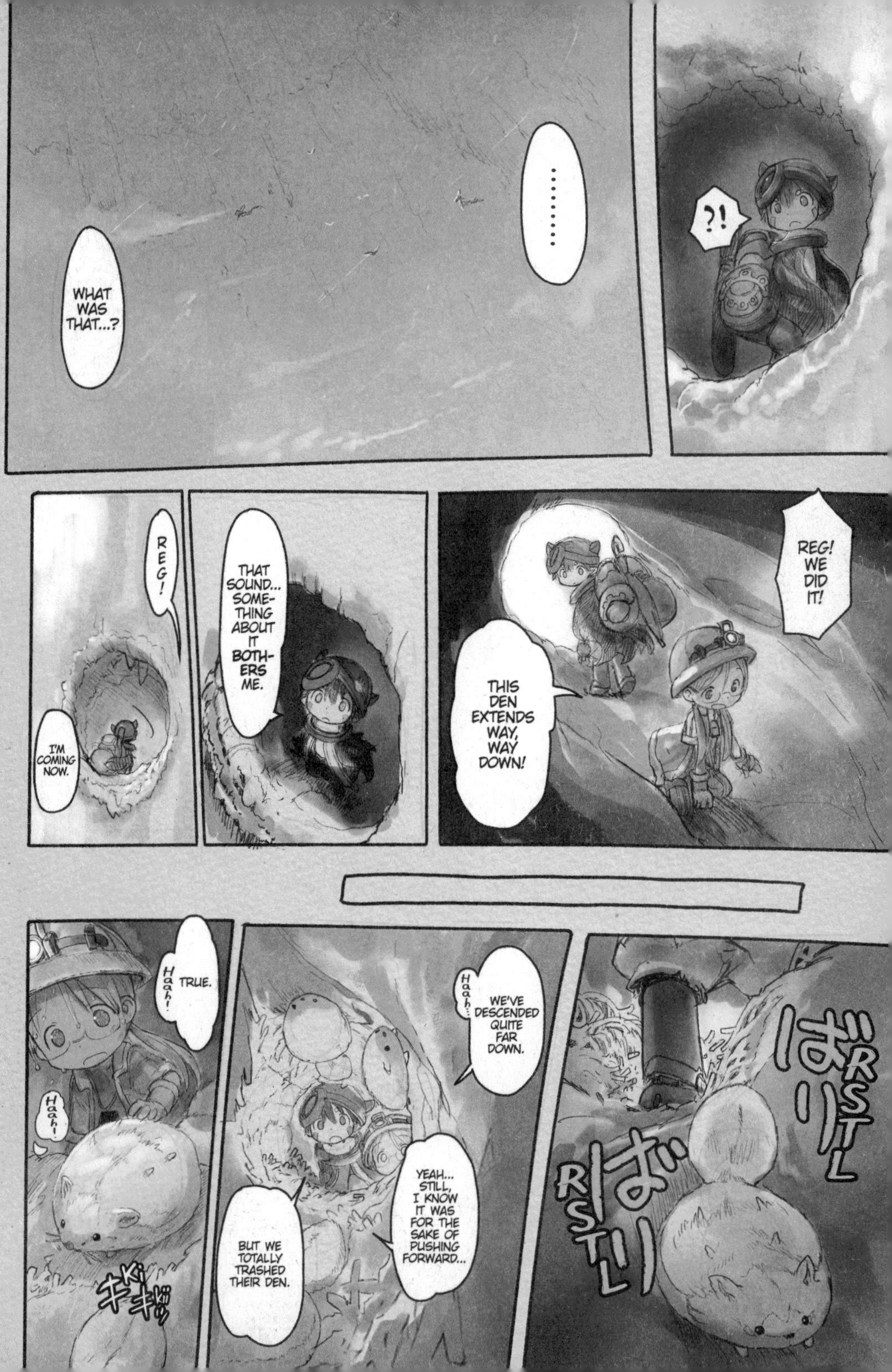
?!
......
WHAT WAS THAT...?
REG! WE DID IT!
THIS DEN EXTENDS WAY, WAY DOWN!
THAT SOUND... SOMETHING ABOUT IT BOTHERS ME.
REG!
I'M COMING NOW.
ばり RSTL
ばり RSTL
Haah... WE'VE DESCENDED QUITE FAR DOWN.
YEAH... STILL, I KNOW IT WAS FOR THE SAKE OF PUSHING FORWARD...
BUT WE TOTALLY TRASHED THEIR DEN.
Haah! TRUE.
Haah!
キキッ Ki

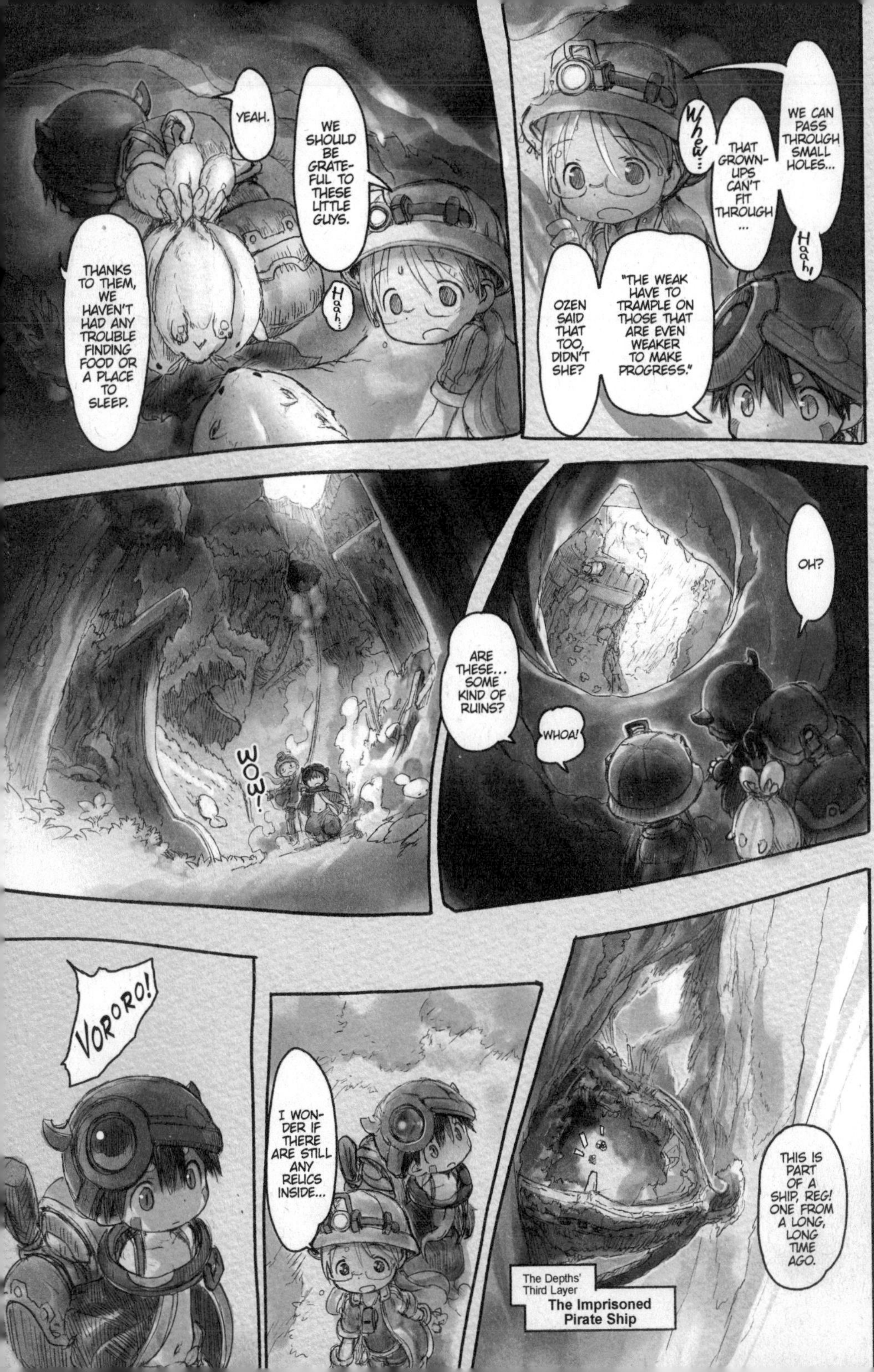
WE CAN PASS THROUGH SMALL HOLES...
Whew...
THAT GROWN-UPS CAN'T FIT THROUGH...
Haah!
"THE WEAK HAVE TO TRAMPLE ON THOSE THAT ARE EVEN WEAKER TO MAKE PROGRESS."
OZEN SAID THAT TOO, DIDN'T SHE?
WE SHOULD BE GRATEFUL TO THESE LITTLE GUYS.
YEAH.
Haah...
THANKS TO THEM, WE HAVEN'T HAD ANY TROUBLE FINDING FOOD OR A PLACE TO SLEEP.
OH?
ARE THESE... SOME KIND OF RUINS?
WHOA!
WOW!
THIS IS PART OF A SHIP, REG! ONE FROM A LONG, LONG TIME AGO.
The Depths' Third Layer
The Imprisoned Pirate Ship
I WONDER IF THERE ARE STILL ANY RELICS INSIDE...
VORORO!

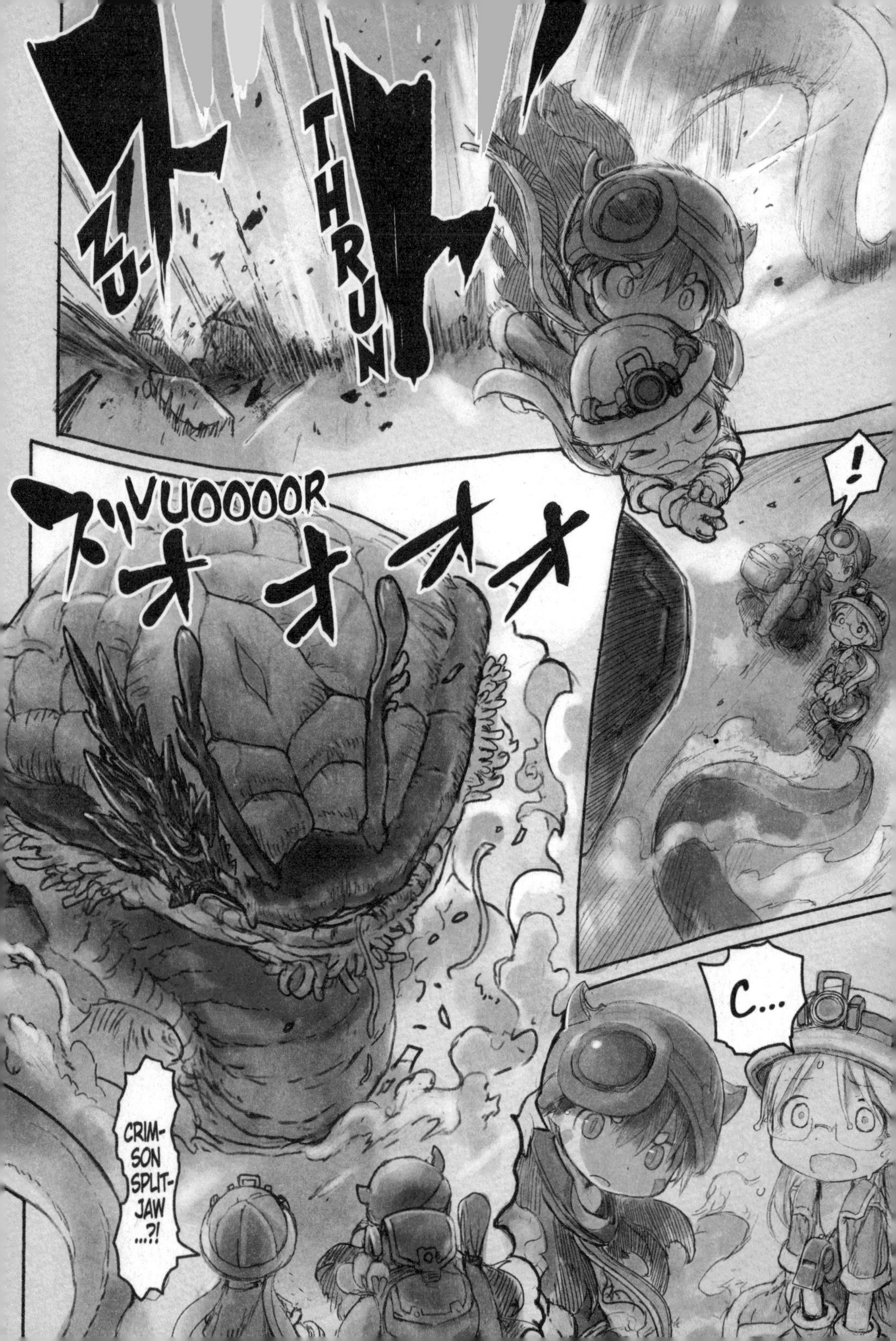
ZU-THRUN
!
VUOOOR
ズォォォ
C...
CRIM-SON SPLIT-JAW ...?!

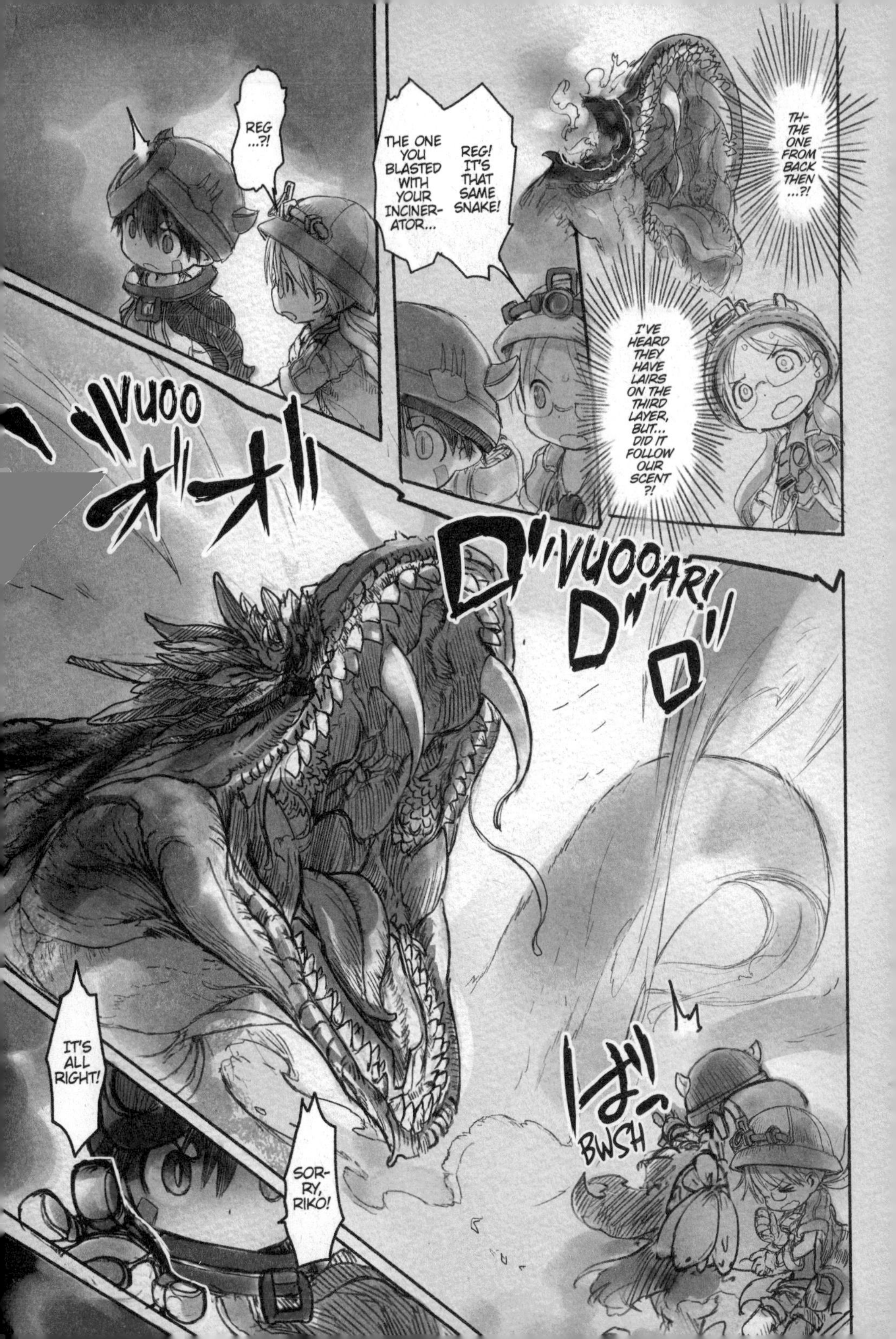
TH-THE ONE FROM BACK THEN...?!
REG! IT'S THAT SAME SNAKE!
THE ONE YOU BLASTED WITH YOUR INCINER-ATOR...
I'VE HEARD THEY HAVE LAIRS ON THE THIRD LAYER, BUT... DID IT FOLLOW OUR SCENT?!
REG...?!
VUOO
オオ
D'VUOOARI
D'D
ばっ
BWSH
IT'S ALL RIGHT!
SORRY, RIKO!

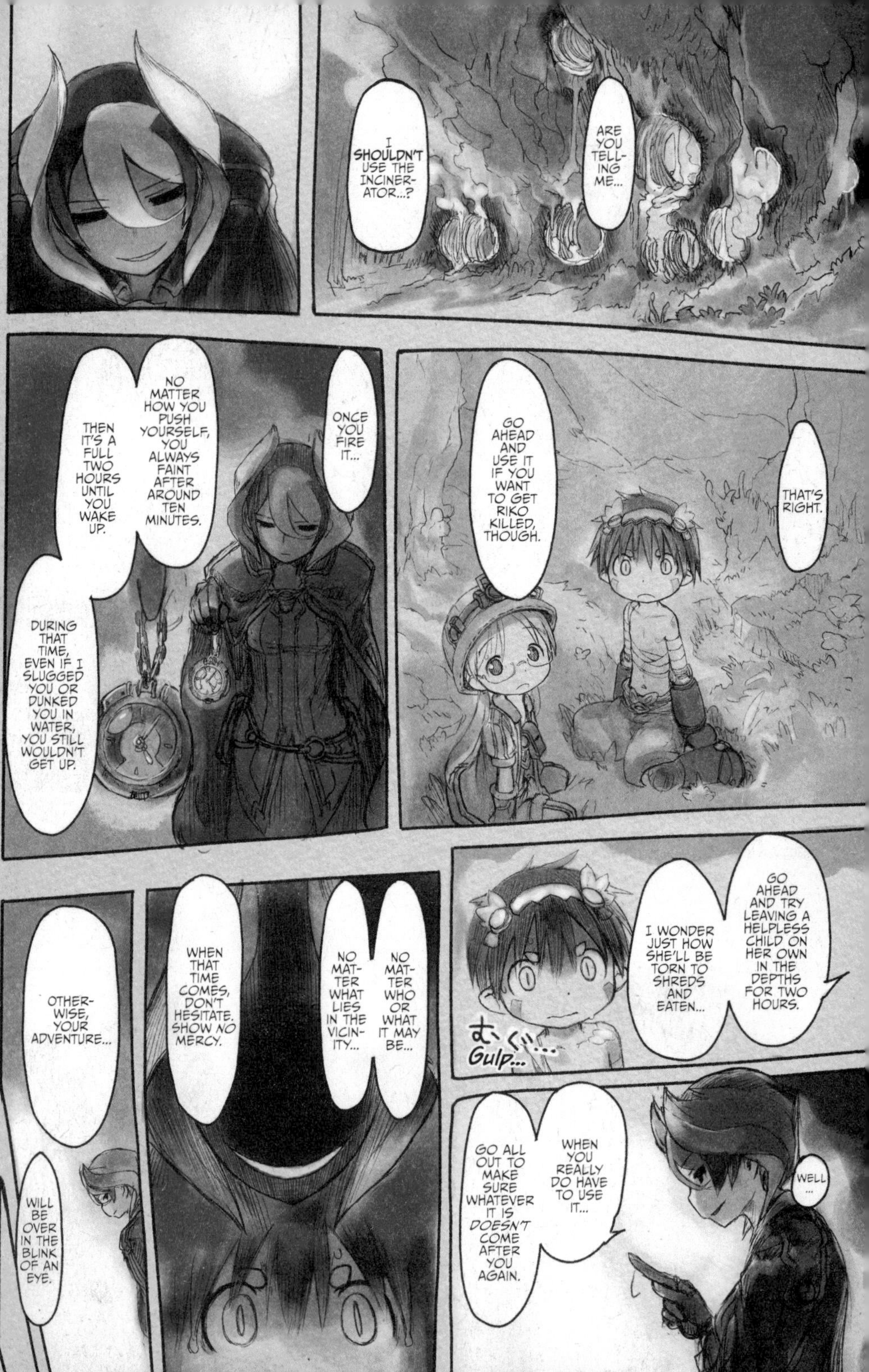
ARE YOU TELLING ME...
I **SHOULDN'T** USE THE INCINERATOR...?
THAT'S RIGHT.
GO AHEAD AND USE IT IF YOU WANT TO GET RIKO KILLED, THOUGH.
ONCE YOU FIRE IT...
NO MATTER HOW YOU PUSH YOURSELF, YOU ALWAYS FAINT AFTER AROUND TEN MINUTES.
THEN IT'S A FULL TWO HOURS UNTIL YOU WAKE UP.
DURING THAT TIME, EVEN IF I SLUGGED YOU OR DUNKED YOU IN WATER, YOU STILL WOULDN'T GET UP.
GO AHEAD AND TRY LEAVING A HELPLESS CHILD ON HER OWN IN THE DEPTHS FOR TWO HOURS.
I WONDER JUST HOW SHE'LL BE TORN TO SHREDS AND EATEN...
Gulp...
WELL...
WHEN YOU REALLY DO HAVE TO USE IT...
GO ALL OUT TO MAKE SURE WHATEVER IT IS *DOESN'T* COME AFTER YOU AGAIN.
NO MATTER WHO OR WHAT IT MAY BE...
NO MATTER WHAT LIES IN THE VICINITY...
WHEN THAT TIME COMES, DON'T HESITATE. SHOW *NO* MERCY.
OTHERWISE, YOUR ADVENTURE...
WILL BE OVER IN THE BLINK OF AN EYE.

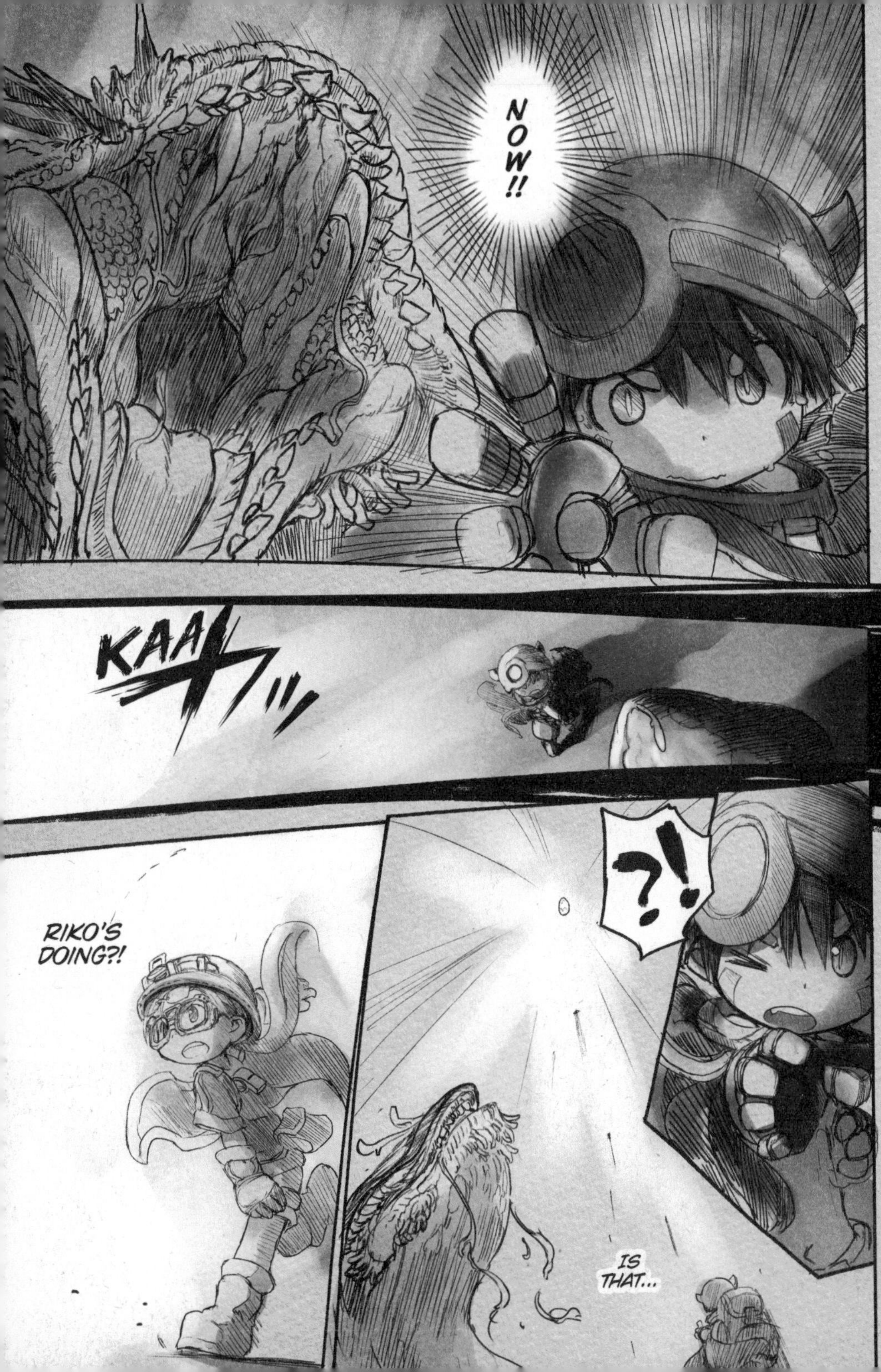
NOW!!
KAAX
?!
IS THAT...
RIKO'S DOING?!

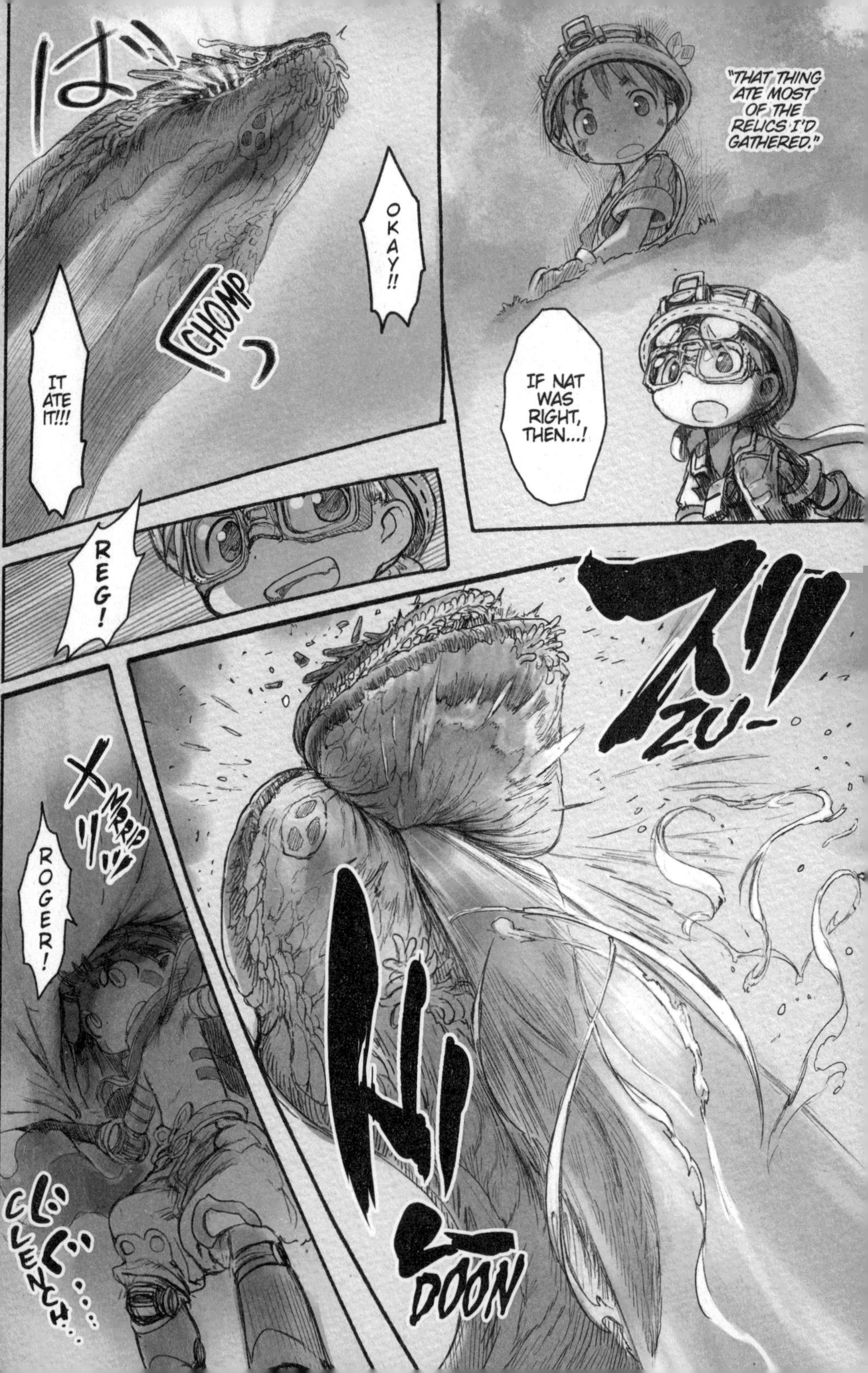
"THAT THING ATE MOST OF THE RELICS I'D GATHERED."
IF NAT WAS RIGHT, THEN...!
OKAY!!
CHOMP
IT ATE IT!!!
REG!
ZU-
DOON
MRRIP
ROGER!
CLENCH...

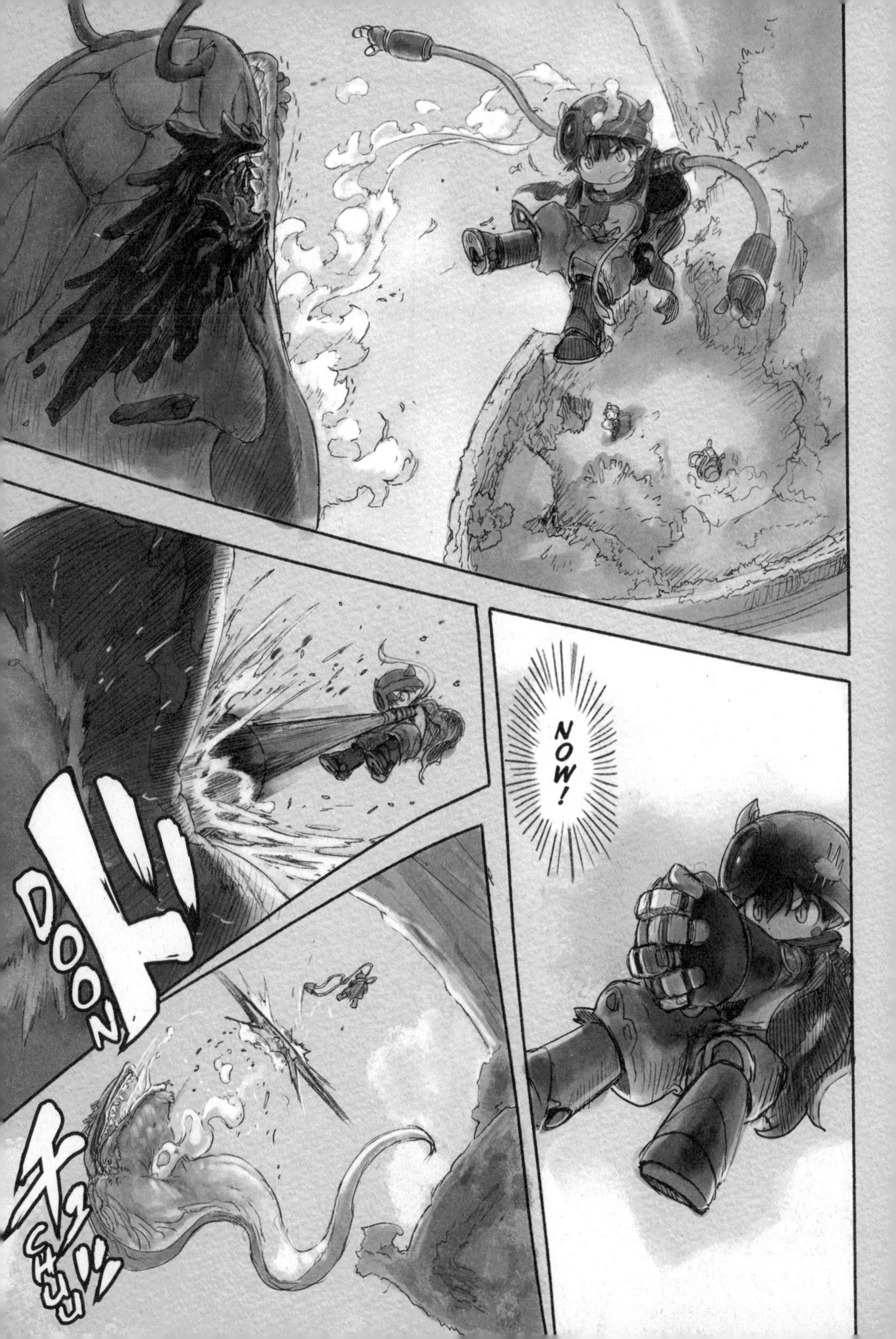
NOW!
DOON
CHUU

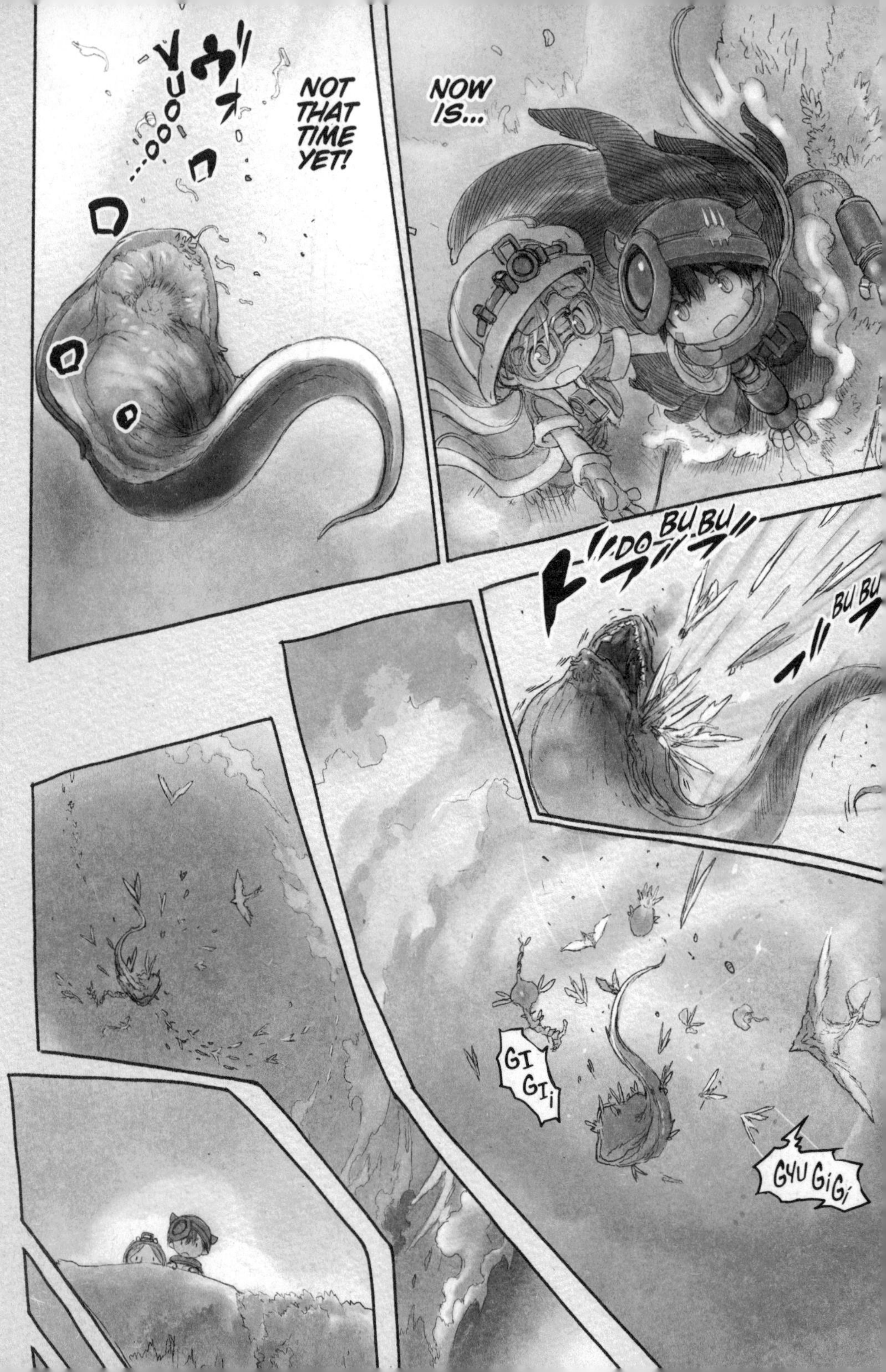
NOW IS...
NOT THAT TIME YET!
YUOO...OO
DOBUBU
BUBU
GI GIi
GYU GiGi

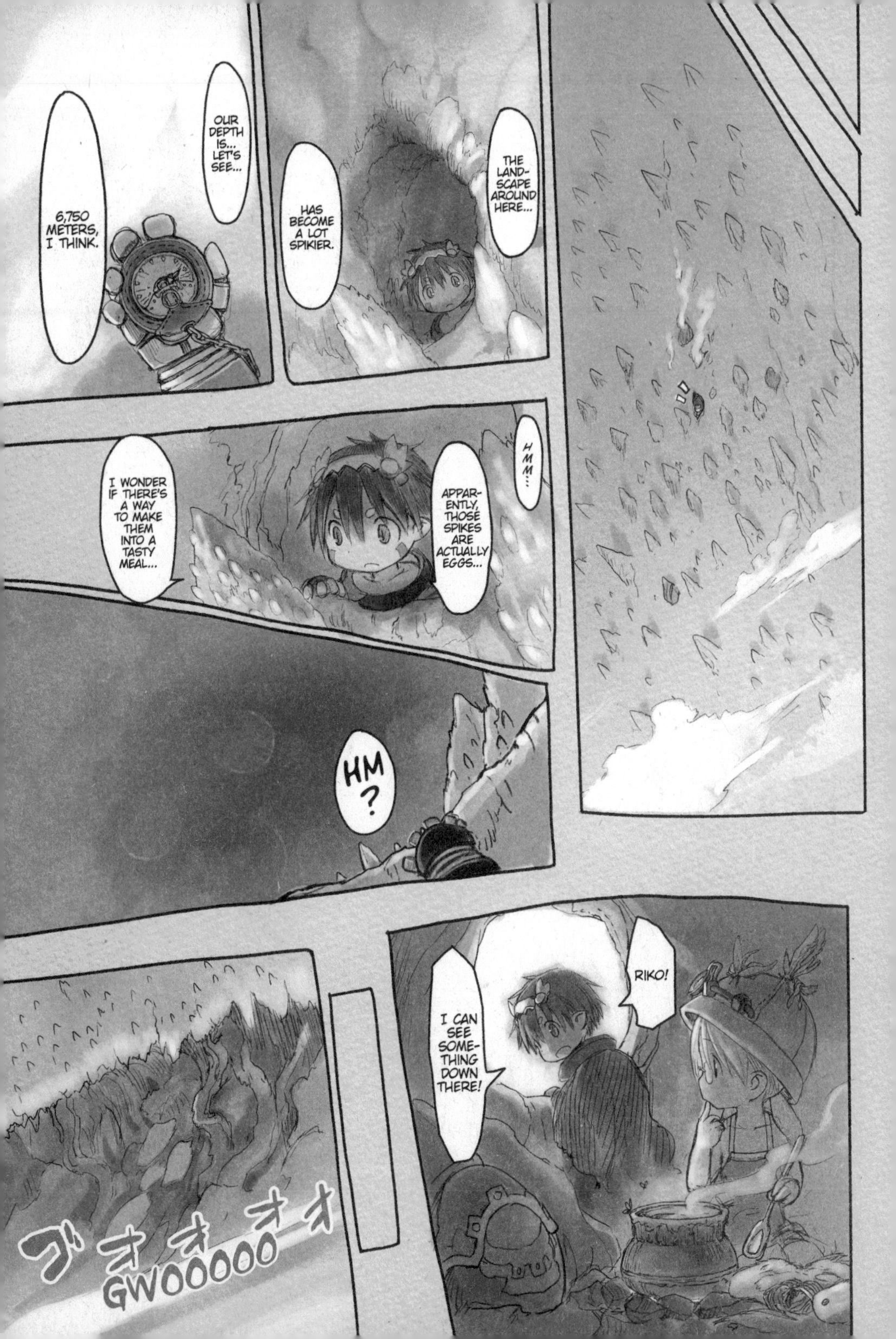

THE LANDSCAPE AROUND HERE...
HAS BECOME A LOT SPIKIER.
OUR DEPTH IS... LET'S SEE...
6,750 METERS, I THINK.
HMM...
APPARENTLY, THOSE SPIKES ARE ACTUALLY EGGS...
I WONDER IF THERE'S A WAY TO MAKE THEM INTO A TASTY MEAL...
HM?
RIKO!
I CAN SEE SOMETHING DOWN THERE!
ゴオオオオ
GWOOOOO

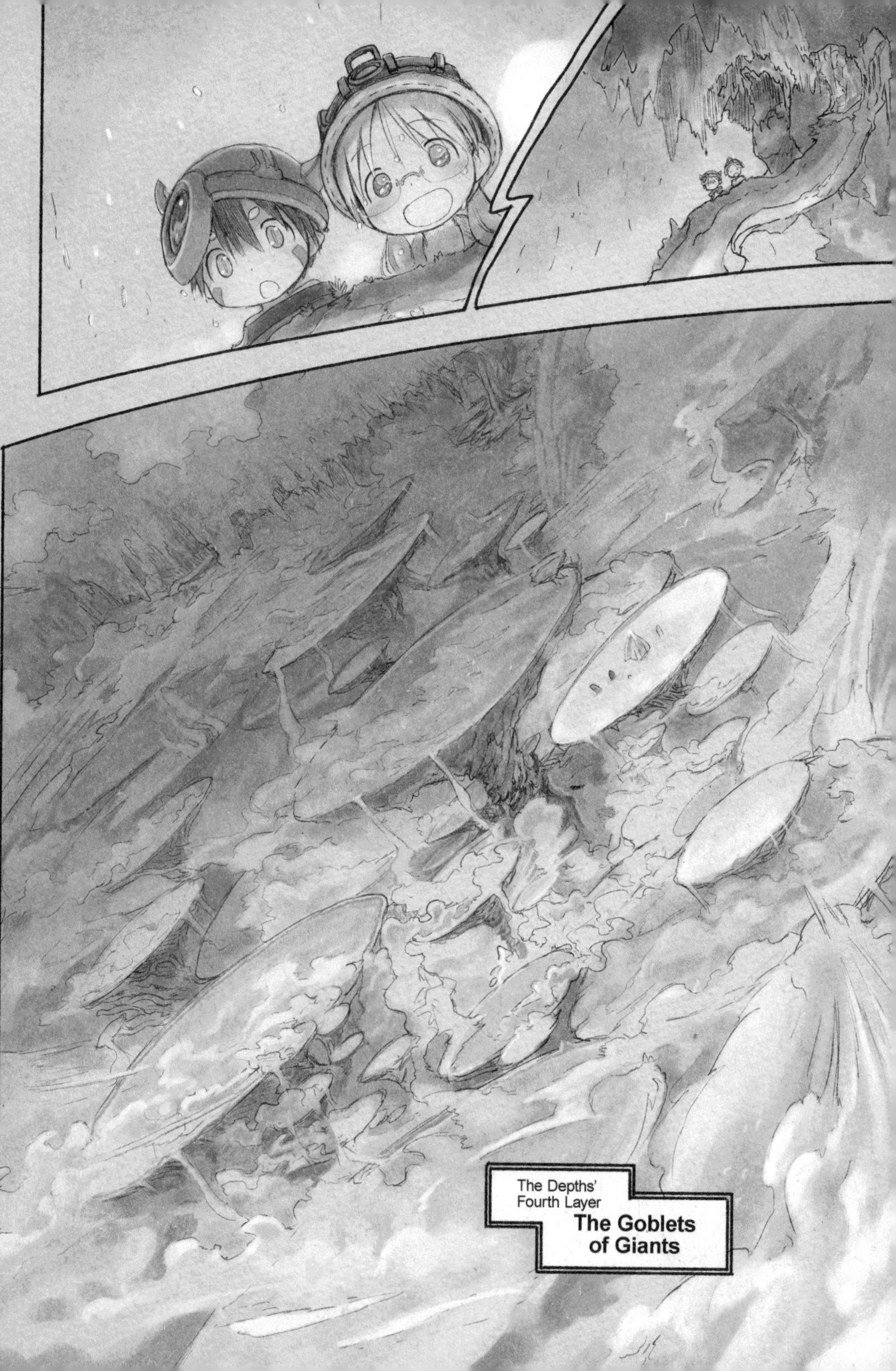
The Depths' Fourth Layer
The Goblets of Giants

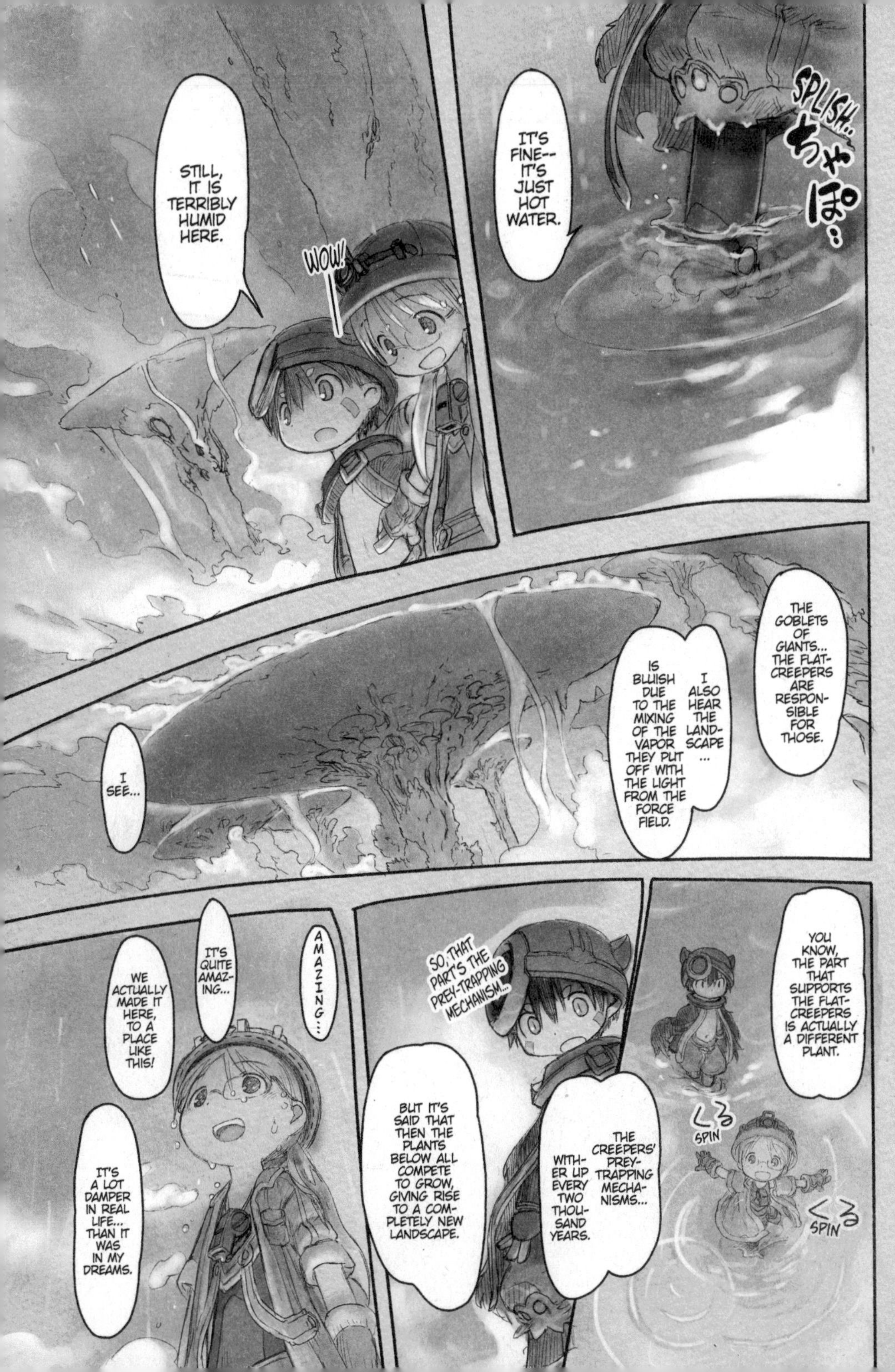
SPLISH..
ちゃぽ…
IT'S FINE-- IT'S JUST HOT WATER.
WOW!
STILL, IT IS TERRIBLY HUMID HERE.
THE GOBLETS OF GIANTS... THE FLAT-CREEPERS ARE RESPONSIBLE FOR THOSE.
I ALSO HEAR THE LANDSCAPE...
IS BLUISH DUE TO THE MIXING OF THE VAPOR THEY PUT OFF WITH THE LIGHT FROM THE FORCE FIELD.
I SEE...
YOU KNOW, THE PART THAT SUPPORTS THE FLAT-CREEPERS IS ACTUALLY A DIFFERENT PLANT.
くる
SPIN
くる
SPIN
SO, THAT PART'S THE PREY-TRAPPING MECHANISM...
THE CREEPERS' PREY-TRAPPING MECHANISMS...
WITHER UP EVERY TWO THOUSAND YEARS.
BUT IT'S SAID THAT THEN THE PLANTS BELOW ALL COMPETE TO GROW, GIVING RISE TO A COMPLETELY NEW LANDSCAPE.
AMAZING...
IT'S QUITE AMAZING...
WE ACTUALLY MADE IT HERE, TO A PLACE LIKE THIS!
IT'S A LOT DAMPER IN REAL LIFE... THAN IT WAS IN MY DREAMS.

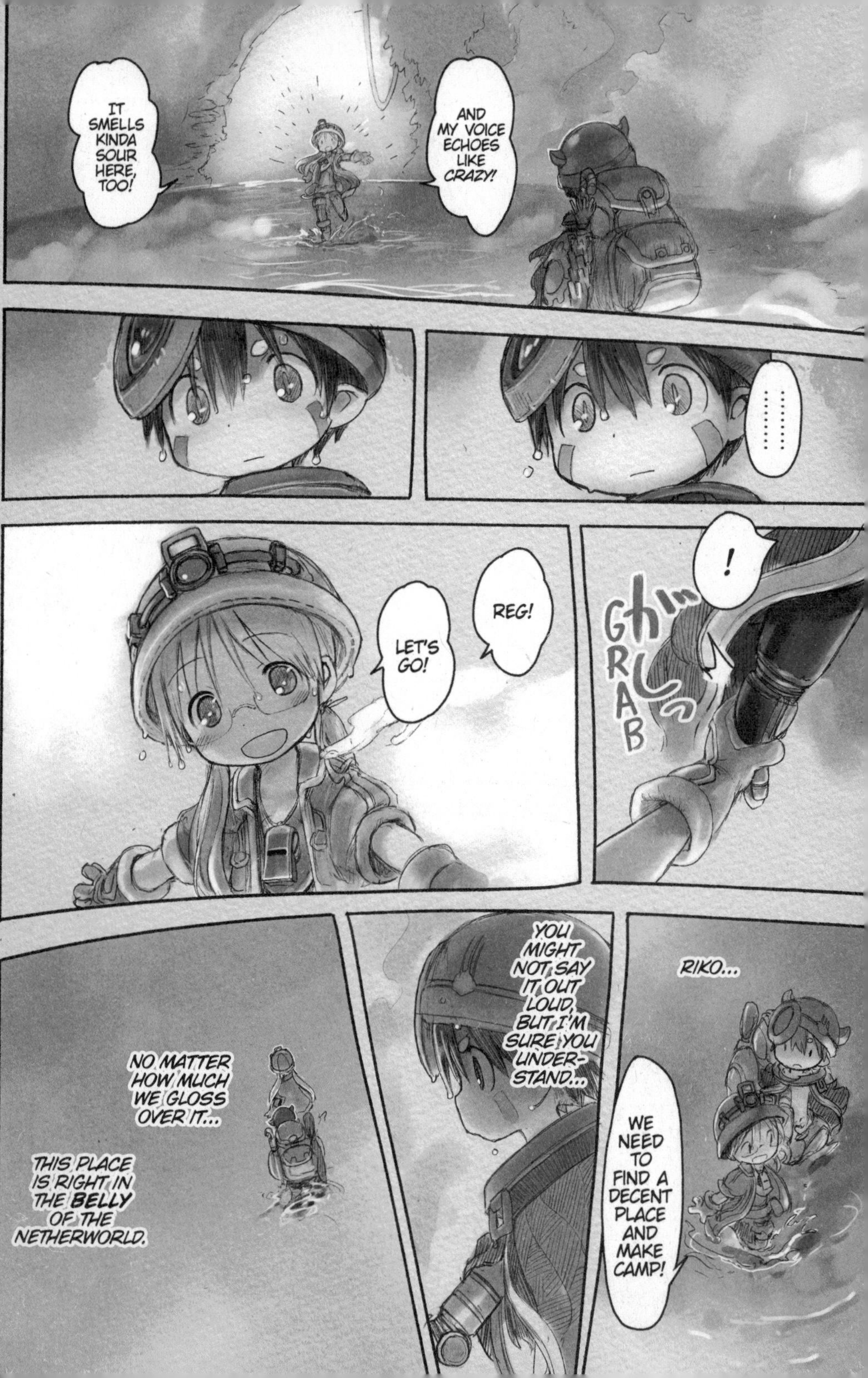
IT SMELLS KINDA SOUR HERE, TOO!
AND MY VOICE ECHOES LIKE CRAZY!
......
!
GRAB
REG!
LET'S GO!
RIKO...
WE NEED TO FIND A DECENT PLACE AND MAKE CAMP!
YOU MIGHT NOT SAY IT OUT LOUD, BUT I'M SURE YOU UNDERSTAND...
NO MATTER HOW MUCH WE GLOSS OVER IT...
THIS PLACE IS RIGHT IN THE BELLY OF THE NETHERWORLD.

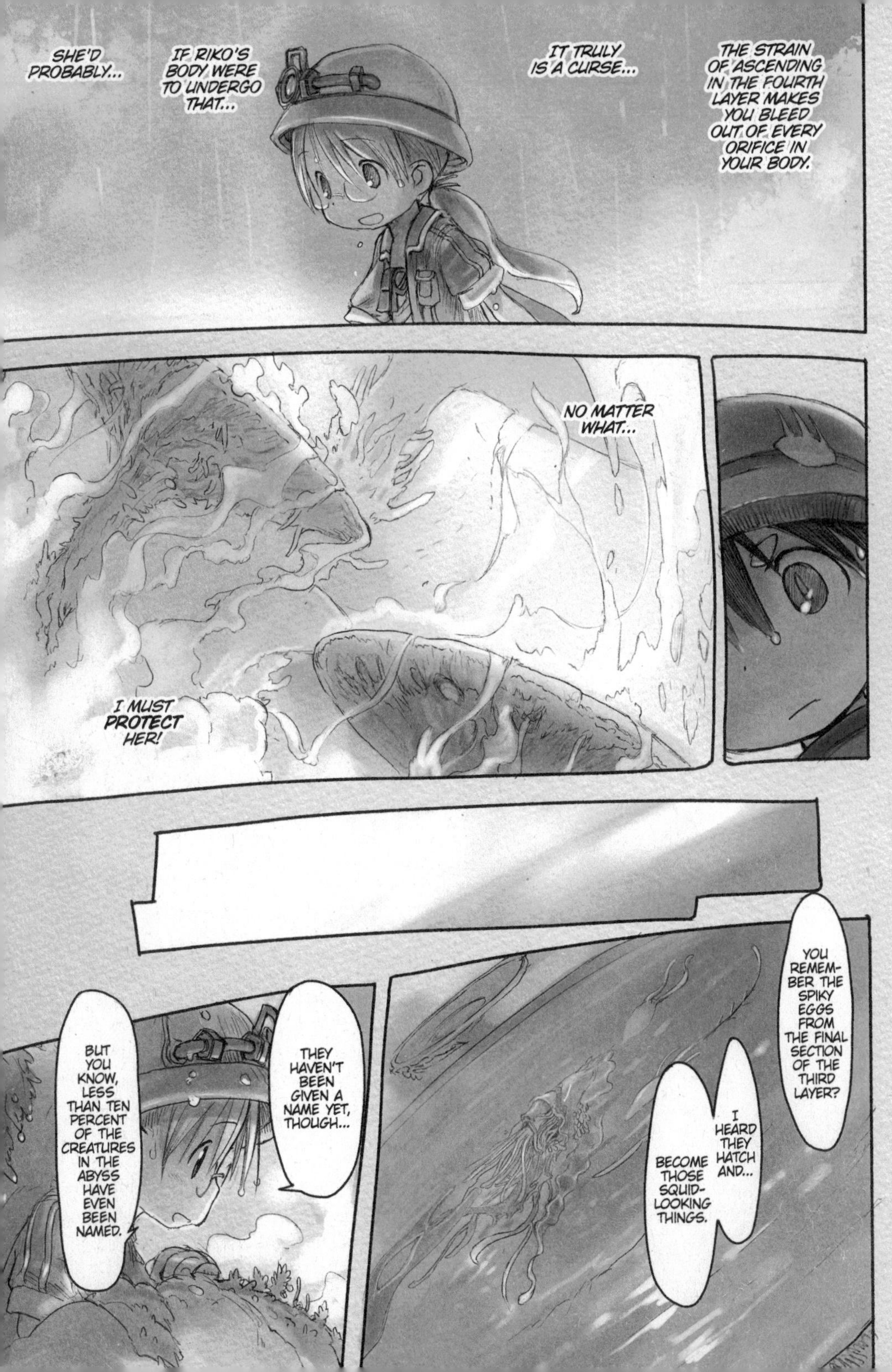
THE STRAIN OF ASCENDING IN THE FOURTH LAYER MAKES YOU BLEED OUT OF EVERY ORIFICE IN YOUR BODY.
IT TRULY IS A CURSE...
IF RIKO'S BODY WERE TO UNDERGO THAT...
SHE'D PROBABLY...
NO MATTER WHAT...
I MUST **PROTECT** HER!
YOU REMEMBER THE SPIKY EGGS FROM THE FINAL SECTION OF THE THIRD LAYER?
I HEARD THEY HATCH AND...
BECOME THOSE SQUID-LOOKING THINGS.
THEY HAVEN'T BEEN GIVEN A NAME YET, THOUGH...
BUT YOU KNOW, LESS THAN TEN PERCENT OF THE CREATURES IN THE ABYSS HAVE EVEN BEEN NAMED.

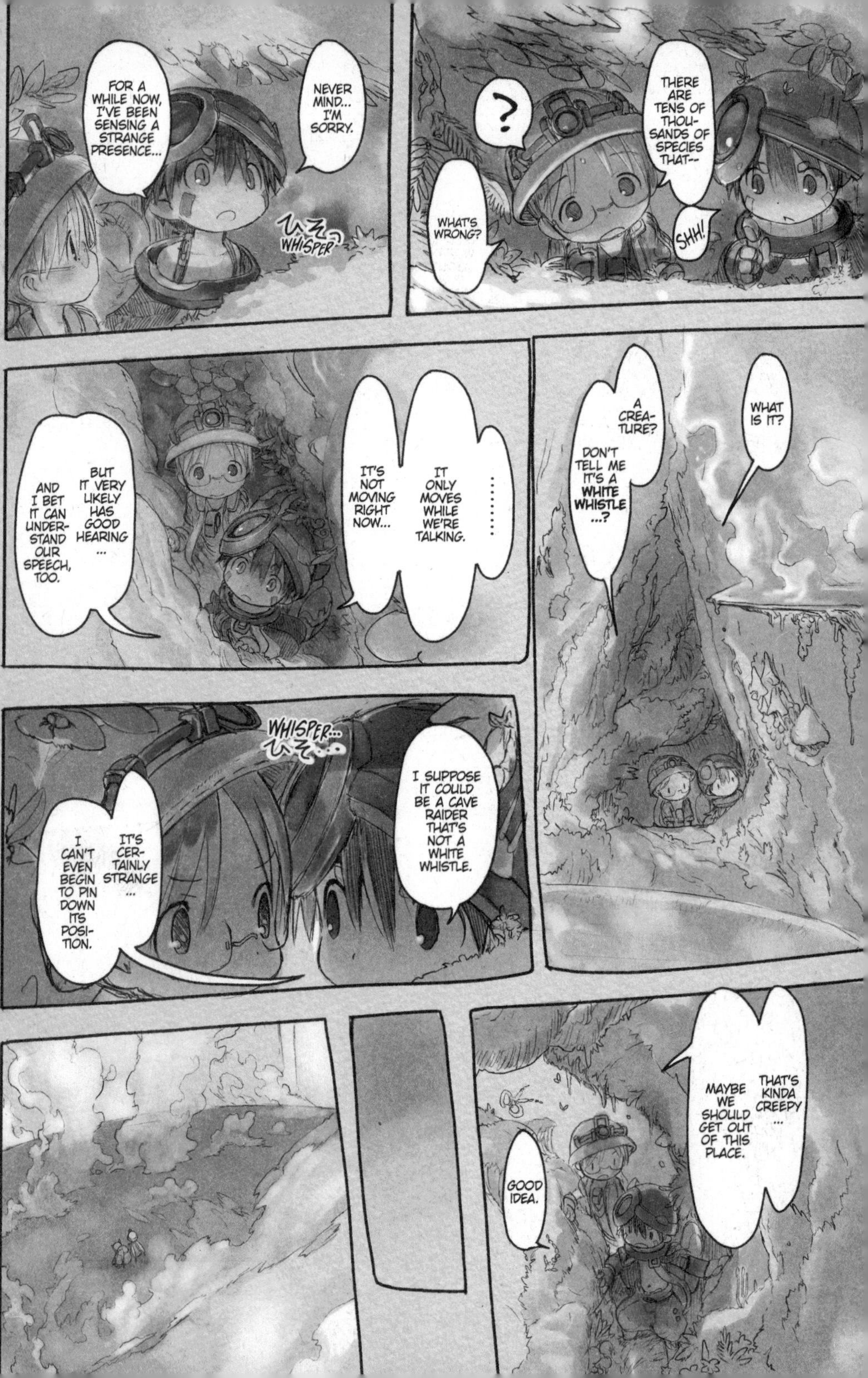
THERE ARE TENS OF THOUSANDS OF SPECIES THAT--
SHH!
?
WHAT'S WRONG?
NEVER MIND... I'M SORRY.
FOR A WHILE NOW, I'VE BEEN SENSING A STRANGE PRESENCE...
WHISPER
WHAT IS IT?
A CREATURE?
DON'T TELL ME IT'S A WHITE WHISTLE...?
....
IT ONLY MOVES WHILE WE'RE TALKING.
IT'S NOT MOVING RIGHT NOW...
BUT IT VERY LIKELY HAS GOOD HEARING...
AND I BET IT CAN UNDERSTAND OUR SPEECH, TOO.
WHISPER...
I SUPPOSE IT COULD BE A CAVE RAIDER THAT'S NOT A WHITE WHISTLE.
IT'S CERTAINLY STRANGE...
I CAN'T EVEN BEGIN TO PIN DOWN ITS POSITION.
THAT'S KINDA CREEPY...
MAYBE WE SHOULD GET OUT OF THIS PLACE.
GOOD IDEA.

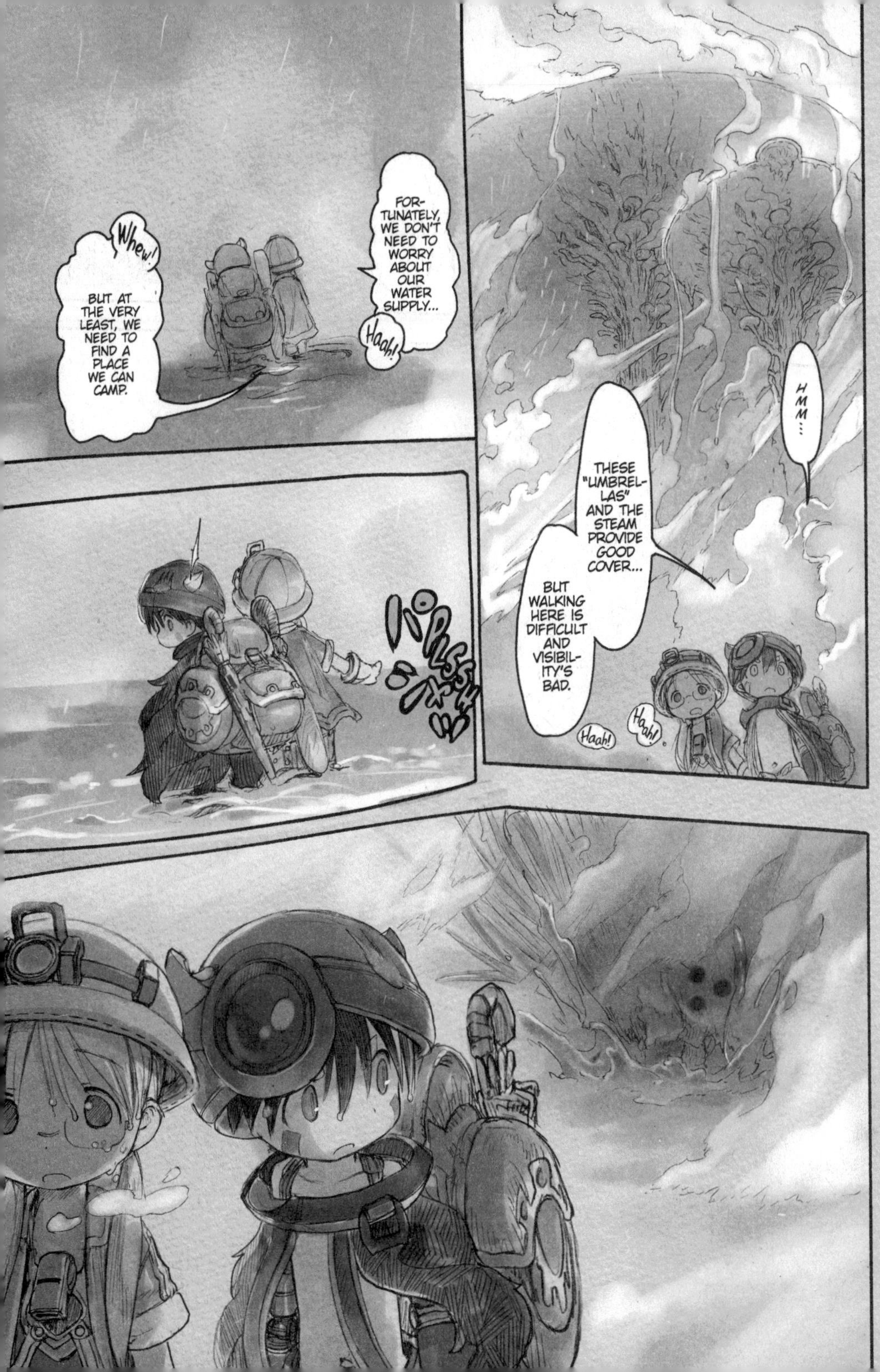
HMM...
THESE "UMBRELLAS" AND THE STEAM PROVIDE GOOD COVER...
BUT WALKING HERE IS DIFFICULT AND VISIBILITY'S BAD.
Haah!
Haah!
FORTUNATELY, WE DON'T NEED TO WORRY ABOUT OUR WATER SUPPLY...
Haah!
Whew!
BUT AT THE VERY LEAST, WE NEED TO FIND A PLACE WE CAN CAMP.
PUSSH

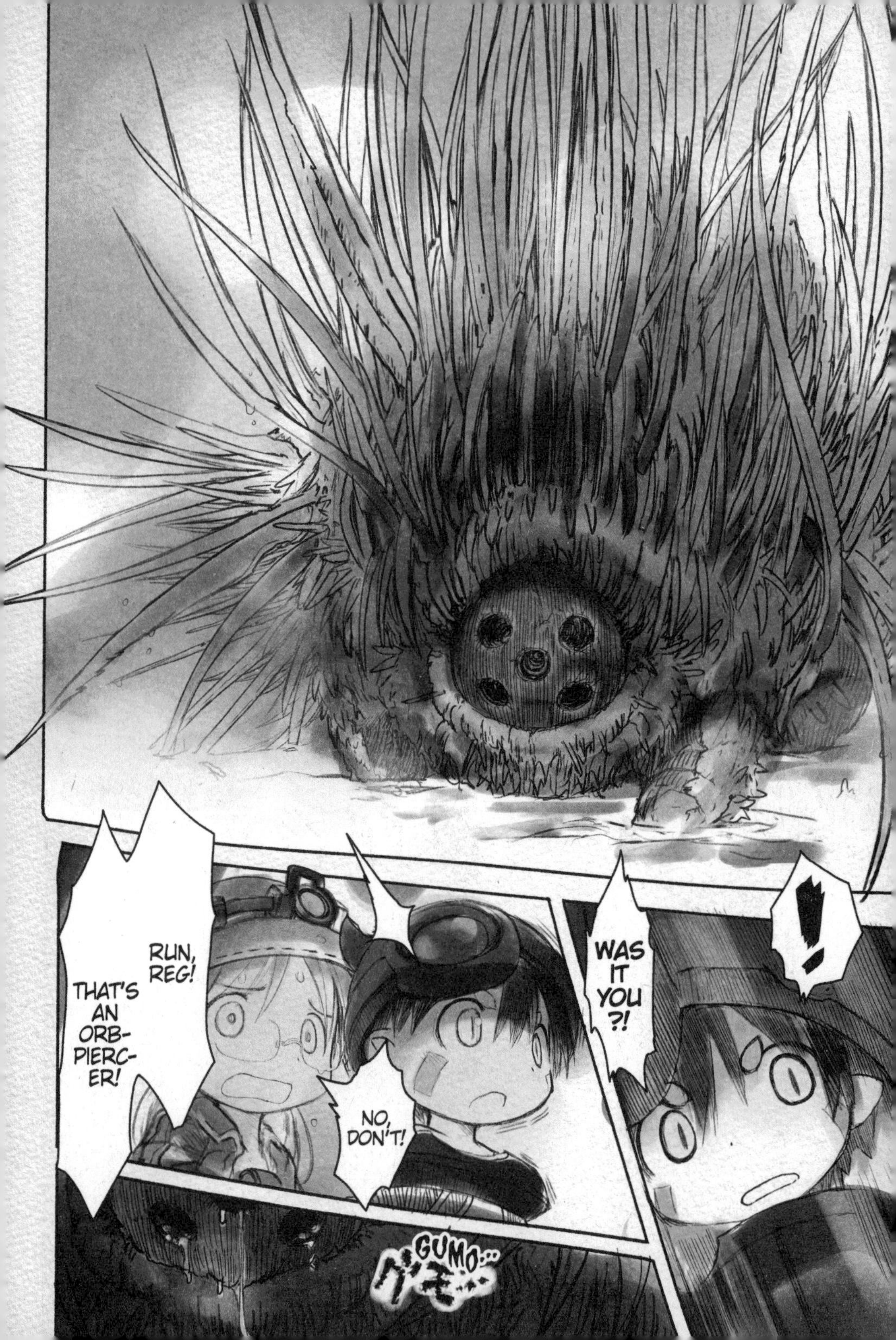
!
WAS IT YOU?!
RUN, REG!
THAT'S AN ORB-PIERCER!
NO, DON'T!
GUMO...

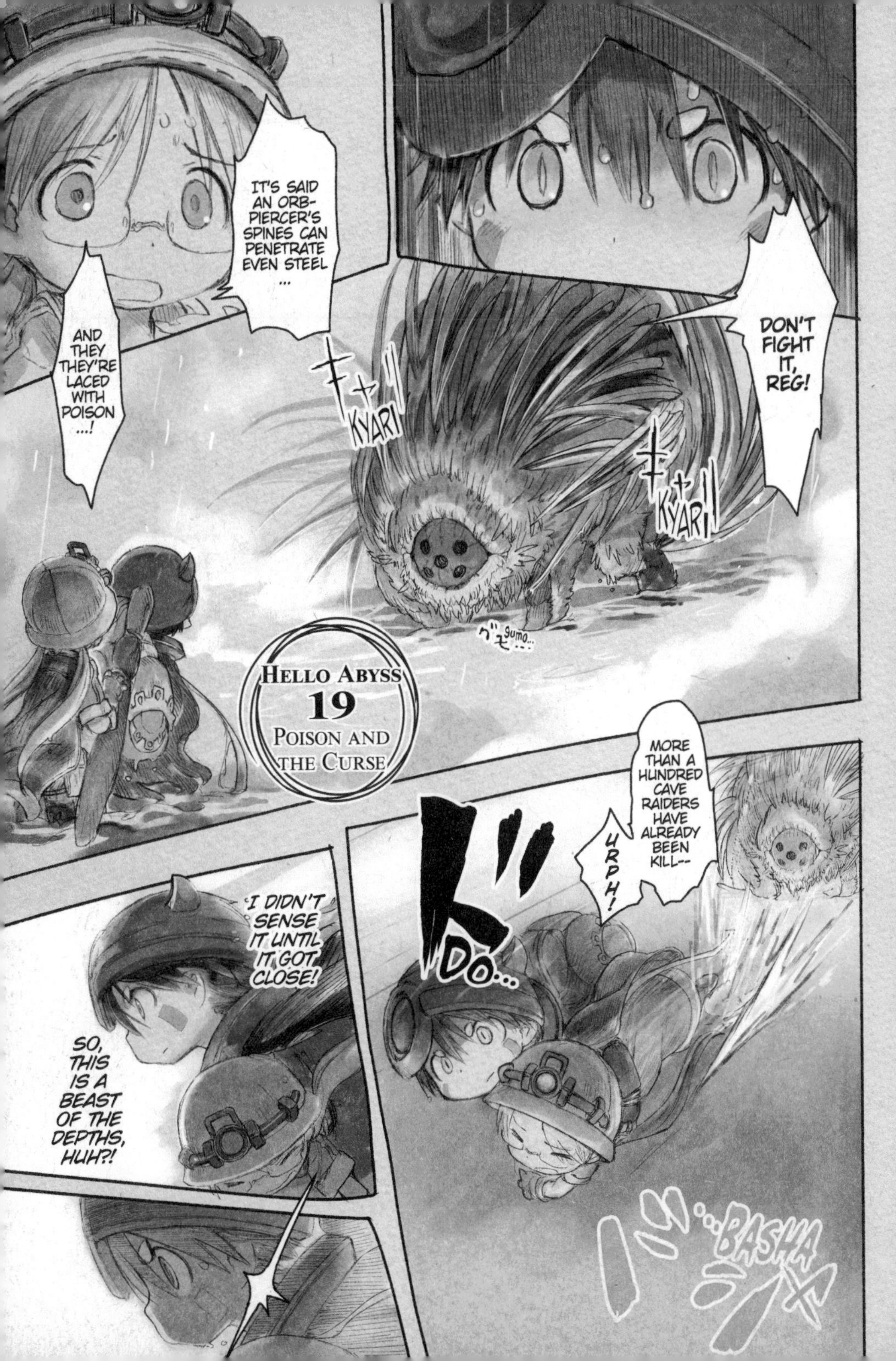
DON'T FIGHT IT, REG!
IT'S SAID AN ORB-PIERCER'S SPINES CAN PENETRATE EVEN STEEL ...
AND THEY THEY'RE LACED WITH POISON ...!
KYARI
KYARI
gumo...
HELLO ABYSS
19
POISON AND THE CURSE
MORE THAN A HUNDRED CAVE RAIDERS HAVE ALREADY BEEN KILL--
URPH!
DO...
BASHA
I DIDN'T SENSE IT UNTIL IT GOT CLOSE!
SO, THIS IS A BEAST OF THE DEPTHS, HUH?!

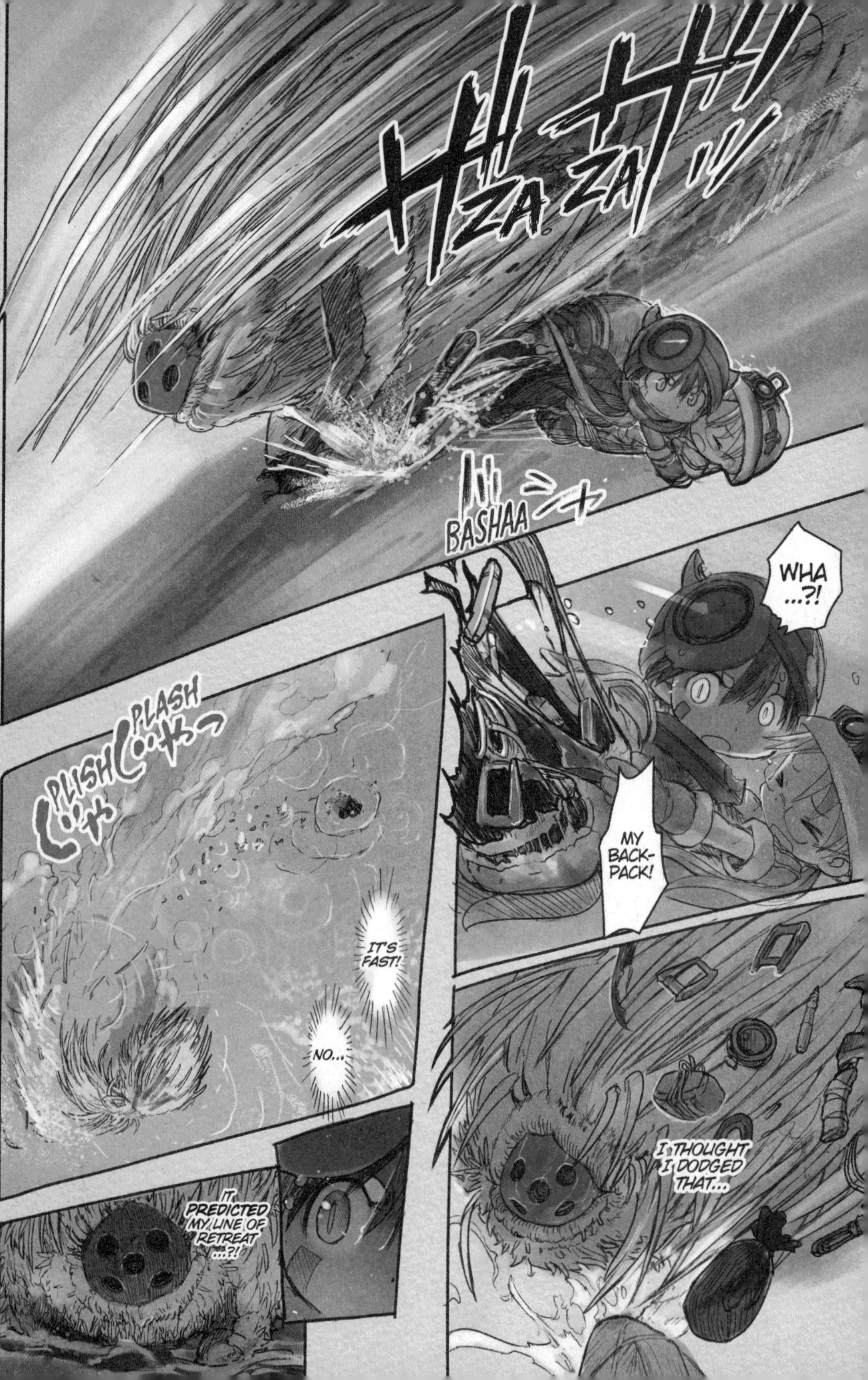
ZA ZA
BASHAA
WHA ...?!
MY BACKPACK!
PLISH
PLASH
IT'S FAST!
NO...
I THOUGHT I DODGED THAT...
IT PREDICTED MY LINE OF RETREAT ...?!

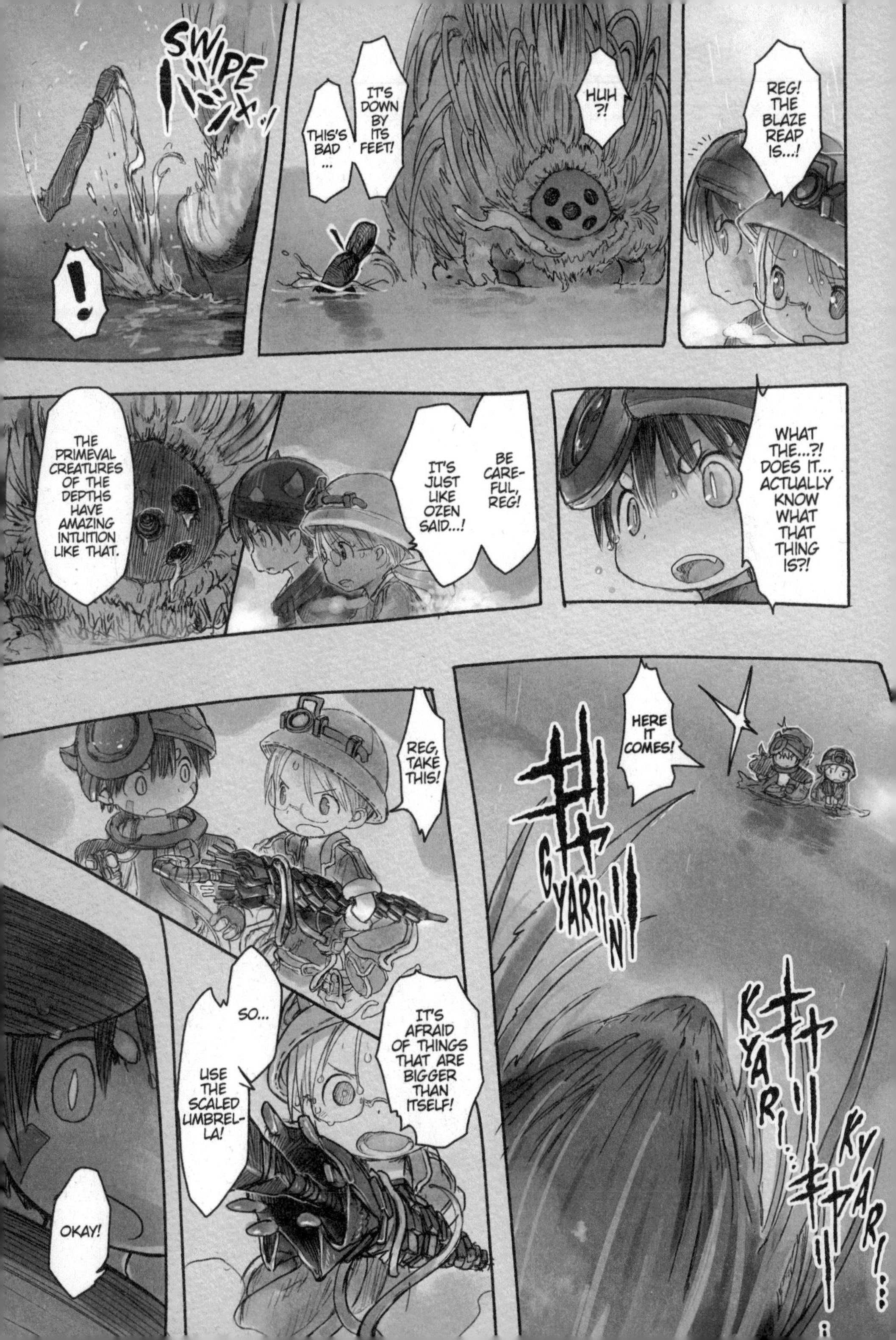

REG! THE BLAZE REAP IS...!
HUH ?!
IT'S DOWN BY ITS FEET!
THIS'S BAD ...
SWIPE
!
WHAT THE...?! DOES IT... ACTUALLY KNOW WHAT THAT THING IS?!
BE CARE-FUL, REG!
IT'S JUST LIKE OZEN SAID...!
THE PRIMEVAL CREATURES OF THE DEPTHS HAVE AMAZING INTUITION LIKE THAT.
HERE IT COMES!
GYARIIIN!
KYARI... KYARI...
REG, TAKE THIS!
IT'S AFRAID OF THINGS THAT ARE BIGGER THAN ITSELF!
SO...
USE THE SCALED UMBREL-LA!
OKAY!

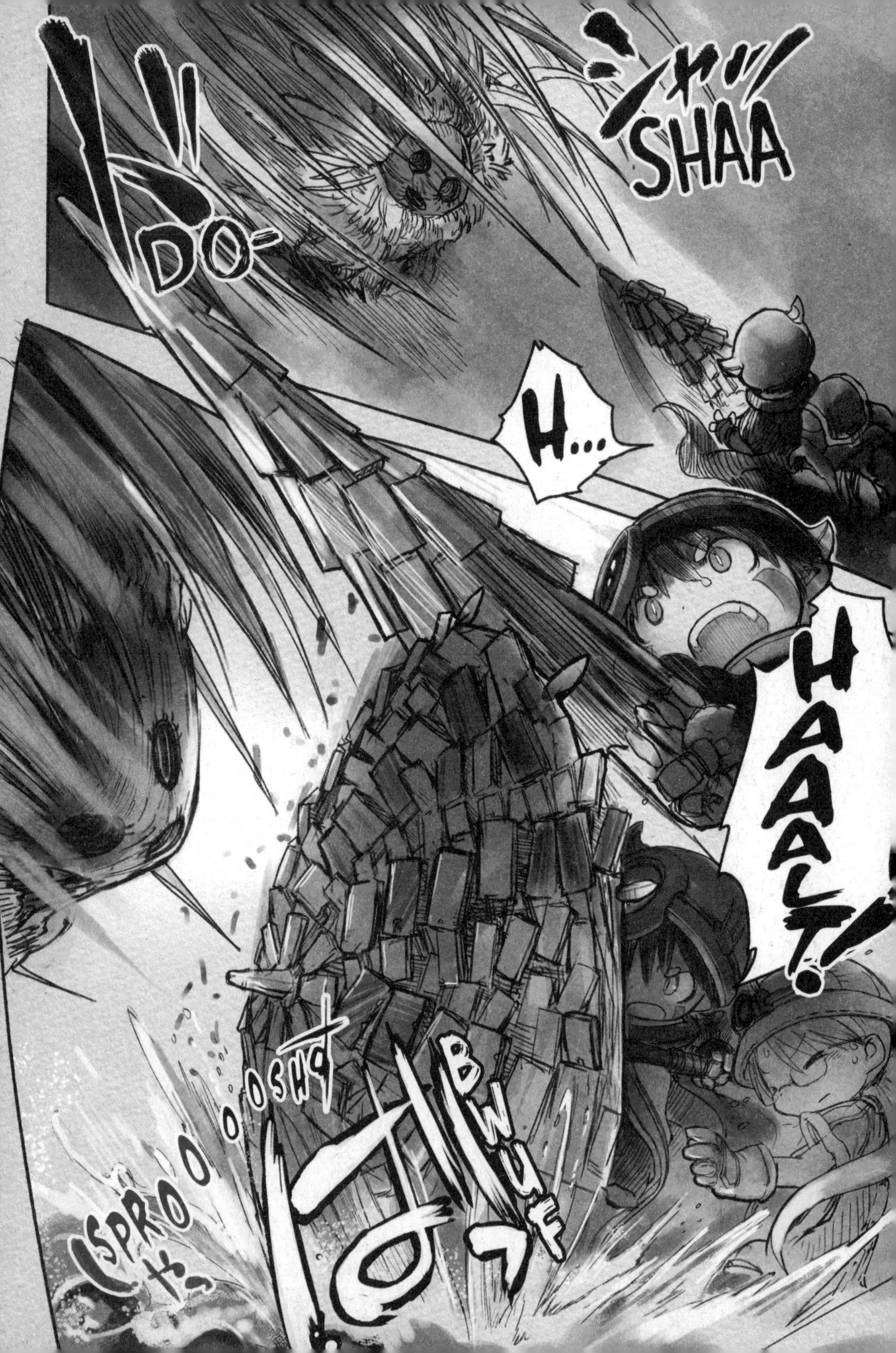
SHAA
DO-
H...
HAAALT!
BWUF
SPROOOOSH

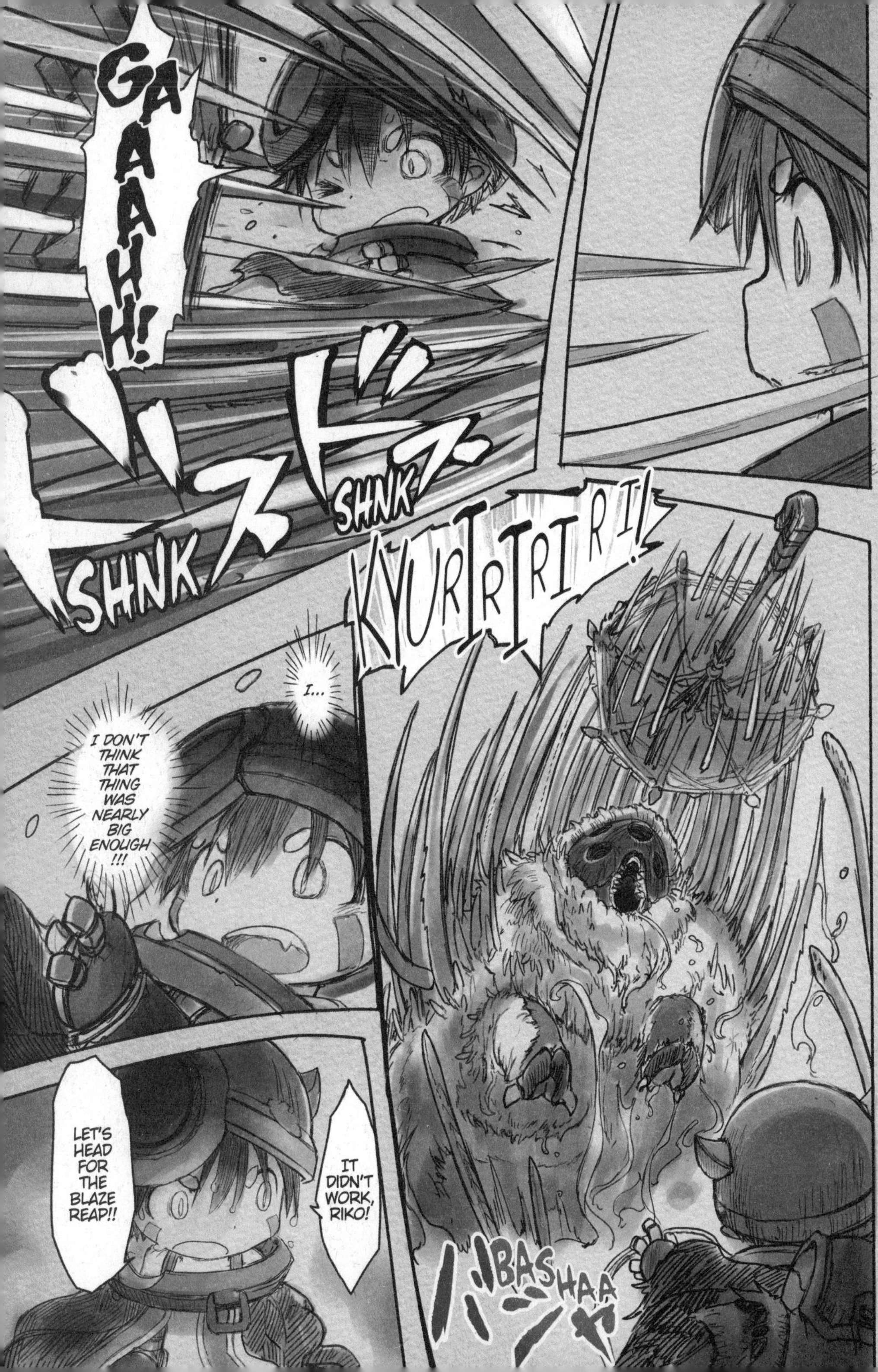
GAAAHH!
SHNK
SHNK
KYURIRIRI!
BASHAA
I...
I DON'T THINK THAT THING WAS NEARLY BIG ENOUGH!!!
IT DIDN'T WORK, RIKO!
LET'S HEAD FOR THE BLAZE REAP!!

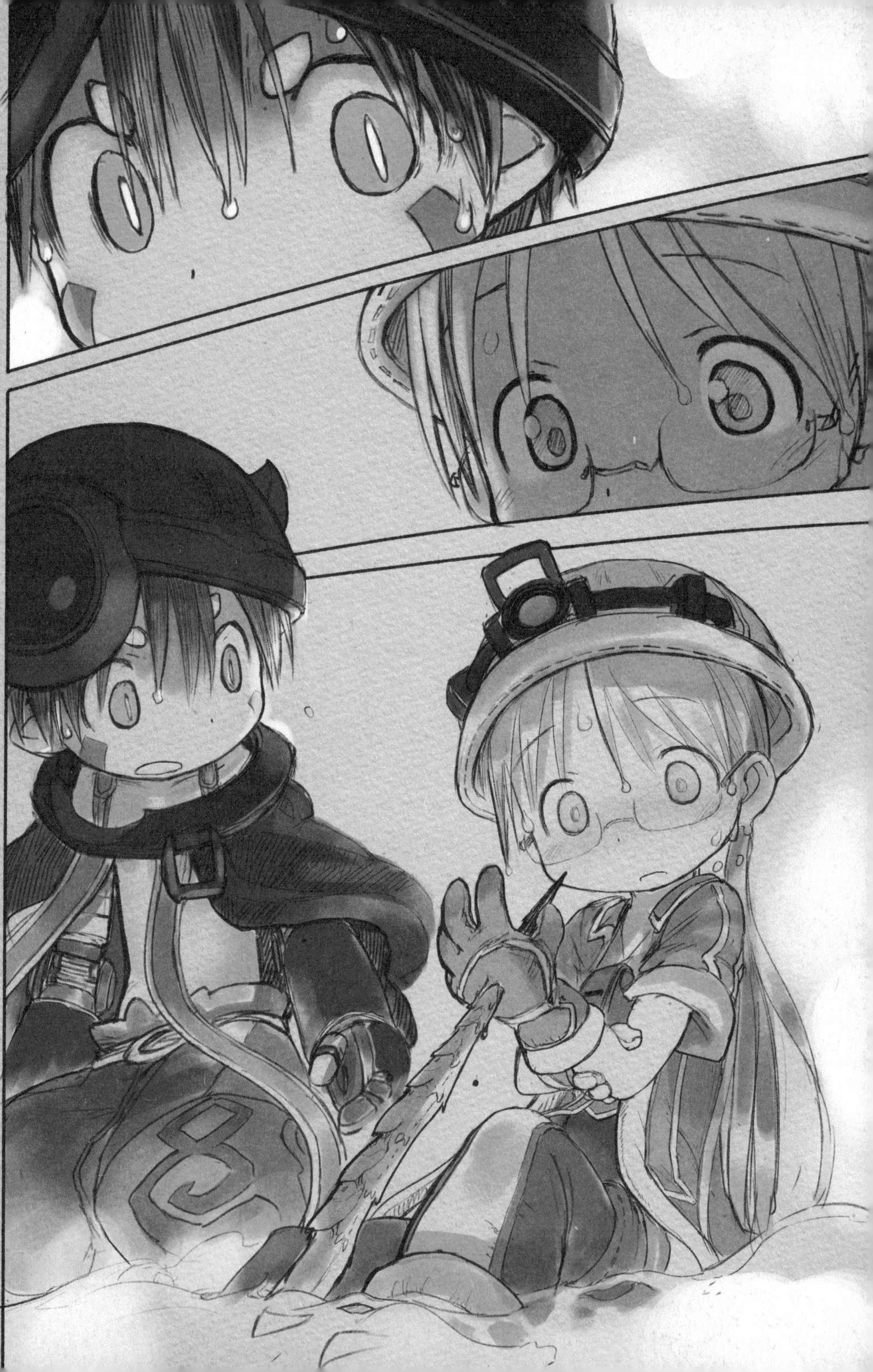

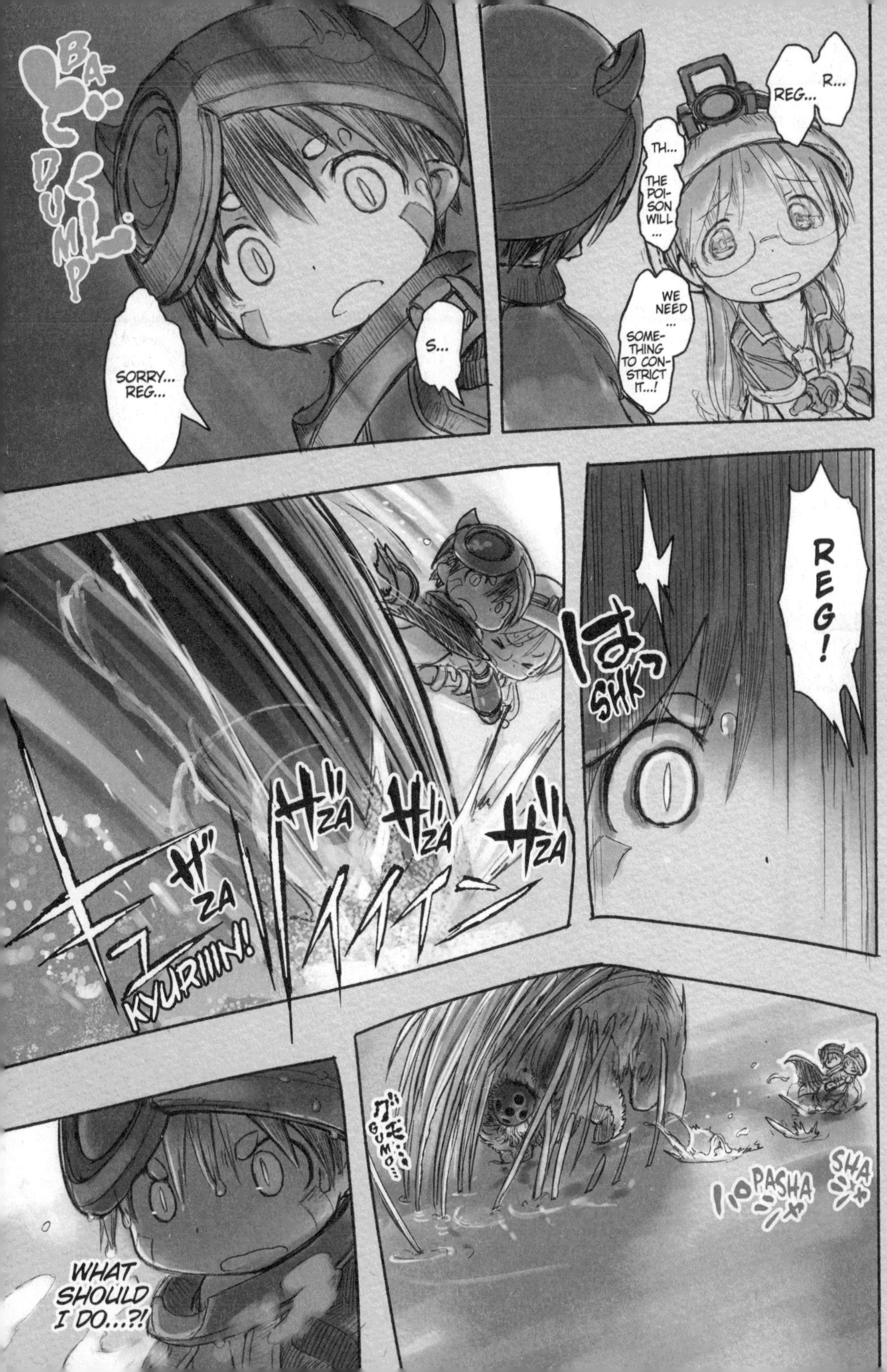

R...
REG...
TH...
THE POISON WILL...
WE NEED... SOMETHING TO CONSTRICT IT...!
BA-DUMP
S...
SORRY... REG...
REG!
はっ
SHK
ZA
ZA
ZA
ZA
KYURIIIN!
SHA
PASHA
GUMO...
WHAT SHOULD I DO...?!

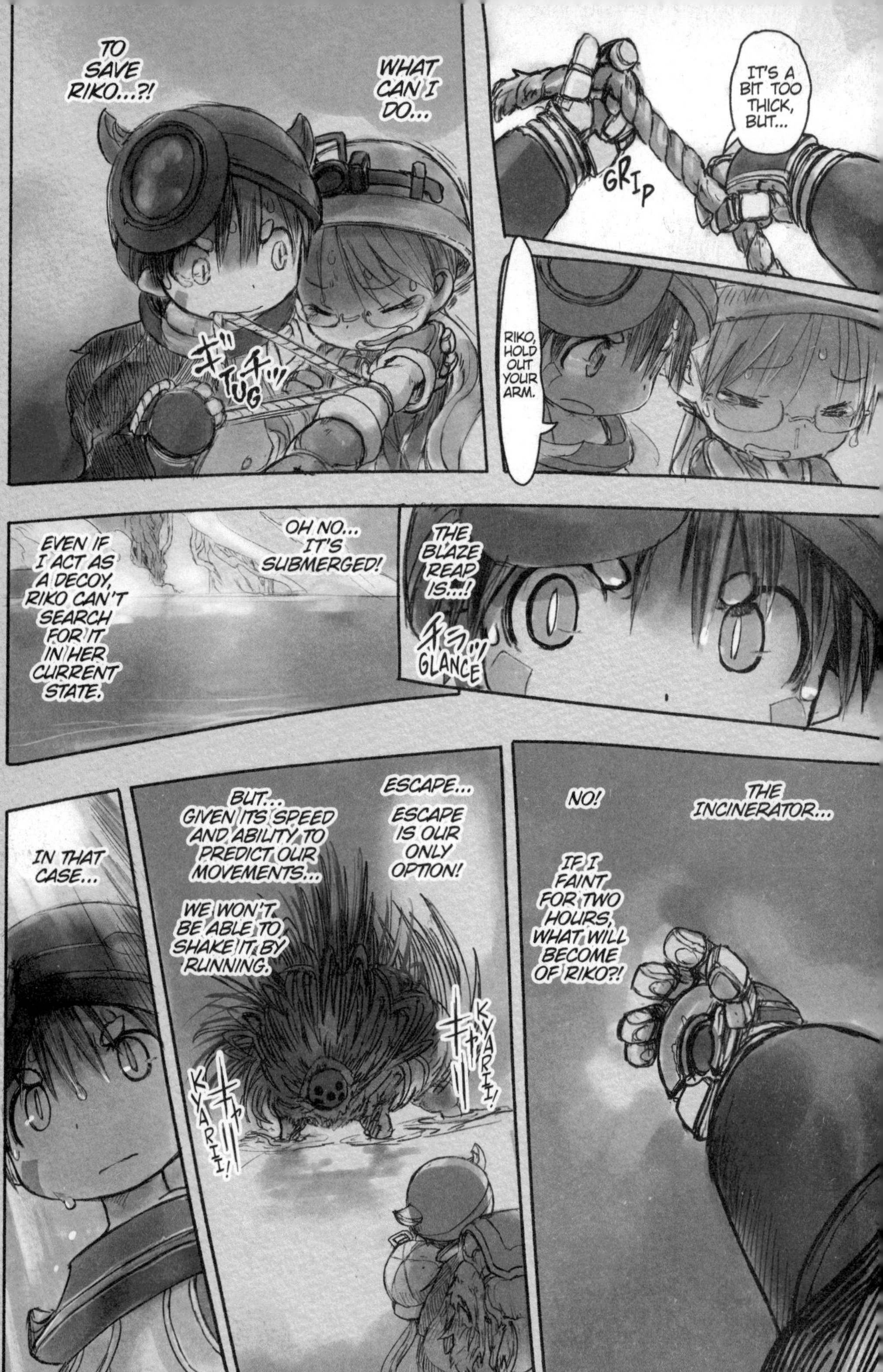
IT'S A BIT TOO THICK, BUT...
GRIP
RIKO, HOLD OUT YOUR ARM.
WHAT CAN I DO...
TO SAVE RIKO...?!
ギチッ
TUG
THE BLAZE REAP IS...!
チラッ
GLANCE
OH NO... IT'S SUBMERGED!
EVEN IF I ACT AS A DECOY, RIKO CAN'T SEARCH FOR IT IN HER CURRENT STATE.
THE INCINERATOR...
NO!
IF I FAINT FOR TWO HOURS, WHAT WILL BECOME OF RIKO?!
ESCAPE...
ESCAPE IS OUR ONLY OPTION!
BUT... GIVEN ITS SPEED AND ABILITY TO PREDICT OUR MOVEMENTS...
WE WON'T BE ABLE TO SHAKE IT BY RUNNING.
KYARII!
KYARII!
IN THAT CASE...

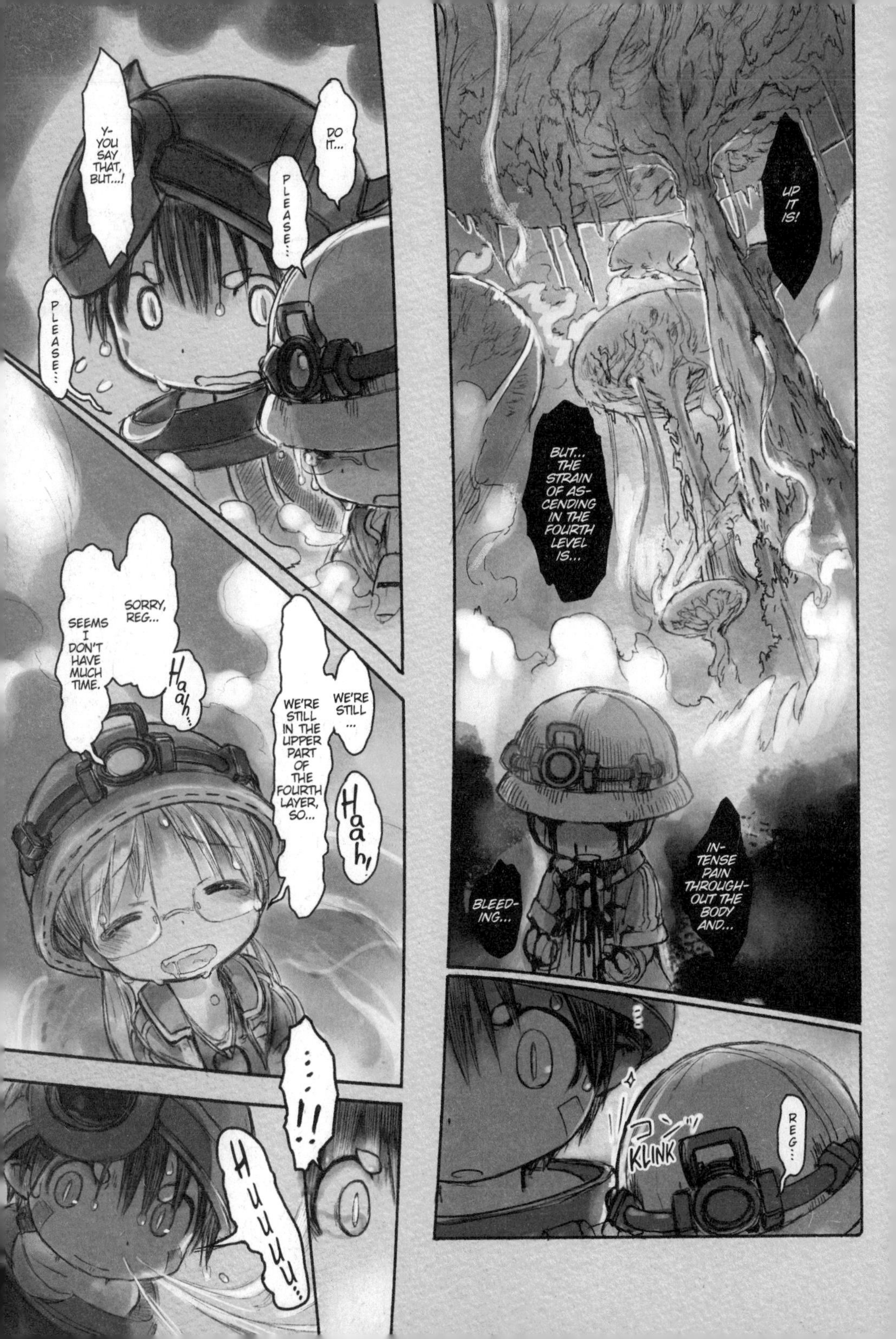
UP IT IS!
BUT... THE STRAIN OF ASCENDING IN THE FOURTH LEVEL IS...
INTENSE PAIN THROUGHOUT THE BODY AND...
BLEEDING...
REG...
KLINK
DO IT...
PLEASE...
Y-YOU SAY THAT, BUT...!
PLEASE...
WE'RE STILL...
WE'RE STILL IN THE UPPER PART OF THE FOURTH LAYER, SO...
Haah!
SORRY, REG...
SEEMS I DON'T HAVE MUCH TIME.
Haah...
...!!
Huuuuu...

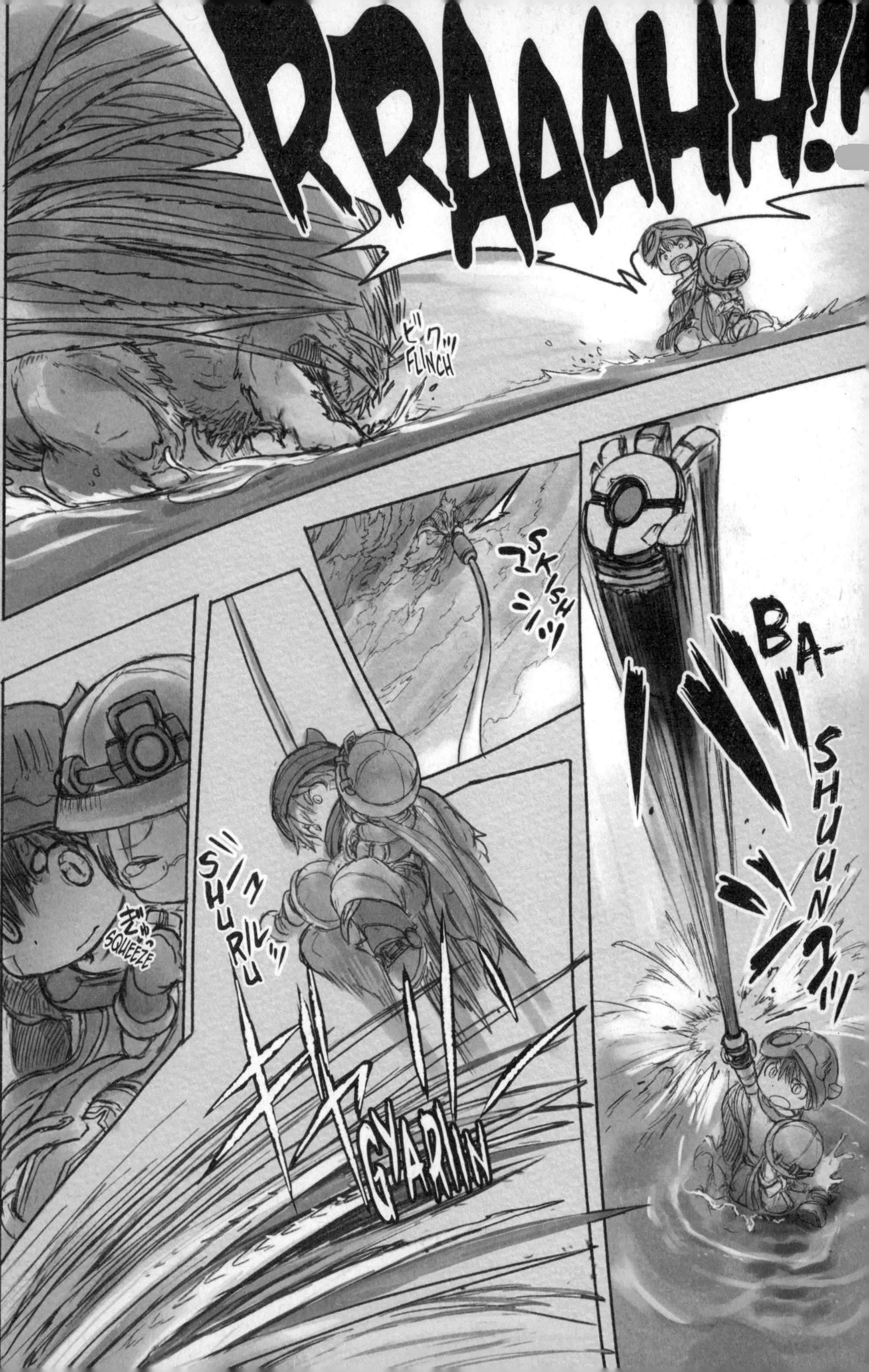
RRAAAHH!!
ビクッ
FLINCH
BA-SHUUN
SKISH
SHURURU
GYARIN
SQUEEZE

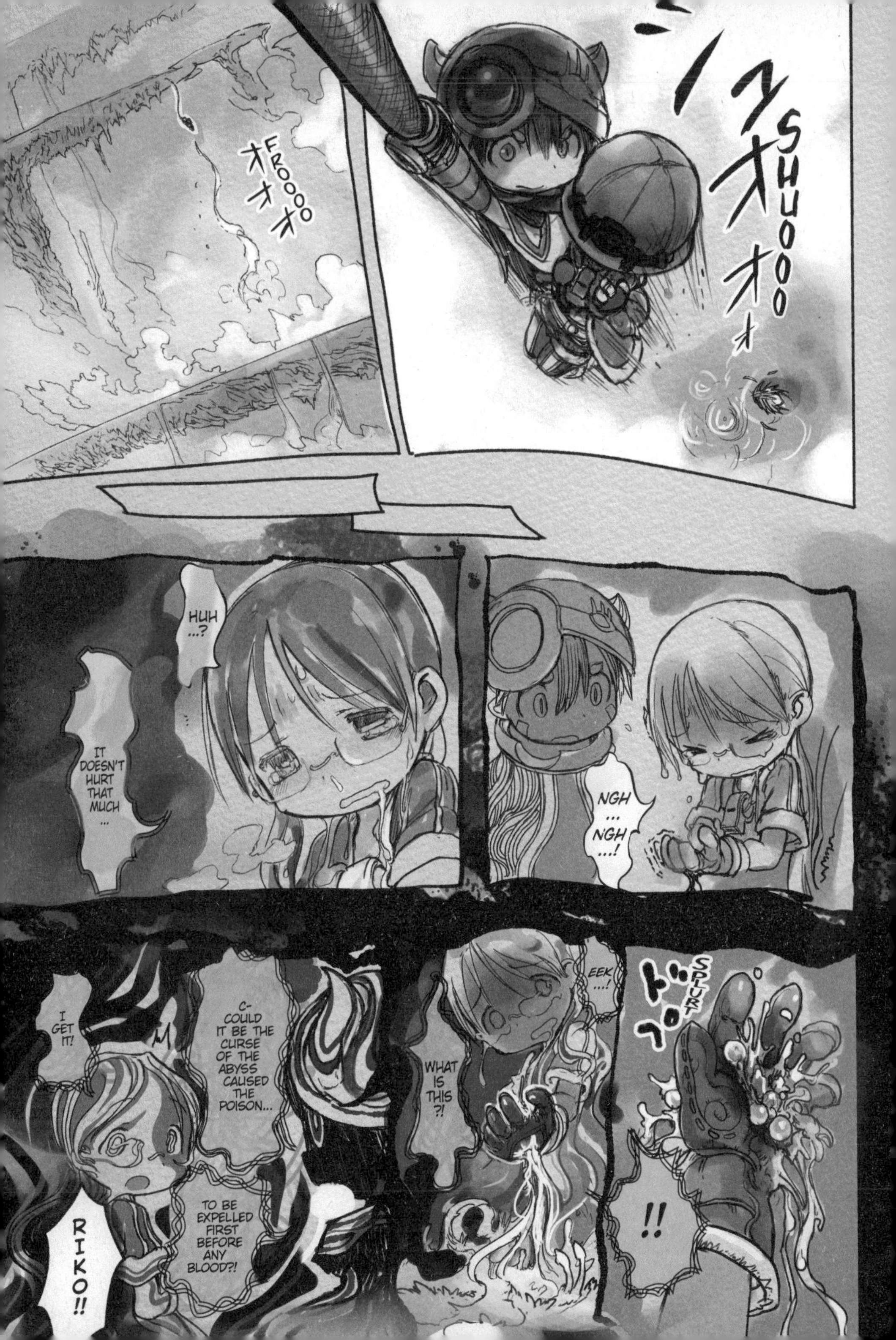
SHUOOOO
FROOOOO
NGH ...NGH ...!
HUH ...?
IT DOESN'T HURT THAT MUCH ...
SPLURT
!!
EEK ...!
WHAT IS THIS?!
C-COULD IT BE THE CURSE OF THE ABYSS CAUSED THE POISON...
I GET IT!
TO BE EXPELLED FIRST BEFORE ANY BLOOD?!
RIKO!!

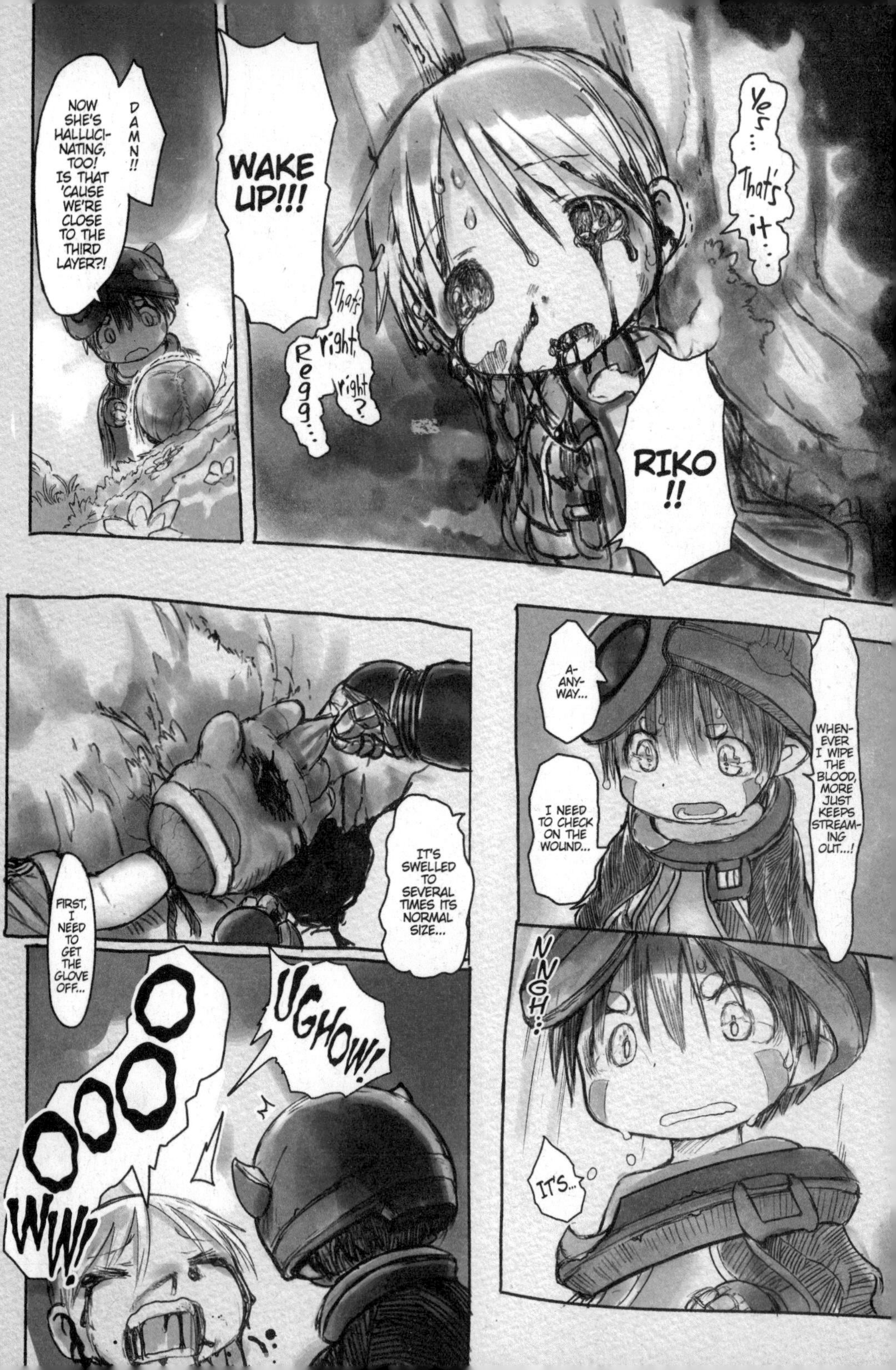

Yes... That's it...
That's right, right? Regg...
RIKO!!
WAKE UP!!!
DAMN!!
NOW SHE'S HALLUCINATING, TOO! IS THAT 'CAUSE WE'RE CLOSE TO THE THIRD LAYER?!
WHENEVER I WIPE THE BLOOD, MORE JUST KEEPS STREAMING OUT...!
A-ANYWAY...
I NEED TO CHECK ON THE WOUND...
IT'S SWELLED TO SEVERAL TIMES ITS NORMAL SIZE...
FIRST, I NEED TO GET THE GLOVE OFF...
NNGH...
IT'S...
UGHOW!
OOOOWW!

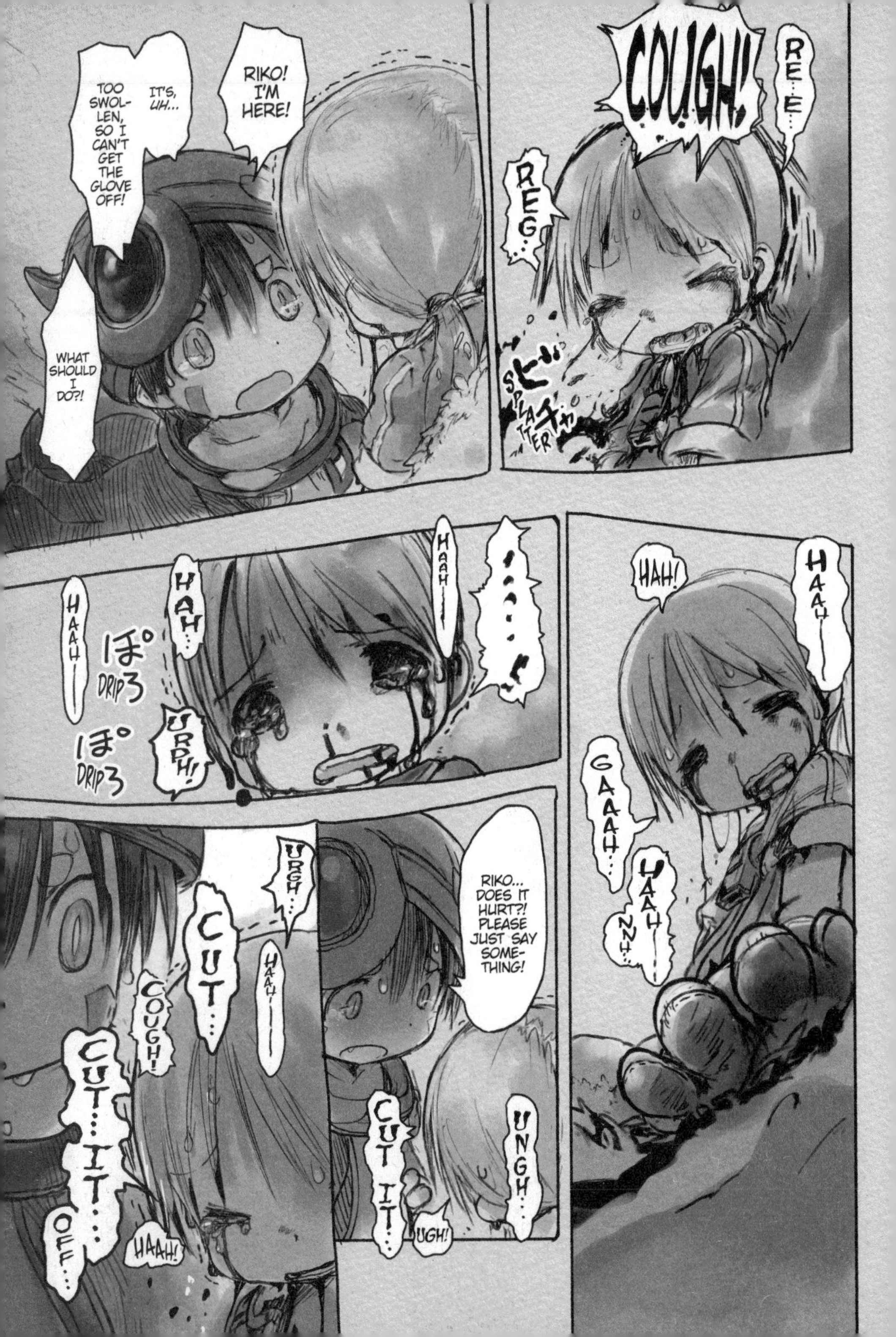
COUGH!
RE...E...
REG...
ビチャ SPLATTER
RIKO! I'M HERE!
IT'S, UH...
TOO SWOLLEN, SO I CAN'T GET THE GLOVE OFF!
WHAT SHOULD I DO?!
HAH!
HAAAH--
GAAAH...
HAAAH
NNH...
...!
HAAH--
HAH...
HAAAH--
ぽろ DRIP
ぽろ DRIP
URGH!
RIKO... DOES IT HURT?! PLEASE JUST SAY SOMETHING!
URGH...
HAAH--
UNGH...
CUT IT...
UGH!
CUT...
COUGH!
CUT... IT... OFF...
HAAH!

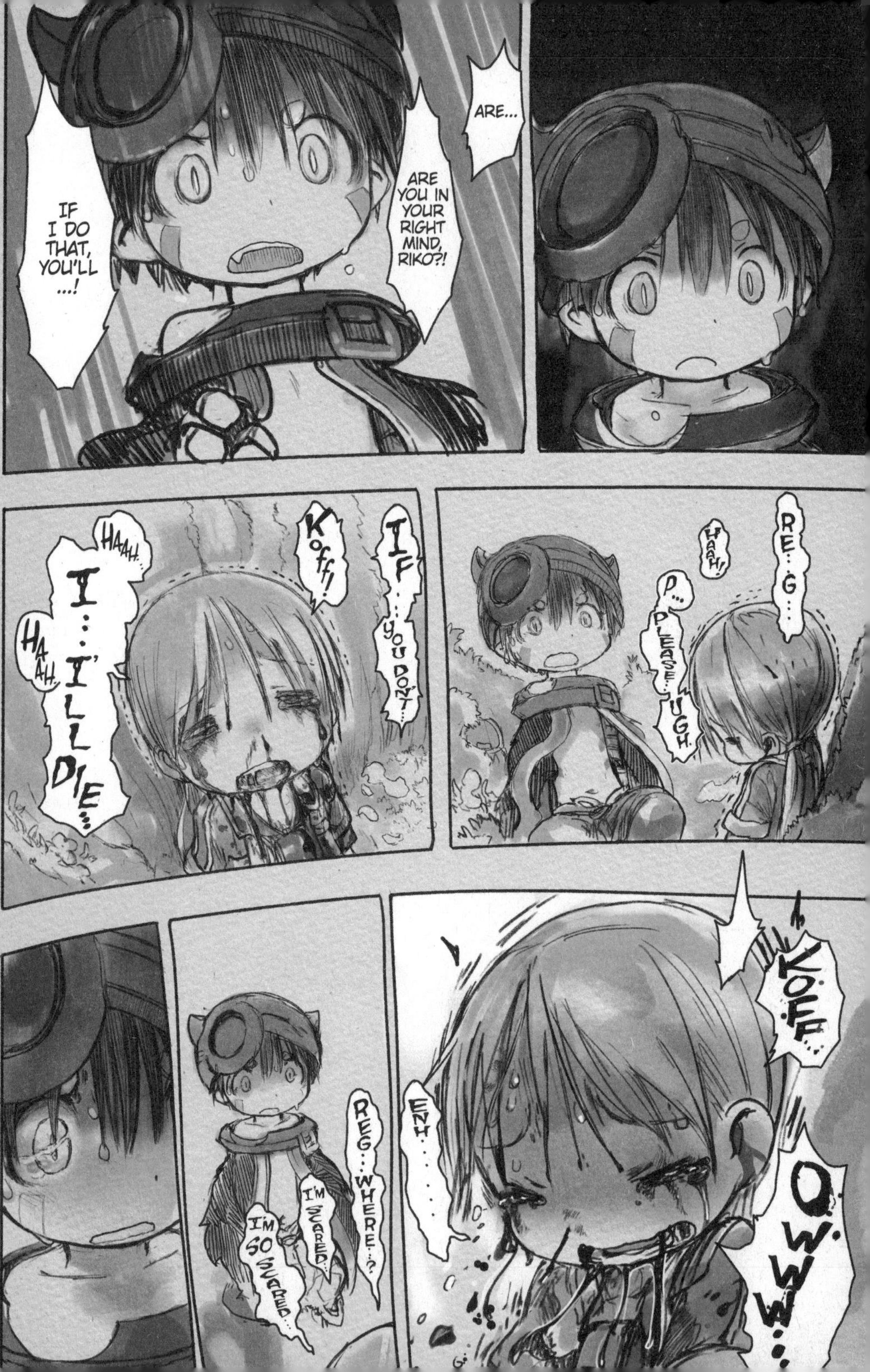
ARE...
ARE YOU IN YOUR RIGHT MIND, RIKO?!
IF I DO THAT, YOU'LL ...!
RE... G...
HAAH!
P... PLEASE... UGH.
IF... YOU DON'T...
KOFF!
HAAH.
I... I'LL DIE...
HAAH.
KOFF...
OWWW...
ENH......
REG... WHERE...?
I'M SCARED...
I'M SO SCARED...

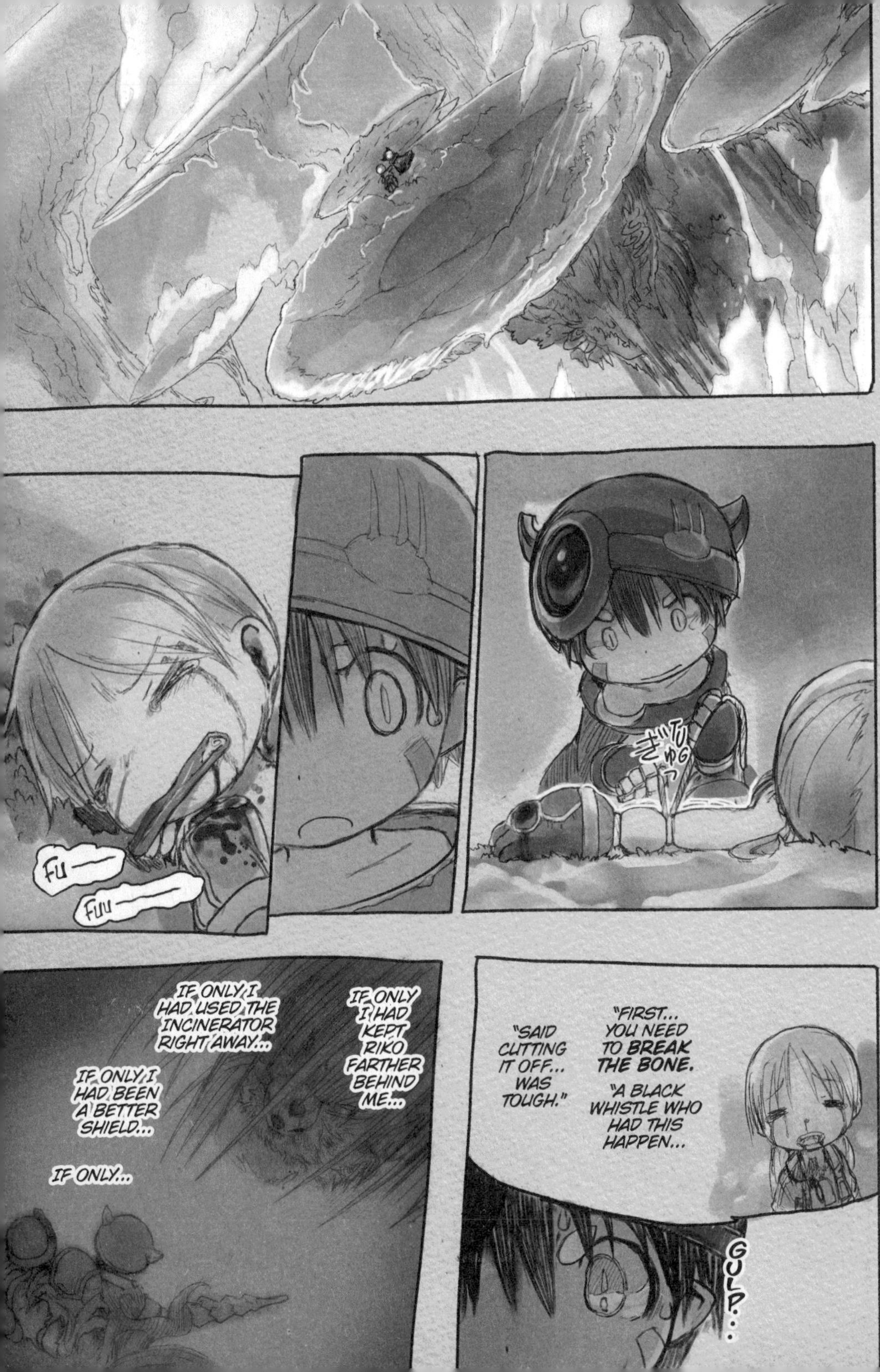
TUG
Fu—
Fuu—
"FIRST... YOU NEED TO BREAK THE BONE.
"A BLACK WHISTLE WHO HAD THIS HAPPEN...
"SAID CUTTING IT OFF... WAS TOUGH."
GULP...
IF ONLY I HAD KEPT RIKO FARTHER BEHIND ME...
IF ONLY I HAD USED THE INCINERATOR RIGHT AWAY...
IF ONLY I HAD BEEN A BETTER SHIELD...
IF ONLY...

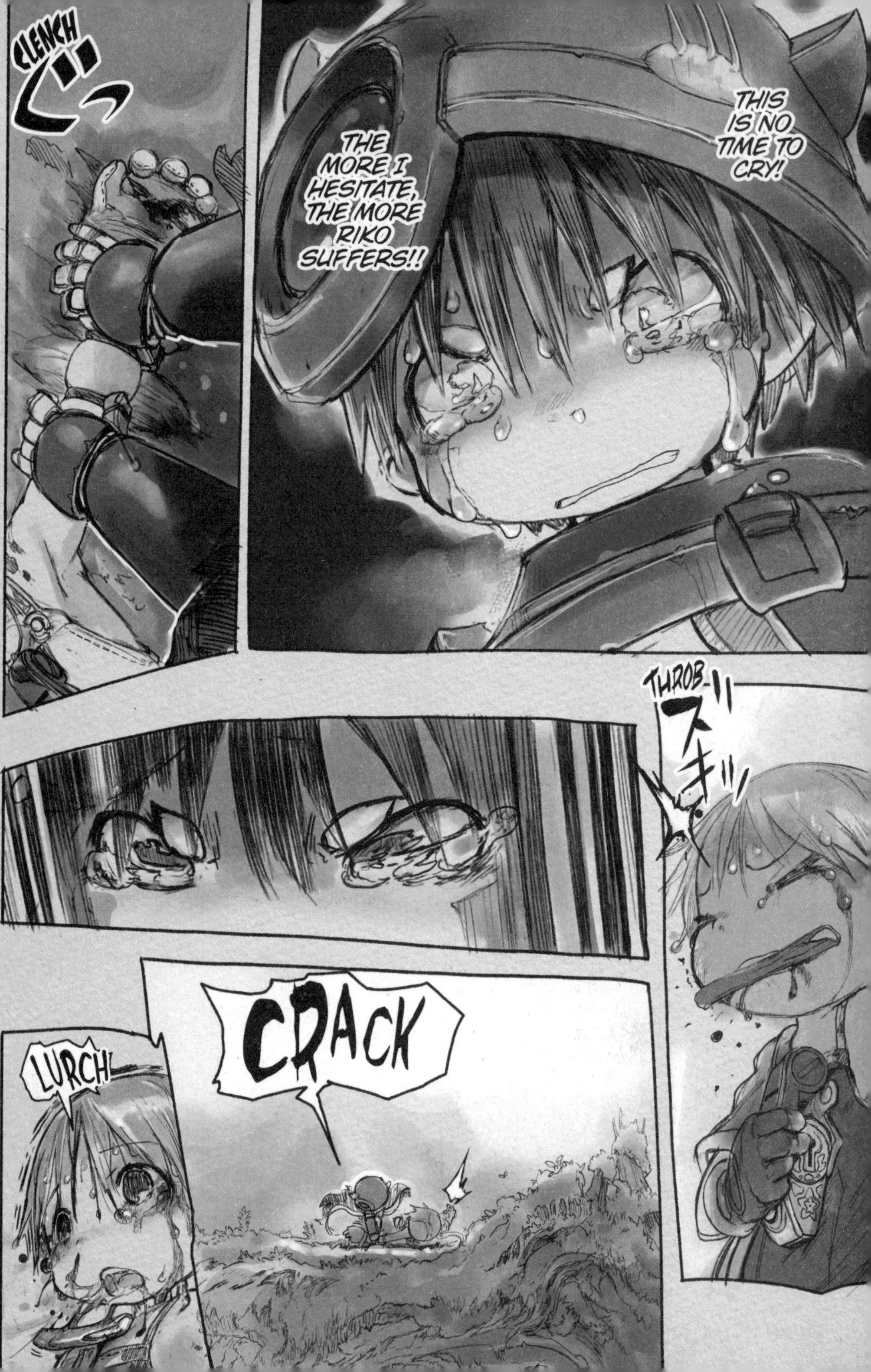

THIS IS NO TIME TO CRY!
THE MORE I HESITATE, THE MORE RIKO SUFFERS!!
CLENCH
ぐっ
THROB
ズキッ
CRACK
LURCH

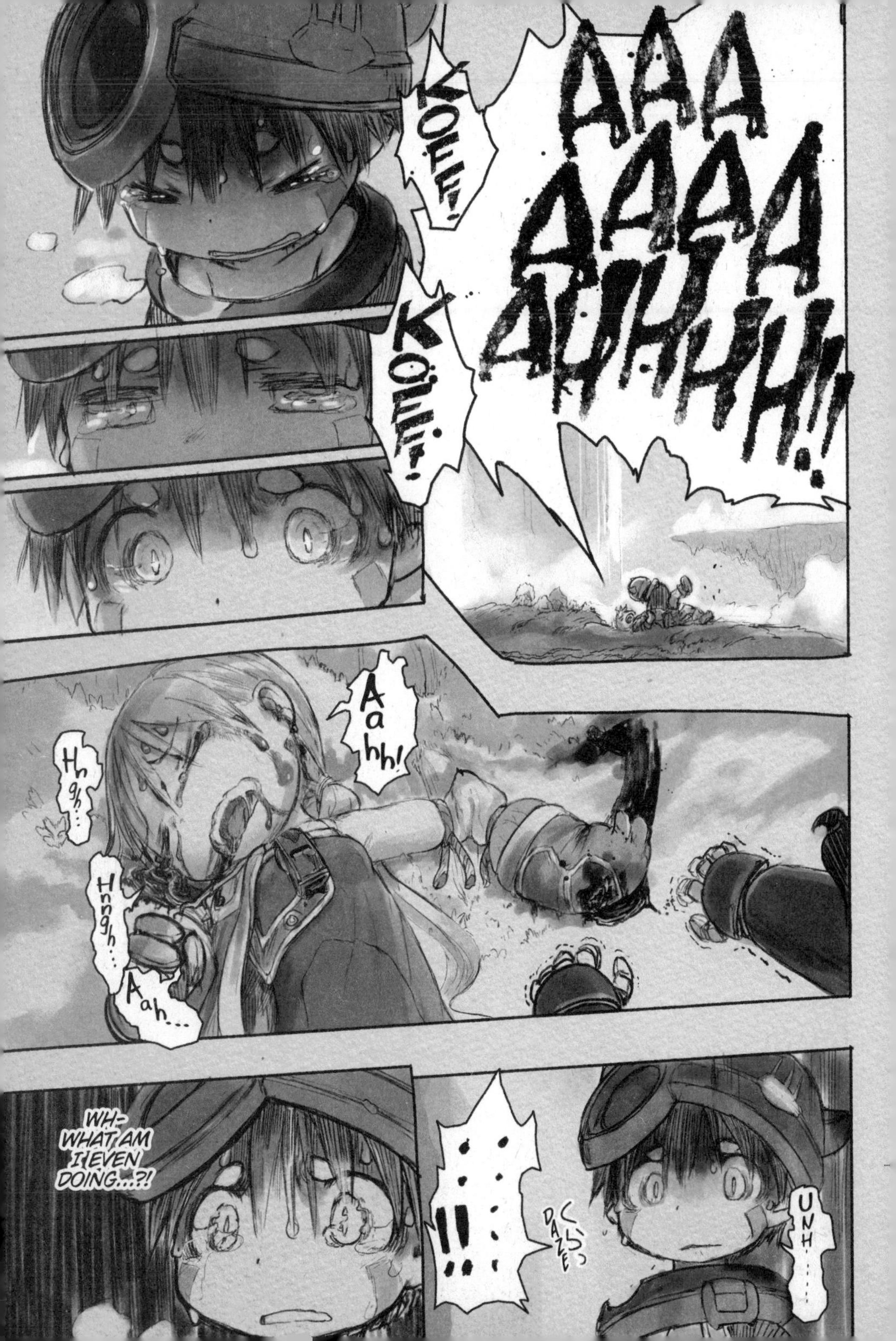
AAAAAAAAHHHHH!!
KOFF!
KOFF!
Aahh!
Hngh...
Hnngh...
Aah...
UNH......
DAZE
...!!
WH-WHAT AM I EVEN DOING...?!

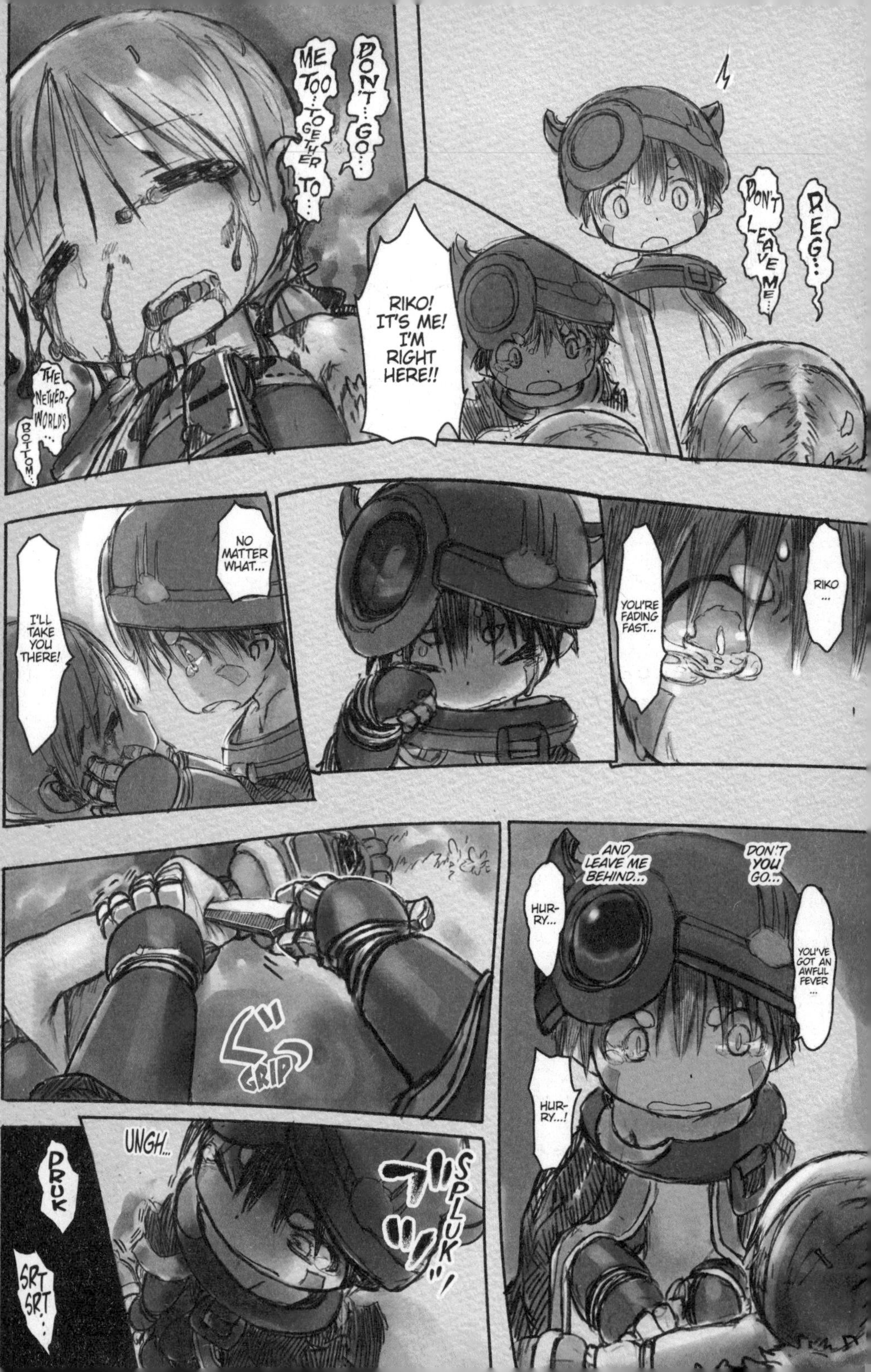
REG...
DON'T LEAVE ME...
RIKO! IT'S ME! I'M RIGHT HERE!!
DON'T...GO...
ME TOO...TOGETHER TO...
THE NETHER-WORLD'S BOTTOM...
RIKO...
YOU'RE FADING FAST...
NO MATTER WHAT...
I'LL TAKE YOU THERE!
DON'T YOU GO...
AND LEAVE ME BEHIND...
YOU'VE GOT AN AWFUL FEVER...
HUR-RY...
HUR-RY...!
GRIP
SPLUK
UNGH...
DRUK
SRT SRT...

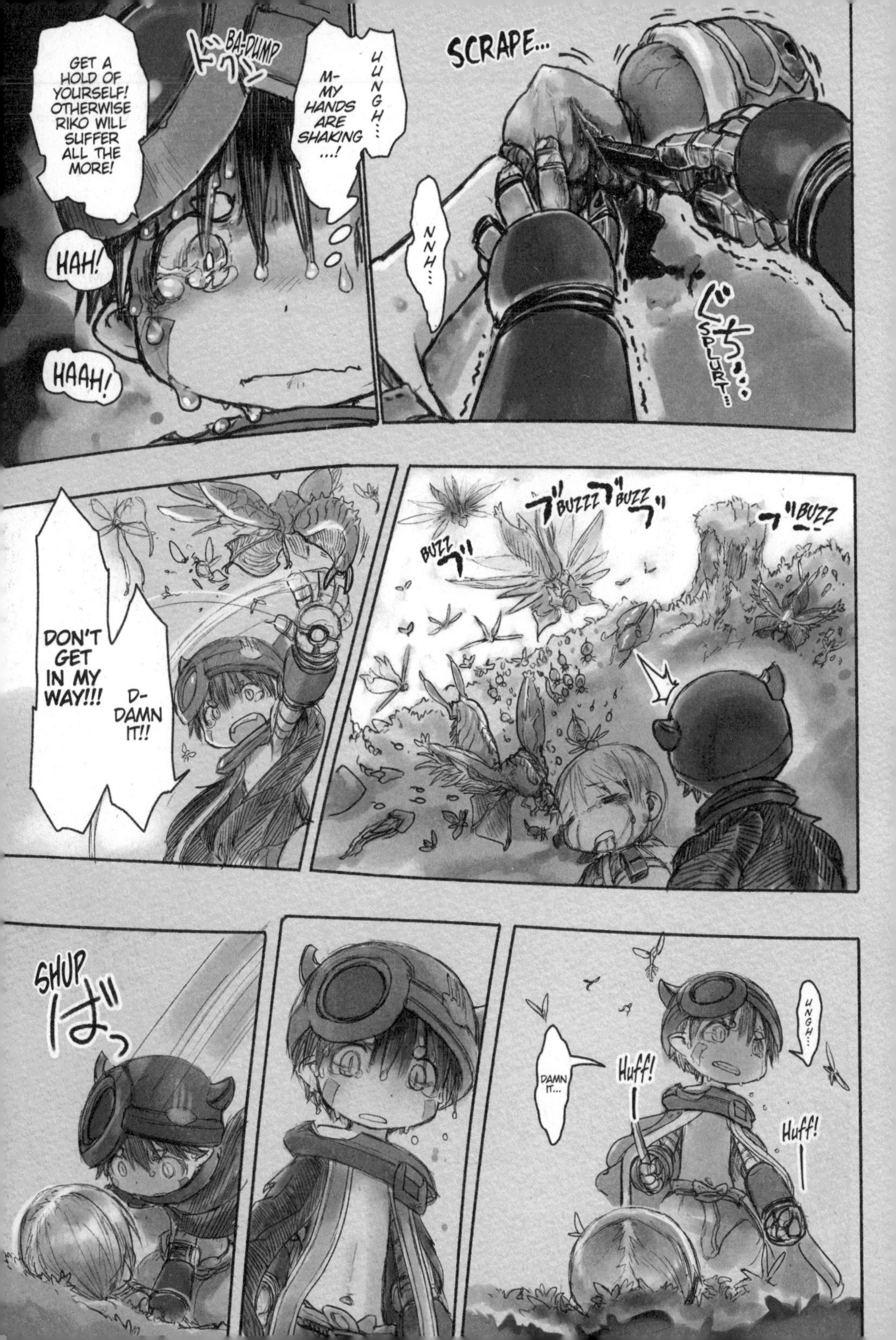
SCRAPE...
NNH...
ぐちっ
SPLURT...
UUNGH...
M-MY HANDS ARE SHAKING...!
BA-DUMP
GET A HOLD OF YOURSELF! OTHERWISE RIKO WILL SUFFER ALL THE MORE!
HAH!
HAAH!
BUZZ
BUZZZ BUZZ
BUZZ
D-DAMN IT!!
DON'T GET IN MY WAY!!!
UNGH...
Huff!
Huff!
DAMN IT...
SHUP
ばっ

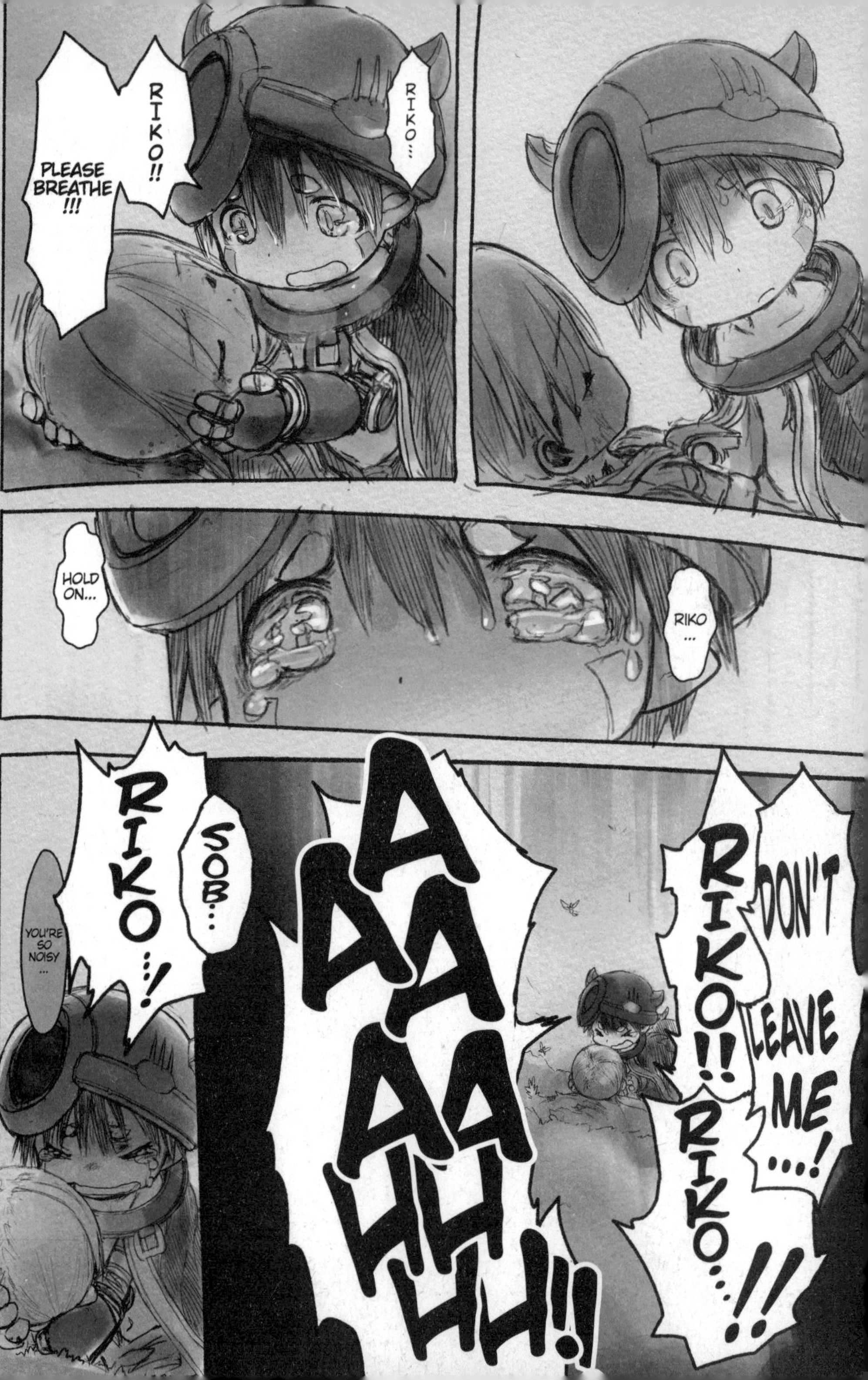
RIKO…
RIKO!!
PLEASE BREATHE!!!
RIKO…
HOLD ON…
DON'T LEAVE ME…!
RIKO!! RIKO…!!
AAAAAAAHHHH!!
SOB…
RIKO…!
YOU'RE SO NOISY…

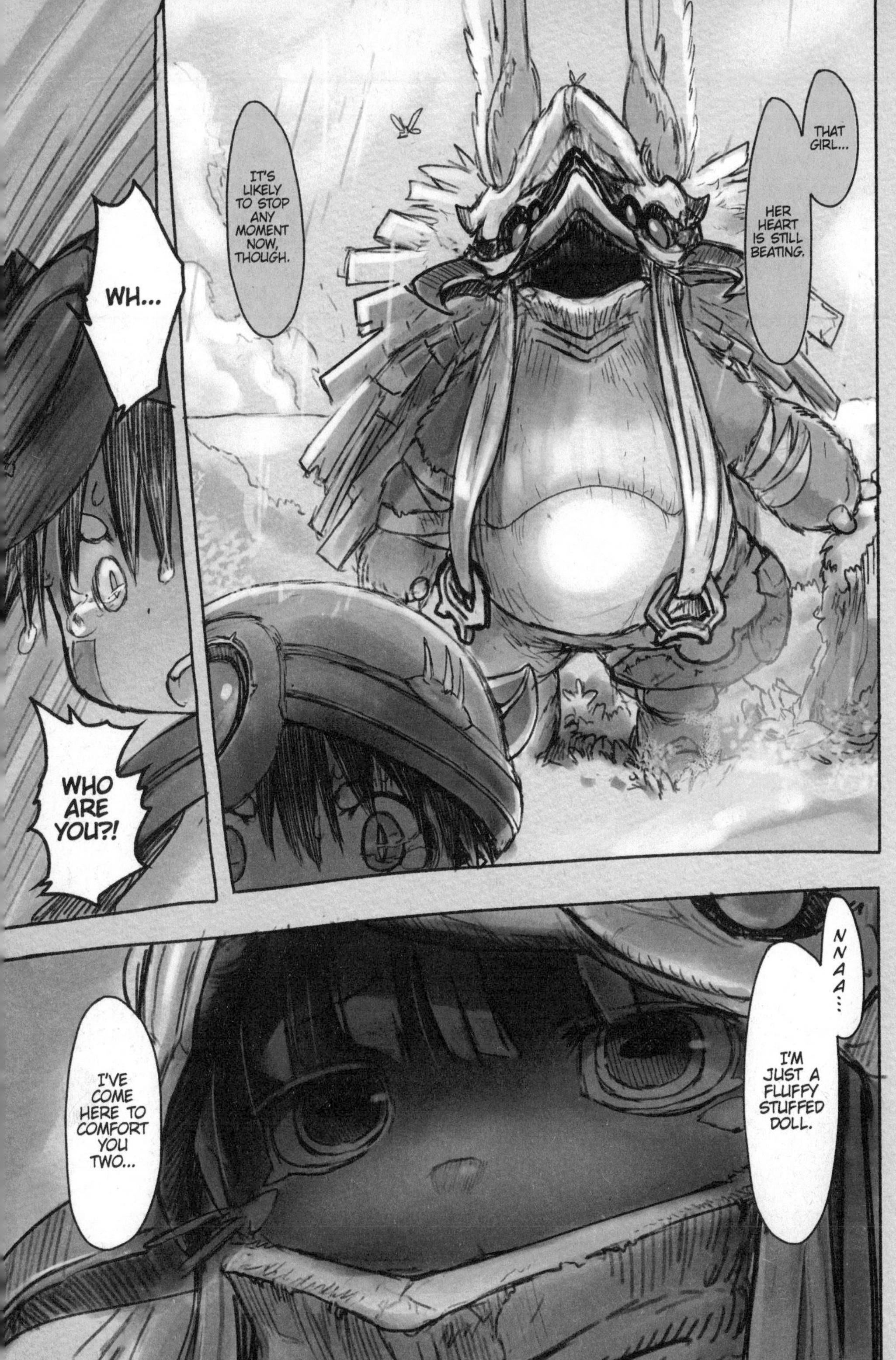
THAT GIRL...
HER HEART IS STILL BEATING.
IT'S LIKELY TO STOP ANY MOMENT NOW, THOUGH.
WH...
WHO ARE YOU?!
NNAAA...
I'M JUST A FLUFFY STUFFED DOLL.
I'VE COME HERE TO COMFORT YOU TWO...

NERITANTAN

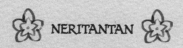

THESE SMALL, FLAT-BODIED ANIMALS LIVE IN THE ROOTS OF THE PLANTS THAT
GROW HAPHAZARDLY WITHIN THE CLIFF FACES OF THE DEPTHS' THIRD LAYER.

THE INTERIORS OF THE HOLLOW PLANT ROOTS WHERE NERITANTANS
LIVE COMMONLY CONTAIN LEAVES (WHICH ARE BRITTLE LIKE COOKIES),
FLOWERS, AND EVEN FRUITS.

NERITANTANS AND THESE PLANTS HAVE A SYMBIOTIC RELATIONSHIP,
IN WHICH NERITANTANS DISPERSE THE SEEDS OF THE PLANTS WITH THEIR EXCREMENT.

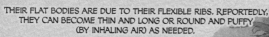

THEIR FLAT BODIES ARE DUE TO THEIR FLEXIBLE RIBS. REPORTEDLY,
THEY CAN BECOME THIN AND LONG OR ROUND AND PUFFY
(BY INHALING AIR) AS NEEDED.

PERHAPS BECAUSE OF THEIR DIET OF FRUIT,
THEIR FLESH IS DELICIOUS, WHICH MAKES IT
SUITABLE FOR A WIDE RANGE OF DISHES.

* THIS ILLUSTRATION SHOWS HOW THEY CHANGE
THE SHAPE OF THEIR BODIES AND BUNCH UP
IN CLOSE FORMATION TO PROTECT
THEIR DEN FROM PREDATORS.

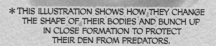

DANGER LEVEL: ☆ (HARMLESS)

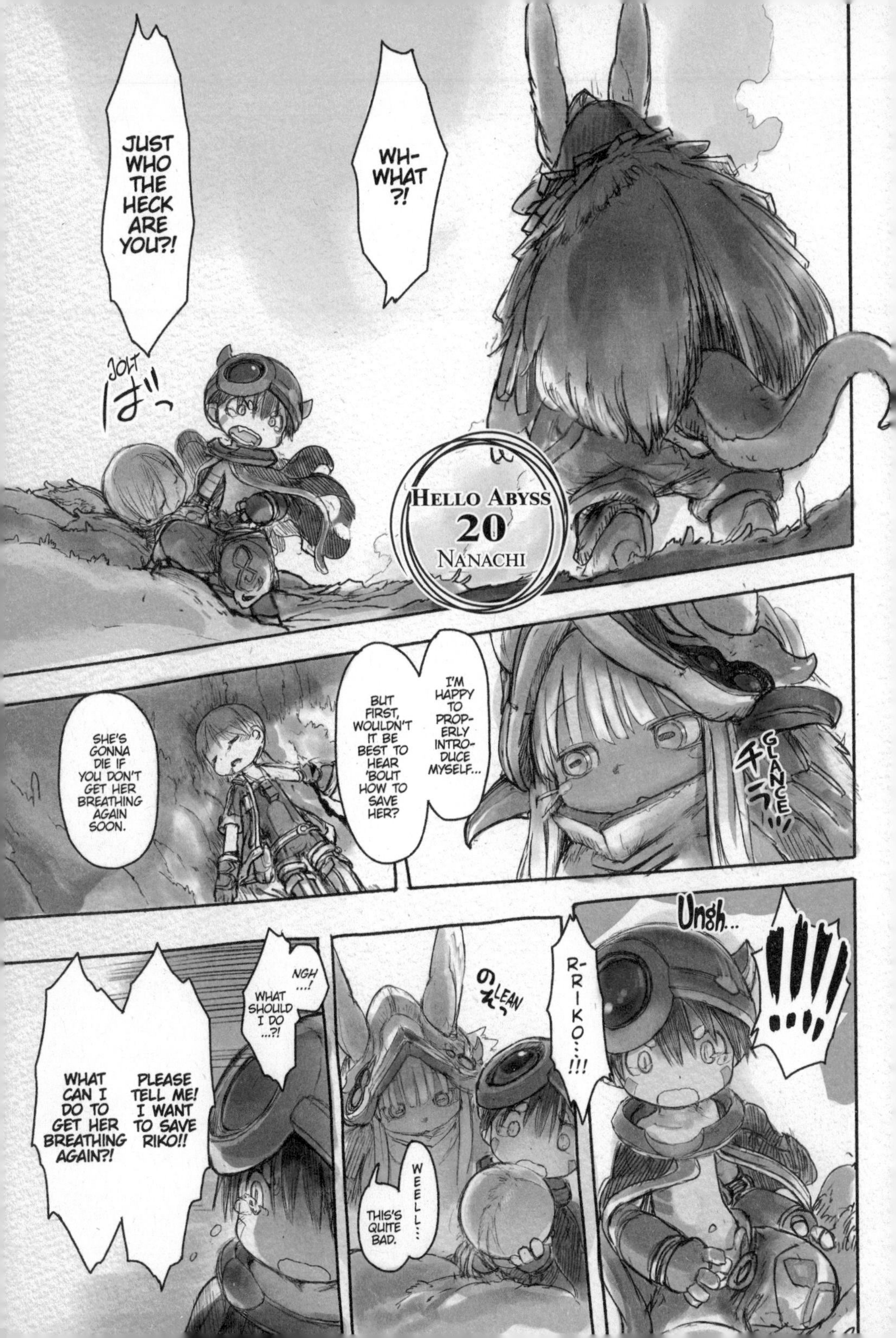
WH-WHAT?!
JUST WHO THE HECK ARE YOU?!
JOLT ぱっ
HELLO ABYSS 20 NANACHI
GLANCE チラッ
I'M HAPPY TO PROPERLY INTRO-DUCE MYSELF...
BUT FIRST, WOULDN'T IT BE BEST TO HEAR 'BOUT HOW TO SAVE HER?
SHE'S GONNA DIE IF YOU DON'T GET HER BREATHING AGAIN SOON.
Ungh...
!!!!!
R-RIKO...!!!
LEAN のそっ
NGH...!
WHAT SHOULD I DO...?!
WEELL...
THIS'S QUITE BAD.
PLEASE TELL ME! I WANT TO SAVE RIKO!!
WHAT CAN I DO TO GET HER BREATHING AGAIN?!

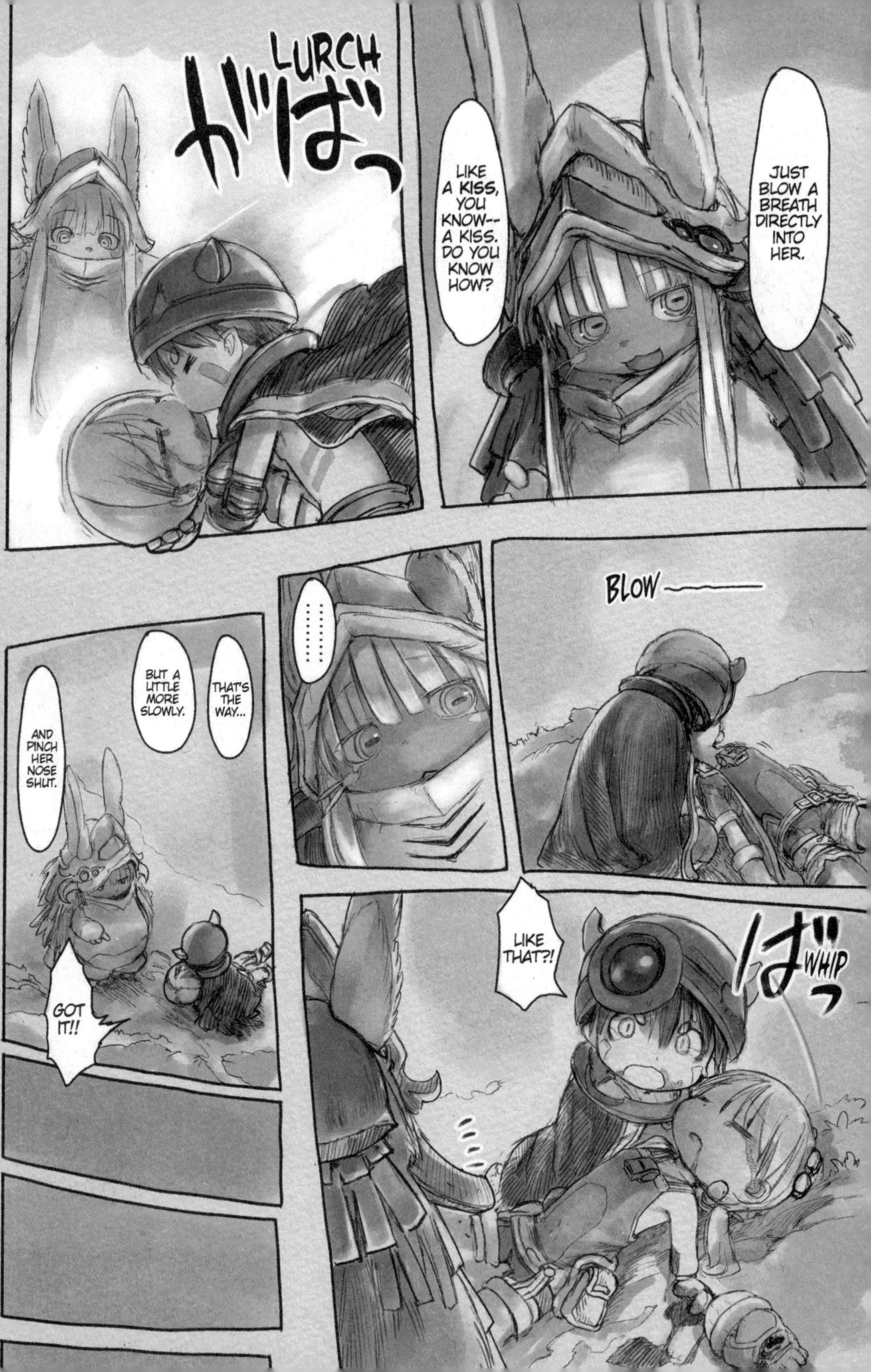
JUST BLOW A BREATH DIRECTLY INTO HER.
LIKE A KISS, YOU KNOW-- A KISS. DO YOU KNOW HOW?
LURCH
がばっ
BLOW
......
LIKE THAT?!
ばっ
WHIP
THAT'S THE WAY...
BUT A LITTLE MORE SLOWLY.
AND PINCH HER NOSE SHUT.
GOT IT!!

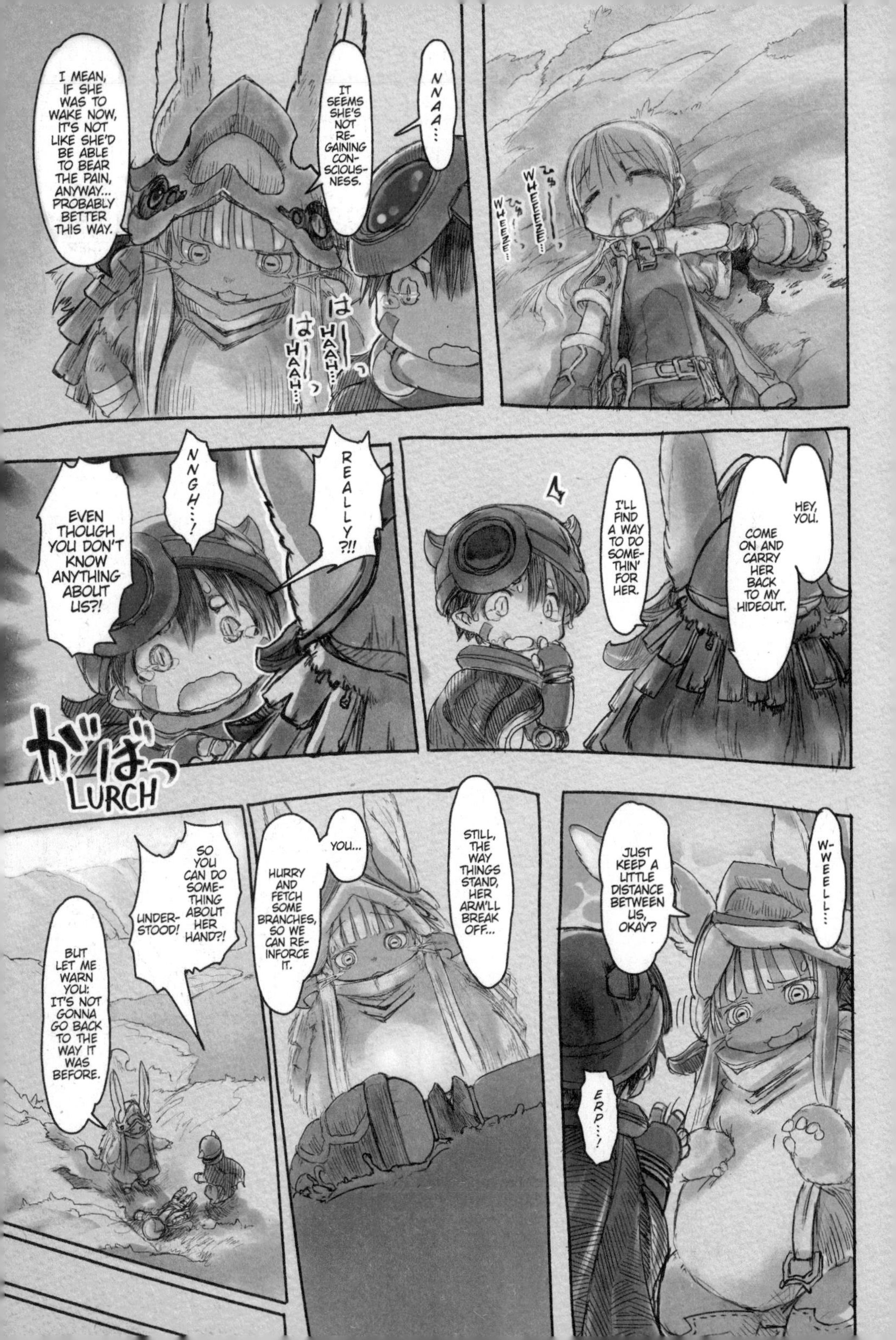

WHEEEZE—,
WHEEZE…
NNAA…
IT SEEMS SHE'S NOT RE-GAINING CON-SCIOUS-NESS.
I MEAN, IF SHE WAS TO WAKE NOW, IT'S NOT LIKE SHE'D BE ABLE TO BEAR THE PAIN, ANYWAY... PROBABLY BETTER THIS WAY.
は— HAAH…っ
は— HAAH…っ
HEY, YOU. COME ON AND CARRY HER BACK TO MY HIDEOUT.
I'LL FIND A WAY TO DO SOME-THIN' FOR HER.
REALLY?!!
NNGH…!
EVEN THOUGH YOU DON'T KNOW ANYTHING ABOUT US?!
がばっ LURCH
W-WEELL…
JUST KEEP A LITTLE DISTANCE BETWEEN US, OKAY?
ERP…!
STILL, THE WAY THINGS STAND, HER ARM'LL BREAK OFF…
YOU…
HURRY AND FETCH SOME BRANCHES, SO WE CAN RE-INFORCE IT.
SO YOU CAN DO SOME-THING ABOUT HER HAND?!
UNDER-STOOD!
BUT LET ME WARN YOU: IT'S NOT GONNA GO BACK TO THE WAY IT WAS BEFORE.

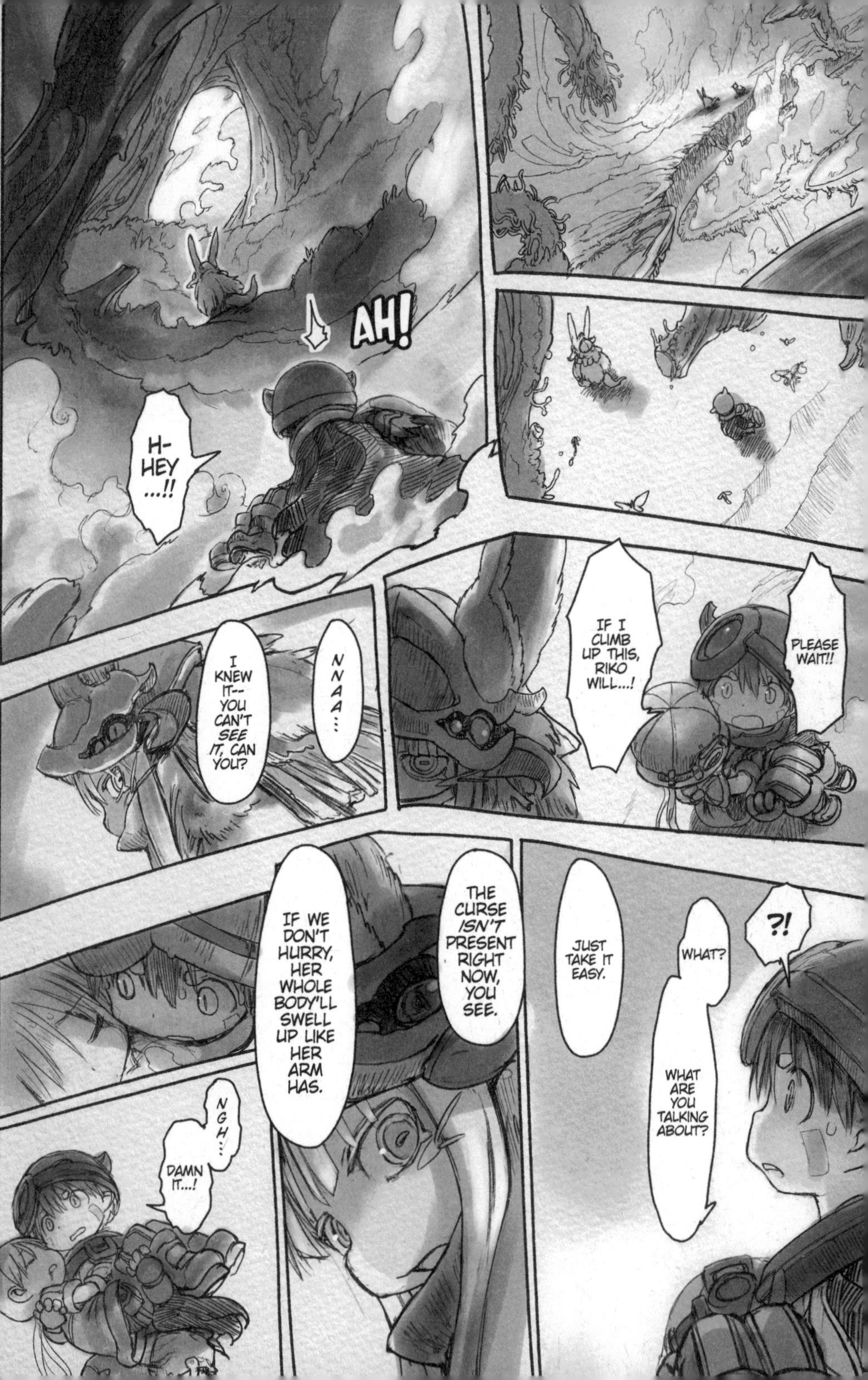
AH!
H-HEY ...!!
PLEASE WAIT!!
IF I CLIMB UP THIS, RIKO WILL...!
NNAAA...
I KNEW IT-- YOU CAN'T *SEE* IT, CAN YOU?
?!
WHAT?
WHAT ARE YOU TALKING ABOUT?
JUST TAKE IT EASY.
THE CURSE *ISN'T* PRESENT RIGHT NOW, YOU SEE.
IF WE DON'T HURRY, HER WHOLE BODY'LL SWELL UP LIKE HER ARM HAS.
NGH...
DAMN IT...!

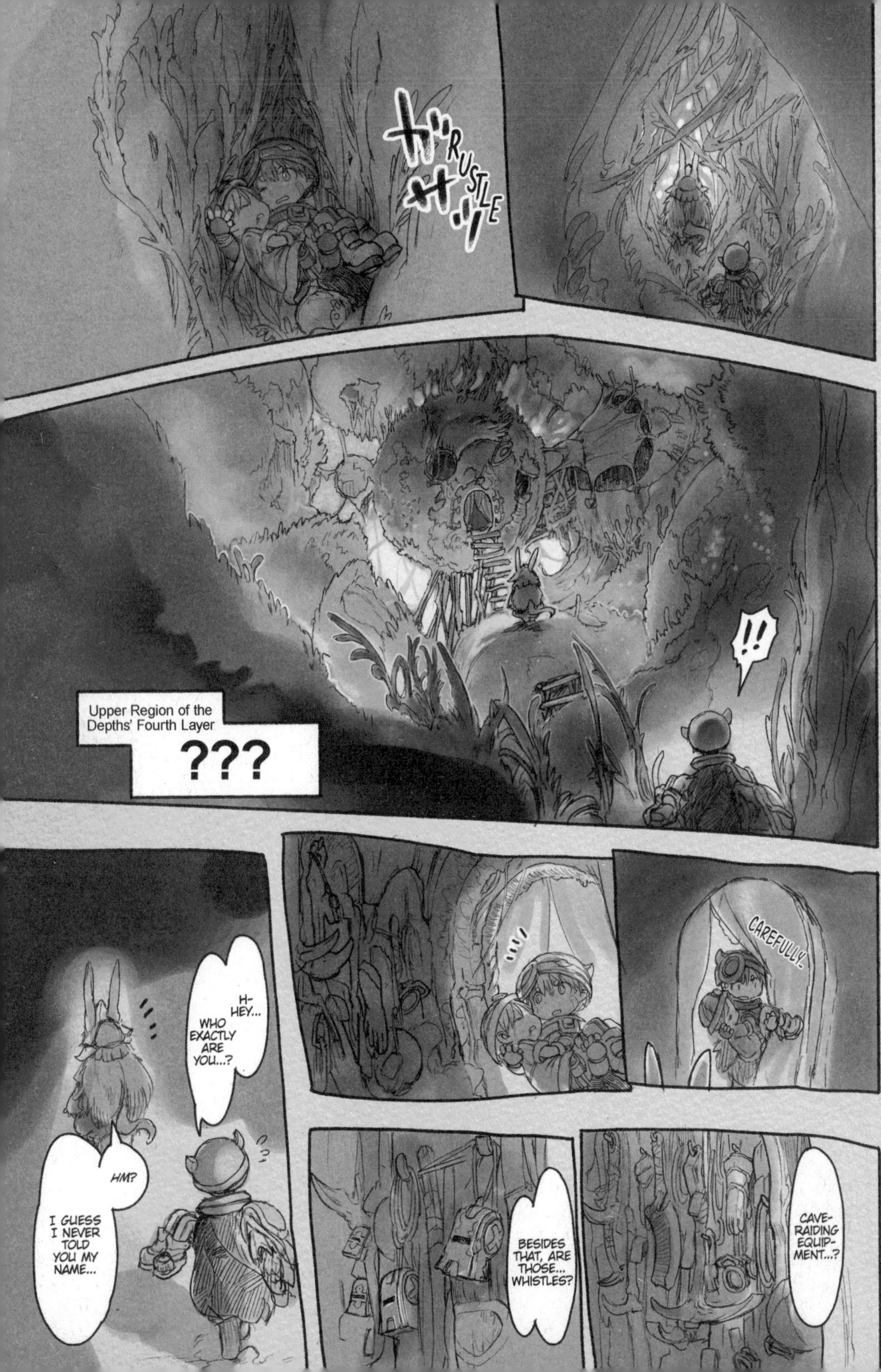
RUSTLE
!!
Upper Region of the Depths' Fourth Layer
???
CAREFULLY.
CAVE-RAIDING EQUIPMENT...?
BESIDES THAT, ARE THOSE... WHISTLES?
H-HEY... WHO EXACTLY ARE YOU...?
HM?
I GUESS I NEVER TOLD YOU MY NAME...

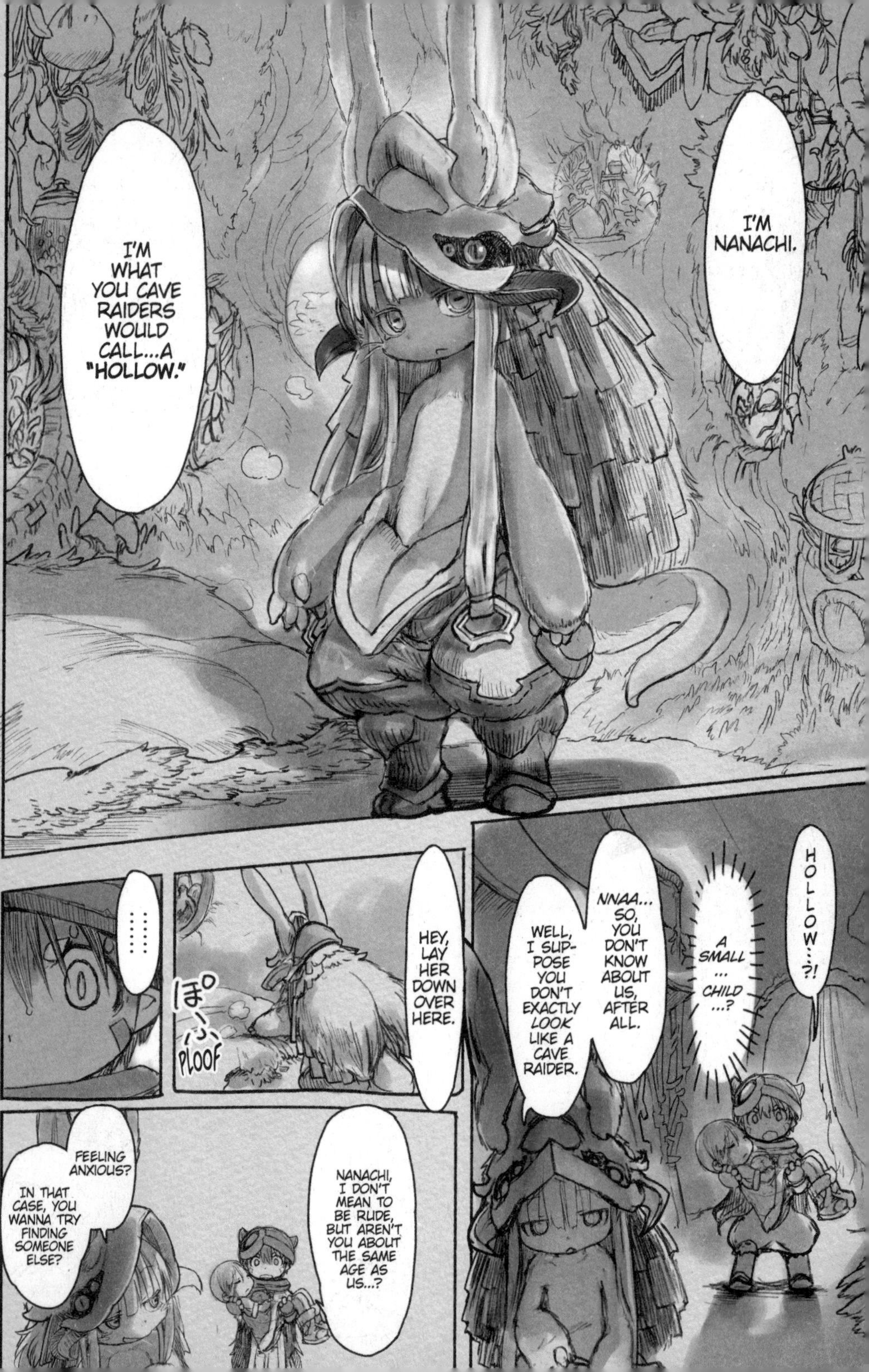
I'M NANACHI.
I'M WHAT YOU CAVE RAIDERS WOULD CALL...A "HOLLOW."
HOLLOW...?!
A SMALL ... CHILD ...?
NNAA... SO, YOU DON'T KNOW ABOUT US, AFTER ALL.
WELL, I SUP-POSE YOU DON'T EXACTLY LOOK LIKE A CAVE RAIDER.
HEY, LAY HER DOWN OVER HERE.
ぽふ
PLOOF
......
NANACHI, I DON'T MEAN TO BE RUDE, BUT AREN'T YOU ABOUT THE SAME AGE AS US...?
FEELING ANXIOUS?
IN THAT CASE, YOU WANNA TRY FINDING SOMEONE ELSE?

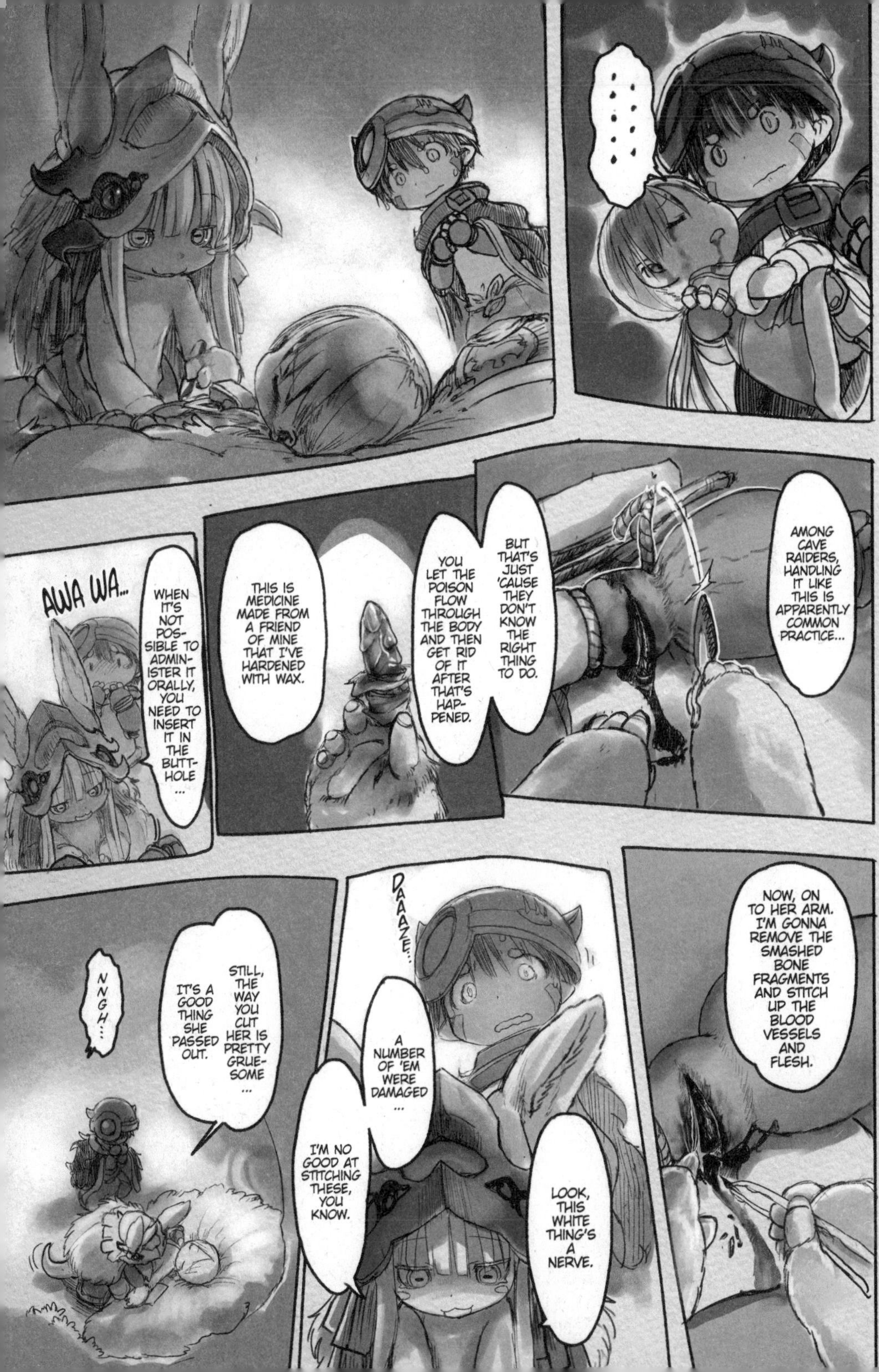
· · · · ·
AMONG CAVE RAIDERS, HANDLING IT LIKE THIS IS APPARENTLY COMMON PRACTICE...
BUT THAT'S JUST 'CAUSE THEY DON'T KNOW THE RIGHT THING TO DO.
YOU LET THE POISON FLOW THROUGH THE BODY AND THEN GET RID OF IT AFTER THAT'S HAPPENED.
THIS IS MEDICINE MADE FROM A FRIEND OF MINE THAT I'VE HARDENED WITH WAX.
WHEN IT'S NOT POSSIBLE TO ADMINISTER IT ORALLY, YOU NEED TO INSERT IT IN THE BUTTHOLE...
AWA WA...
NOW, ON TO HER ARM. I'M GONNA REMOVE THE SMASHED BONE FRAGMENTS AND STITCH UP THE BLOOD VESSELS AND FLESH.
DAAAAZE...
LOOK, THIS WHITE THING'S A NERVE.
A NUMBER OF 'EM WERE DAMAGED...
I'M NO GOOD AT STITCHING THESE, YOU KNOW.
STILL, THE WAY YOU CUT HER IS PRETTY GRUESOME...
IT'S A GOOD THING SHE PASSED OUT.
NNGH...

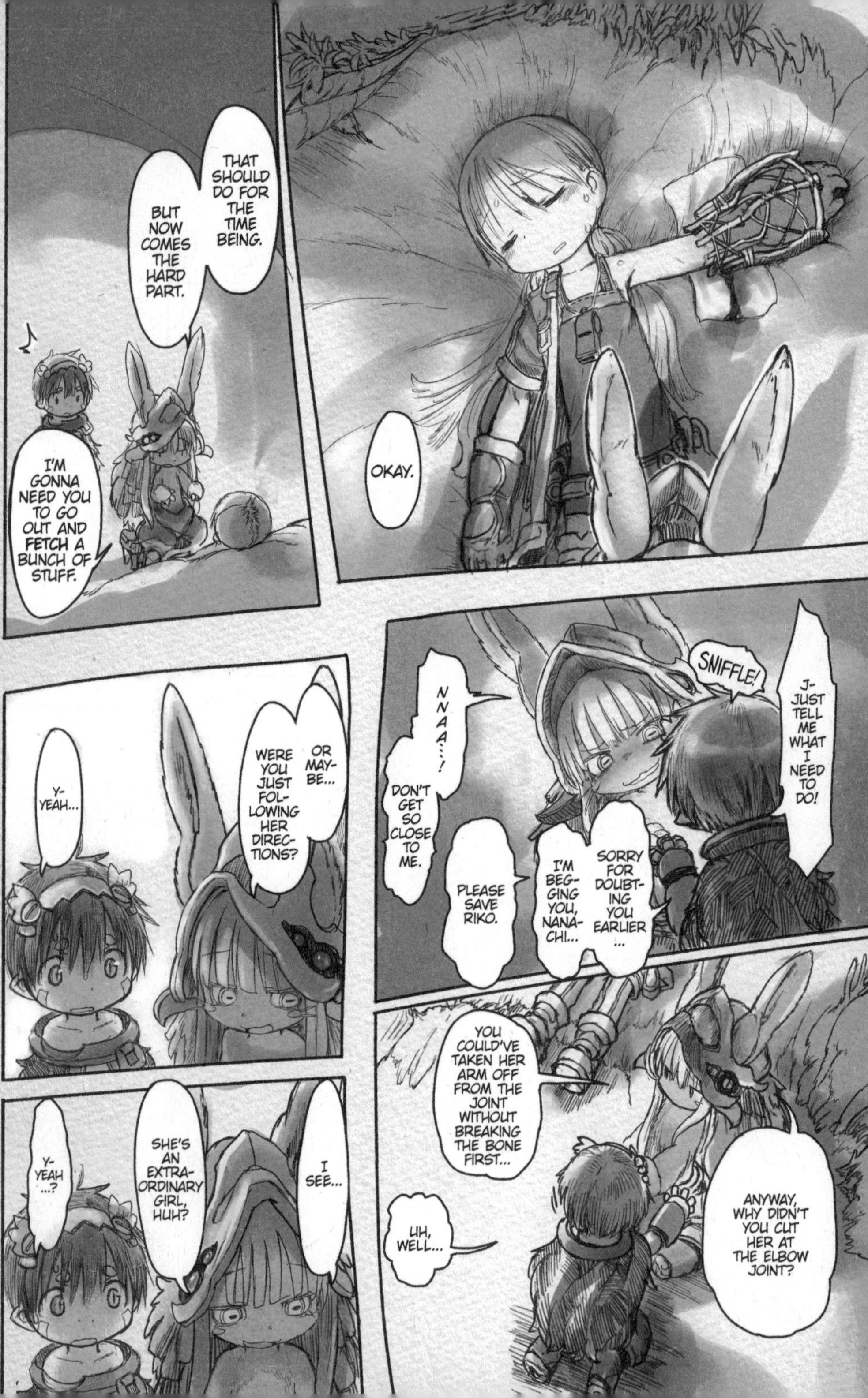
OKAY.
THAT SHOULD DO FOR THE TIME BEING.
BUT NOW COMES THE HARD PART.
I'M GONNA NEED YOU TO GO OUT AND FETCH A BUNCH OF STUFF.
J-JUST TELL ME WHAT I NEED TO DO!
SNIFFLE!
NNAA...!
DON'T GET SO CLOSE TO ME.
SORRY FOR DOUBTING YOU EARLIER...
I'M BEGGING YOU, NANACHI...
PLEASE SAVE RIKO.
ANYWAY, WHY DIDN'T YOU CUT HER AT THE ELBOW JOINT?
YOU COULD'VE TAKEN HER ARM OFF FROM THE JOINT WITHOUT BREAKING THE BONE FIRST...
UH, WELL...
OR MAYBE...
WERE YOU JUST FOLLOWING HER DIRECTIONS?
Y-YEAH...
I SEE...
SHE'S AN EXTRAORDINARY GIRL, HUH?
Y-YEAH...?

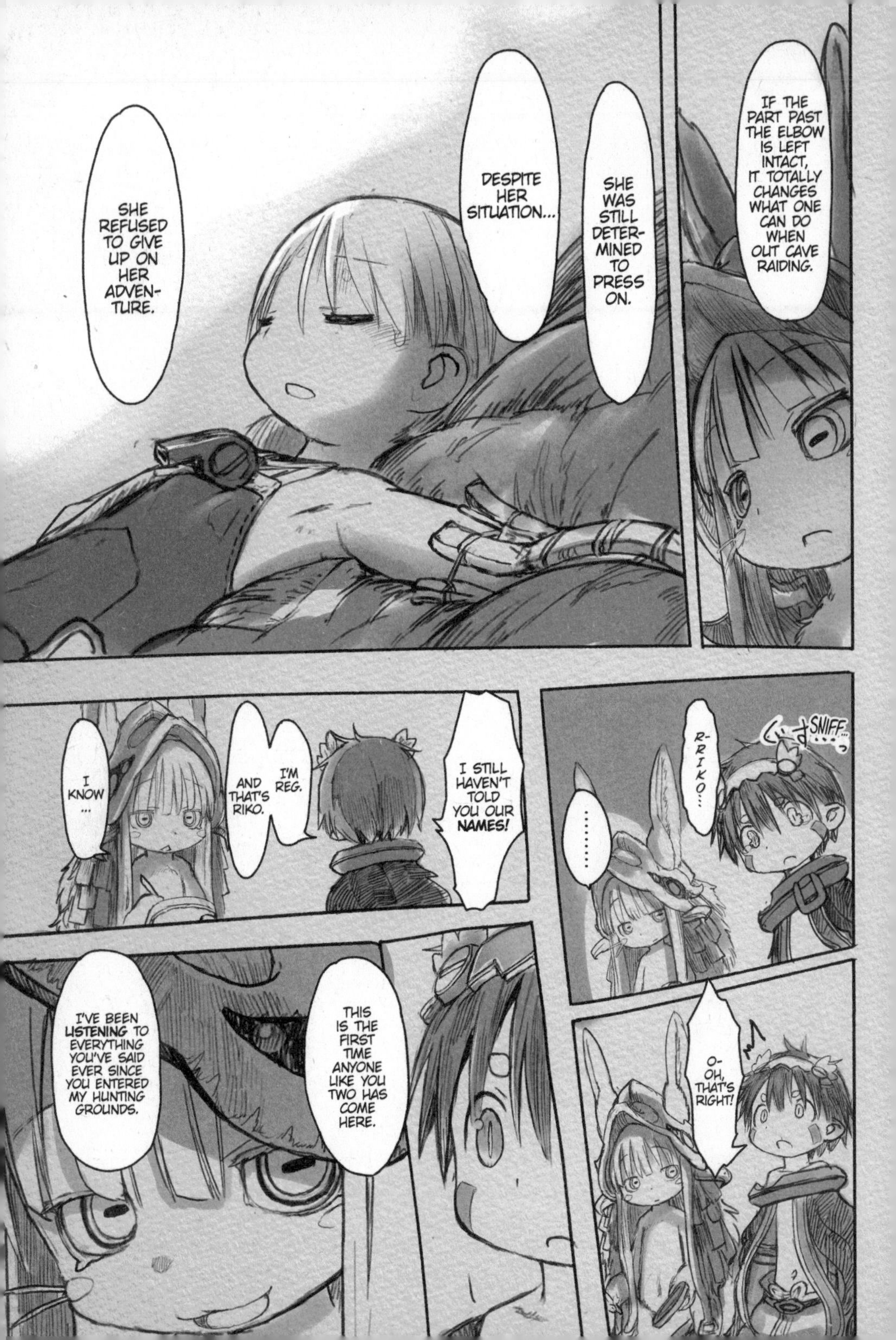
IF THE PART PAST THE ELBOW IS LEFT INTACT, IT TOTALLY CHANGES WHAT ONE CAN DO WHEN OUT CAVE RAIDING.
DESPITE HER SITUATION...
SHE WAS STILL DETERMINED TO PRESS ON.
SHE REFUSED TO GIVE UP ON HER ADVENTURE.
くす…っ SNIFF...
R-RIKO...
......
I STILL HAVEN'T TOLD YOU OUR **NAMES!**
I'M REG.
AND THAT'S RIKO.
I KNOW...
O-OH, THAT'S RIGHT!
THIS IS THE FIRST TIME ANYONE LIKE YOU TWO HAS COME HERE.
I'VE BEEN **LISTENING** TO EVERYTHING YOU'VE SAID EVER SINCE YOU ENTERED MY HUNTING GROUNDS.

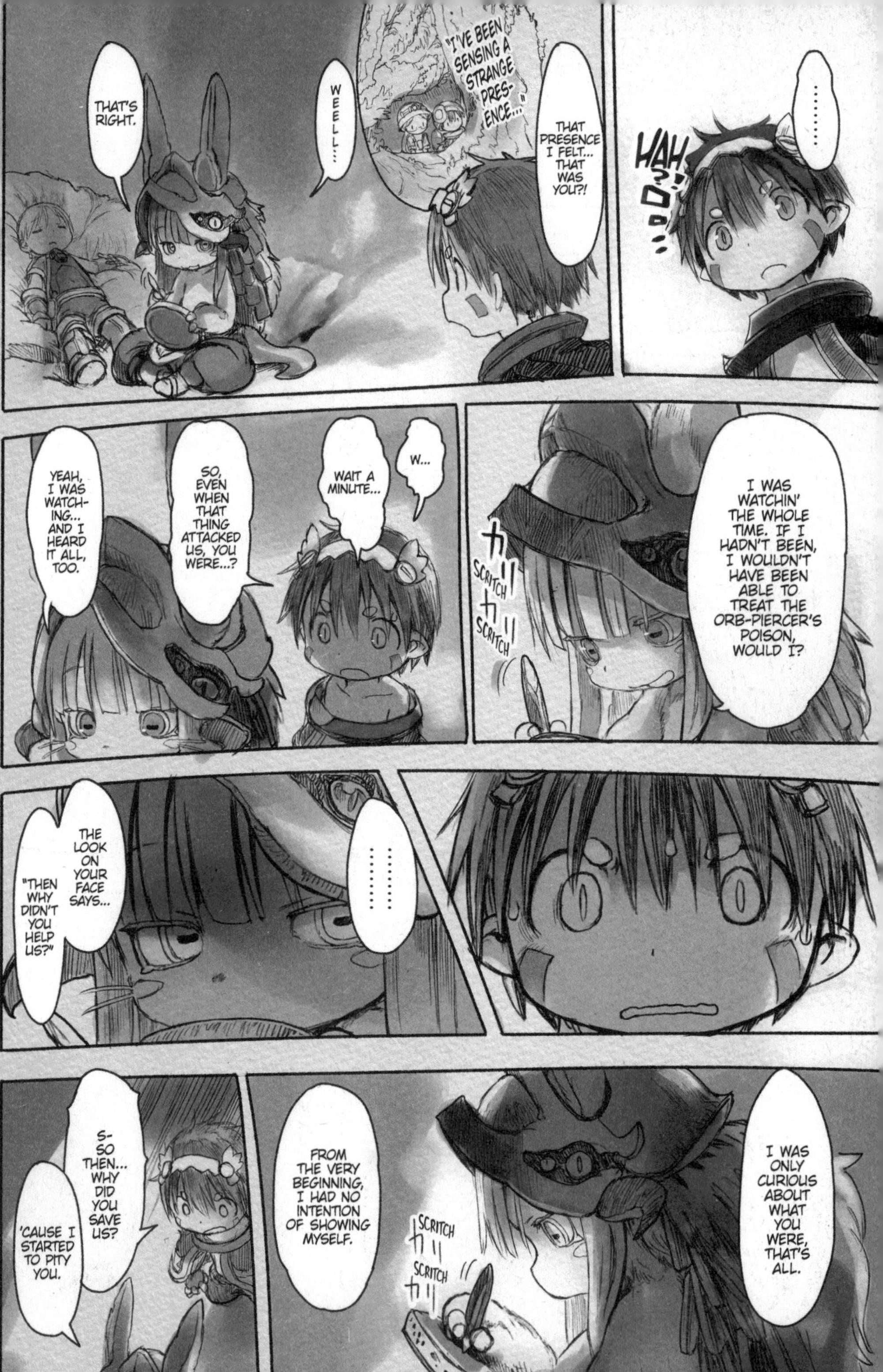
......
HAH?!
D...
"I'VE BEEN SENSING A STRANGE PRESENCE..."
THAT PRESENCE I FELT... THAT WAS YOU?!
WEELL...
THAT'S RIGHT.
I WAS WATCHIN' THE WHOLE TIME. IF I HADN'T BEEN, I WOULDN'T HAVE BEEN ABLE TO TREAT THE ORB-PIERCER'S POISON, WOULD I?
カリ SCRITCH
カリ SCRITCH
W...
WAIT A MINUTE...
SO, EVEN WHEN THAT THING ATTACKED US, YOU WERE...?
YEAH, I WAS WATCHING... AND I HEARD IT ALL, TOO.
......
THE LOOK ON YOUR FACE SAYS...
"THEN WHY DIDN'T YOU HELP US?"
I WAS ONLY CURIOUS ABOUT WHAT YOU WERE, THAT'S ALL.
カリ SCRITCH
カリ SCRITCH
FROM THE VERY BEGINNING, I HAD NO INTENTION OF SHOWING MYSELF.
S-SO THEN... WHY DID YOU SAVE US?
'CAUSE I STARTED TO PITY YOU.

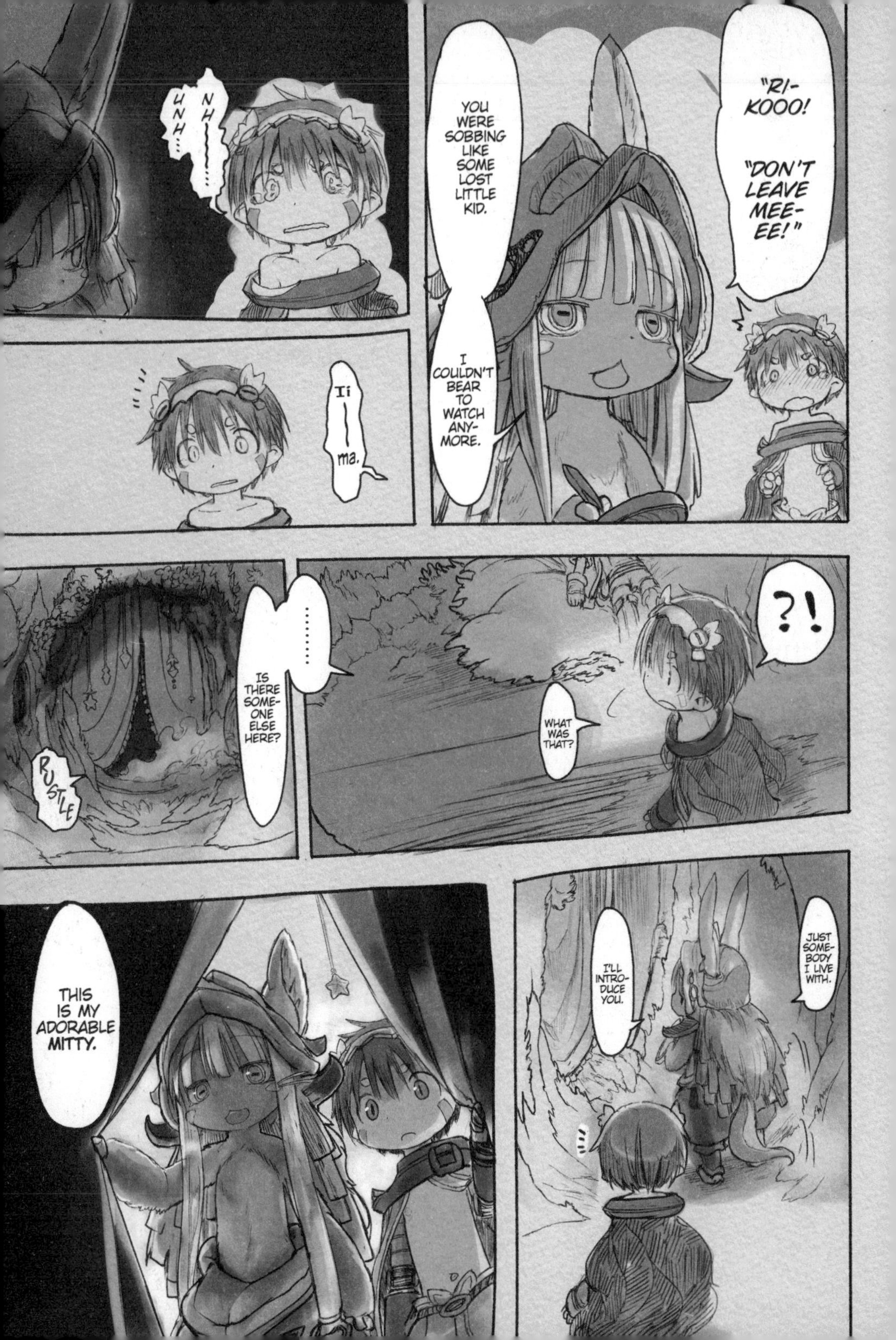
"RI-KOOO!
"DON'T LEAVE MEE-EE!"
YOU WERE SOBBING LIKE SOME LOST LITTLE KID.
I COULDN'T BEAR TO WATCH ANY-MORE.
NH————...
UNH...
Ti——ma.
?!
WHAT WAS THAT?
....
IS THERE SOME-ONE ELSE HERE?
RUSTLE
JUST SOME-BODY I LIVE WITH.
I'LL INTRO-DUCE YOU.
THIS IS MY ADORABLE MITTY.

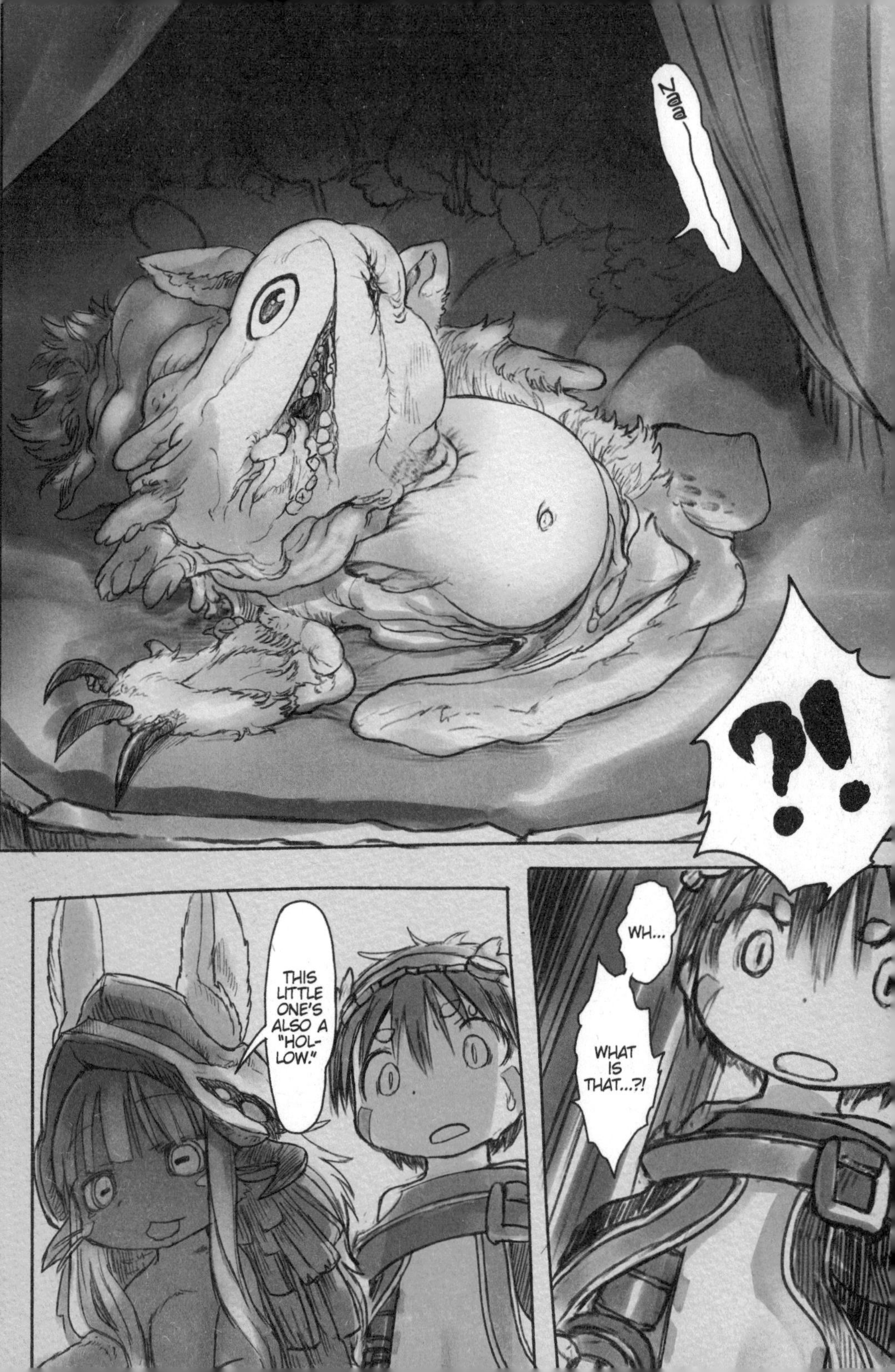
Naaa—
?!
WH...
WHAT IS THAT...?!
THIS LITTLE ONE'S ALSO A "HOLLOW."

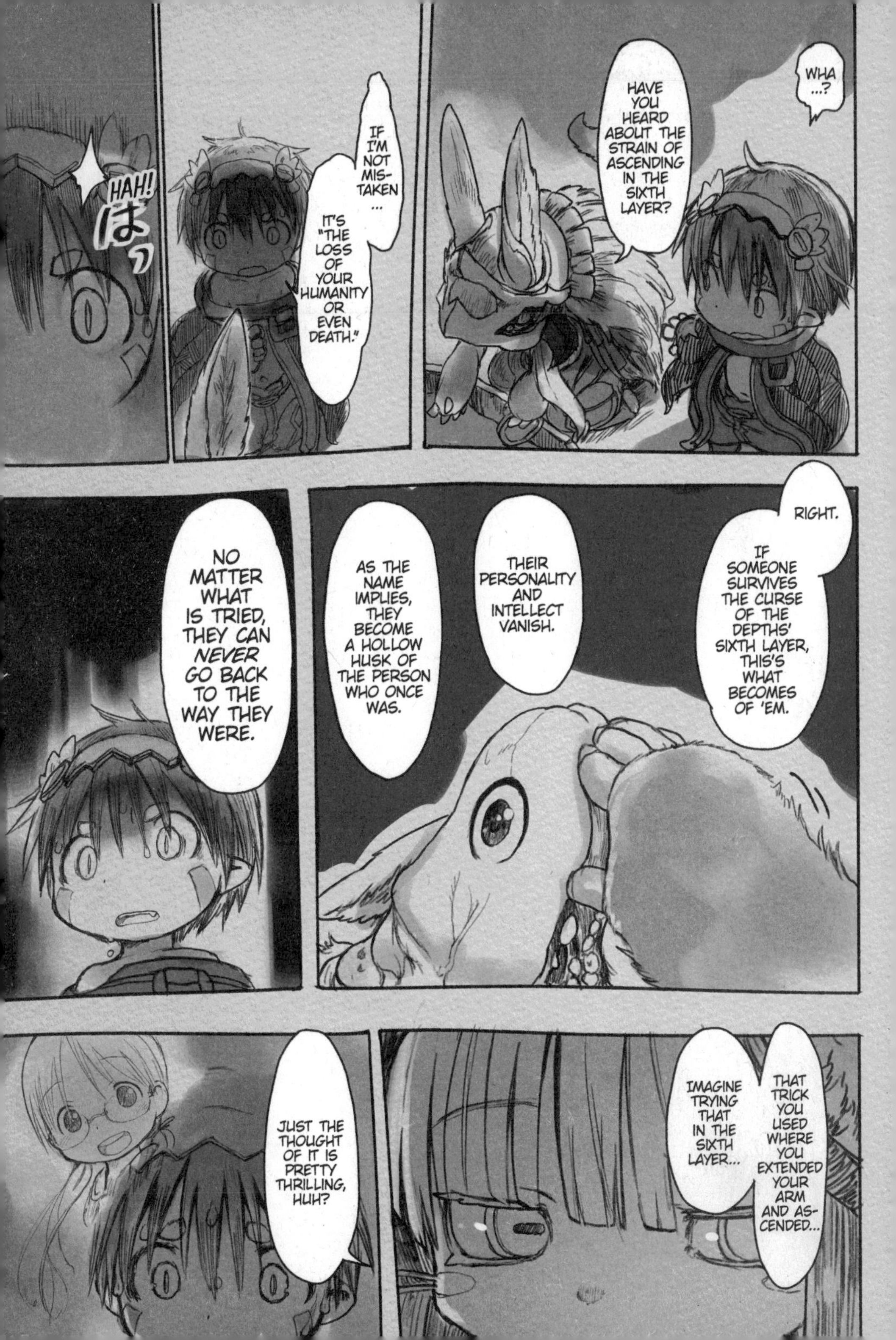
WHA ...?
HAVE YOU HEARD ABOUT THE STRAIN OF ASCENDING IN THE SIXTH LAYER?
IF I'M NOT MIS-TAKEN ...
IT'S "THE LOSS OF YOUR HUMANITY OR EVEN DEATH."
HAH!
はっ
RIGHT.
IF SOMEONE SURVIVES THE CURSE OF THE DEPTHS' SIXTH LAYER, THIS'S WHAT BECOMES OF 'EM.
THEIR PERSONALITY AND INTELLECT VANISH.
AS THE NAME IMPLIES, THEY BECOME A HOLLOW HUSK OF THE PERSON WHO ONCE WAS.
NO MATTER WHAT IS TRIED, THEY CAN *NEVER* GO BACK TO THE WAY THEY WERE.
THAT TRICK YOU USED WHERE YOU EXTENDED YOUR ARM AND AS-CENDED...
IMAGINE TRYING THAT IN THE SIXTH LAYER...
JUST THE THOUGHT OF IT IS PRETTY THRILLING, HUH?

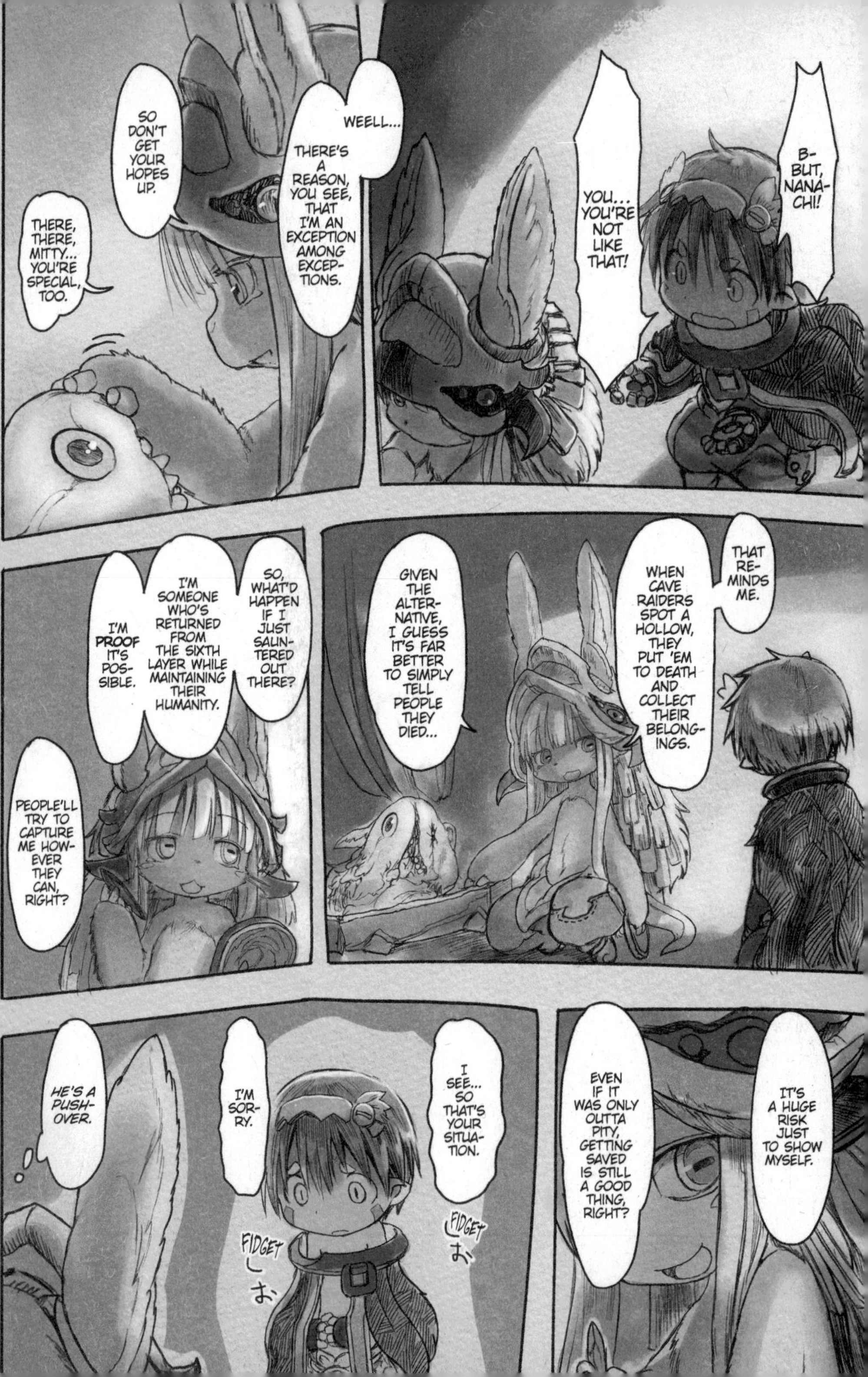
B-BUT, NANACHI!
YOU... YOU'RE NOT LIKE THAT!
WEELL...
THERE'S A REASON, YOU SEE, THAT I'M AN EXCEPTION AMONG EXCEPTIONS.
SO DON'T GET YOUR HOPES UP.
THERE, THERE, MITTY... YOU'RE SPECIAL, TOO.
THAT REMINDS ME.
WHEN CAVE RAIDERS SPOT A HOLLOW, THEY PUT 'EM TO DEATH AND COLLECT THEIR BELONGINGS.
GIVEN THE ALTERNATIVE, I GUESS IT'S FAR BETTER TO SIMPLY TELL PEOPLE THEY DIED...
SO, WHAT'D HAPPEN IF I JUST SAUNTERED OUT THERE?
I'M SOMEONE WHO'S RETURNED FROM THE SIXTH LAYER WHILE MAINTAINING THEIR HUMANITY.
I'M **PROOF** IT'S POSSIBLE.
PEOPLE'LL TRY TO CAPTURE ME HOWEVER THEY CAN, RIGHT?
IT'S A HUGE RISK JUST TO SHOW MYSELF.
EVEN IF IT WAS ONLY OUTTA PITY, GETTING SAVED IS STILL A GOOD THING, RIGHT?
I SEE... SO THAT'S YOUR SITUATION.
FIDGET
I'M SORRY.
FIDGET
HE'S A PUSHOVER.

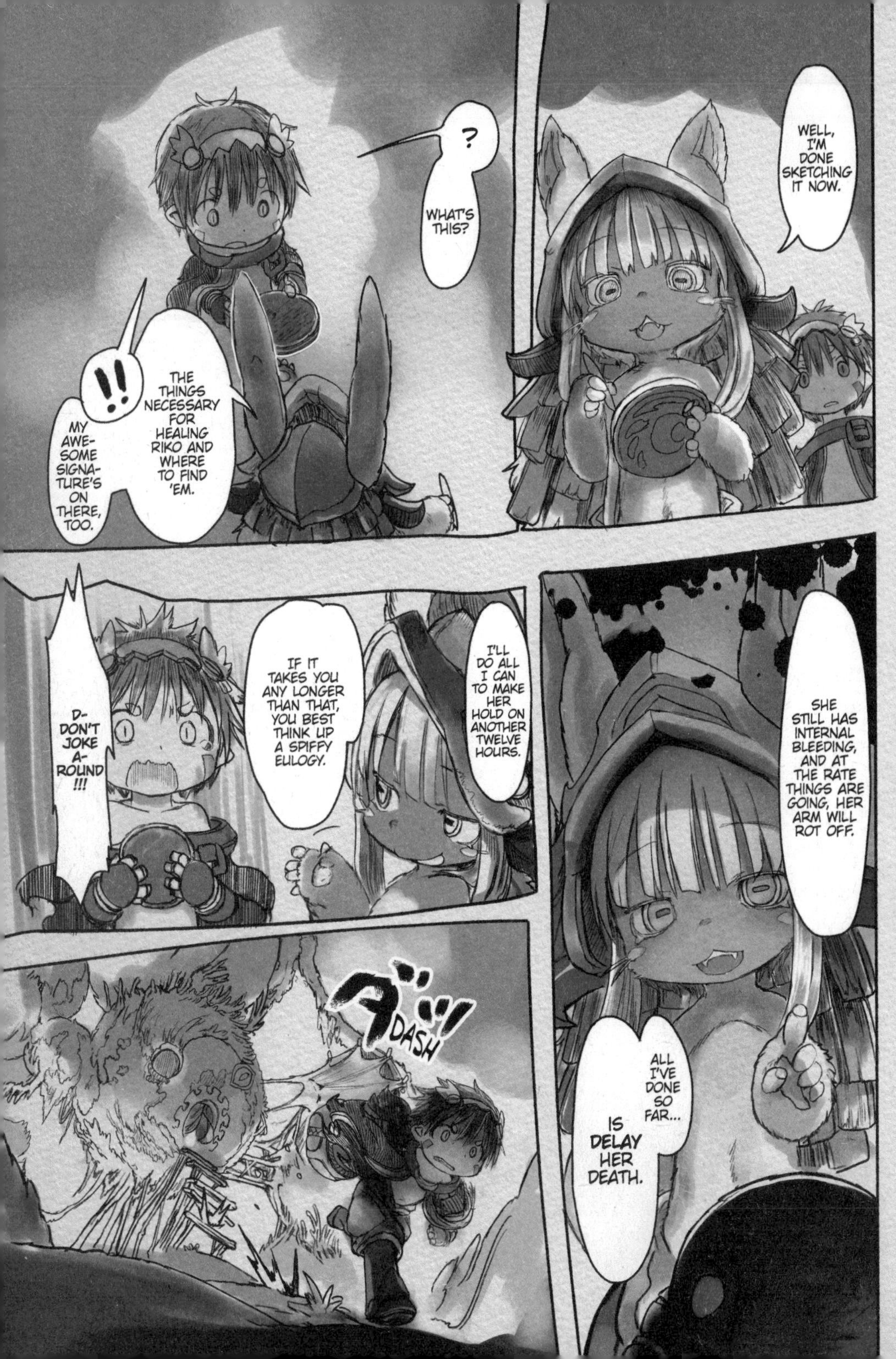
WELL, I'M DONE SKETCHING IT NOW.
?
WHAT'S THIS?
THE THINGS NECESSARY FOR HEALING RIKO AND WHERE TO FIND 'EM.
!!
MY AWESOME SIGNATURE'S ON THERE, TOO.
SHE STILL HAS INTERNAL BLEEDING, AND AT THE RATE THINGS ARE GOING, HER ARM WILL ROT OFF.
ALL I'VE DONE SO FAR...
IS **DELAY** HER DEATH.
I'LL DO ALL I CAN TO MAKE HER HOLD ON ANOTHER TWELVE HOURS.
IF IT TAKES YOU ANY LONGER THAN THAT, YOU BEST THINK UP A SPIFFY EULOGY.
D-DON'T JOKE A-ROUND!!!
ダッ!!
DASH

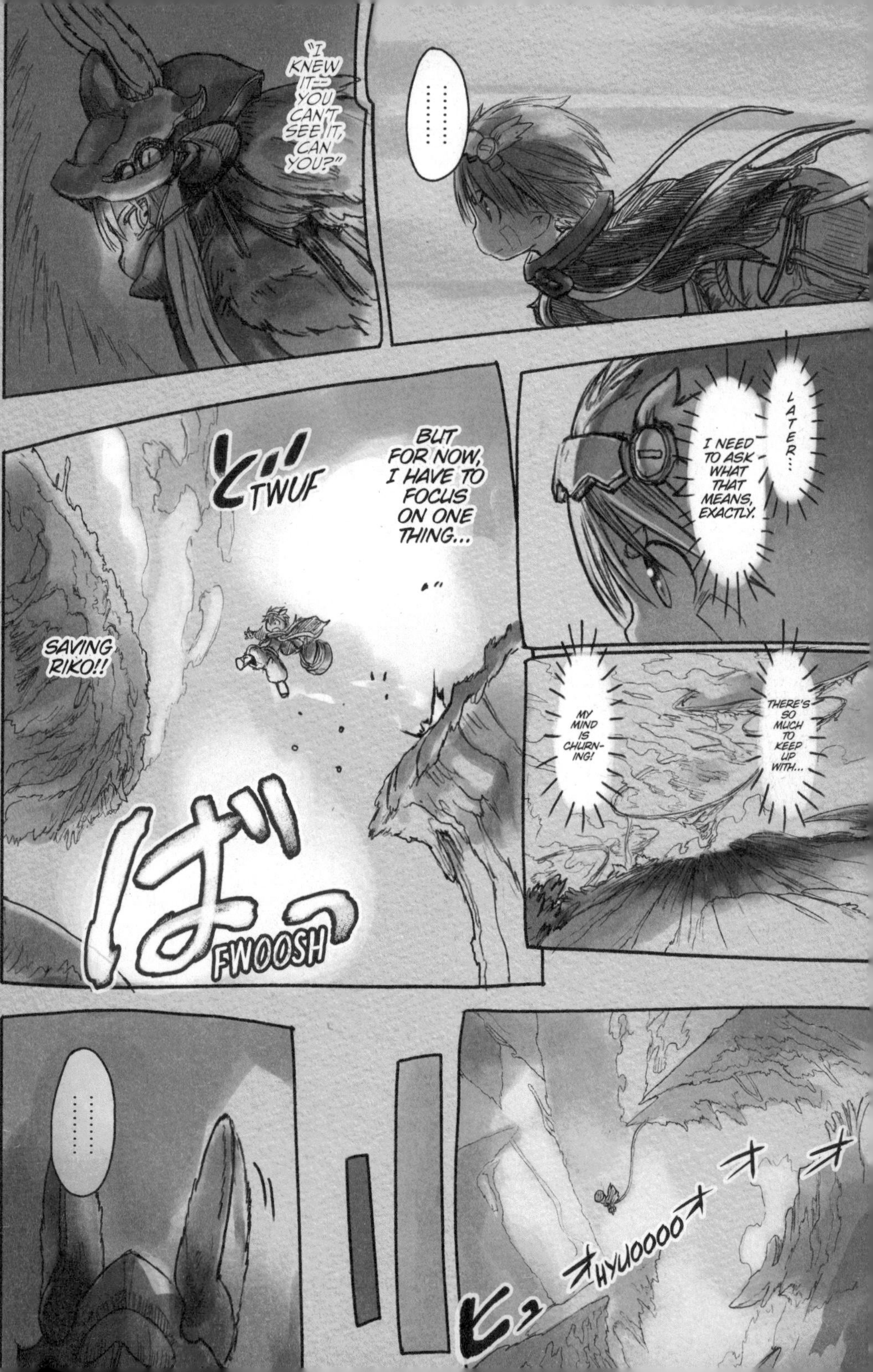
……
"I KNEW IT— YOU CAN'T SEE IT, CAN YOU?"
LATER… I NEED TO ASK WHAT THAT MEANS, EXACTLY.
THERE'S SO MUCH TO KEEP UP WITH…
MY MIND IS CHURNING!
TWUF
BUT FOR NOW, I HAVE TO FOCUS ON ONE THING…
SAVING RIKO!!
FWOOSH
HYUOOOO
……

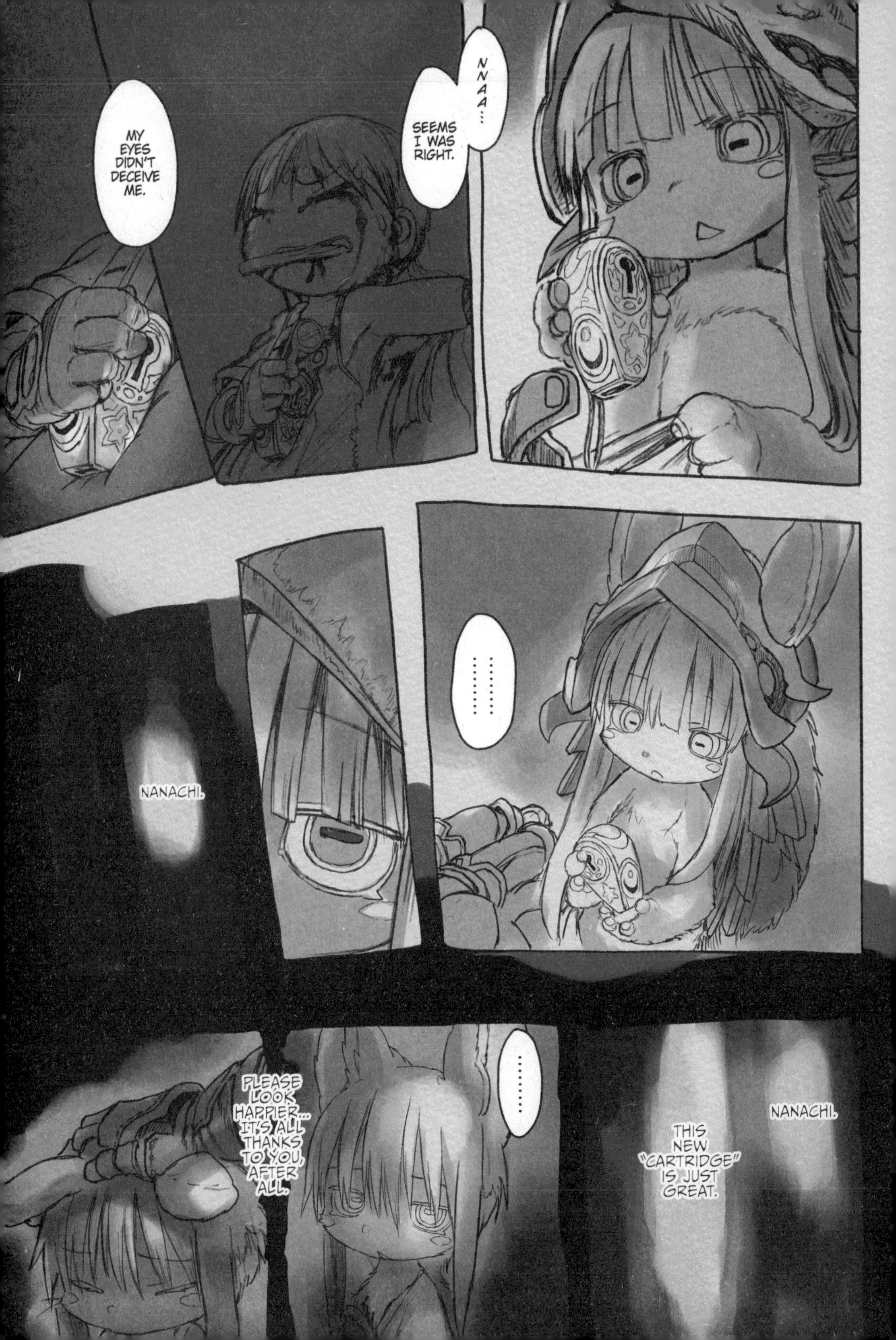
NNAA... SEEMS I WAS RIGHT.
MY EYES DIDN'T DECEIVE ME.
......
NANACHI.
NANACHI.
THIS NEW "CARTRIDGE" IS JUST GREAT.
......
PLEASE LOOK HAPPIER... IT'S ALL THANKS TO YOU, AFTER ALL.

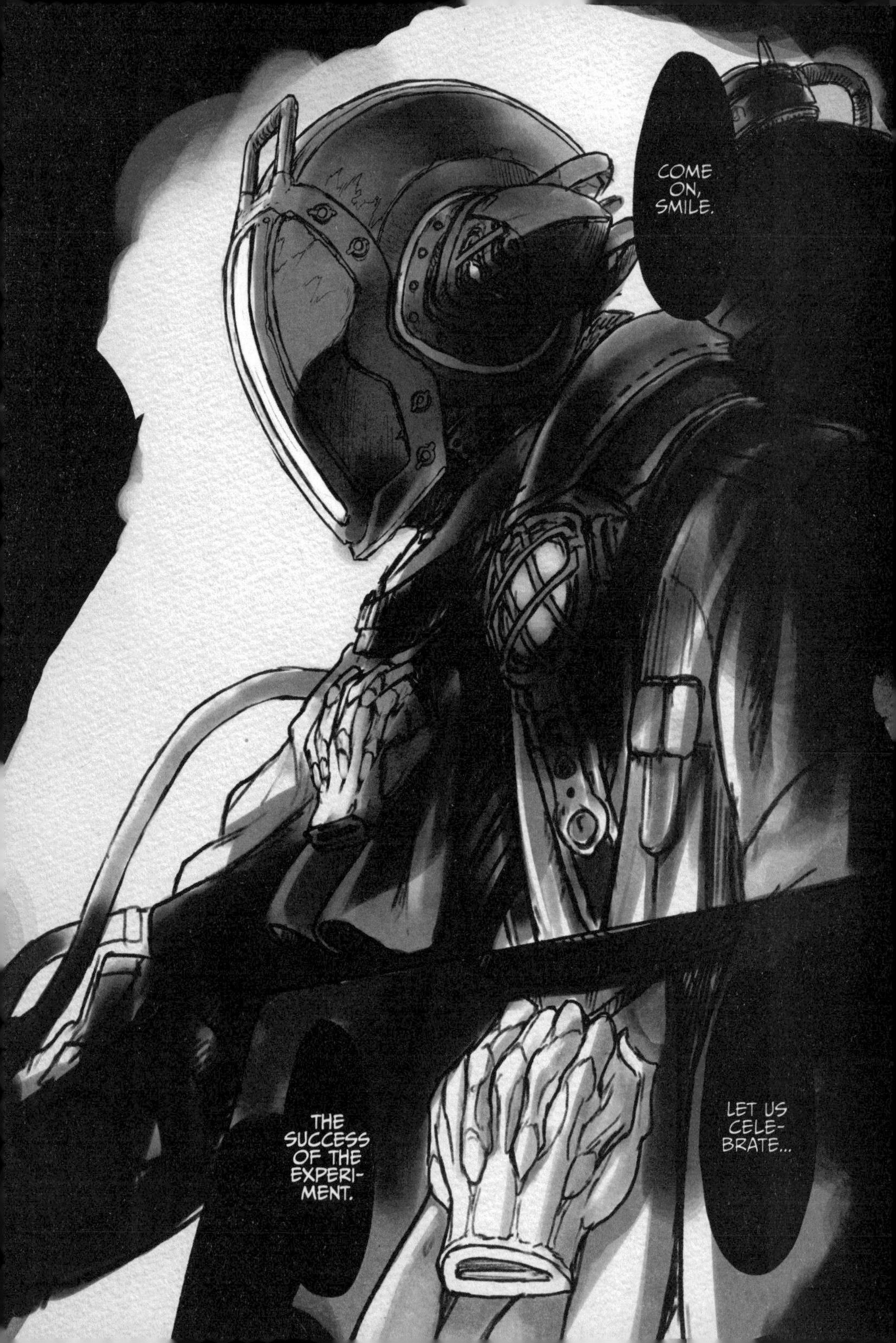
COME ON, SMILE.
LET US CELEBRATE...
THE SUCCESS OF THE EXPERIMENT.

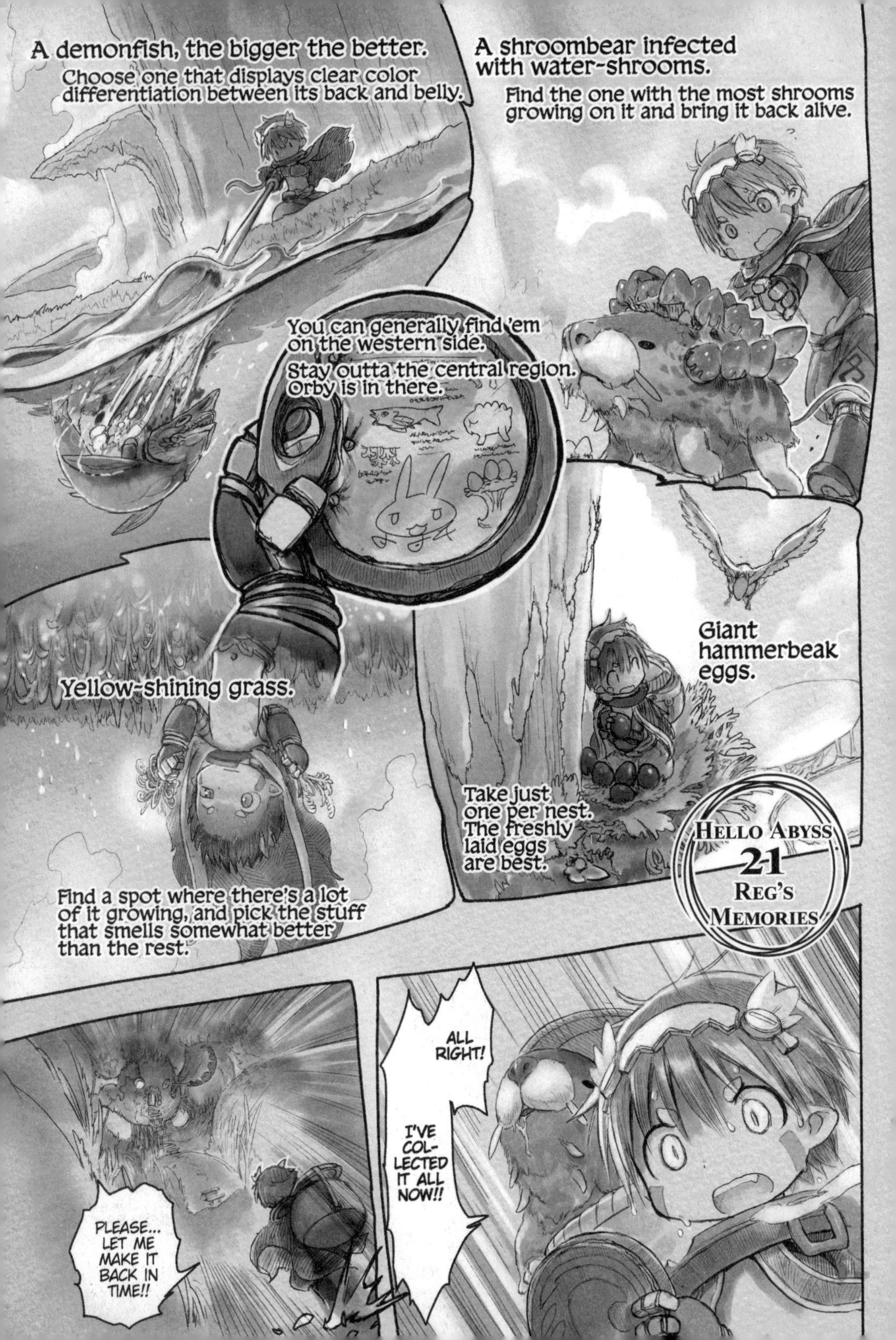
A shroombear infected with water-shrooms.
Find the one with the most shrooms growing on it and bring it back alive.
A demonfish, the bigger the better.
Choose one that displays clear color differentiation between its back and belly.
You can generally find 'em on the western side.
Stay outta the central region. Orby is in there.
Giant hammerbeak eggs.
Take just one per nest. The freshly laid eggs are best.
Yellow-shining grass.
Find a spot where there's a lot of it growing, and pick the stuff that smells somewhat better than the rest.
HELLO ABYSS 21 REG'S MEMORIES
ALL RIGHT!
I'VE COL-LECTED IT ALL NOW!!
PLEASE... LET ME MAKE IT BACK IN TIME!!

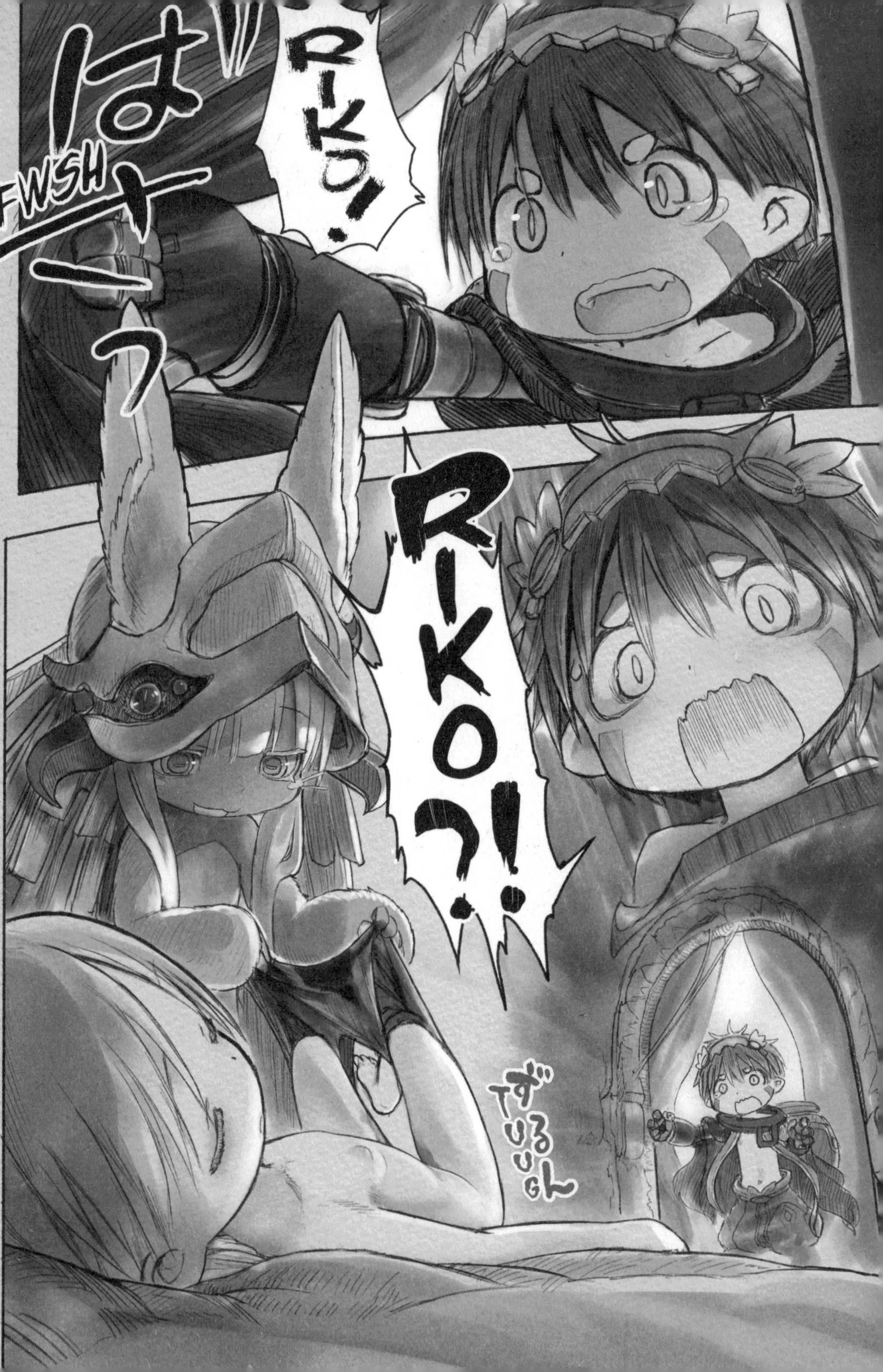
RIKO!
はっ
FWSH
RIKO?!
ずるん
TUUG

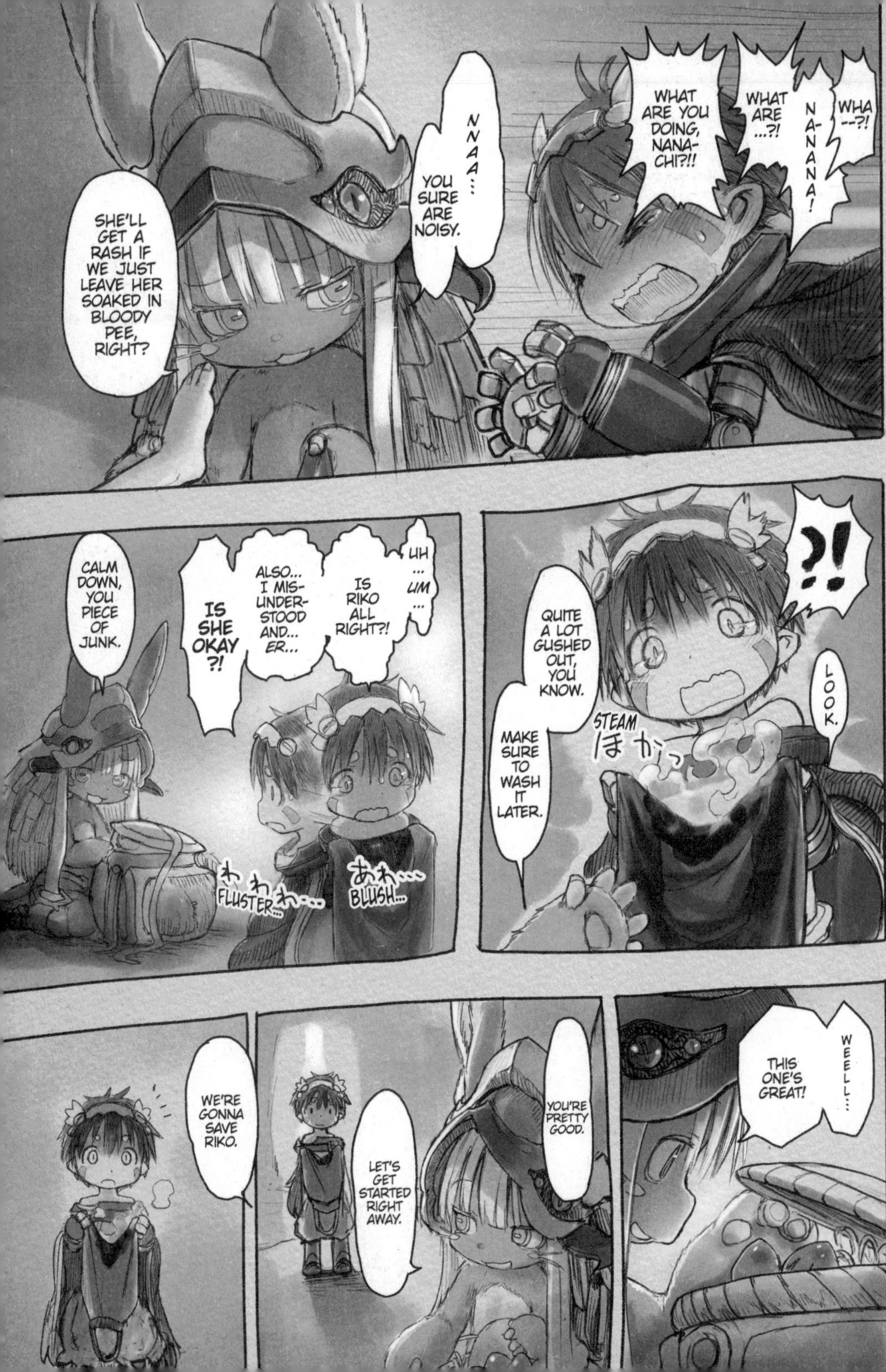

WHA--?!
NANANA!
WHAT ARE ...?!
WHAT ARE YOU DOING, NANACHI?!!
NNAA... YOU SURE ARE NOISY.
SHE'LL GET A RASH IF WE JUST LEAVE HER SOAKED IN BLOODY PEE, RIGHT?
?!
LOOK.
QUITE A LOT GUSHED OUT, YOU KNOW.
MAKE SURE TO WASH IT LATER.
STEAM
ほかっ
UH... UM...
IS RIKO ALL RIGHT?!
ALSO... I MISUNDERSTOOD AND... ER...
IS SHE OKAY?!
CALM DOWN, YOU PIECE OF JUNK.
あわ...
BLUSH...
わわわ...
FLUSTER...
WEELL...
THIS ONE'S GREAT!
YOU'RE PRETTY GOOD.
LET'S GET STARTED RIGHT AWAY.
WE'RE GONNA SAVE RIKO.

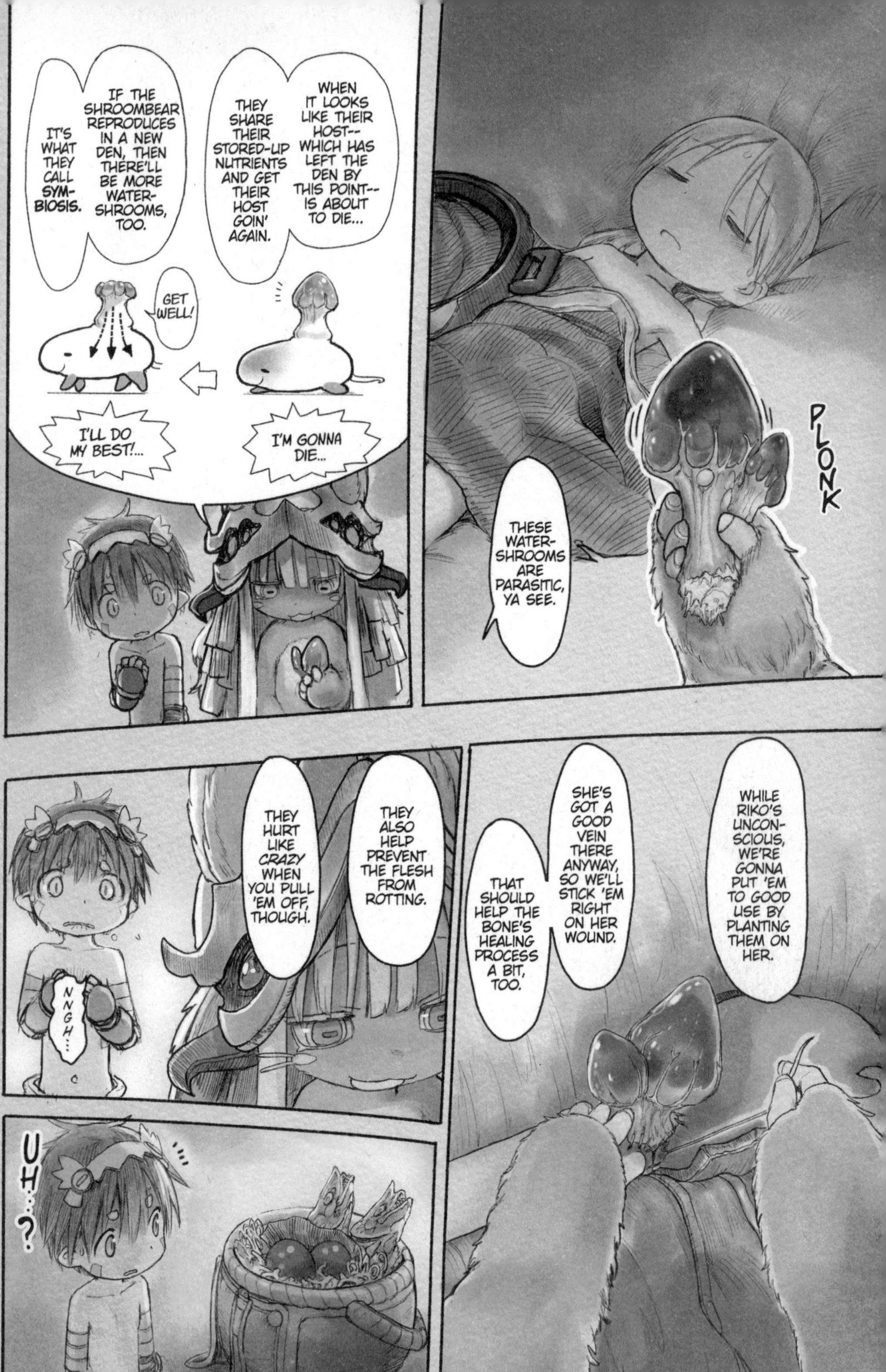
PLONK
THESE WATER-SHROOMS ARE PARASITIC, YA SEE.
WHEN IT LOOKS LIKE THEIR HOST--WHICH HAS LEFT THE DEN BY THIS POINT--IS ABOUT TO DIE...
THEY SHARE THEIR STORED-UP NUTRIENTS AND GET THEIR HOST GOIN' AGAIN.
IF THE SHROOMBEAR REPRODUCES IN A NEW DEN, THEN THERE'LL BE MORE WATER-SHROOMS, TOO.
IT'S WHAT THEY CALL SYMBIOSIS.
I'M GONNA DIE...
GET WELL!
I'LL DO MY BEST!...
WHILE RIKO'S UNCONSCIOUS, WE'RE GONNA PUT 'EM TO GOOD USE BY PLANTING THEM ON HER.
SHE'S GOT A GOOD VEIN THERE ANYWAY, SO WE'LL STICK 'EM RIGHT ON HER WOUND.
THAT SHOULD HELP THE BONE'S HEALING PROCESS A BIT, TOO.
THEY ALSO HELP PREVENT THE FLESH FROM ROTTING.
THEY HURT LIKE CRAZY WHEN YOU PULL 'EM OFF, THOUGH.
NNGH...
UH...?

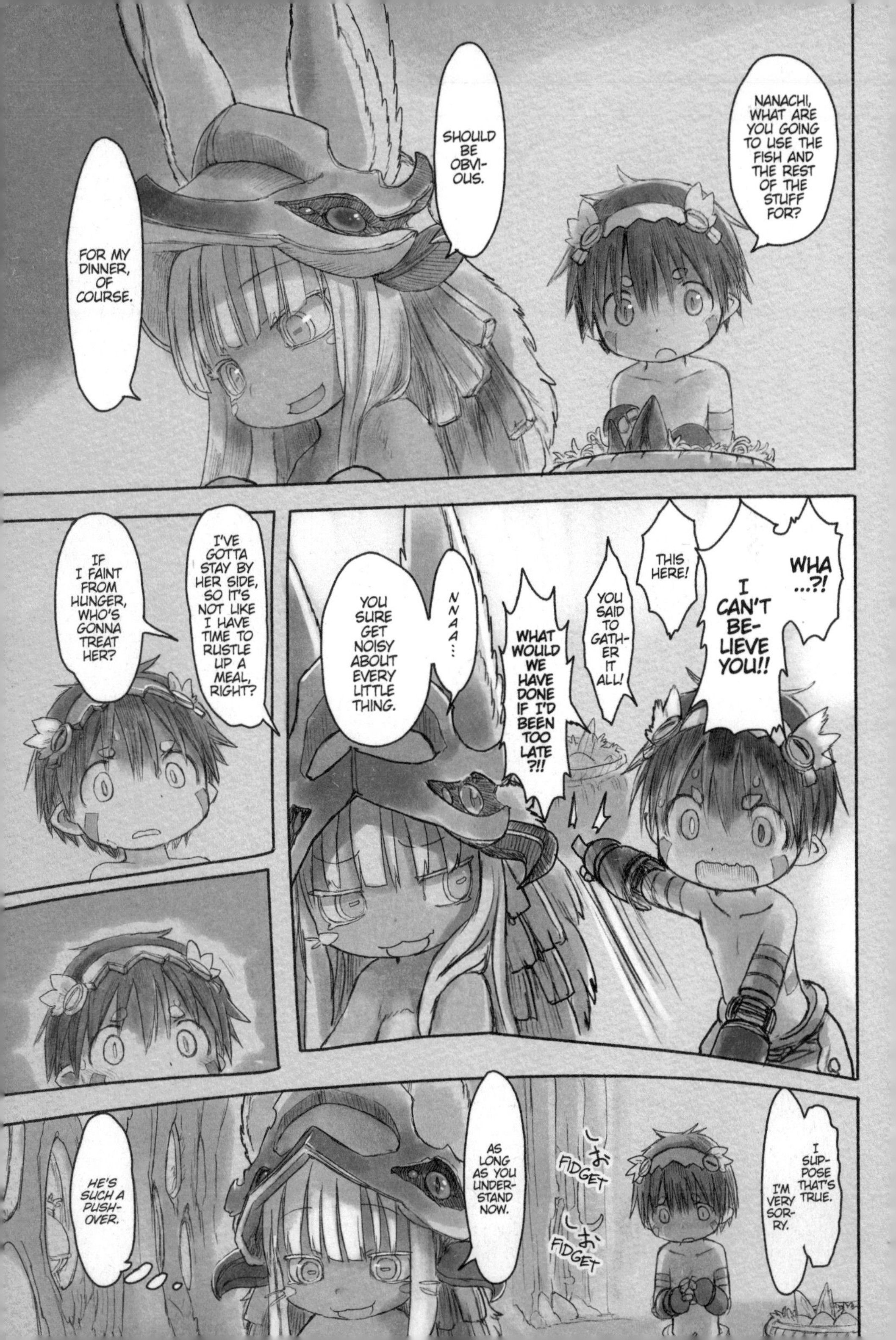
NANACHI, WHAT ARE YOU GOING TO USE THE FISH AND THE REST OF THE STUFF FOR?
SHOULD BE OBVIOUS.
FOR MY DINNER, OF COURSE.
WHA...?!
I CAN'T BELIEVE YOU!!
THIS HERE!
YOU SAID TO GATHER IT ALL!
WHAT WOULD WE HAVE DONE IF I'D BEEN TOO LATE?!!
NNAAA...
YOU SURE GET NOISY ABOUT EVERY LITTLE THING.
I'VE GOTTA STAY BY HER SIDE, SO IT'S NOT LIKE I HAVE TIME TO RUSTLE UP A MEAL, RIGHT?
IF I FAINT FROM HUNGER, WHO'S GONNA TREAT HER?
I SUPPOSE THAT'S TRUE.
I'M VERY SORRY.
FIDGET
FIDGET
AS LONG AS YOU UNDERSTAND NOW.
HE'S SUCH A PUSHOVER.

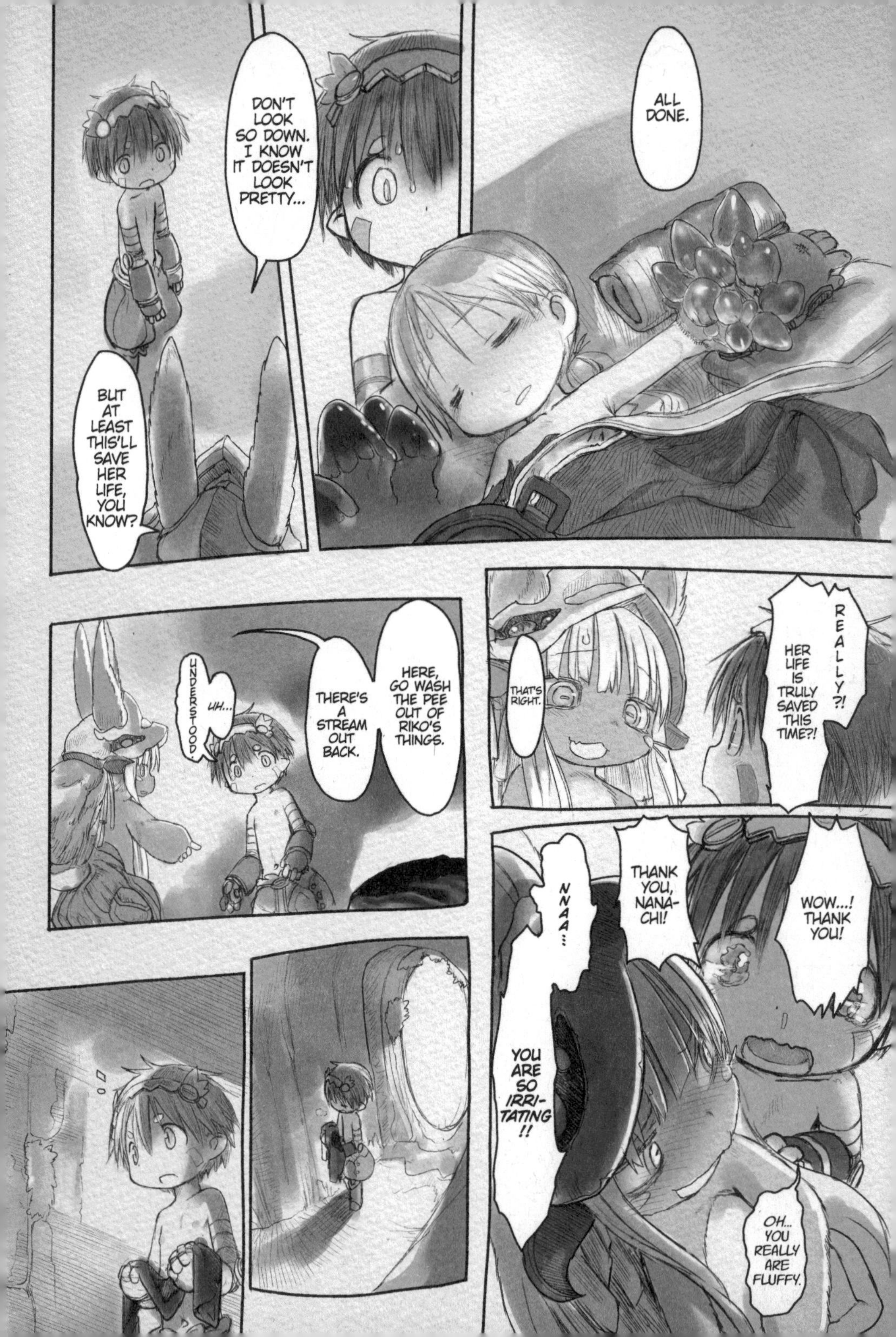
ALL DONE.
DON'T LOOK SO DOWN. I KNOW IT DOESN'T LOOK PRETTY...
BUT AT LEAST THIS'LL SAVE HER LIFE, YOU KNOW?
REALLY?!
HER LIFE IS TRULY SAVED THIS TIME?!
THAT'S RIGHT.
HERE, GO WASH THE PEE OUT OF RIKO'S THINGS.
THERE'S A STREAM OUT BACK.
UH...
UNDERSTOOD.
WOW...! THANK YOU!
THANK YOU, NANA-CHI!
NNAAA...
YOU ARE SO IRRITATING!!
OH... YOU REALLY ARE FLUFFY.

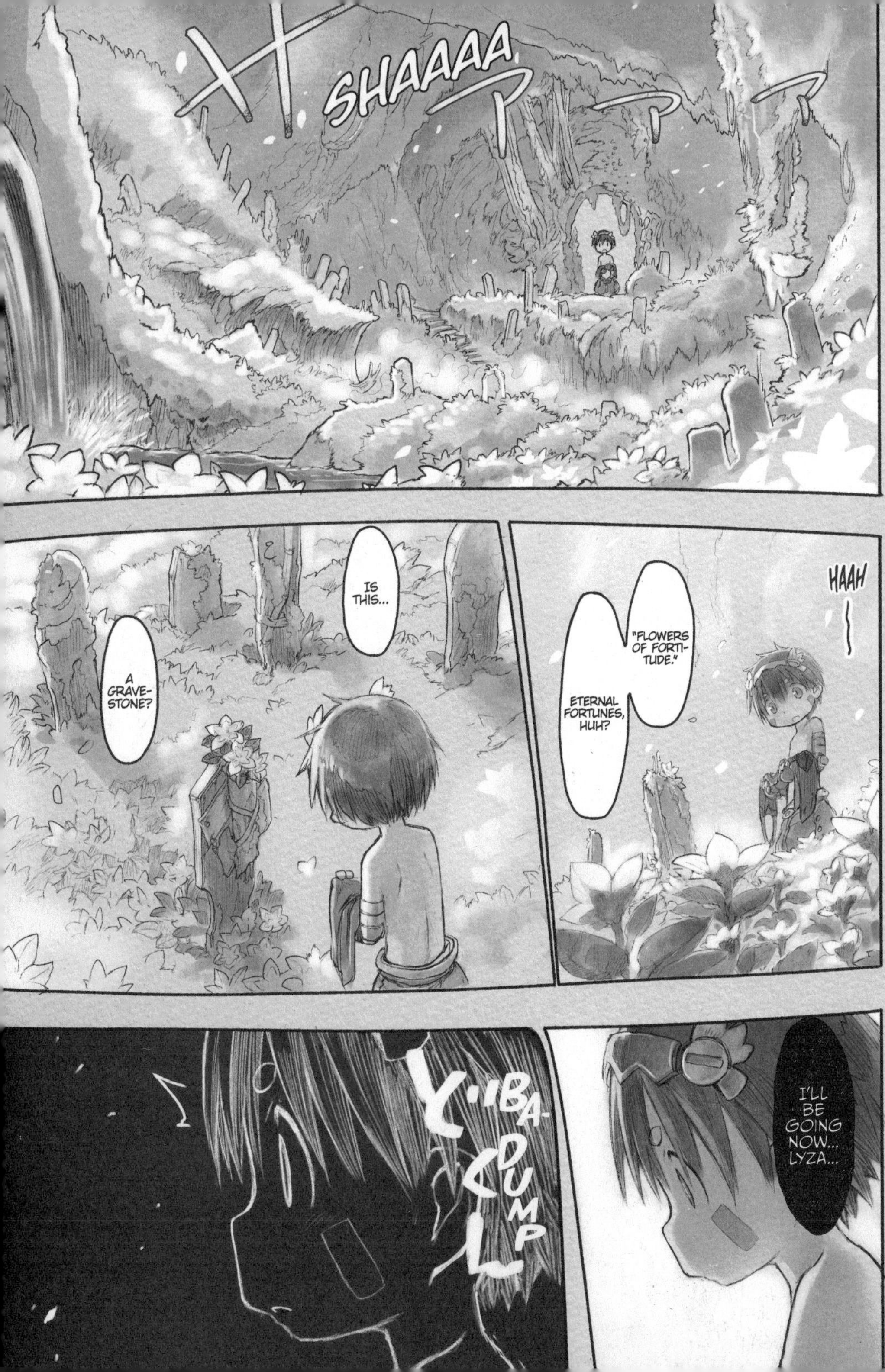
SHAAAA
HAAAH
"FLOWERS OF FORTITUDE."
ETERNAL FORTUNES, HUH?
IS THIS...
A GRAVESTONE?
I'LL BE GOING NOW... LYZA...
BA-DUMP

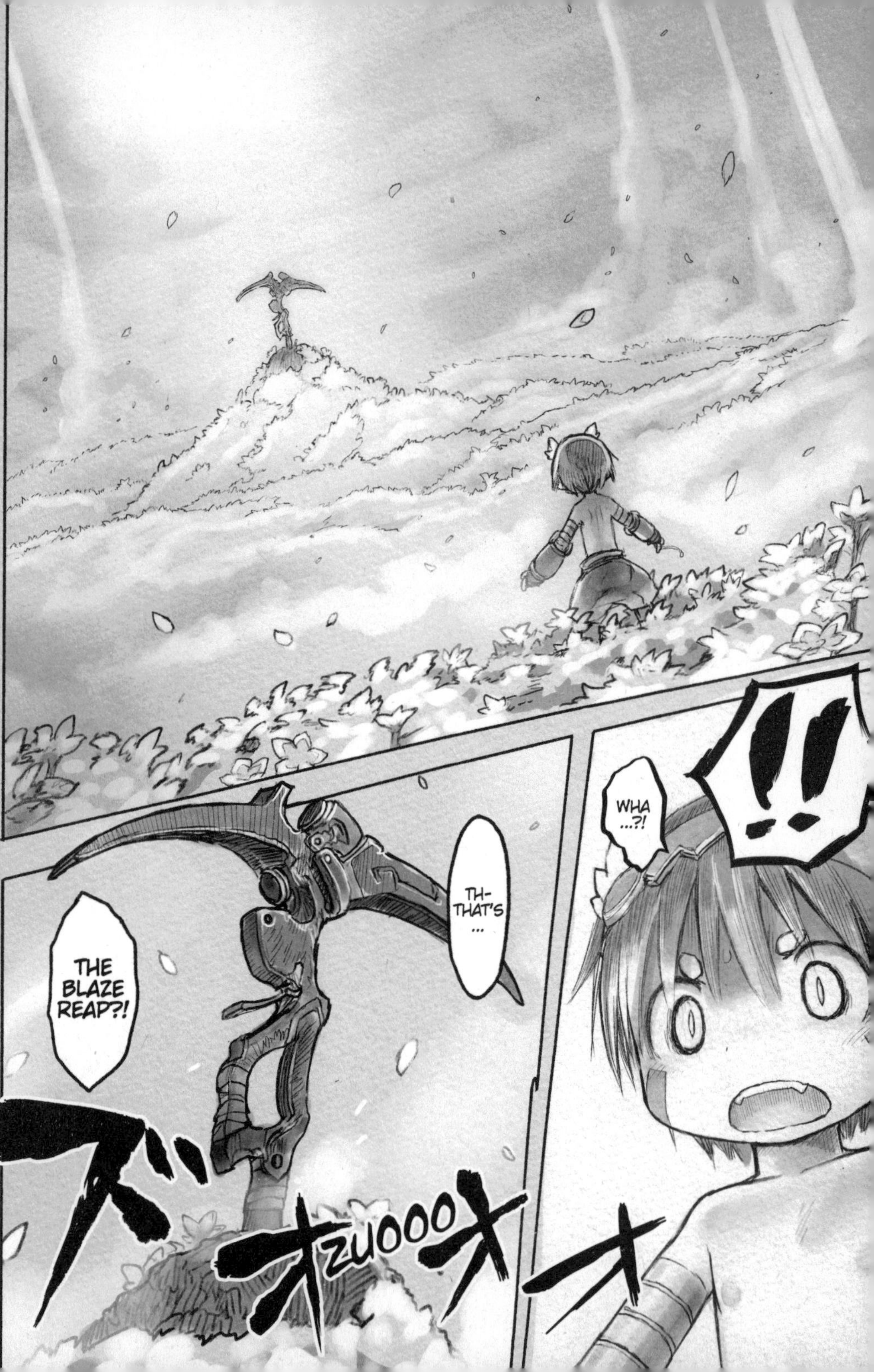
!!
WHA ...?!
TH- THAT'S ...
THE BLAZE REAP?!
ZUOOO

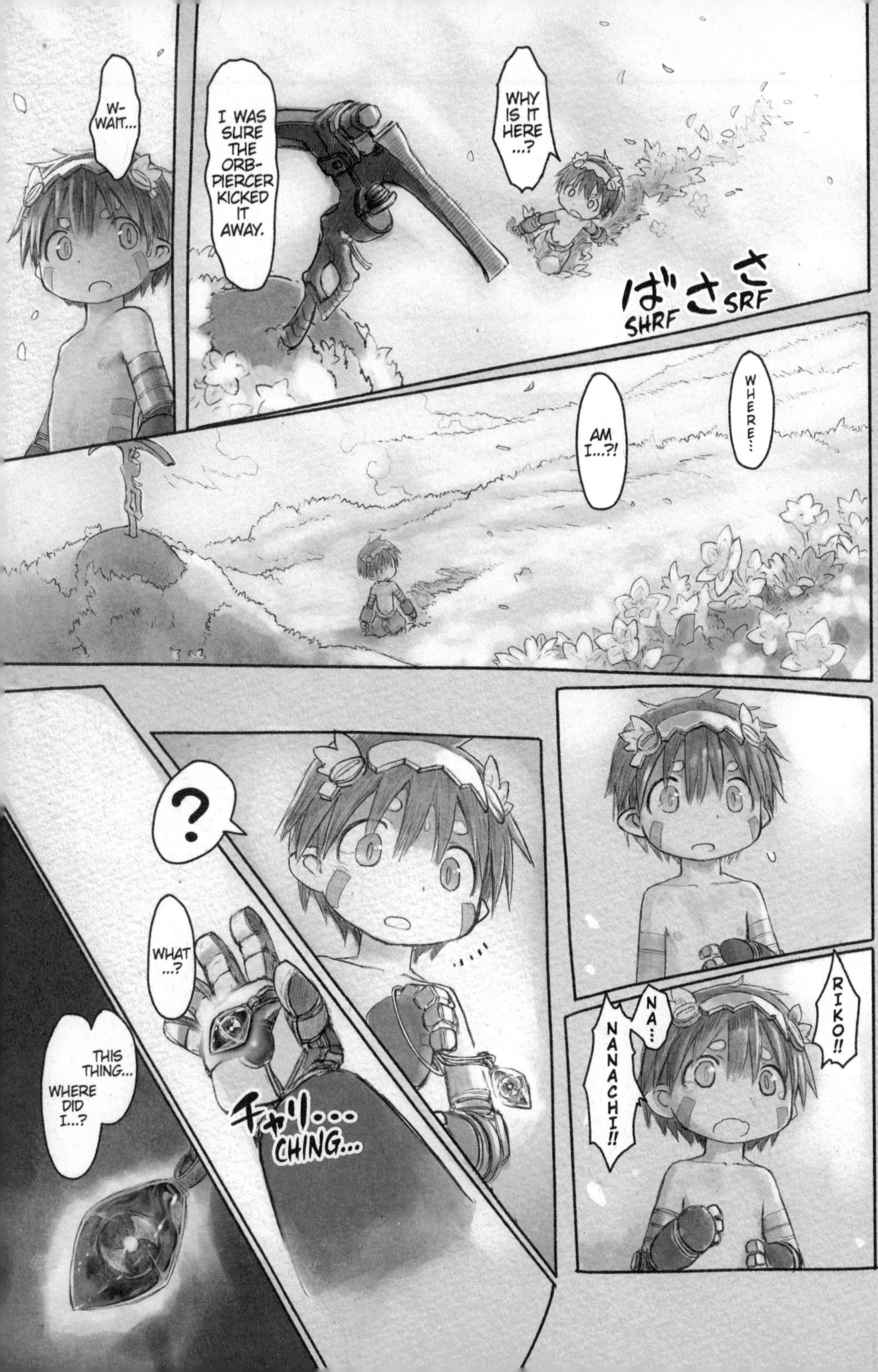
WHY IS IT HERE ...?
I WAS SURE THE ORB-PIERCER KICKED IT AWAY.
ばさ さ
SHRF SRF
W-WAIT...
WHERE...
AM I...?!
RIKO!!
NA...
NANACHI!!
?
WHAT ...?
チャリ...
CHING...
THIS THING... WHERE DID I...?

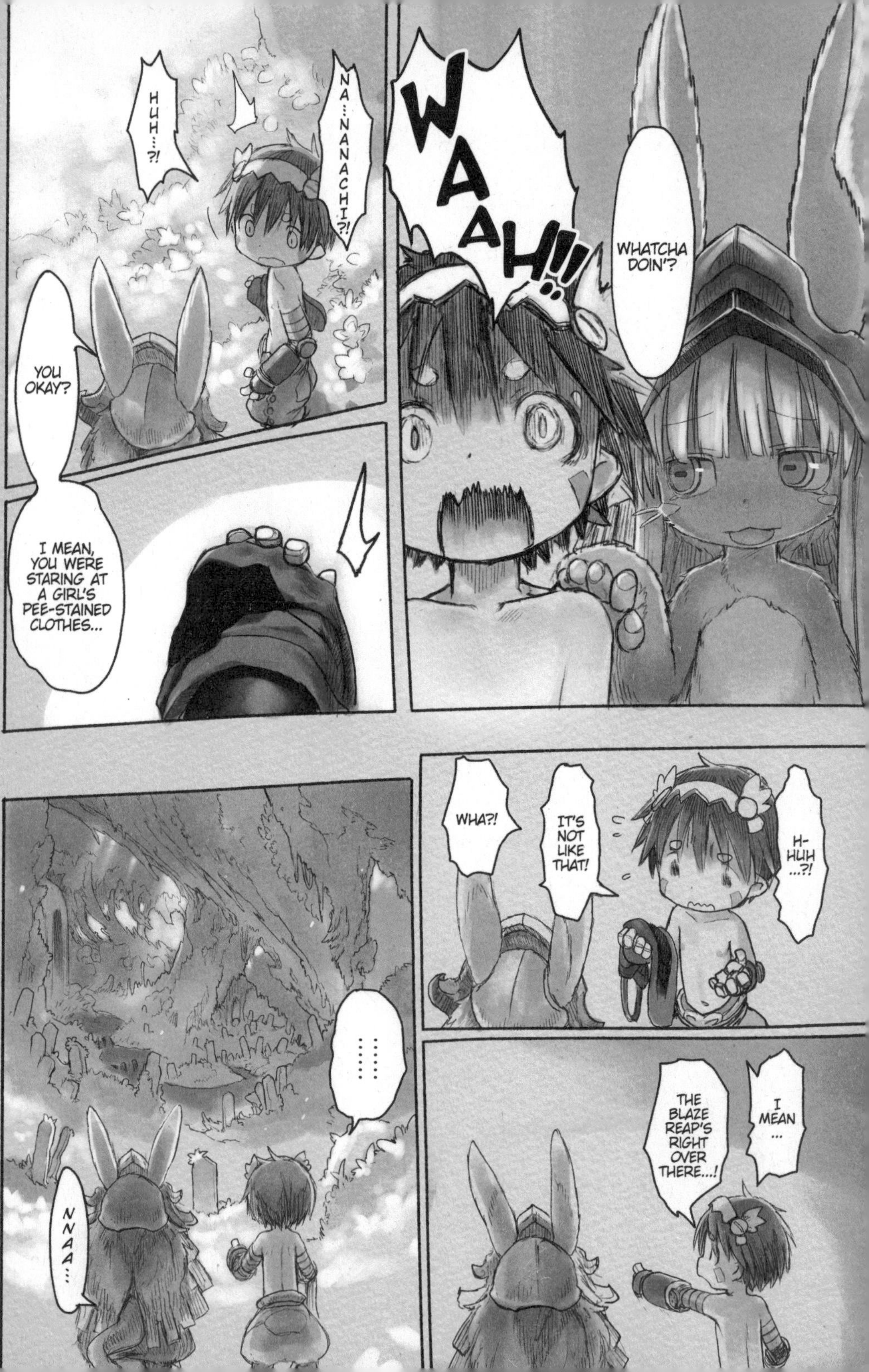
WHATCHA DOIN'?
WAAH!!
NA...NANACHI?!
HUH...?!
YOU OKAY?
I MEAN, YOU WERE STARING AT A GIRL'S PEE-STAINED CLOTHES...
H-HUH...?!
IT'S NOT LIKE THAT!
WHA?!
I MEAN...
THE BLAZE REAP'S RIGHT OVER THERE...!
......
NNAA...

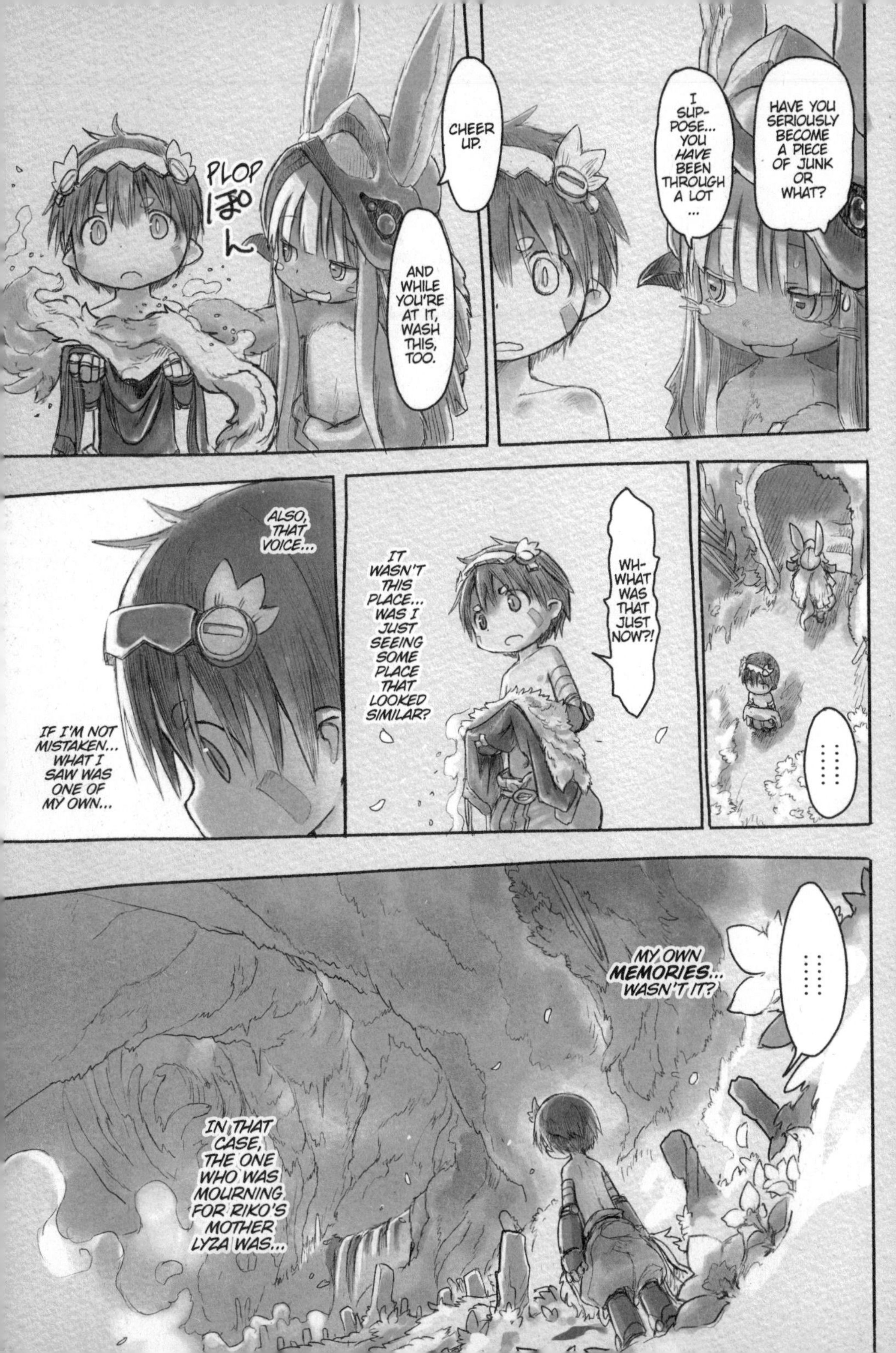
HAVE YOU SERIOUSLY BECOME A PIECE OF JUNK OR WHAT?
I SUPPOSE... YOU HAVE BEEN THROUGH A LOT...
CHEER UP.
AND WHILE YOU'RE AT IT, WASH THIS, TOO.
PLOP ぽん
......
WH-WHAT WAS THAT JUST NOW?!
IT WASN'T THIS PLACE... WAS I JUST SEEING SOME PLACE THAT LOOKED SIMILAR?
ALSO, THAT VOICE...
IF I'M NOT MISTAKEN... WHAT I SAW WAS ONE OF MY OWN...
......
MY OWN **MEMORIES**... WASN'T IT?
IN THAT CASE, THE ONE WHO WAS MOURNING FOR RIKO'S MOTHER LYZA WAS...

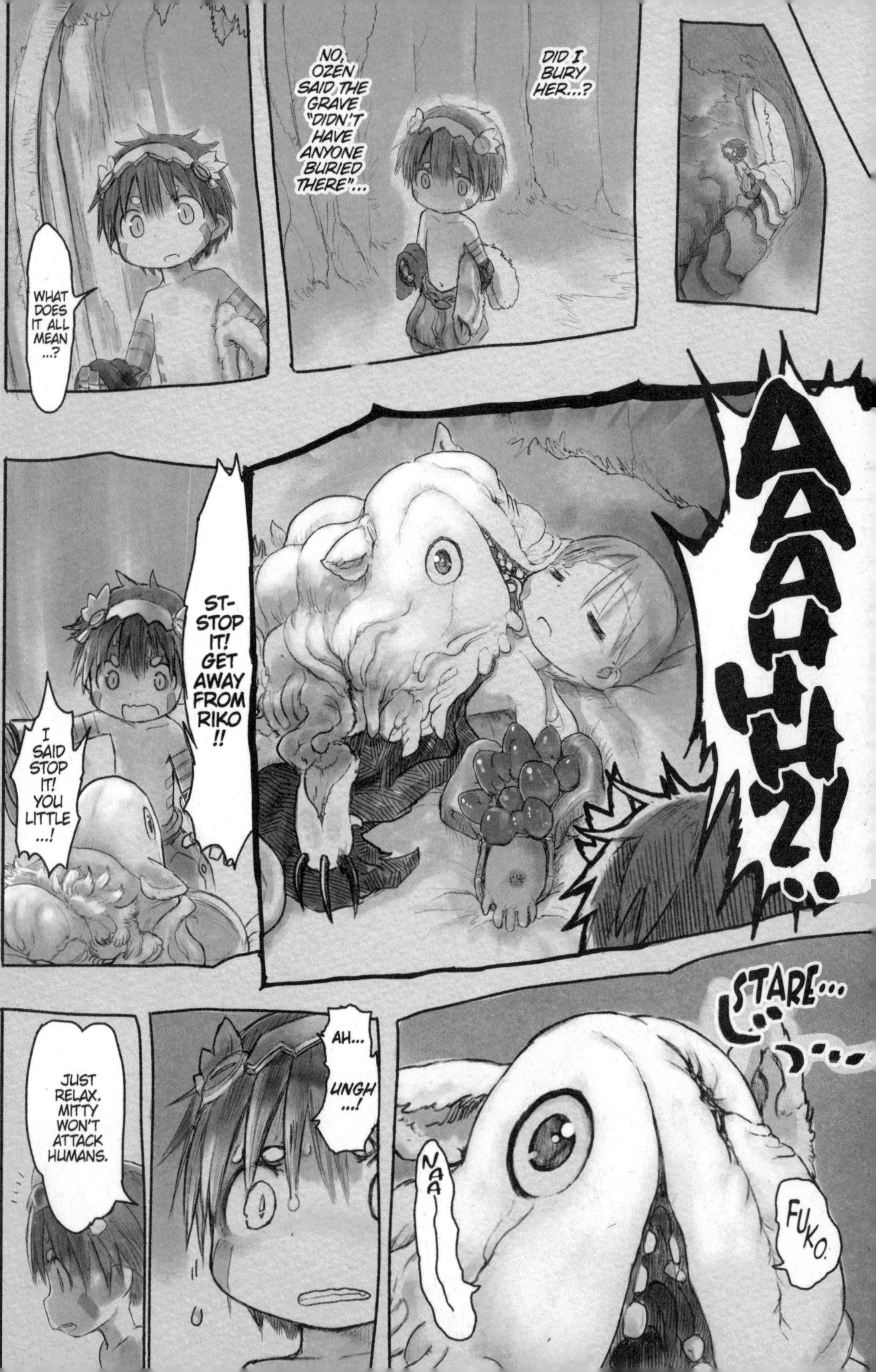
DID I BURY HER...?
NO, OZEN SAID THE GRAVE "DIDN'T HAVE ANYONE BURIED THERE"...
WHAT DOES IT ALL MEAN ...?
AAAHH?!
ST- STOP IT! GET AWAY FROM RIKO !!
I SAID STOP IT! YOU LITTLE ...!
STARE...
FUKO.
NAA
AH... UNGH ...!
JUST RELAX. MITTY WON'T ATTACK HUMANS.

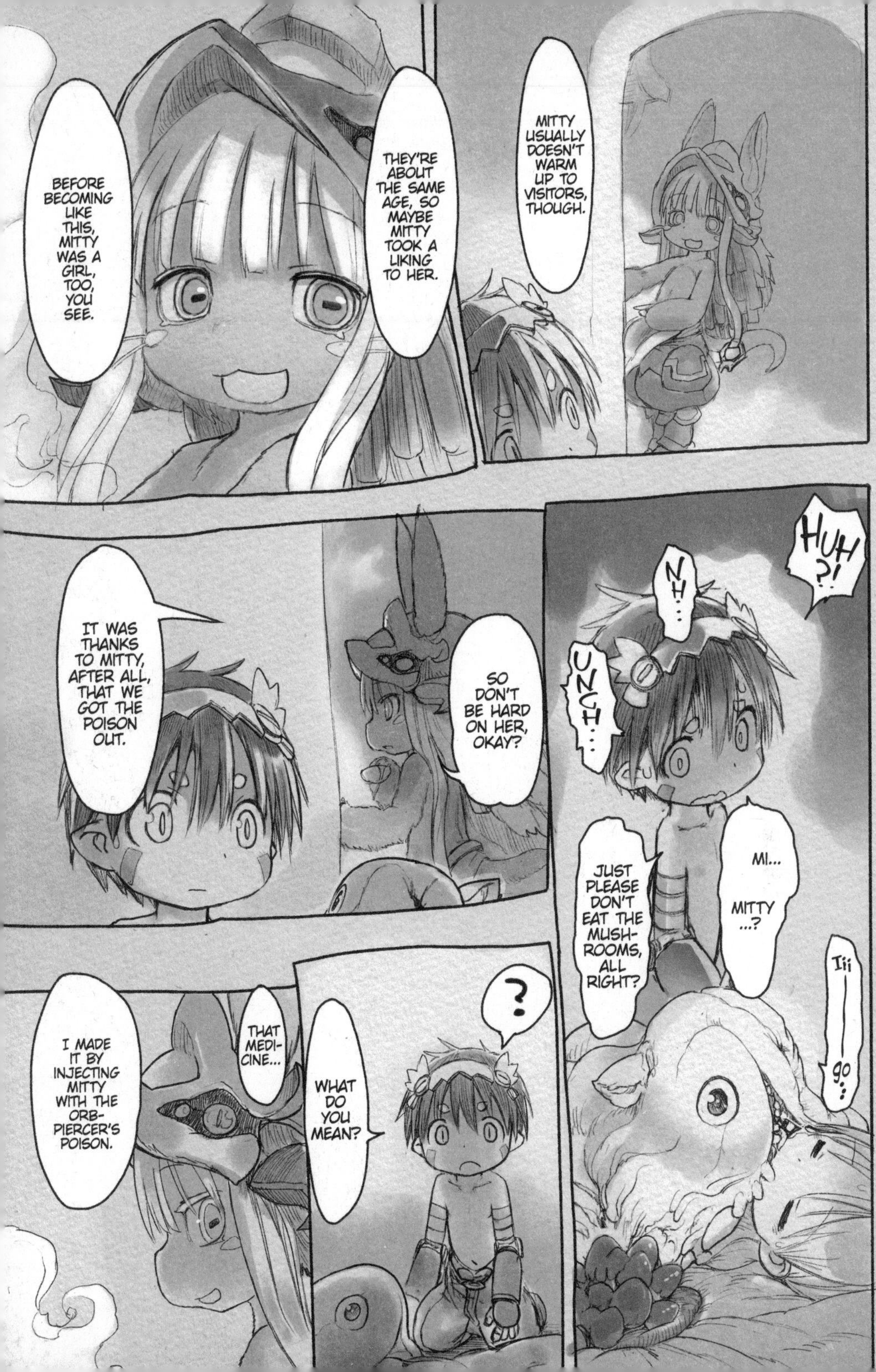
MITTY USUALLY DOESN'T WARM UP TO VISITORS, THOUGH.
THEY'RE ABOUT THE SAME AGE, SO MAYBE MITTY TOOK A LIKING TO HER.
BEFORE BECOMING LIKE THIS, MITTY WAS A GIRL, TOO, YOU SEE.
HUH?!
NH...
UNGH...
MI...
MITTY ...?
JUST PLEASE DON'T EAT THE MUSHROOMS, ALL RIGHT?
IT WAS THANKS TO MITTY, AFTER ALL, THAT WE GOT THE POISON OUT.
SO DON'T BE HARD ON HER, OKAY?
Iii——go...
?
WHAT DO YOU MEAN?
THAT MEDICINE...
I MADE IT BY INJECTING MITTY WITH THE ORB-PIERCER'S POISON.

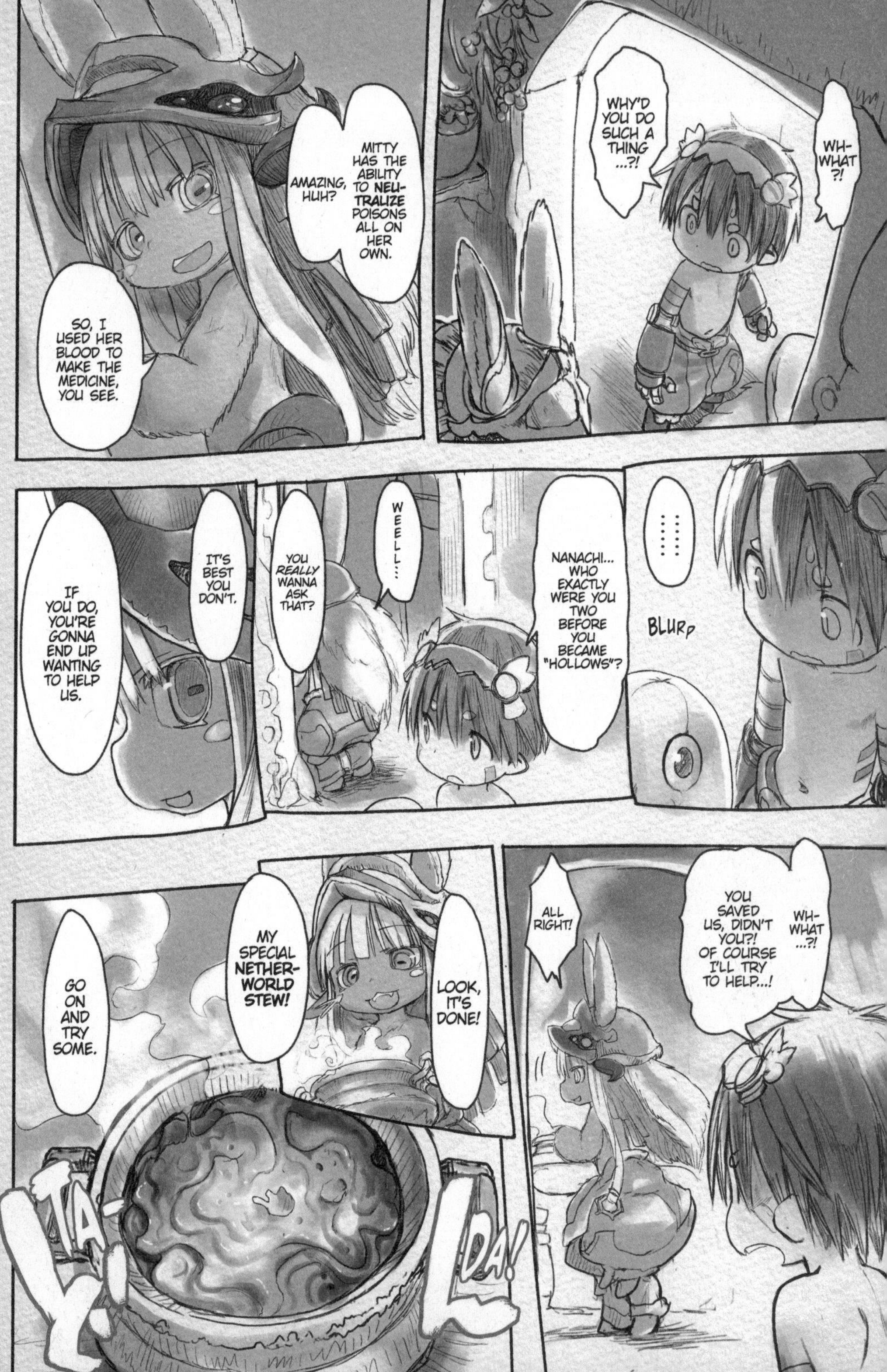
WH-WHAT ?!
WHY'D YOU DO SUCH A THING ...?!
MITTY HAS THE ABILITY TO **NEU-TRALIZE** POISONS ALL ON HER OWN.
AMAZING, HUH?
SO, I USED HER BLOOD TO MAKE THE MEDICINE, YOU SEE.
......
BLURP
NANACHI... WHO EXACTLY WERE YOU TWO BEFORE YOU BECAME "HOLLOWS"?
WEELL...
YOU *REALLY* WANNA ASK THAT?
IT'S BEST YOU DON'T.
IF YOU DO, YOU'RE GONNA END UP WANTING TO HELP US.
WH-WHAT ...?!
YOU SAVED US, DIDN'T YOU?! OF COURSE I'LL TRY TO HELP...!
ALL RIGHT!
LOOK, IT'S DONE!
MY SPECIAL **NETHER-WORLD STEW!**
GO ON AND TRY SOME.
TA-
DA!

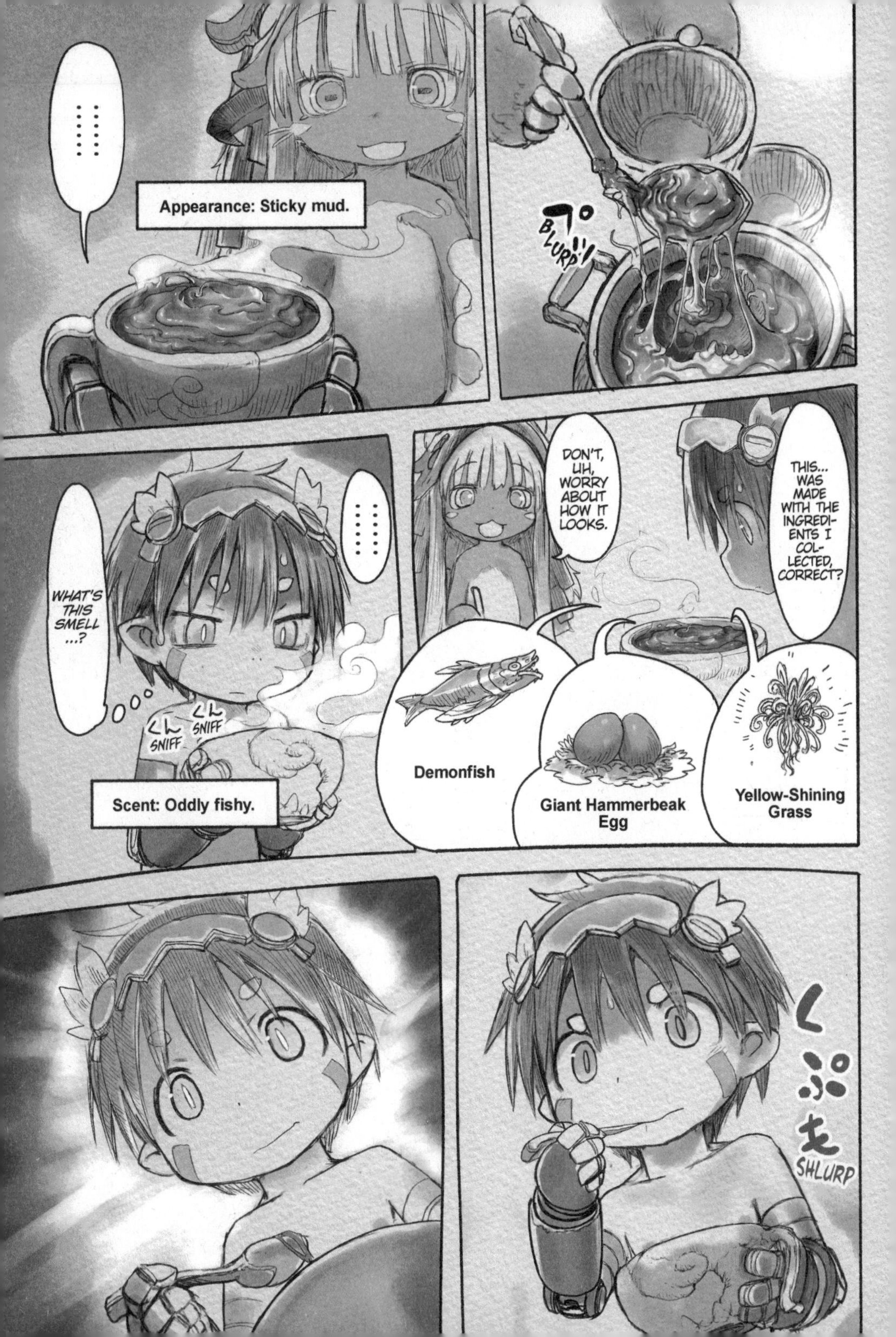
BLURP
......
Appearance: Sticky mud.
THIS... WAS MADE WITH THE INGREDI-ENTS I COL-LECTED, CORRECT?
DON'T, UH, WORRY ABOUT HOW IT LOOKS.
Yellow-Shining Grass
Giant Hammerbeak Egg
Demonfish
......
WHAT'S THIS SMELL ...?
くん SNIFF
くん SNIFF
Scent: Oddly fishy.
SHLURP

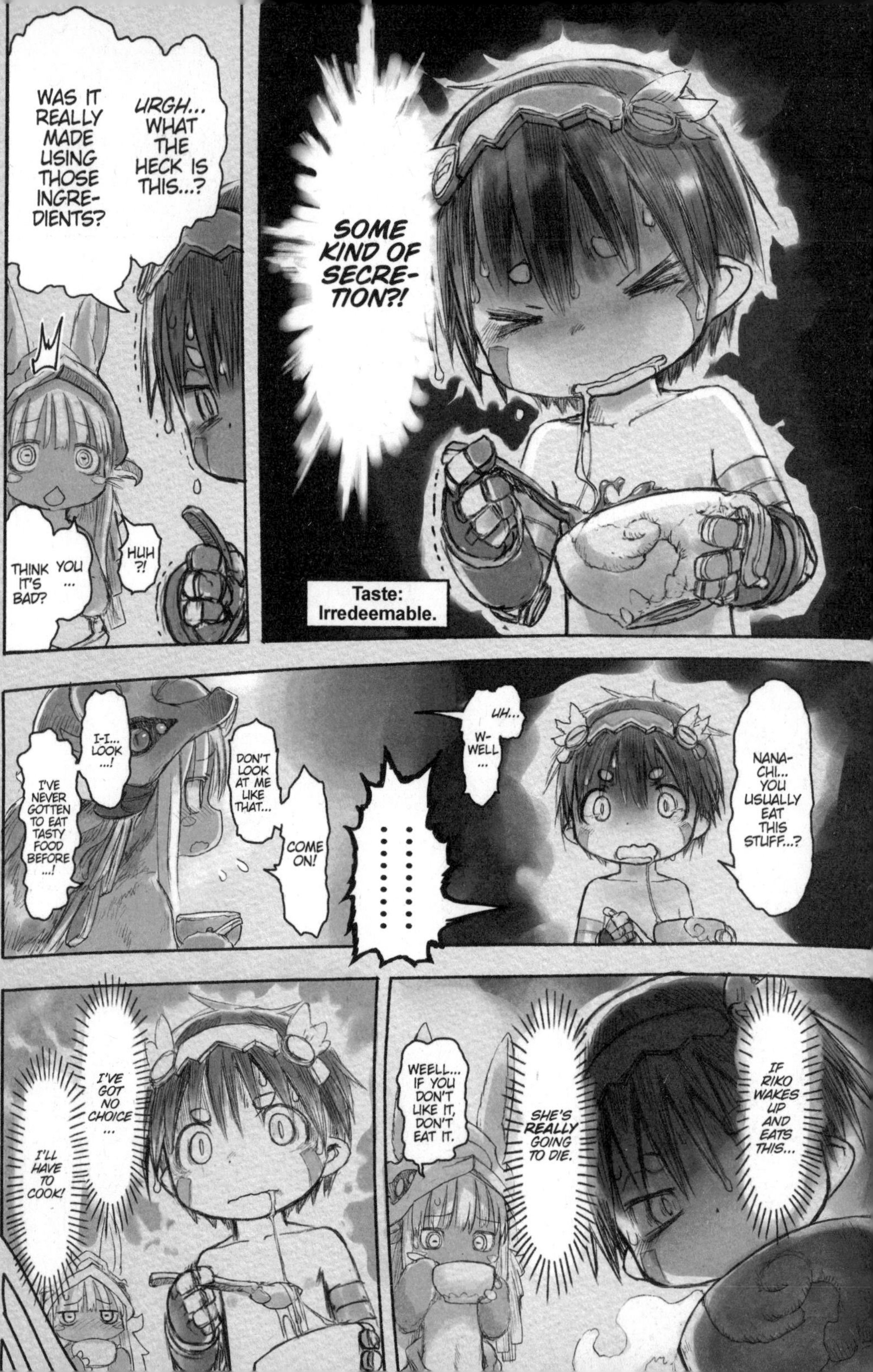
SOME KIND OF SECRETION?!
Taste: Irredeemable.
URGH... WHAT THE HECK IS THIS...?
WAS IT REALLY MADE USING THOSE INGREDIENTS?
HUH?!
YOU... THINK IT'S BAD?
NANACHI... YOU USUALLY EAT THIS STUFF...?
UH... W-WELL...
....
DON'T LOOK AT ME LIKE THAT...
COME ON!
I-I... LOOK...!
I'VE NEVER GOTTEN TO EAT TASTY FOOD BEFORE...!
IF RIKO WAKES UP AND EATS THIS...
SHE'S REALLY GOING TO DIE.
WEELL... IF YOU DON'T LIKE IT, DON'T EAT IT.
I'VE GOT NO CHOICE...
I'LL HAVE TO COOK!

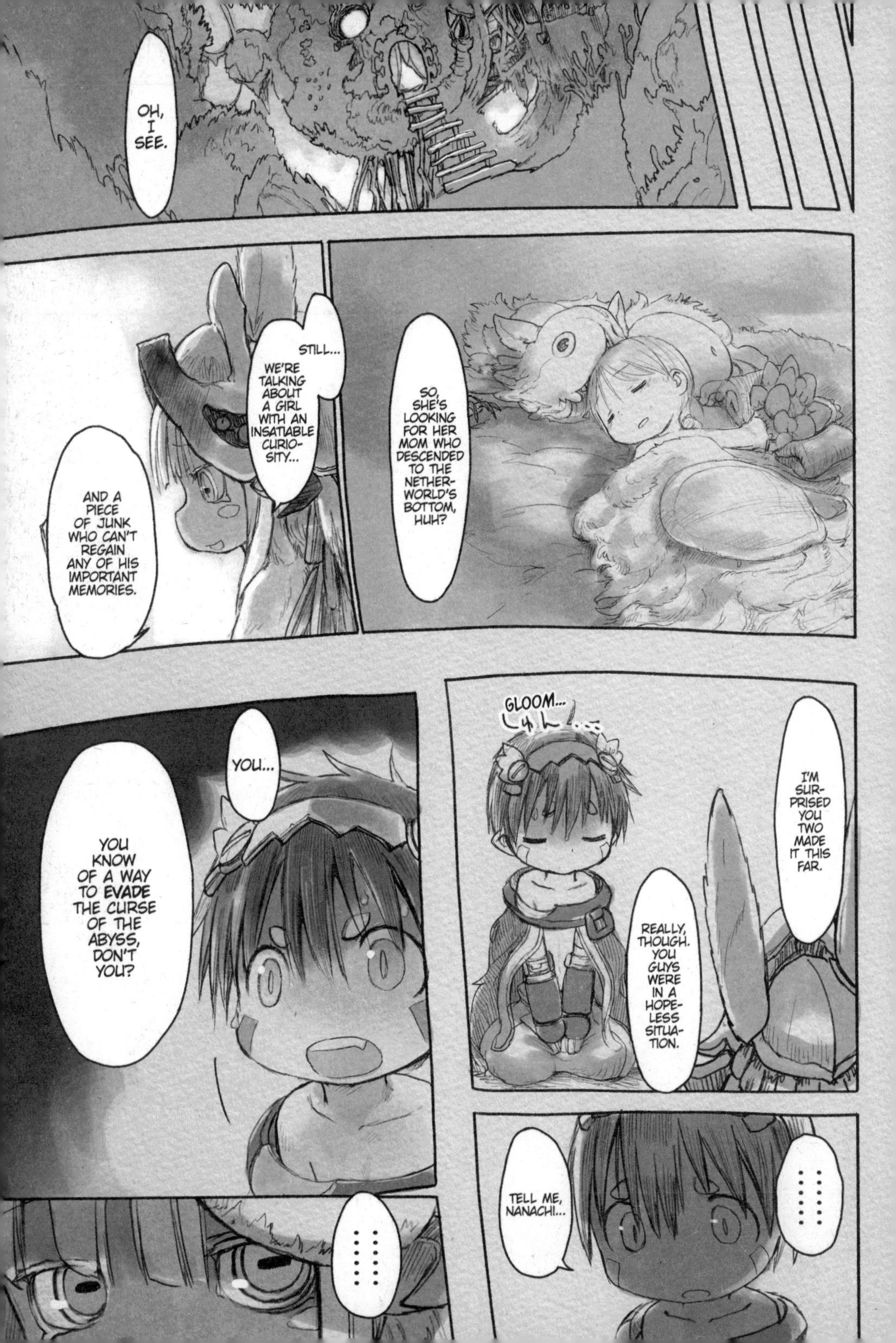
OH, I SEE.
SO, SHE'S LOOKING FOR HER MOM WHO DESCENDED TO THE NETHER-WORLD'S BOTTOM, HUH?
STILL... WE'RE TALKING ABOUT A GIRL WITH AN INSATIABLE CURIO-SITY...
AND A PIECE OF JUNK WHO CAN'T REGAIN ANY OF HIS IMPORTANT MEMORIES.
I'M SUR-PRISED YOU TWO MADE IT THIS FAR.
REALLY, THOUGH. YOU GUYS WERE IN A HOPE-LESS SITUA-TION.
GLOOM...
しゅん...
......
TELL ME, NANACHI...
YOU...
YOU KNOW OF A WAY TO EVADE THE CURSE OF THE ABYSS, DON'T YOU?
......

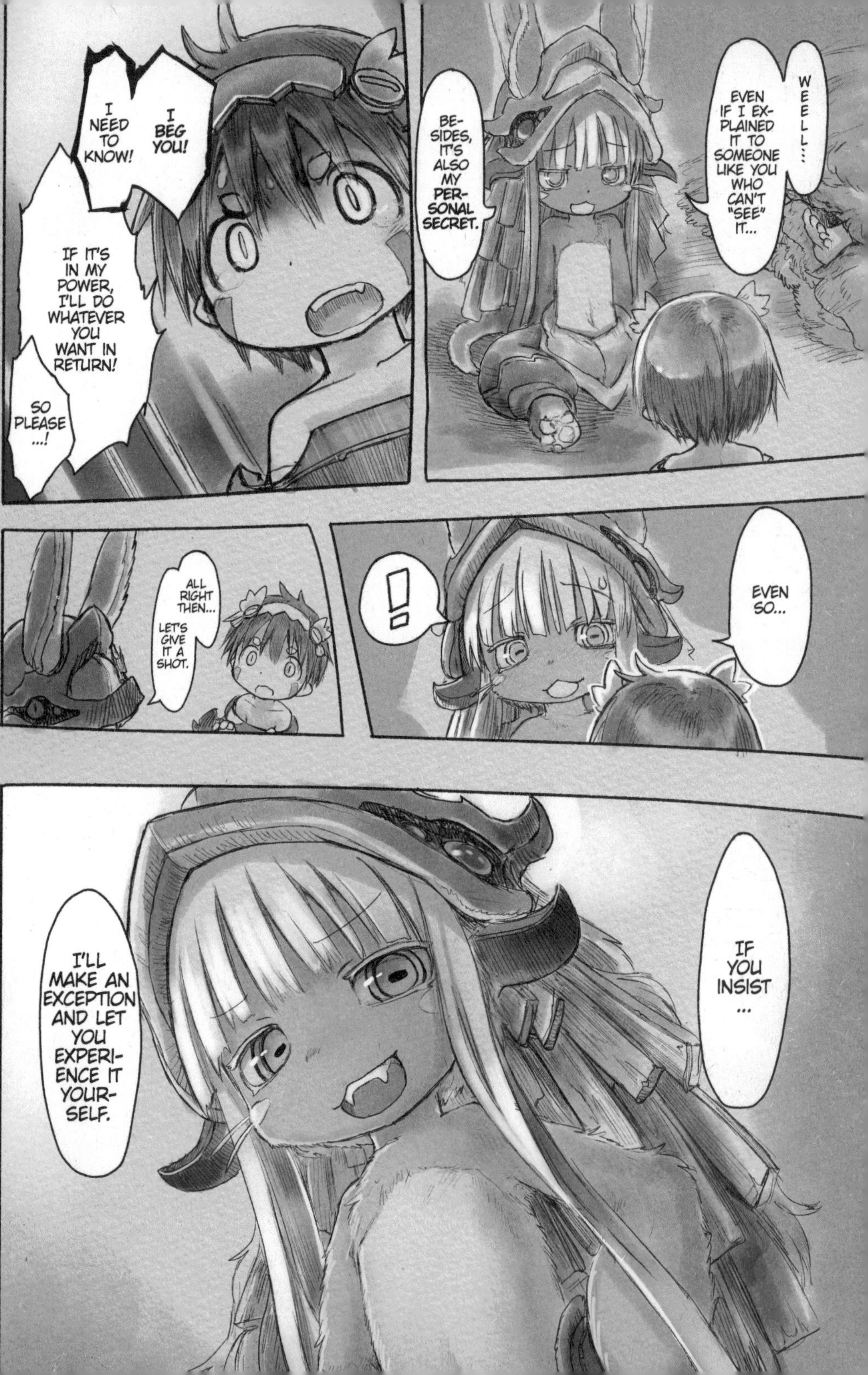
WEELL...
EVEN IF I EXPLAINED IT TO SOMEONE LIKE YOU WHO CAN'T "SEE" IT...
BESIDES, IT'S ALSO MY PERSONAL SECRET.
I BEG YOU!
I NEED TO KNOW!
IF IT'S IN MY POWER, I'LL DO WHATEVER YOU WANT IN RETURN!
SO PLEASE ...!
EVEN SO...
!
ALL RIGHT THEN...
LET'S GIVE IT A SHOT.
IF YOU INSIST ...
I'LL MAKE AN EXCEPTION AND LET YOU EXPERIENCE IT YOURSELF.

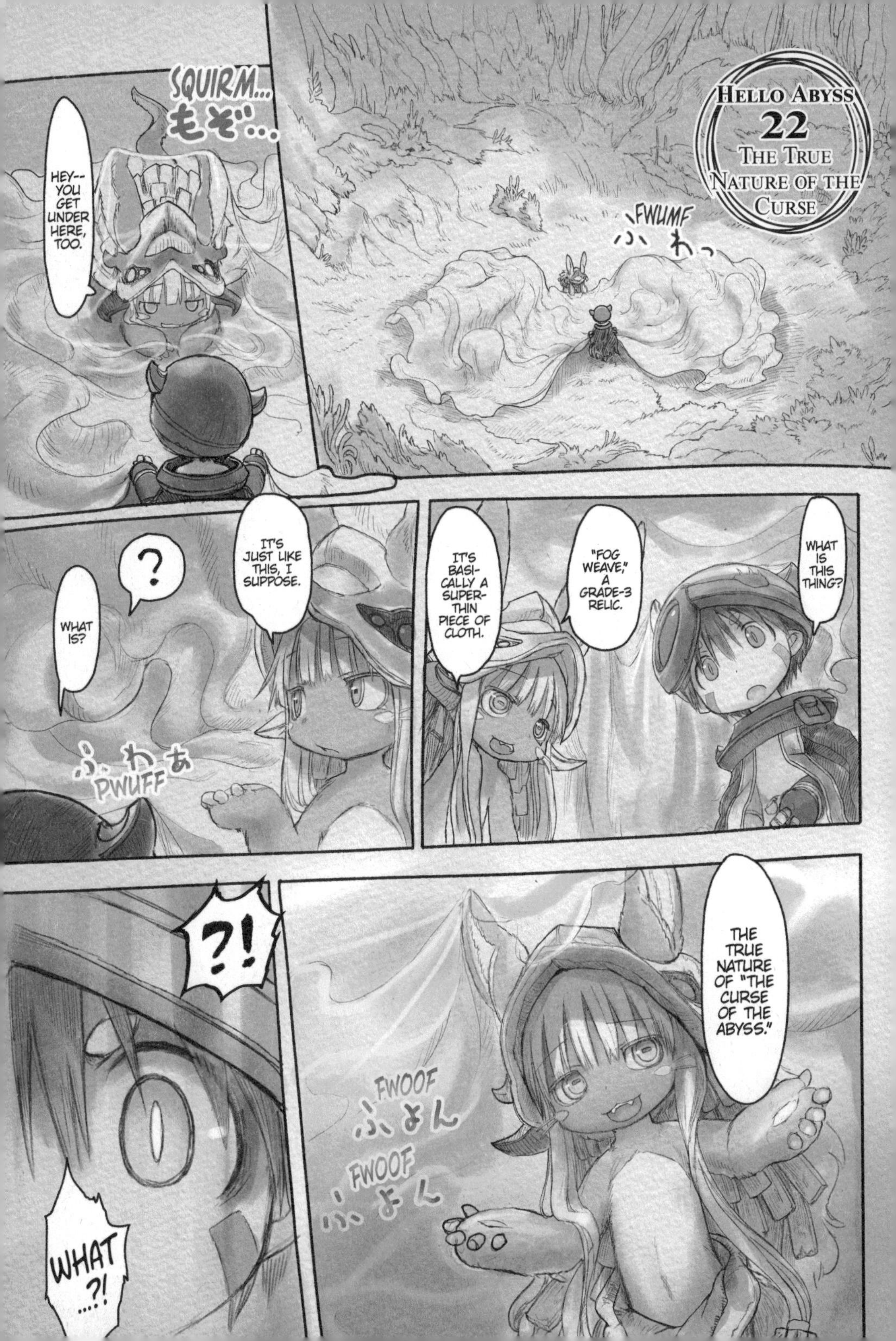
HELLO ABYSS 22
THE TRUE NATURE OF THE CURSE
FWUMF
ふわっ
SQUIRM...
もぞ...
HEY-- YOU GET UNDER HERE, TOO.
WHAT IS THIS THING?
"FOG WEAVE," A GRADE-3 RELIC.
IT'S BASICALLY A SUPER-THIN PIECE OF CLOTH.
IT'S JUST LIKE THIS, I SUPPOSE.
?
WHAT IS?
ふわぁ
PWUFF
THE TRUE NATURE OF "THE CURSE OF THE ABYSS."
FWOOF
ふよん
FWOOF
ふよん
?!
WHAT ...?!

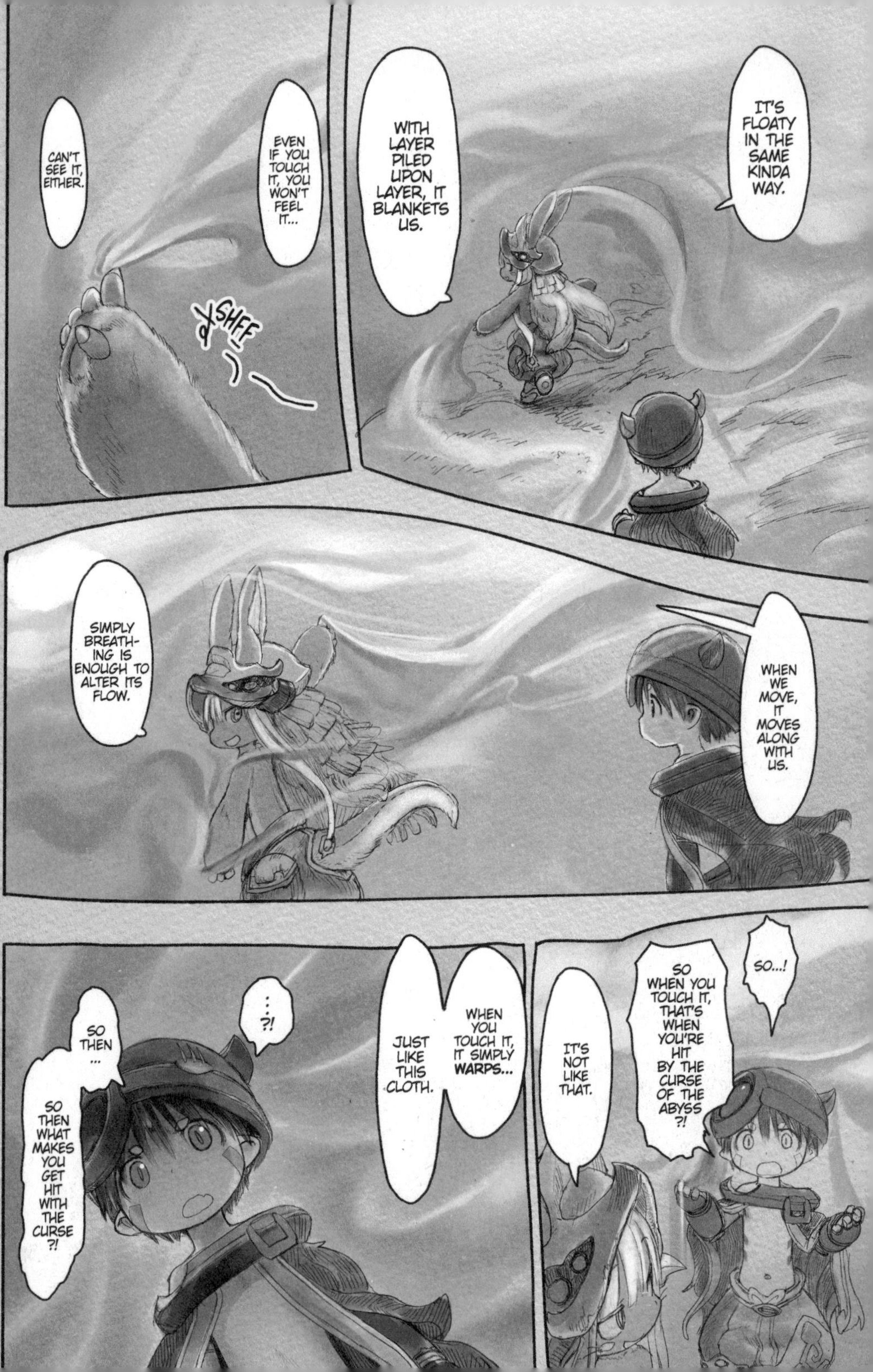
IT'S FLOATY IN THE SAME KINDA WAY.
WITH LAYER PILED UPON LAYER, IT BLANKETS US.
EVEN IF YOU TOUCH IT, YOU WON'T FEEL IT...
CAN'T SEE IT, EITHER.
SHFF
WHEN WE MOVE, IT MOVES ALONG WITH US.
SIMPLY BREATHING IS ENOUGH TO ALTER ITS FLOW.
SO...!
SO WHEN YOU TOUCH IT, THAT'S WHEN YOU'RE HIT BY THE CURSE OF THE ABYSS?!
IT'S NOT LIKE THAT.
WHEN YOU TOUCH IT, IT SIMPLY **WARPS...**
JUST LIKE THIS CLOTH.
...?!
SO THEN...
SO THEN WHAT MAKES YOU GET HIT WITH THE CURSE?!

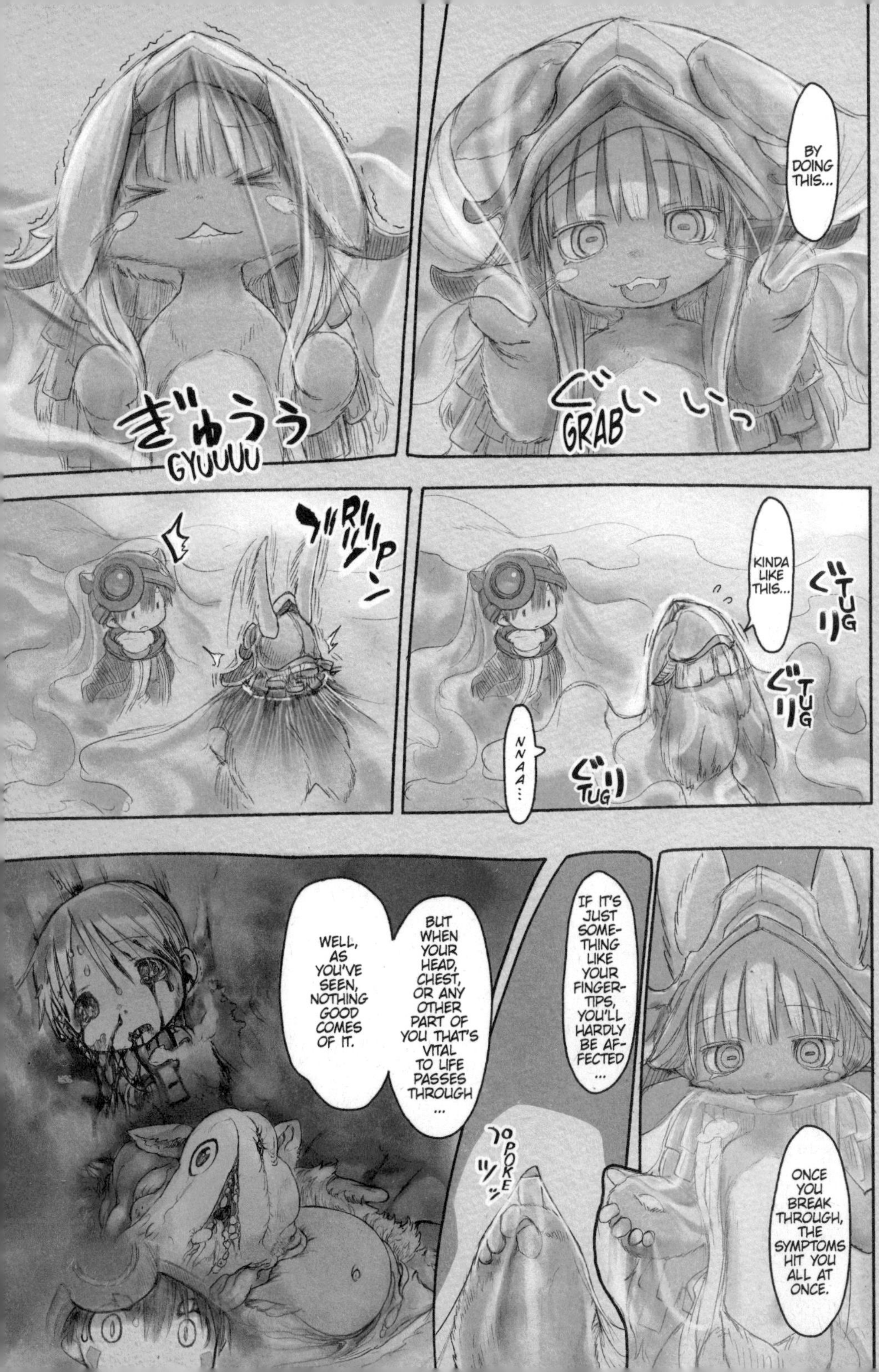
BY DOING THIS...
ぐいいっ
GRAB
ぎゅううう
GYUUUU
KINDA LIKE THIS...
ぐり
TUG
ぐり
TUG
ぐり
TUG
NNAA...
RIIIP
IF IT'S JUST SOME-THING LIKE YOUR FINGER-TIPS, YOU'LL HARDLY BE AF-FECTED...
ONCE YOU BREAK THROUGH, THE SYMPTOMS HIT YOU ALL AT ONCE.
POKE
BUT WHEN YOUR HEAD, CHEST, OR ANY OTHER PART OF YOU THAT'S VITAL TO LIFE PASSES THROUGH...
WELL, AS YOU'VE SEEN, NOTHING GOOD COMES OF IT.

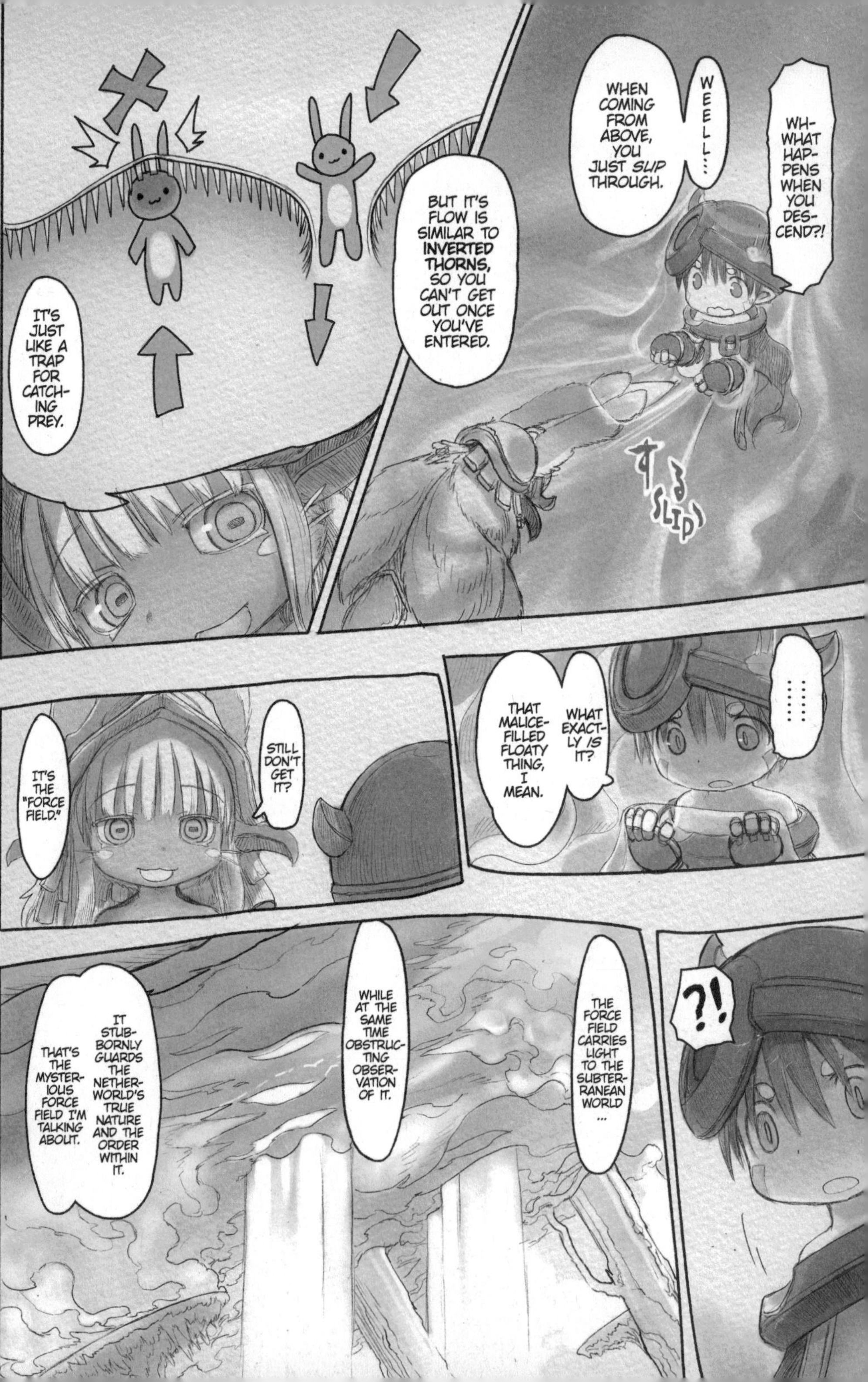
WH-WHAT HAPPENS WHEN YOU DESCEND?!
WEELL...
WHEN COMING FROM ABOVE, YOU JUST *SLIP* THROUGH.
BUT IT'S FLOW IS SIMILAR TO **INVERTED THORNS,** SO YOU CAN'T GET OUT ONCE YOU'VE ENTERED.
する SLIP
IT'S JUST LIKE A TRAP FOR CATCHING PREY.
......
WHAT EXACTLY *IS* IT?
THAT MALICE-FILLED FLOATY THING, I MEAN.
STILL DON'T GET IT?
IT'S THE "FORCE FIELD."
?!
THE FORCE FIELD CARRIES LIGHT TO THE SUBTERRANEAN WORLD ...
WHILE AT THE SAME TIME OBSTRUCTING OBSERVATION OF IT.
IT STUBBORNLY GUARDS THE NETHERWORLD'S TRUE NATURE AND THE ORDER WITHIN IT.
THAT'S THE MYSTERIOUS FORCE FIELD I'M TALKING ABOUT.

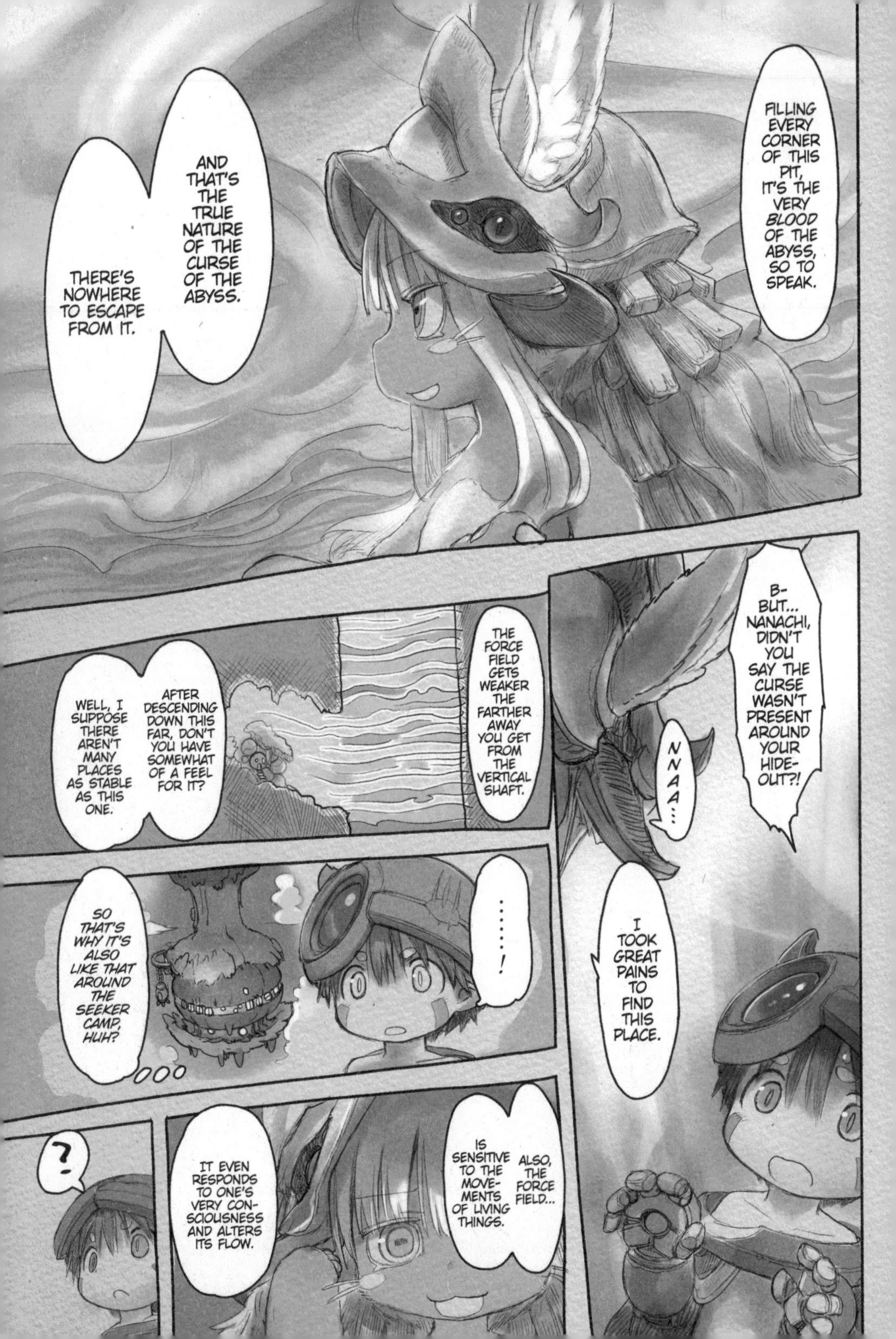
FILLING EVERY CORNER OF THIS PIT, IT'S THE VERY *BLOOD* OF THE ABYSS, SO TO SPEAK.
AND THAT'S THE TRUE NATURE OF THE CURSE OF THE ABYSS.
THERE'S NOWHERE TO ESCAPE FROM IT.
B-BUT... NANACHI, DIDN'T YOU SAY THE CURSE WASN'T PRESENT AROUND YOUR HIDE-OUT?!
NNAA...
I TOOK GREAT PAINS TO FIND THIS PLACE.
THE FORCE FIELD GETS WEAKER THE FARTHER AWAY YOU GET FROM THE VERTICAL SHAFT.
AFTER DESCENDING DOWN THIS FAR, DON'T YOU HAVE SOMEWHAT OF A FEEL FOR IT?
WELL, I SUPPOSE THERE AREN'T MANY PLACES AS STABLE AS THIS ONE.
......!
SO THAT'S WHY IT'S ALSO LIKE THAT AROUND THE SEEKER CAMP, HUH?
ALSO, THE FORCE FIELD...
IS SENSITIVE TO THE MOVEMENTS OF LIVING THINGS.
IT EVEN RESPONDS TO ONE'S VERY CONSCIOUSNESS AND ALTERS ITS FLOW.
?

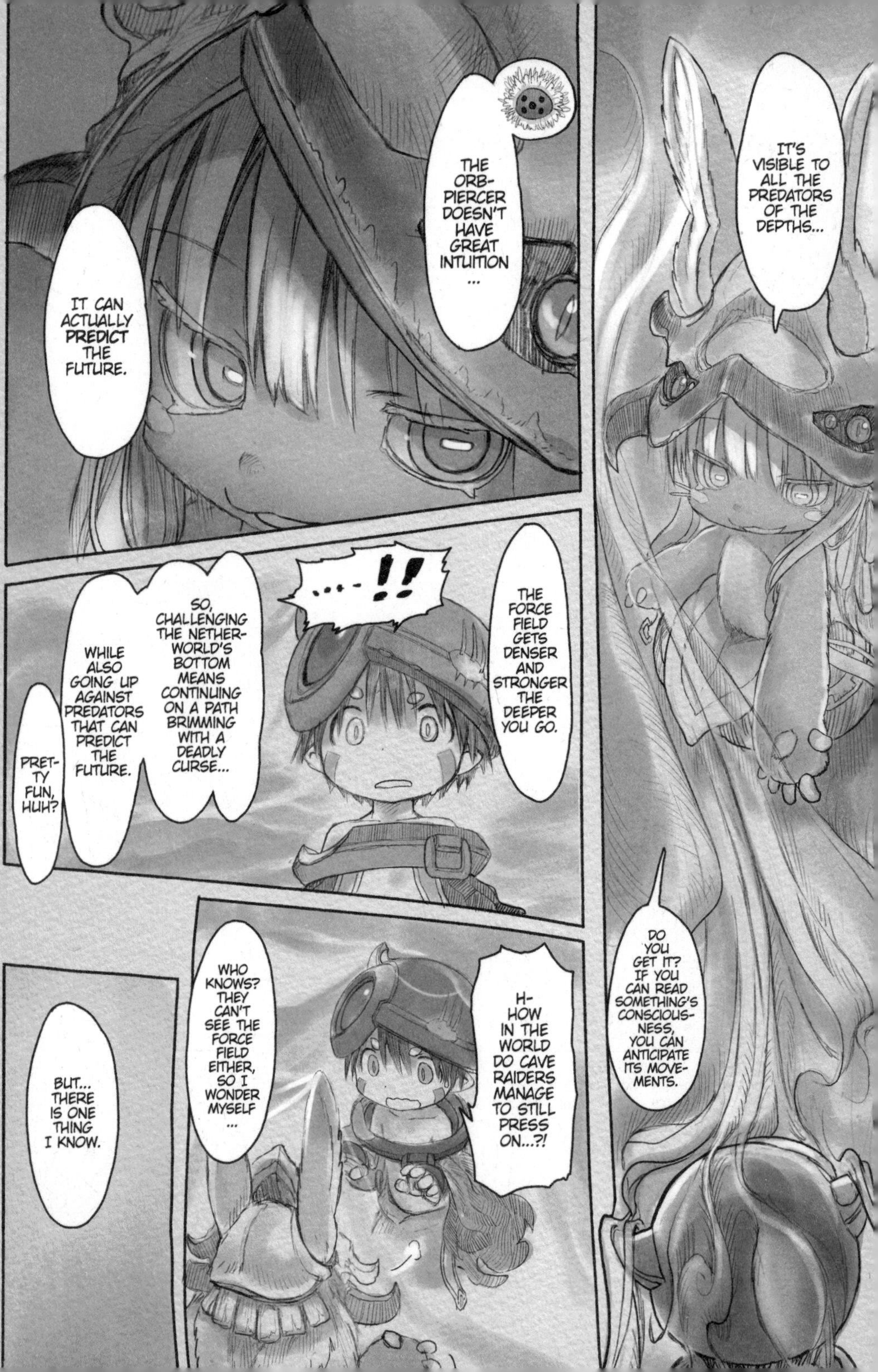
IT'S VISIBLE TO ALL THE PREDATORS OF THE DEPTHS...
DO YOU GET IT? IF YOU CAN READ SOMETHING'S CONSCIOUSNESS, YOU CAN ANTICIPATE ITS MOVEMENTS.
THE ORB-PIERCER DOESN'T HAVE GREAT INTUITION ...
IT CAN ACTUALLY PREDICT THE FUTURE.
THE FORCE FIELD GETS DENSER AND STRONGER THE DEEPER YOU GO.
...-!!
SO, CHALLENGING THE NETHER-WORLD'S BOTTOM MEANS CONTINUING ON A PATH BRIMMING WITH A DEADLY CURSE...
WHILE ALSO GOING UP AGAINST PREDATORS THAT CAN PREDICT THE FUTURE.
PRET-TY FUN, HUH?
H-HOW IN THE WORLD DO CAVE RAIDERS MANAGE TO STILL PRESS ON...?!
WHO KNOWS? THEY CAN'T SEE THE FORCE FIELD EITHER, SO I WONDER MYSELF ...
BUT... THERE IS ONE THING I KNOW.

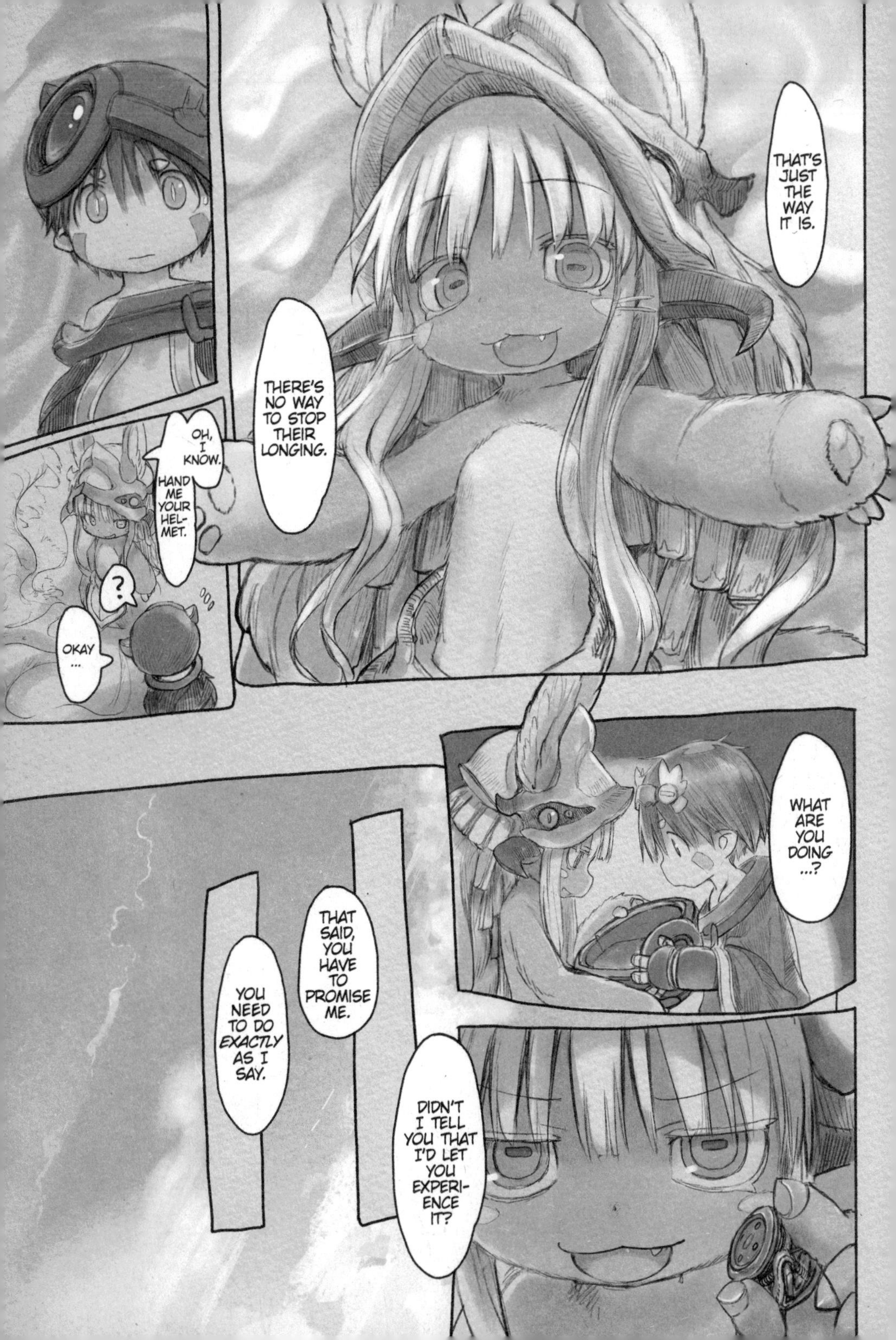
THAT'S JUST THE WAY IT IS.
THERE'S NO WAY TO STOP THEIR LONGING.
OH, I KNOW.
HAND ME YOUR HEL-MET.
?
OKAY ...
WHAT ARE YOU DOING ...?
DIDN'T I TELL YOU THAT I'D LET YOU EXPERI-ENCE IT?
THAT SAID, YOU HAVE TO PROMISE ME.
YOU NEED TO DO *EXACTLY* AS I SAY.

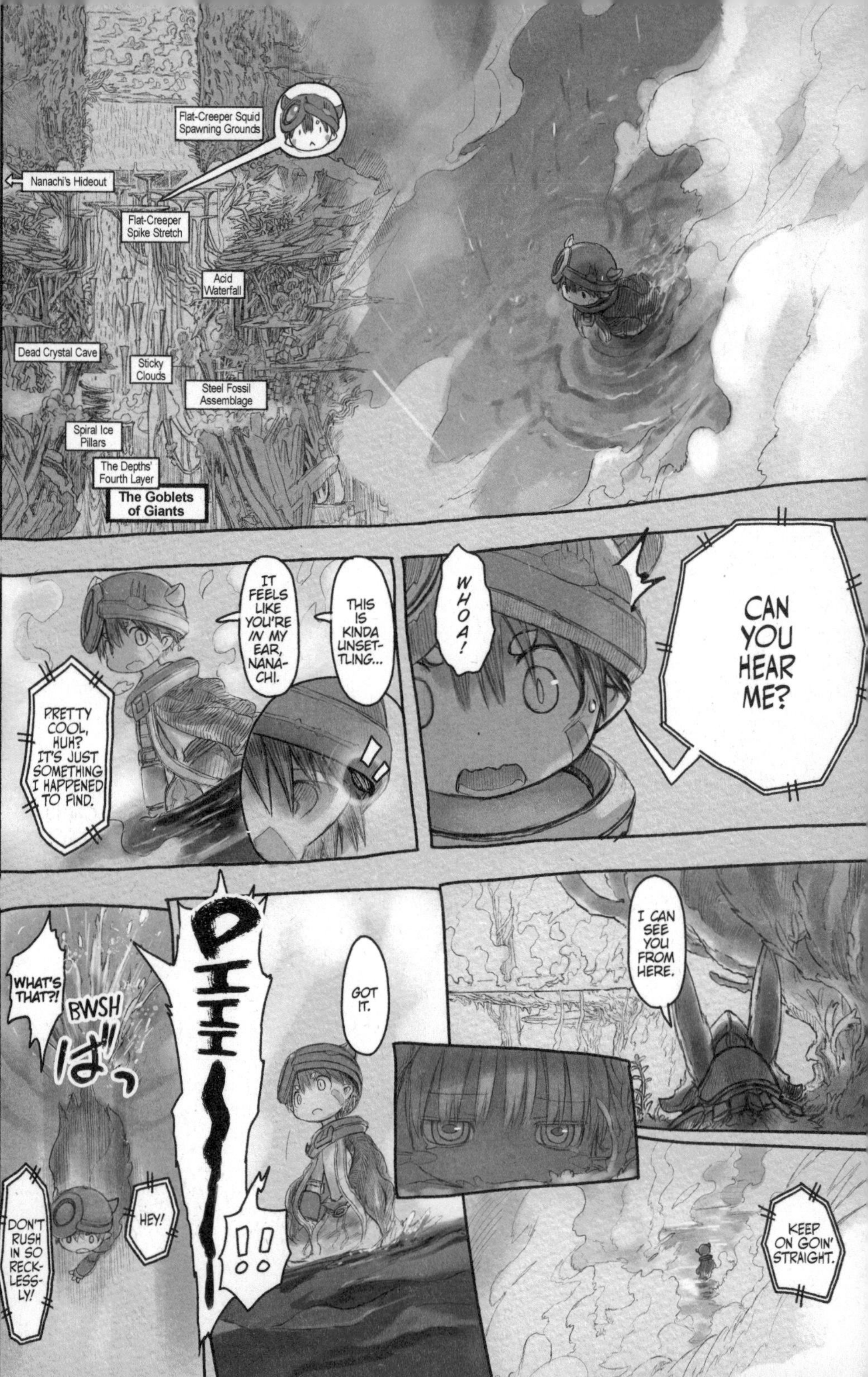
Flat-Creeper Squid Spawning Grounds
Nanachi's Hideout
Flat-Creeper Spike Stretch
Acid Waterfall
Dead Crystal Cave
Sticky Clouds
Steel Fossil Assemblage
Spiral Ice Pillars
The Depths' Fourth Layer
The Goblets of Giants
CAN YOU HEAR ME?
WHOA!
THIS IS KINDA UNSETTLING...
IT FEELS LIKE YOU'RE IN MY EAR, NANACHI.
PRETTY COOL, HUH? IT'S JUST SOMETHING I HAPPENED TO FIND.
I CAN SEE YOU FROM HERE.
KEEP ON GOIN' STRAIGHT.
GOT IT.
DIII—!
!!
WHAT'S THAT?!
BWSH
ばっ
HEY!
DON'T RUSH IN SO RECKLESSLY!

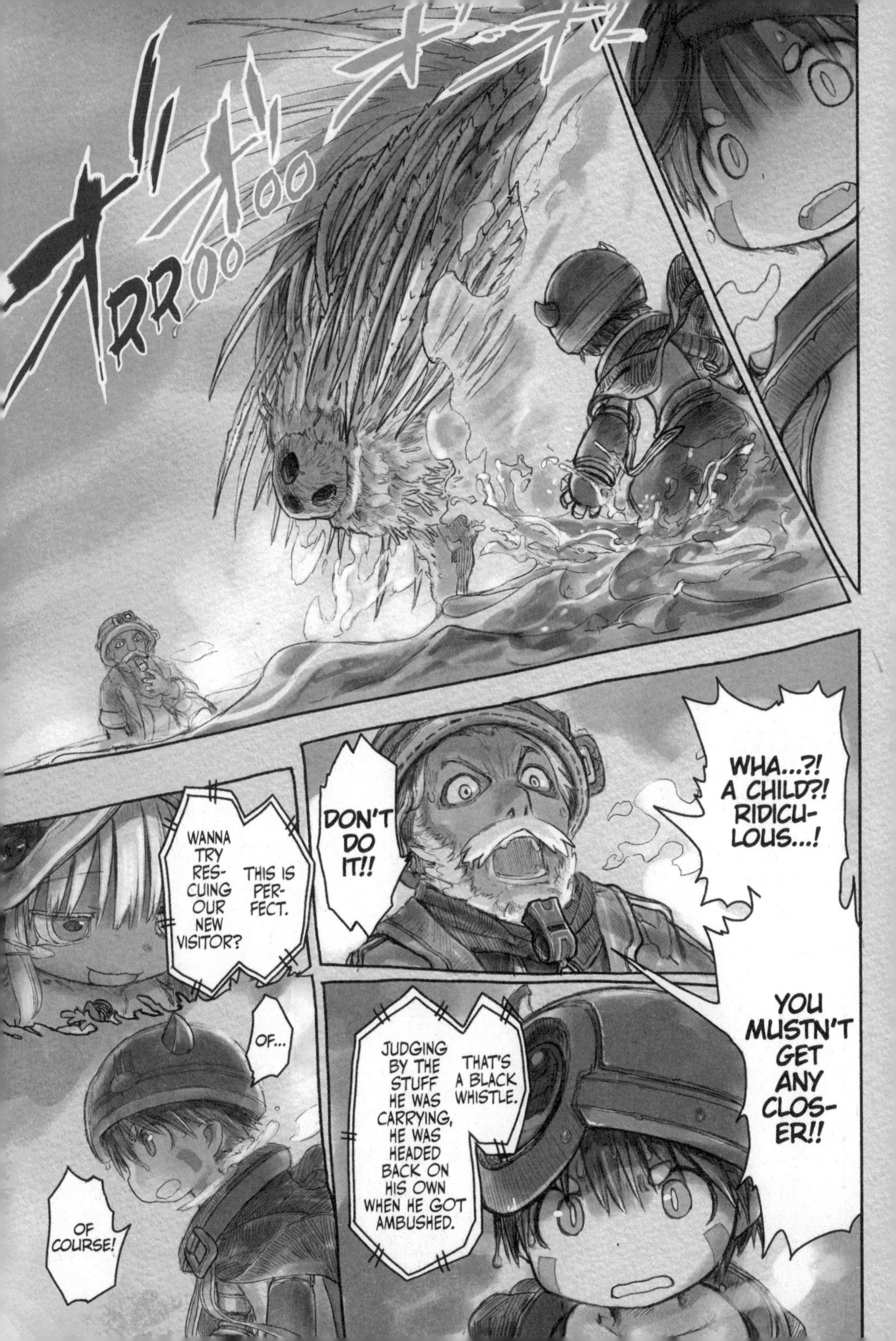
DRROOOO
WHA...?! A CHILD?! RIDICULOUS...!
DON'T DO IT!!
THIS IS PERFECT.
WANNA TRY RESCUING OUR NEW VISITOR?
YOU MUSTN'T GET ANY CLOSER!!
THAT'S A BLACK WHISTLE.
JUDGING BY THE STUFF HE WAS CARRYING, HE WAS HEADED BACK ON HIS OWN WHEN HE GOT AMBUSHED.
OF...
OF COURSE!

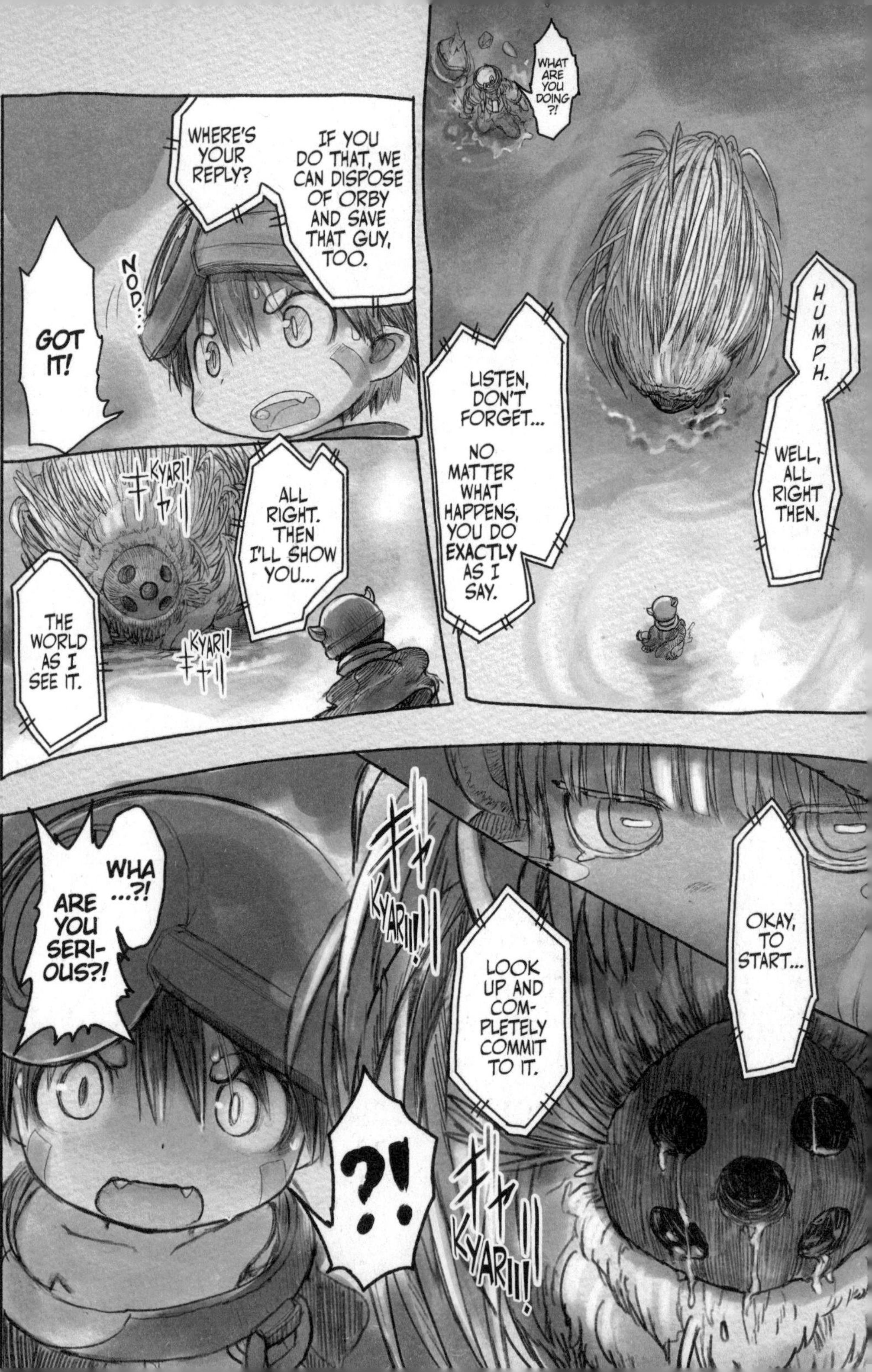
WHAT ARE YOU DOING?!
HUMPH.
WELL, ALL RIGHT THEN.
LISTEN, DON'T FORGET...
NO MATTER WHAT HAPPENS, YOU DO EXACTLY AS I SAY.
IF YOU DO THAT, WE CAN DISPOSE OF ORBY AND SAVE THAT GUY, TOO.
WHERE'S YOUR REPLY?
NOD...
GOT IT!
KYARI!
ALL RIGHT. THEN I'LL SHOW YOU...
KYARI!
THE WORLD AS I SEE IT.
OKAY, TO START...
LOOK UP AND COMPLETELY COMMIT TO IT.
KYARIII!!
KYARIII!!
WHA...?!
ARE YOU SERIOUS?!
?!

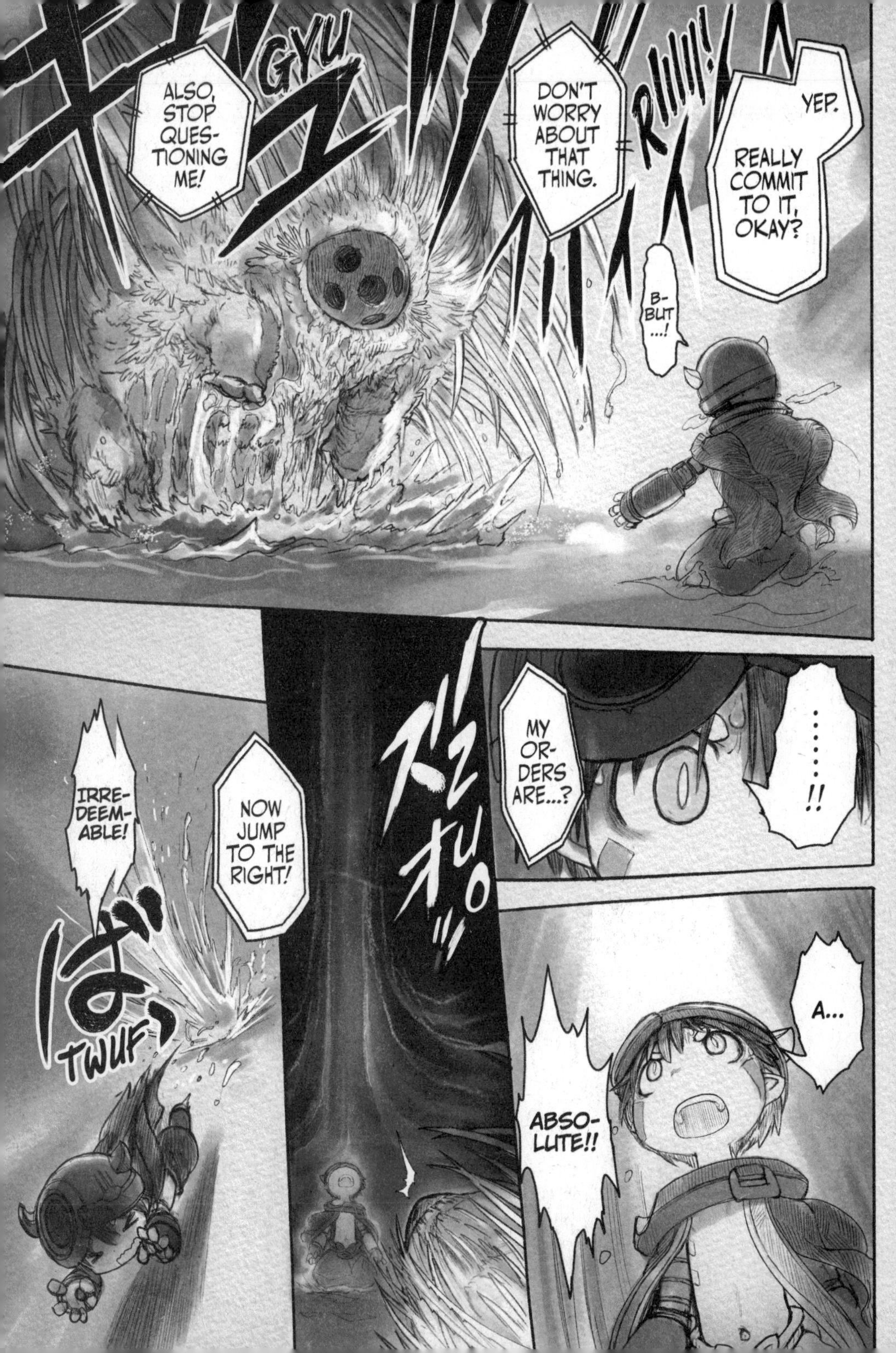
YEP. REALLY COMMIT TO IT, OKAY?
RIIIII!
DON'T WORRY ABOUT THAT THING.
B-BUT...!
GYU
ALSO, STOP QUES-TIONING ME!
......!!
MY OR-DERS ARE...?
A...
ABSO-LUTE!!
NOW JUMP TO THE RIGHT!
IRRE-DEEM-ABLE!
TWUF

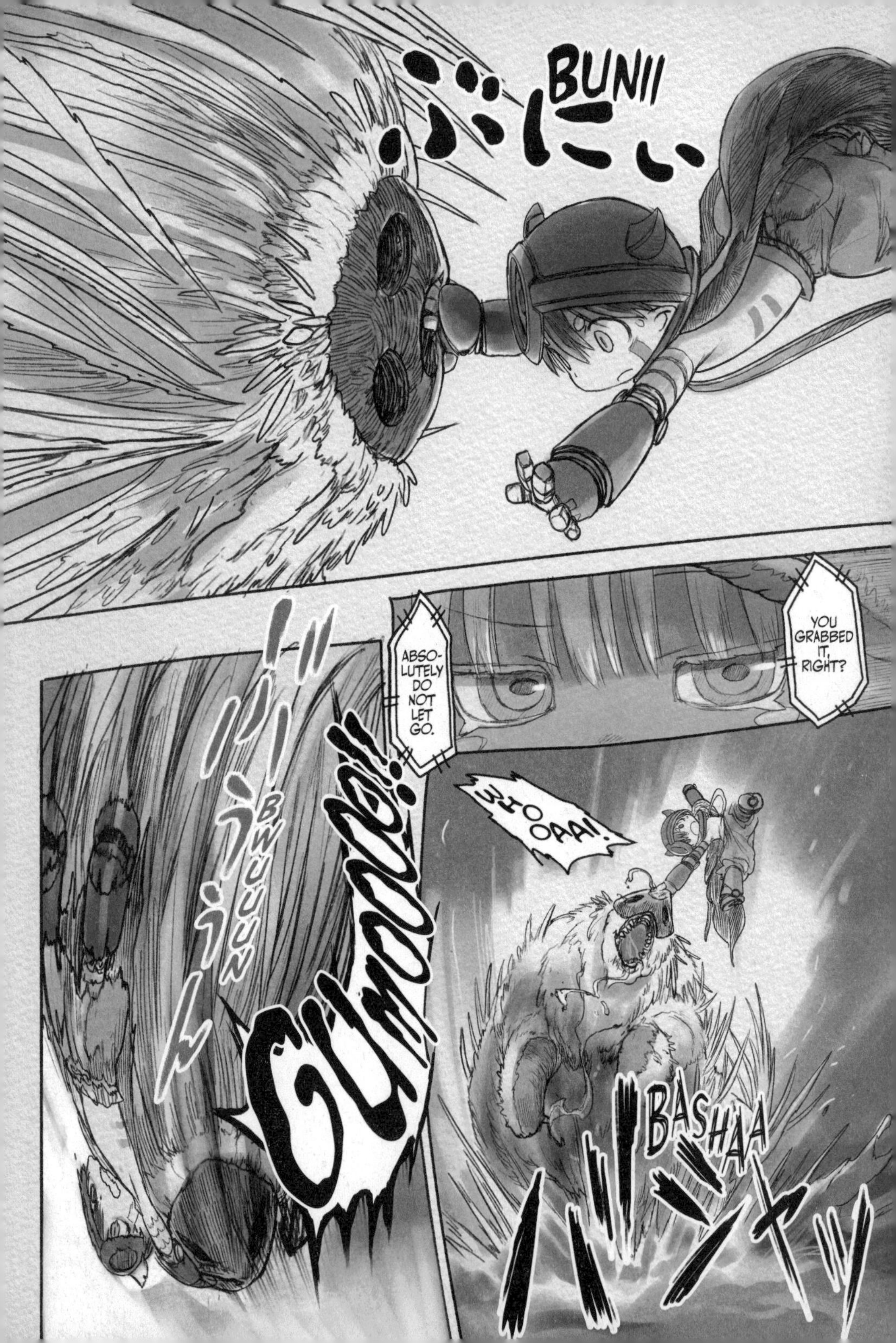
BUNII
YOU GRABBED IT, RIGHT?
ABSOLUTELY DO NOT LET GO.
WHOOAA!
BASHAA
BWUUUUN
GUMOOO!!

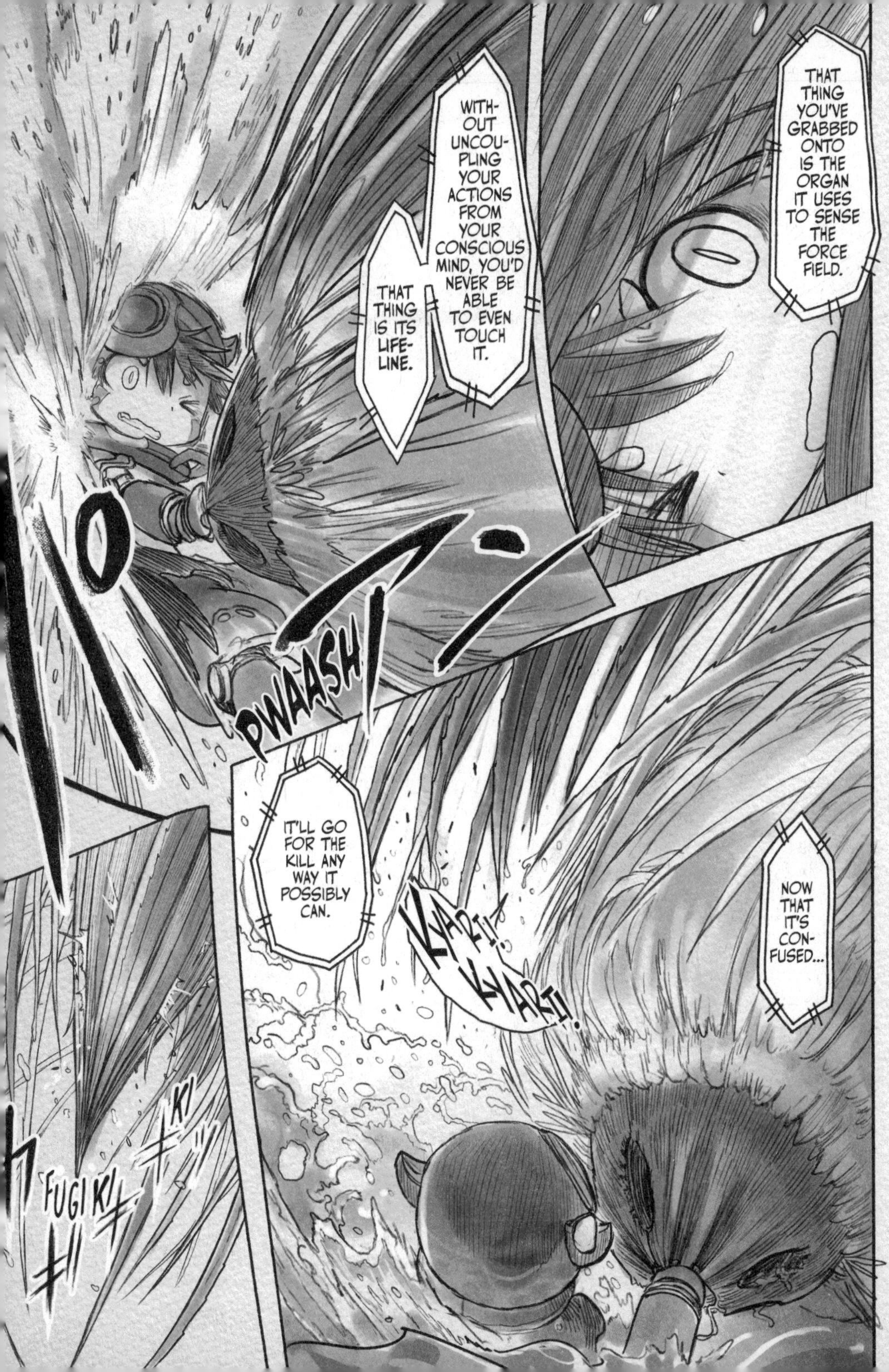
THAT THING YOU'VE GRABBED ONTO IS THE ORGAN IT USES TO SENSE THE FORCE FIELD.
WITHOUT UNCOUPLING YOUR ACTIONS FROM YOUR CONSCIOUS MIND, YOU'D NEVER BE ABLE TO EVEN TOUCH IT.
THAT THING IS ITS LIFELINE.
PWAASH
NOW THAT IT'S CONFUSED...
KYARI! KYARI!
IT'LL GO FOR THE KILL ANY WAY IT POSSIBLY CAN.
FUGI KI KI

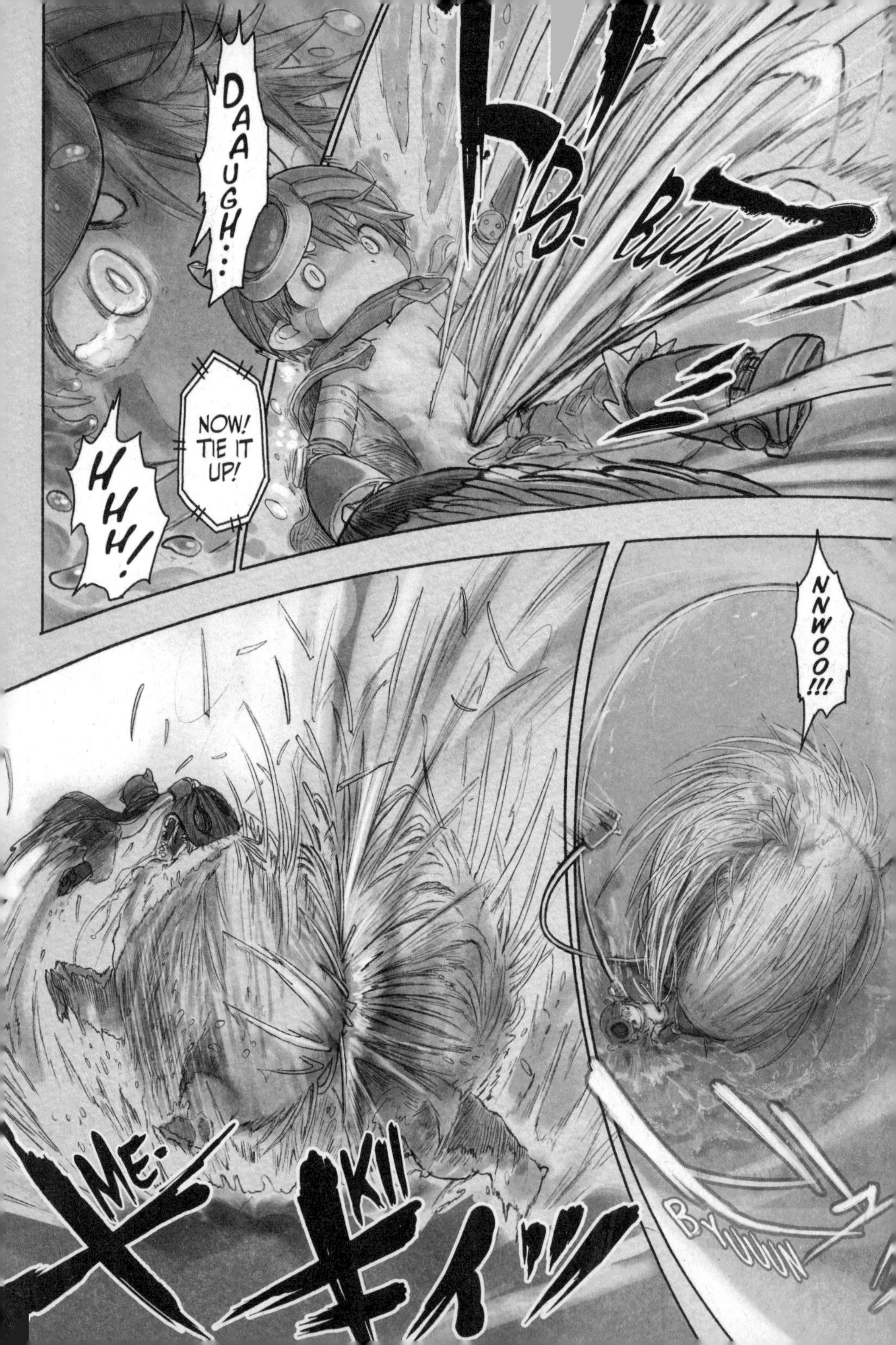
DO- BUUN
DAAUGH...
NOW! TIE IT UP!
HHH!
NNWOOO!!!
BYUUUN
ME- KII

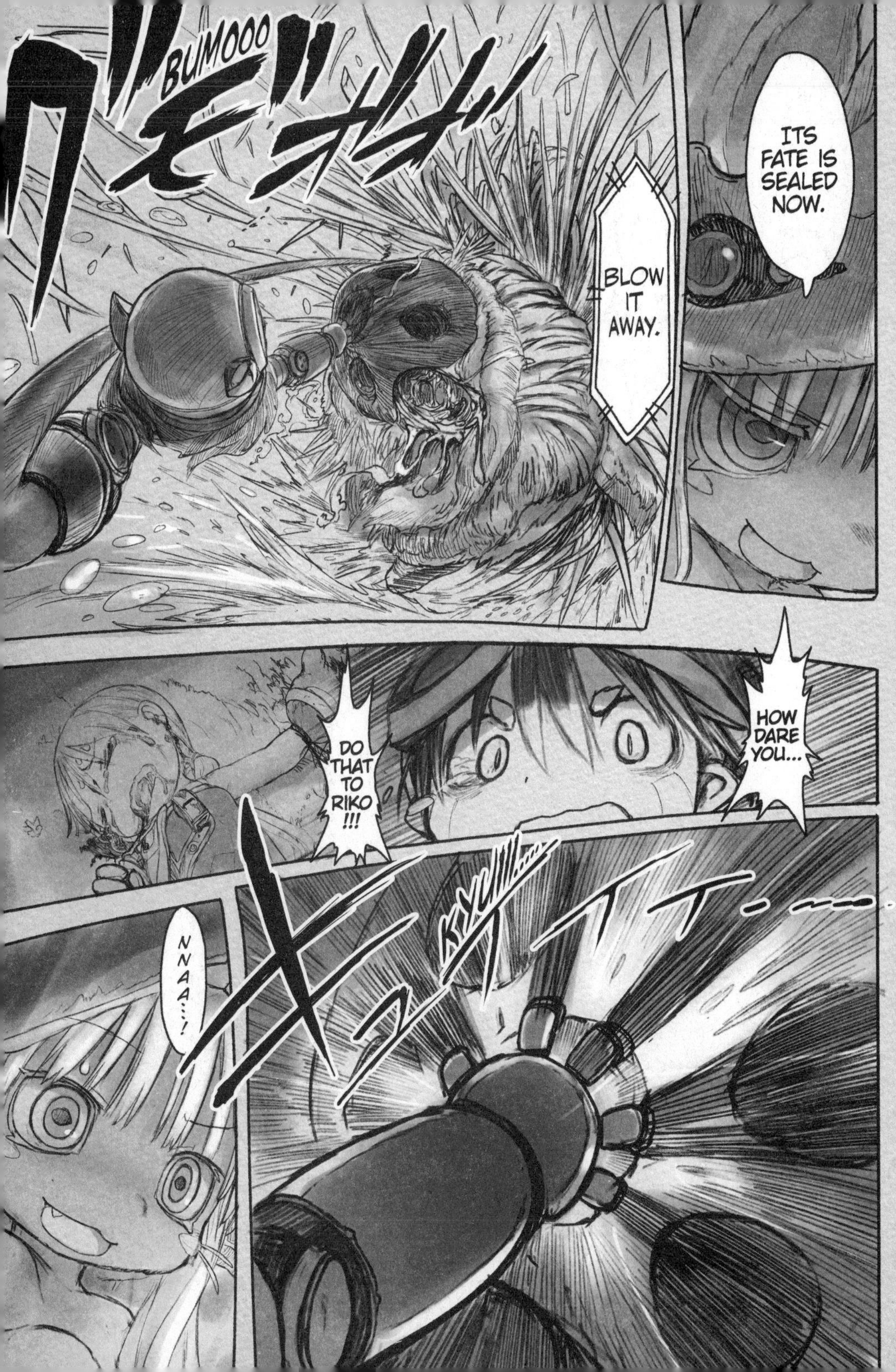
ITS FATE IS SEALED NOW.
BLOW IT AWAY.
BUMOOO
HOW DARE YOU...
DO THAT TO RIKO!!!
KYUIIII....
NNAA...!

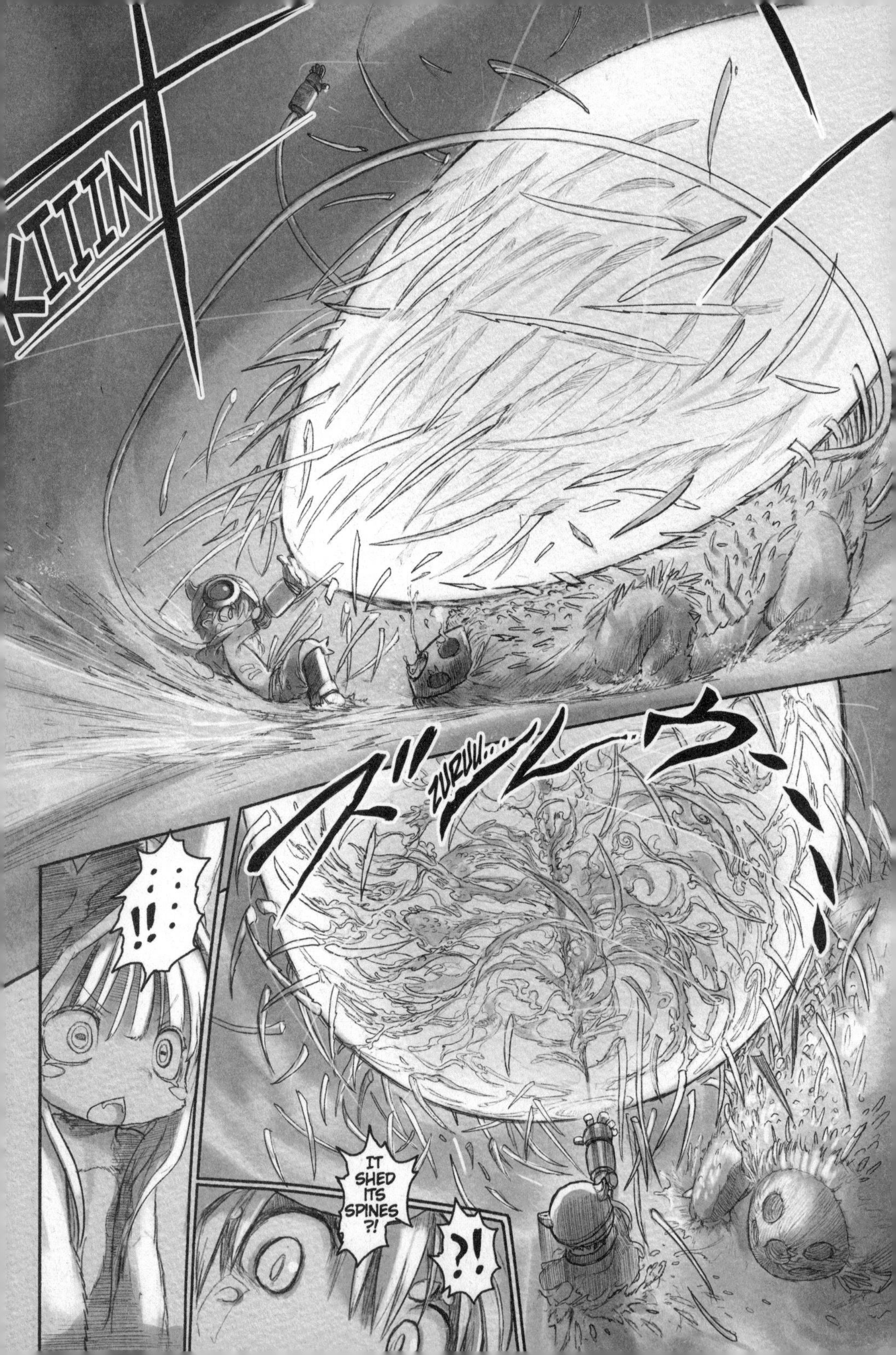

KIIIN
ズルーウ
ZURUU...
...!!
IT SHED ITS SPINES ?!
?!

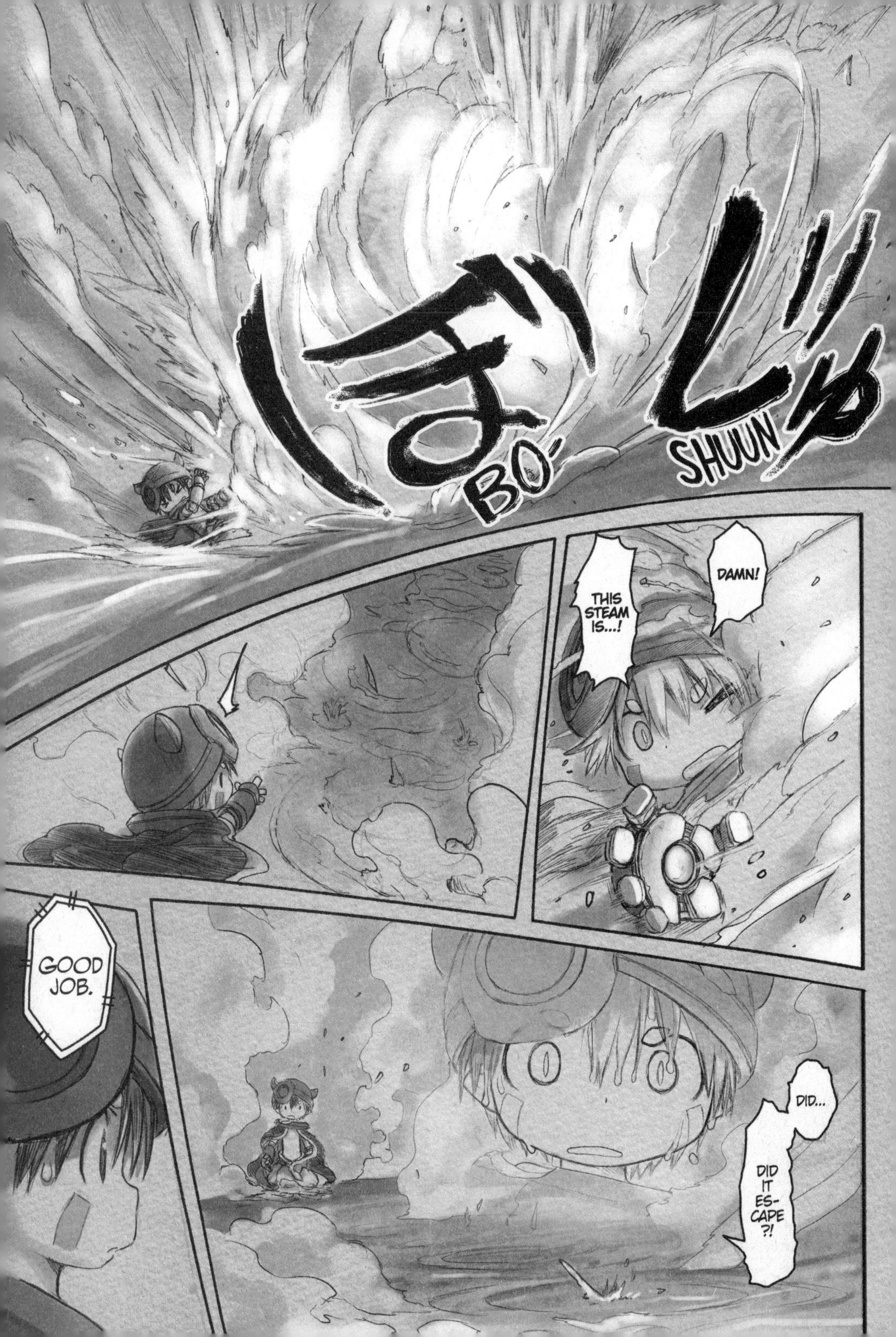
SHUUN
BO
DAMN!
THIS STEAM IS...!
DID...
DID IT ES-CAPE?!
GOOD JOB.

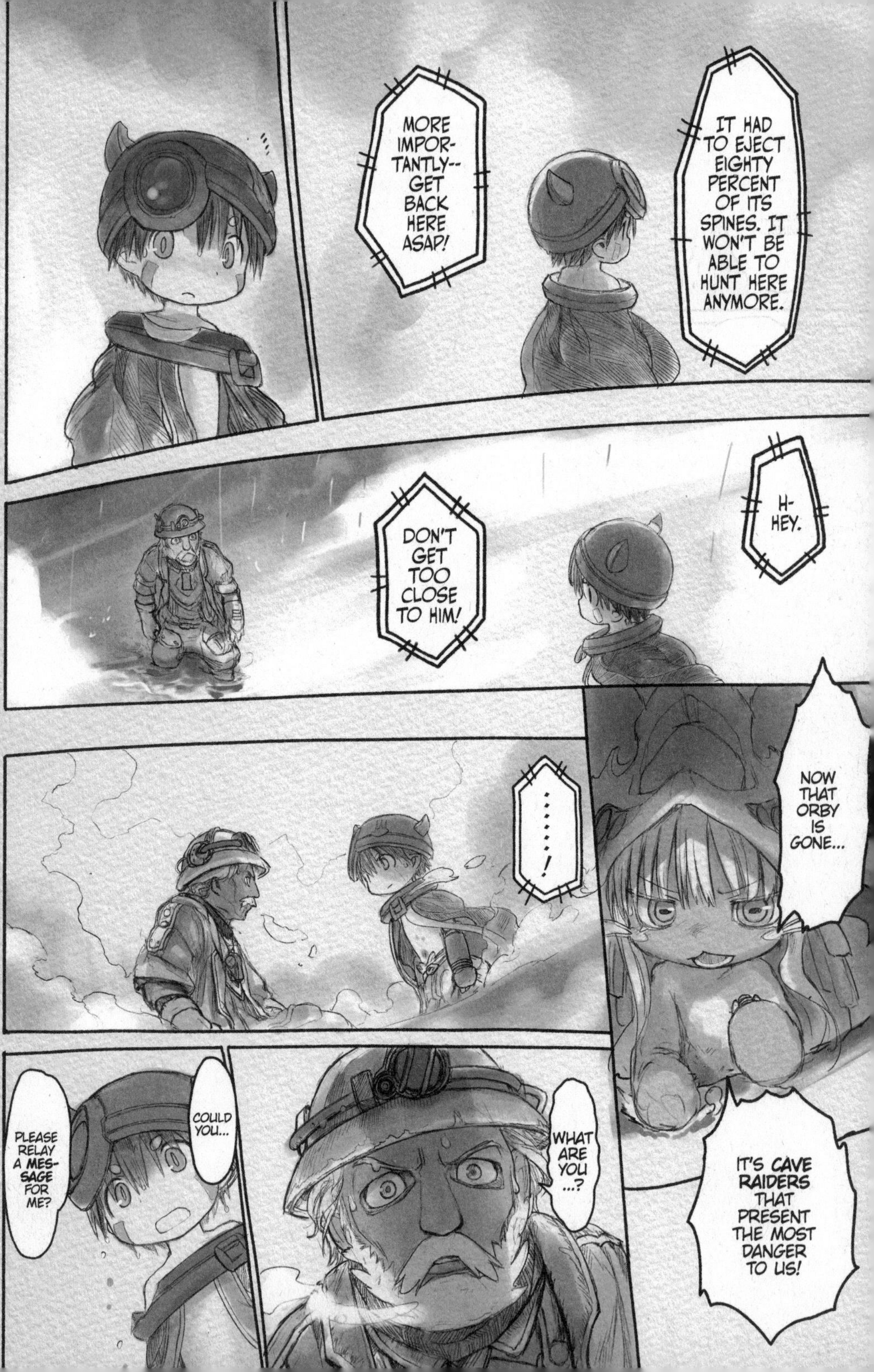
IT HAD TO EJECT EIGHTY PERCENT OF ITS SPINES. IT WON'T BE ABLE TO HUNT HERE ANYMORE.
MORE IMPOR-TANTLY-- GET BACK HERE ASAP!
H-HEY.
DON'T GET TOO CLOSE TO HIM!
NOW THAT ORBY IS GONE...
IT'S CAVE RAIDERS THAT PRESENT THE MOST DANGER TO US!
......!
WHAT ARE YOU ...?
COULD YOU...
PLEASE RELAY A MES-SAGE FOR ME?

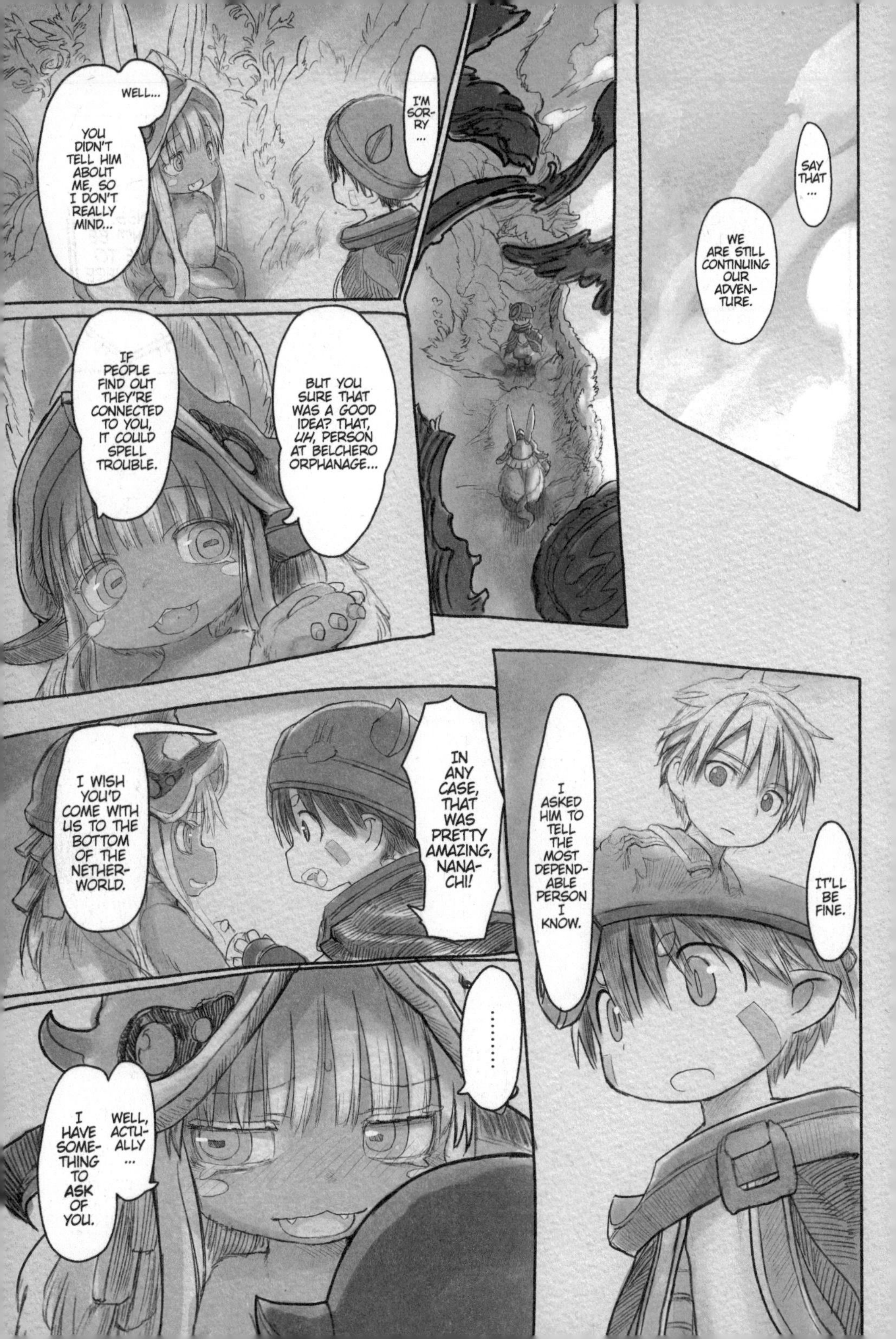
SAY THAT...
WE ARE STILL CONTINUING OUR ADVENTURE.
I'M SORRY...
WELL...
YOU DIDN'T TELL HIM ABOUT ME, SO I DON'T REALLY MIND...
BUT YOU SURE THAT WAS A GOOD IDEA? THAT, *UH*, PERSON AT BELCHERO ORPHANAGE...
IF PEOPLE FIND OUT THEY'RE CONNECTED TO YOU, IT COULD SPELL TROUBLE.
IT'LL BE FINE.
I ASKED HIM TO TELL THE MOST DEPENDABLE PERSON I KNOW.
IN ANY CASE, THAT WAS PRETTY AMAZING, NANACHI!
I WISH YOU'D COME WITH US TO THE BOTTOM OF THE NETHERWORLD.
......
WELL, ACTUALLY...
I HAVE SOMETHING TO ASK OF YOU.

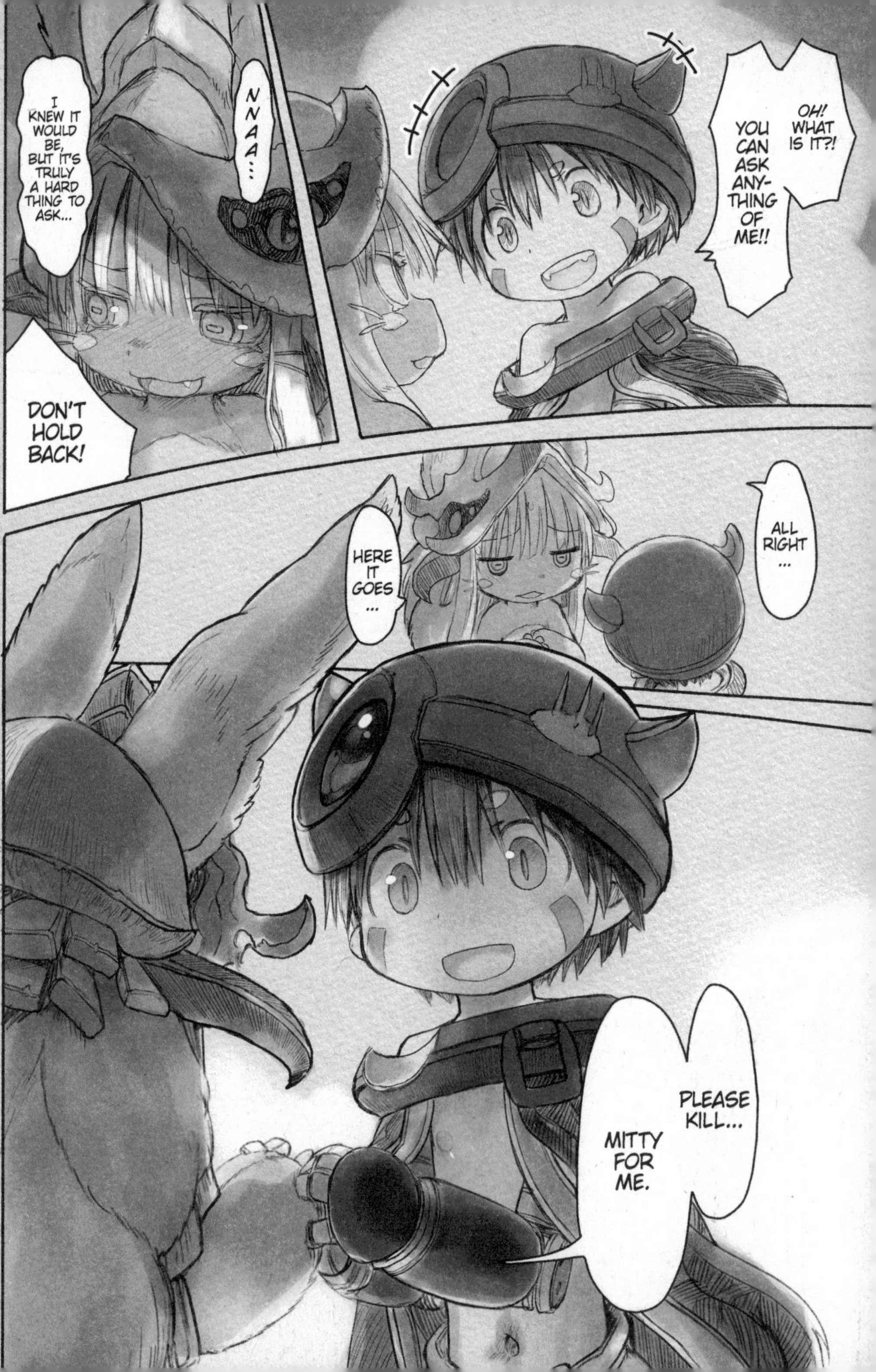
OH! WHAT IS IT?!
YOU CAN ASK ANY-THING OF ME!!
NNAA...
I KNEW IT WOULD BE, BUT IT'S TRULY A HARD THING TO ASK...
DON'T HOLD BACK!
ALL RIGHT ...
HERE IT GOES ...
PLEASE KILL...
MITTY FOR ME.

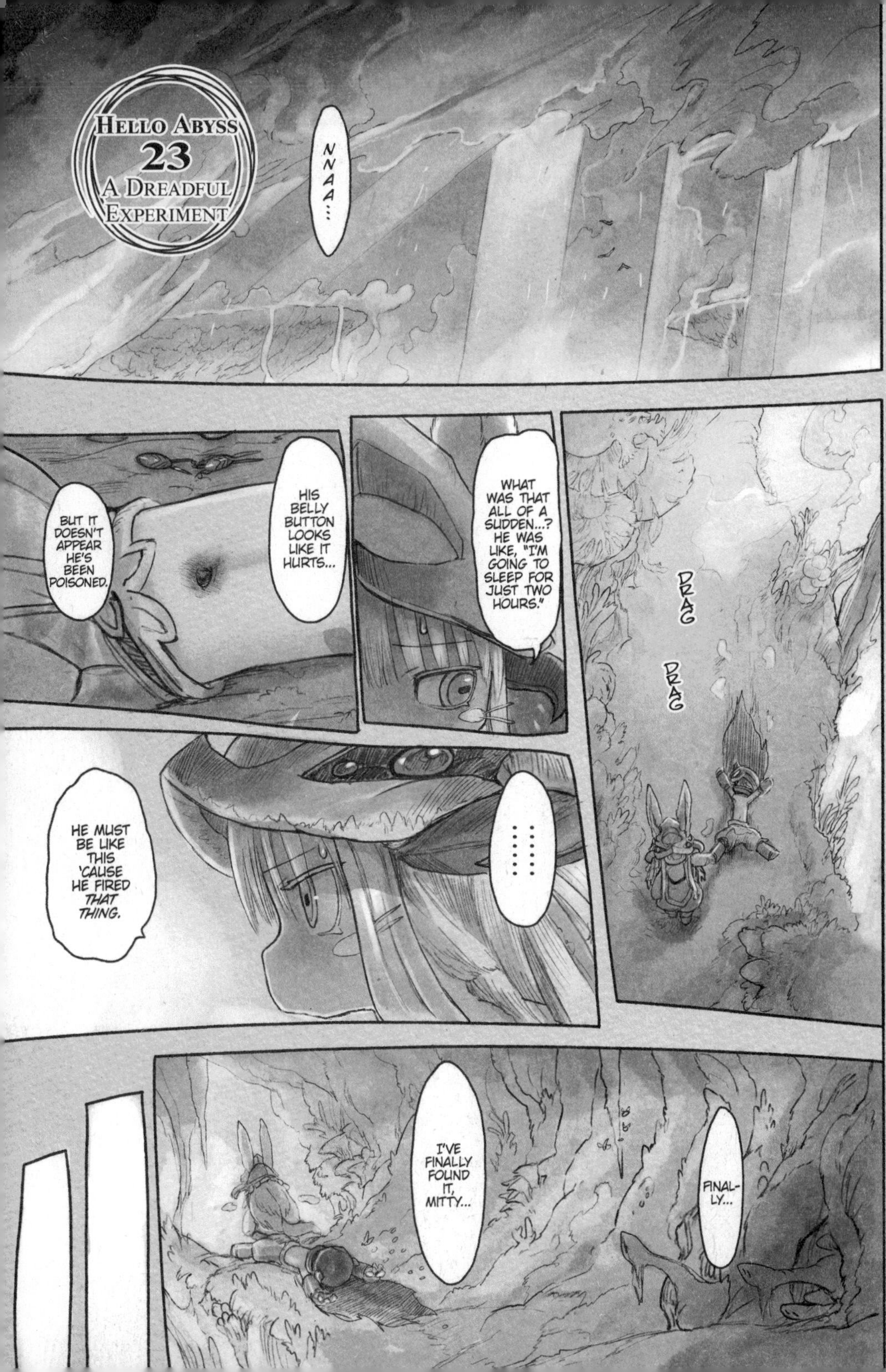
NNAA...
HELLO ABYSS 23 A DREADFUL EXPERIMENT
DRAG DRAG
WHAT WAS THAT ALL OF A SUDDEN...? HE WAS LIKE, "I'M GOING TO SLEEP FOR JUST TWO HOURS."
HIS BELLY BUTTON LOOKS LIKE IT HURTS...
BUT IT DOESN'T APPEAR HE'S BEEN POISONED.
......
HE MUST BE LIKE THIS 'CAUSE HE FIRED *THAT THING*.
FINAL-LY...
I'VE FINALLY FOUND IT, MITTY...

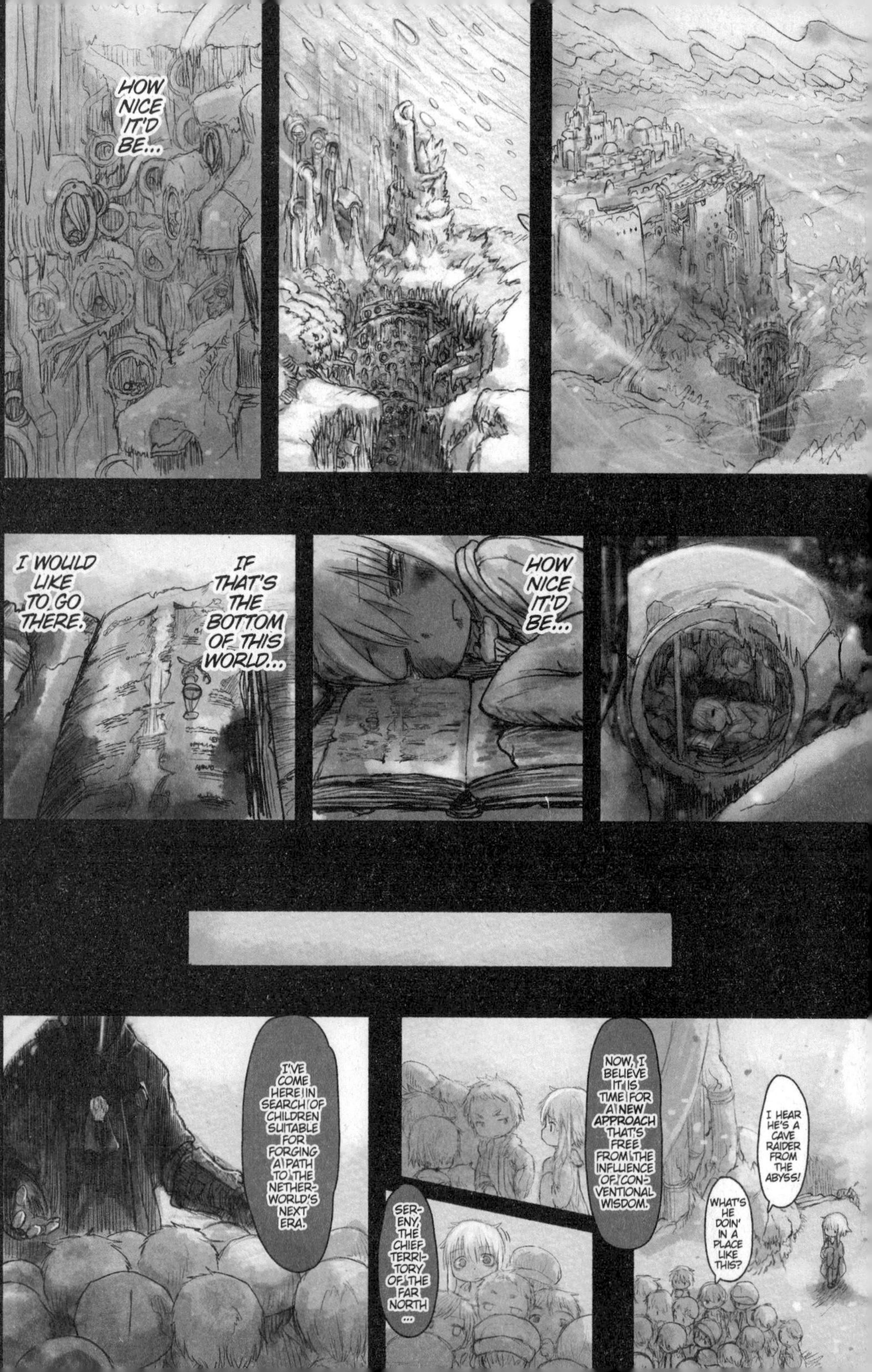
HOW NICE IT'D BE...
HOW NICE IT'D BE...
IF THAT'S THE BOTTOM OF THIS WORLD...
I WOULD LIKE TO GO THERE.
I HEAR HE'S A CAVE RAIDER FROM THE ABYSS!
WHAT'S HE DOIN' IN A PLACE LIKE THIS?
NOW, I BELIEVE IT IS TIME FOR A NEW APPROACH THAT'S FREE FROM THE INFLUENCE OF CON-VENTIONAL WISDOM.
SER-ENY, THE CHIEF TERRI-TORY OF THE FAR NORTH...
I'VE COME HERE IN SEARCH OF CHILDREN SUITABLE FOR FORGING A PATH TO THE NETHER-WORLD'S NEXT ERA.

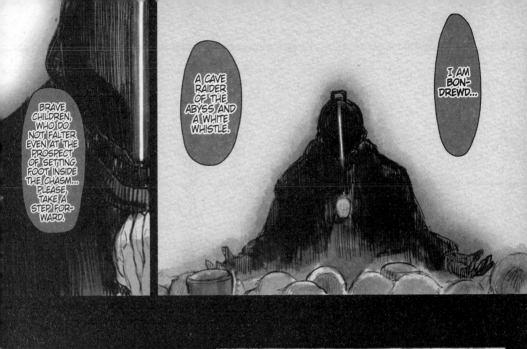

I AM BON-DREWD...
A CAVE RAIDER OF THE ABYSS AND A WHITE WHISTLE.
BRAVE CHILDREN, WHO DO NOT FALTER EVEN AT THE PROSPECT OF SETTING FOOT INSIDE THE CHASM... PLEASE, TAKE A STEP FOR-WARD.
I'M REALLY HERE NOW...
COME ON, LET'S DO IT!
SO, WE'RE NOT THE ONLY ONES, HUH?
SHUT UP!
GET LOST, STUPID!
NOW, EVERY-ONE-- COME AND BOARD THE VES-SEL.
FEAR NOT, FOR MY TEAM OF CAVE RAIDERS WILL ESCORT YOU THROUGH-OUT THE JOURNEY.

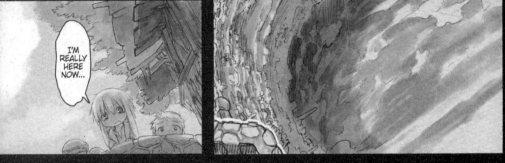

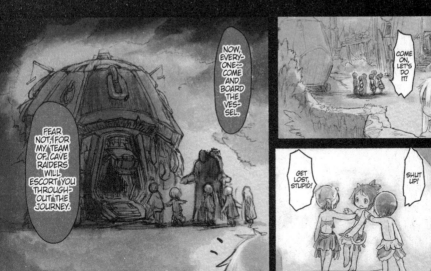

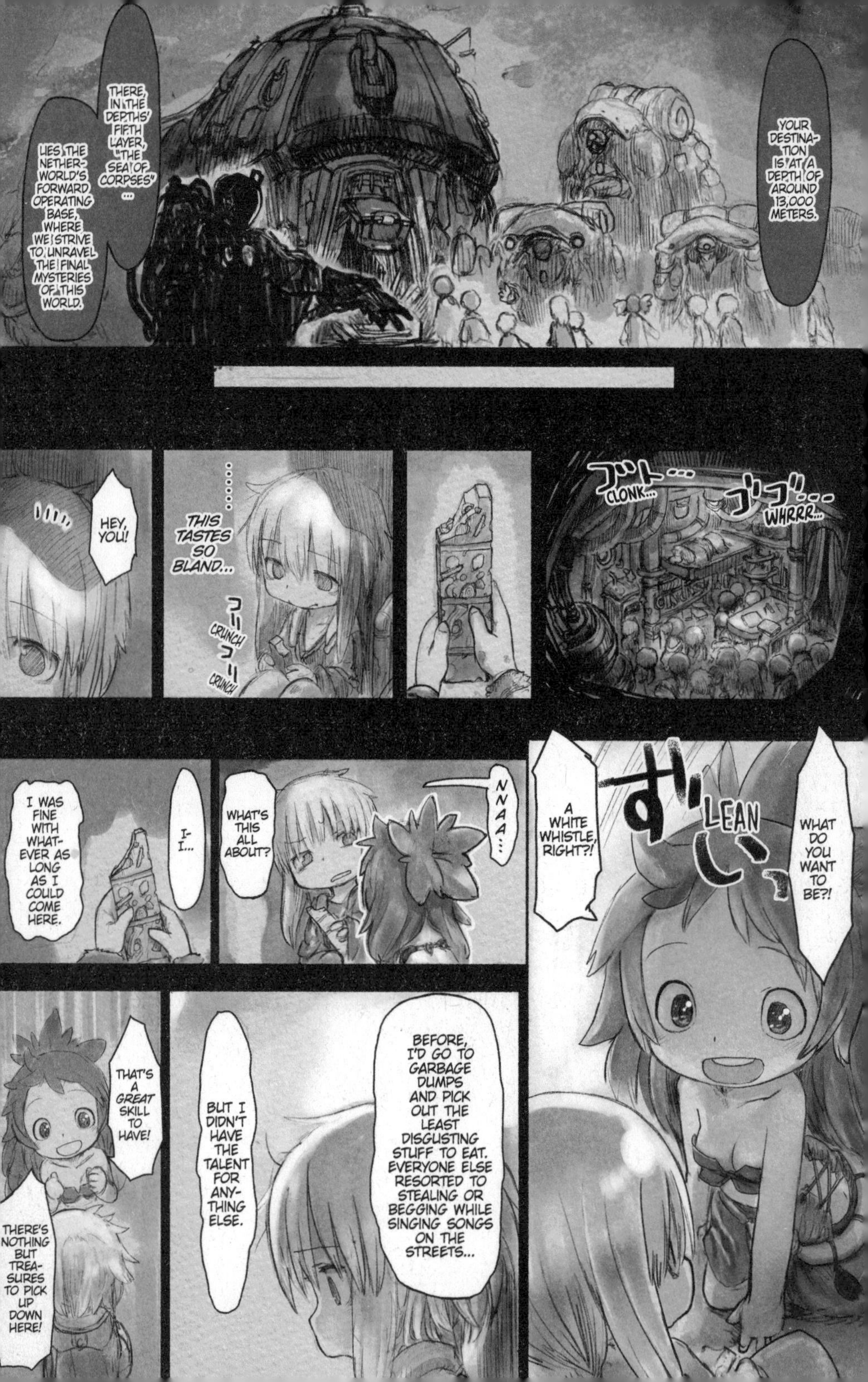
YOUR DESTINATION IS AT A DEPTH OF AROUND 13,000 METERS.
THERE, IN THE DEPTHS' FIFTH LAYER, "THE SEA OF CORPSES"...
LIES THE NETHER-WORLD'S FORWARD OPERATING BASE, WHERE WE STRIVE TO UNRAVEL THE FINAL MYSTERIES OF THIS WORLD.
ゴゴ... WHRRR...
ブト... CLONK...
......
THIS TASTES SO BLAND...
CRUNCH
CRUNCH
HEY, YOU!
WHAT DO YOU WANT TO BE?!
LEAN
A WHITE WHISTLE, RIGHT?!
NNAAA...
WHAT'S THIS ALL ABOUT?
I-I...
I WAS FINE WITH WHATEVER AS LONG AS I COULD COME HERE.
BEFORE, I'D GO TO GARBAGE DUMPS AND PICK OUT THE LEAST DISGUSTING STUFF TO EAT. EVERYONE ELSE RESORTED TO STEALING OR BEGGING WHILE SINGING SONGS ON THE STREETS...
BUT I DIDN'T HAVE THE TALENT FOR ANYTHING ELSE.
THAT'S A GREAT SKILL TO HAVE!
THERE'S NOTHING BUT TREASURES TO PICK UP DOWN HERE!

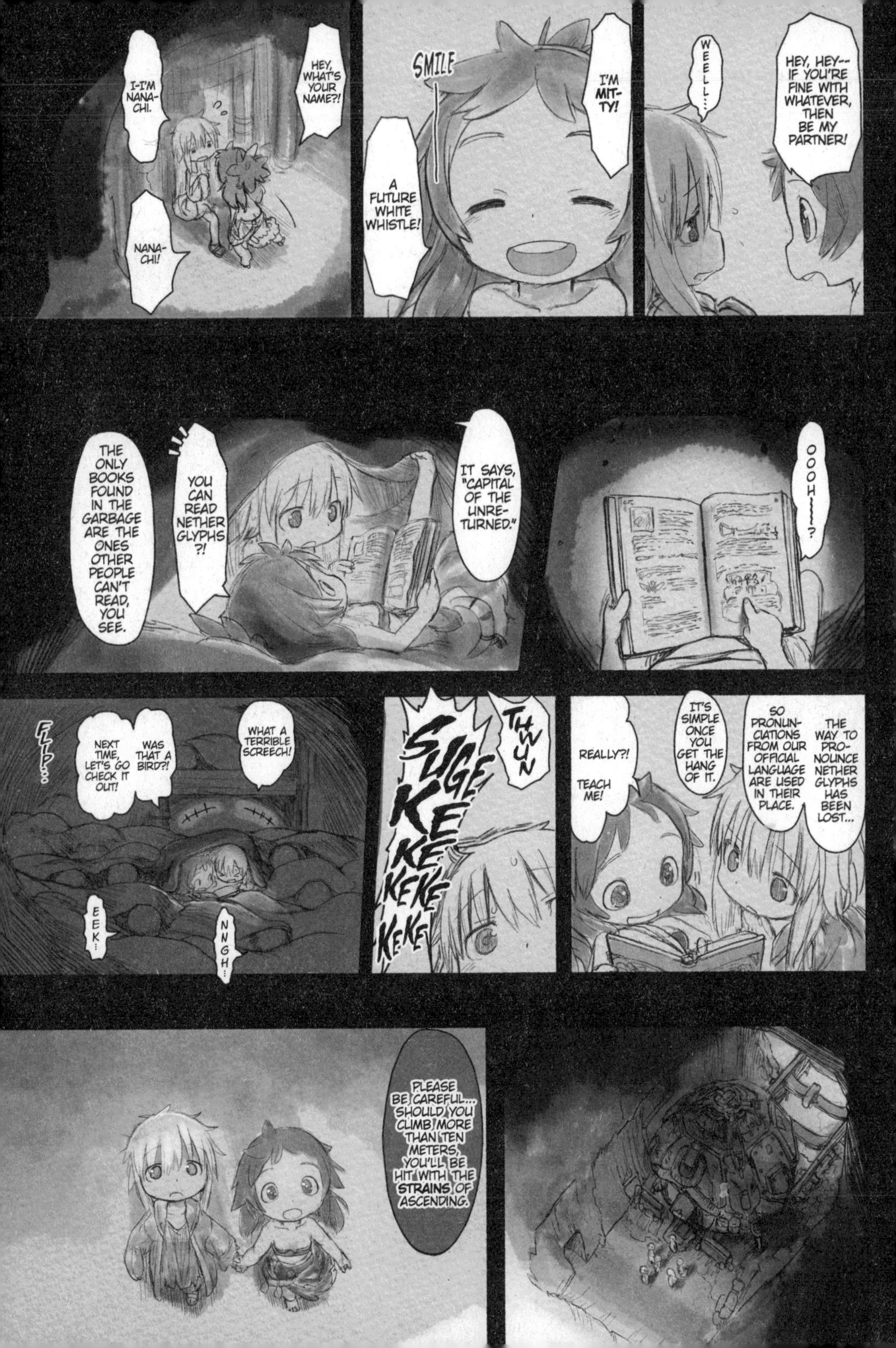
HEY, HEY-- IF YOU'RE FINE WITH WHATEVER, THEN BE MY PARTNER!
WEELL...
I'M MITTY!
SMILE
A FUTURE WHITE WHISTLE!
HEY, WHAT'S YOUR NAME?!
I-I'M NANACHI.
NANACHI!
OOOH~~~?
IT SAYS, "CAPITAL OF THE UNRETURNED."
YOU CAN READ NETHER GLYPHS?!
!!!
THE ONLY BOOKS FOUND IN THE GARBAGE ARE THE ONES OTHER PEOPLE CAN'T READ, YOU SEE.
THE WAY TO PRONOUNCE NETHER GLYPHS HAS BEEN LOST...
SO PRONUNCIATIONS FROM OUR OFFICIAL LANGUAGE ARE USED IN THEIR PLACE.
IT'S SIMPLE ONCE YOU GET THE HANG OF IT.
REALLY?!
TEACH ME!
THWUN
SUGEKEKEKEKEKEKE
WHAT A TERRIBLE SCREECH!
WAS THAT A BIRD?!
NEXT TIME, LET'S GO CHECK IT OUT!
FLIP...
NNGH...
EEK...
PLEASE BE CAREFUL... SHOULD YOU CLIMB MORE THAN TEN METERS, YOU'LL BE HIT WITH THE STRAINS OF ASCENDING.

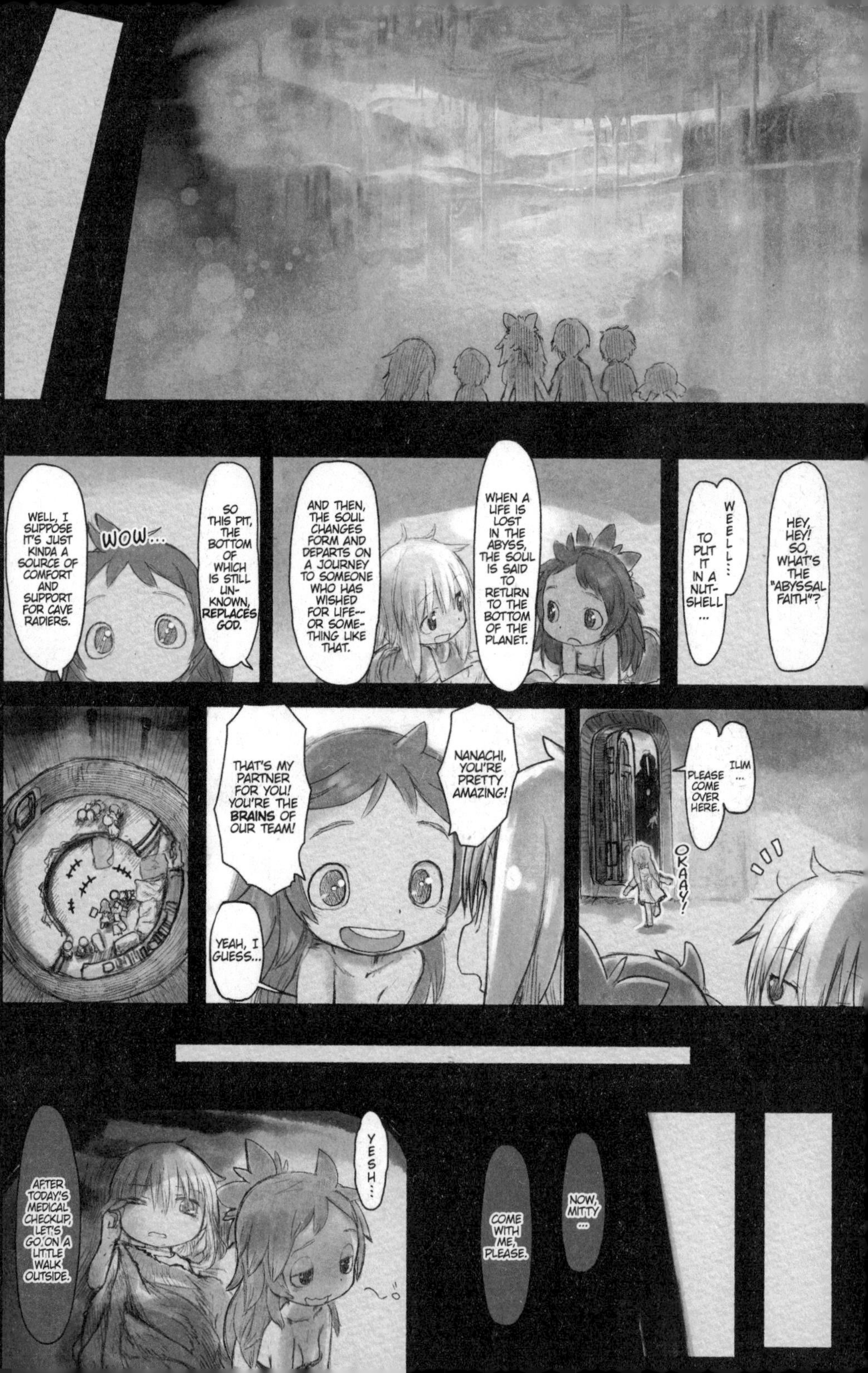
HEY, HEY! SO, WHAT'S THE "ABYSSAL FAITH"?
WEELL... TO PUT IT IN A NUT-SHELL...
WHEN A LIFE IS LOST IN THE ABYSS, THE SOUL IS SAID TO RETURN TO THE BOTTOM OF THE PLANET.
AND THEN, THE SOUL CHANGES FORM AND DEPARTS ON A JOURNEY TO SOMEONE WHO HAS WISHED FOR LIFE--OR SOMETHING LIKE THAT.
SO THIS PIT, THE BOTTOM OF WHICH IS STILL UNKNOWN, **REPLACES** GOD.
WOW...
WELL, I SUPPOSE IT'S JUST KINDA A SOURCE OF COMFORT AND SUPPORT FOR CAVE RADIERS.
ILIM... PLEASE COME OVER HERE.
OKAAY!
NANACHI, YOU'RE PRETTY AMAZING!
THAT'S MY PARTNER FOR YOU! YOU'RE THE **BRAINS** OF OUR TEAM!
YEAH, I GUESS...
NOW, MITTY...
COME WITH ME, PLEASE.
YESH...
AFTER TODAY'S MEDICAL CHECKUP, LET'S GO ON A LITTLE WALK OUTSIDE.

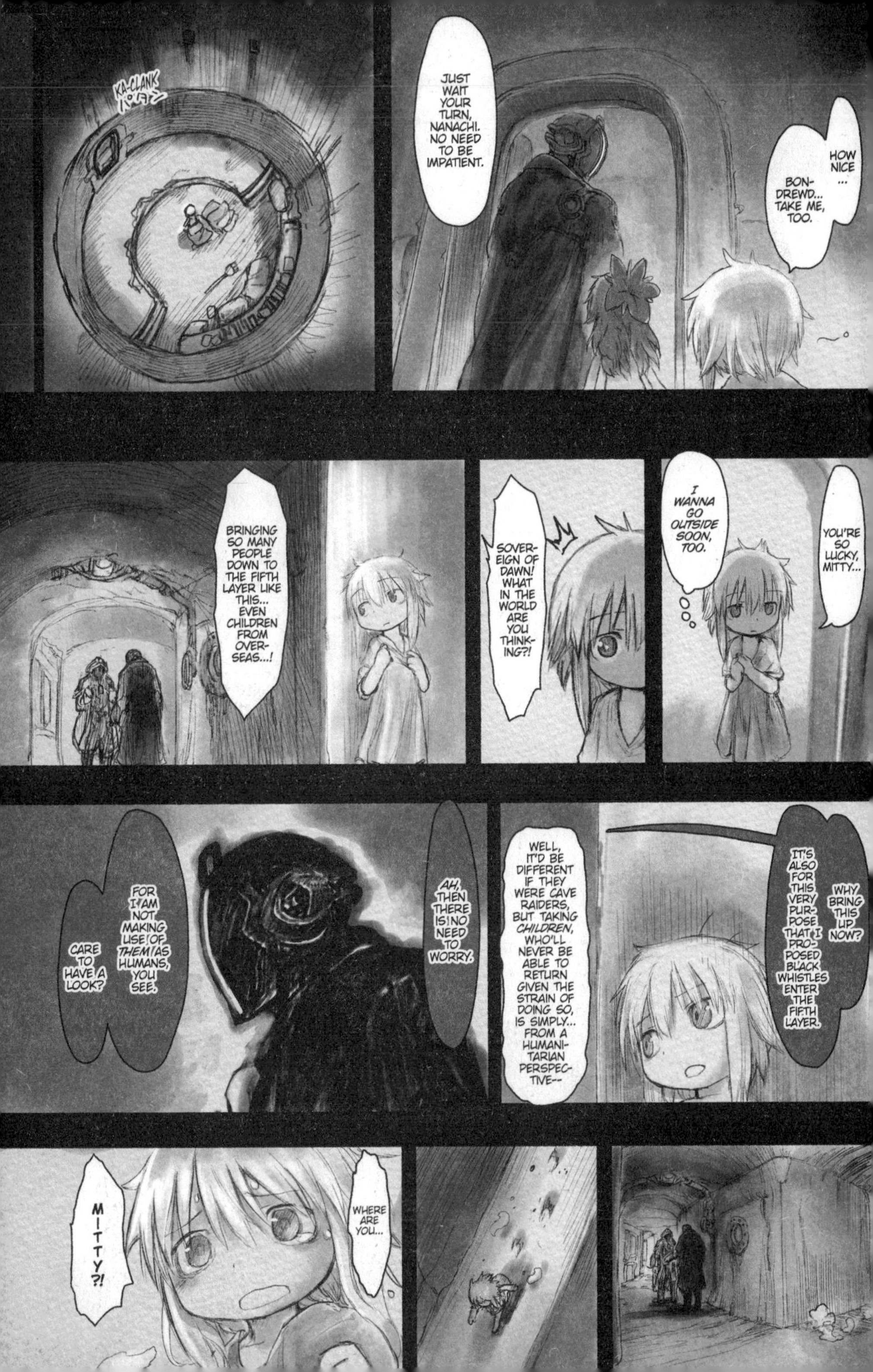
HOW NICE... BONDREWD... TAKE ME, TOO.
JUST WAIT YOUR TURN, NANACHI. NO NEED TO BE IMPATIENT.
KA-CLANK
YOU'RE SO LUCKY, MITTY...
I WANNA GO OUTSIDE SOON, TOO.
SOVEREIGN OF DAWN! WHAT IN THE WORLD ARE YOU THINKING?!
BRINGING SO MANY PEOPLE DOWN TO THE FIFTH LAYER LIKE THIS... EVEN CHILDREN FROM OVERSEAS...!
WHY BRING THIS UP NOW?
IT'S ALSO FOR THIS VERY PURPOSE THAT I PROPOSED BLACK WHISTLES ENTER THE FIFTH LAYER.
WELL, IT'D BE DIFFERENT IF THEY WERE CAVE RAIDERS, BUT TAKING *CHILDREN*, WHO'LL NEVER BE ABLE TO RETURN GIVEN THE STRAIN OF DOING SO, IS SIMPLY... FROM A HUMANITARIAN PERSPECTIVE--
AH, THEN THERE IS NO NEED TO WORRY.
FOR I AM NOT MAKING USE OF *THEM* AS HUMANS, YOU SEE.
CARE TO HAVE A LOOK?
WHERE ARE YOU...
MITTY?!

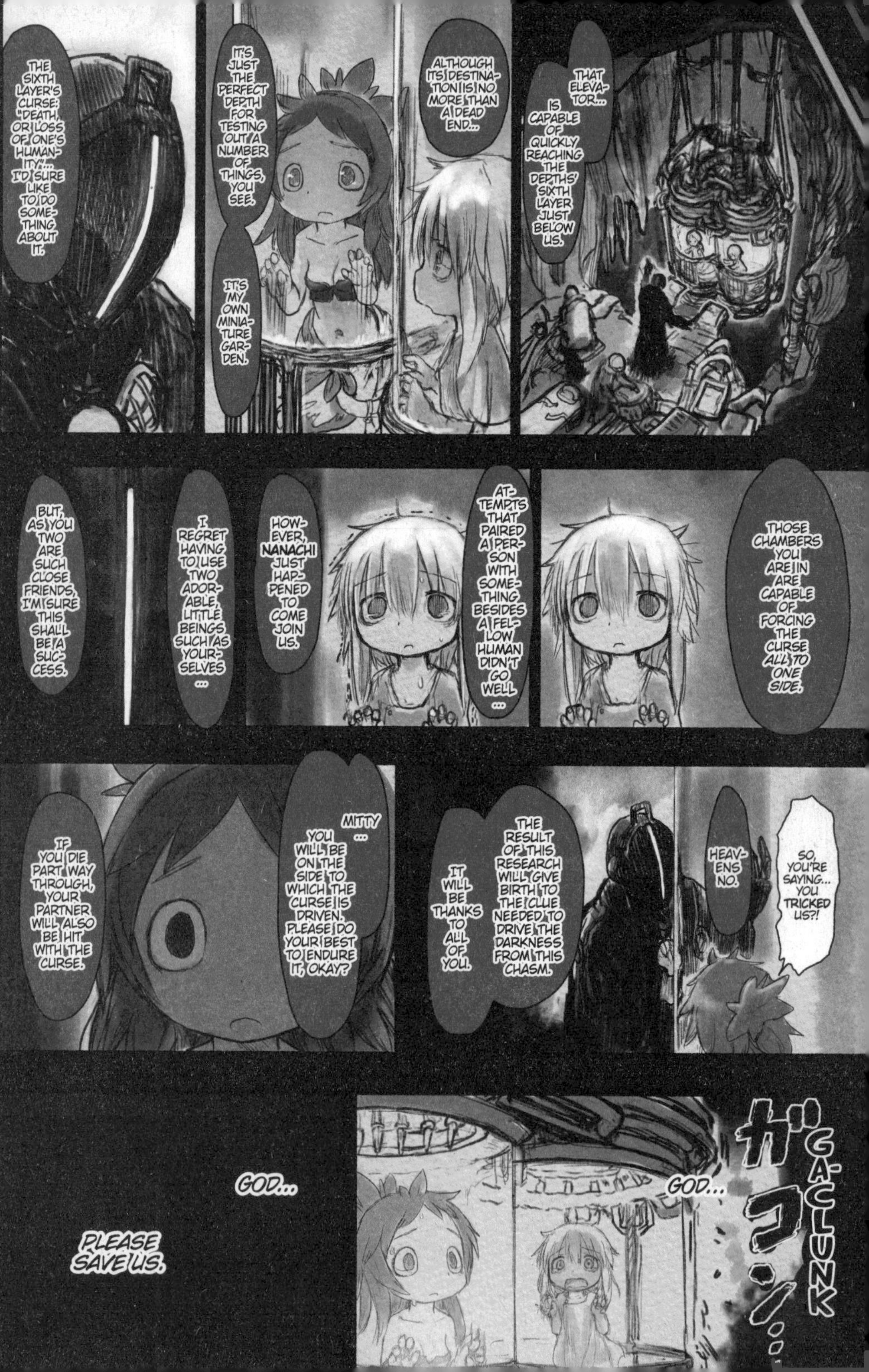
THAT ELEVATOR... IS CAPABLE OF QUICKLY REACHING THE DEPTHS' SIXTH LAYER JUST BELOW US.
ALTHOUGH ITS DESTINATION IS NO MORE THAN A DEAD END...
IT'S JUST THE PERFECT DEPTH FOR TESTING OUT A NUMBER OF THINGS, YOU SEE.
IT'S MY OWN MINIATURE GARDEN.
THE SIXTH LAYER'S CURSE: "DEATH, OR LOSS OF ONE'S HUMANITY"... I'D SURE LIKE TO DO SOMETHING ABOUT IT.
THOSE CHAMBERS YOU ARE IN ARE CAPABLE OF FORCING THE CURSE ALL TO ONE SIDE.
ATTEMPTS THAT PAIRED A PERSON WITH SOMETHING BESIDES A FELLOW HUMAN DIDN'T GO WELL...
HOWEVER, NANACHI JUST HAPPENED TO COME JOIN US.
I REGRET HAVING TO USE TWO ADORABLE LITTLE BEINGS SUCH AS YOURSELVES...
BUT, AS YOU TWO ARE SUCH CLOSE FRIENDS, I'M SURE THIS SHALL BE A SUCCESS.
SO, YOU'RE SAYING... YOU TRICKED US?!
HEAVENS NO.
THE RESULT OF THIS RESEARCH WILL GIVE BIRTH TO THE CLUE NEEDED TO DRIVE THE DARKNESS FROM THIS CHASM.
IT WILL BE THANKS TO ALL OF YOU.
MITTY... YOU WILL BE ON THE SIDE TO WHICH THE CURSE IS DRIVEN. PLEASE DO YOUR BEST TO ENDURE IT, OKAY?
IF YOU DIE PART WAY THROUGH, YOUR PARTNER WILL ALSO BE HIT WITH THE CURSE.
GACLUNK
GOD...
GOD...
PLEASE SAVE US.

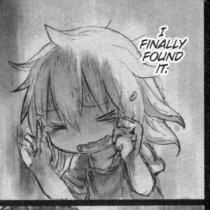

I FINALLY FOUND IT.
I FOUND A TREASURE I HOLD DEAR.
PLEASE...
PLEASE DON'T TAKE HER AWAY FROM ME...!
THWUNK
lieh.
liehpu.
lieh.

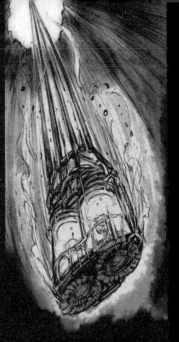

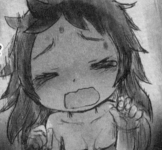

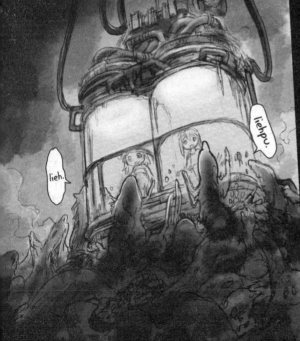

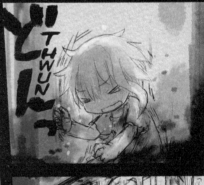

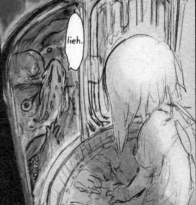

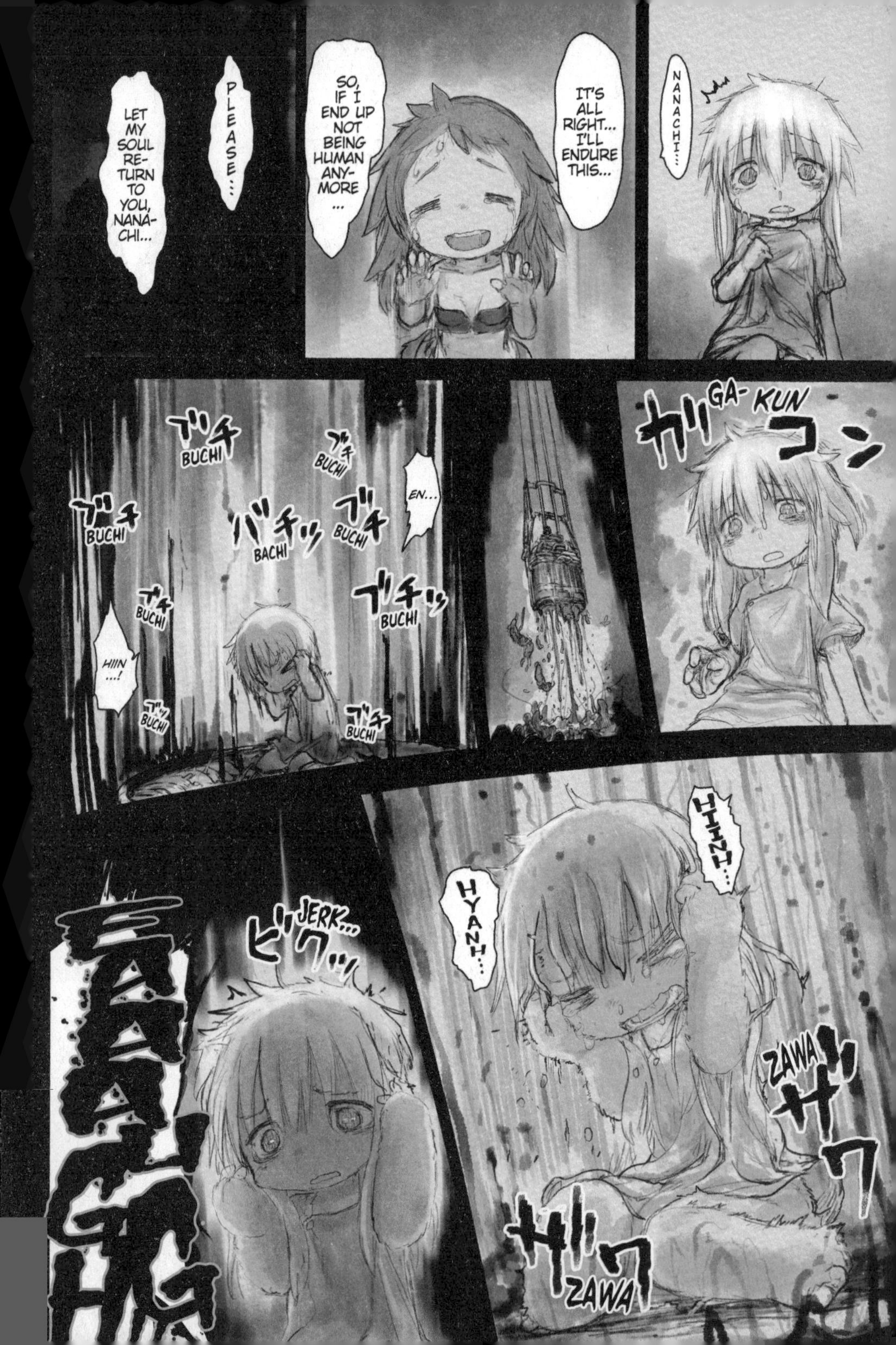

NANACHI...
IT'S ALL RIGHT... I'LL ENDURE THIS...
SO, IF I END UP NOT BEING HUMAN ANYMORE...
PLEASE...
LET MY SOUL RE-TURN TO YOU, NANA-CHI...
ガコン
GA-KUN
EN...
ブチ
BUCHI
ブチ
BUCHI
バチッ
BACHI
ブチ
BUCHI
ブチ
BUCHI
ブチッ
BUCHI
ブチ
BUCHI
HIIN...!
ブッ
BUCHI
ブチ
BUCHI
HIIINH...
HYANH...
ザワ
ZAWA
ザワ
ZAWA
ビクッ
JERK...

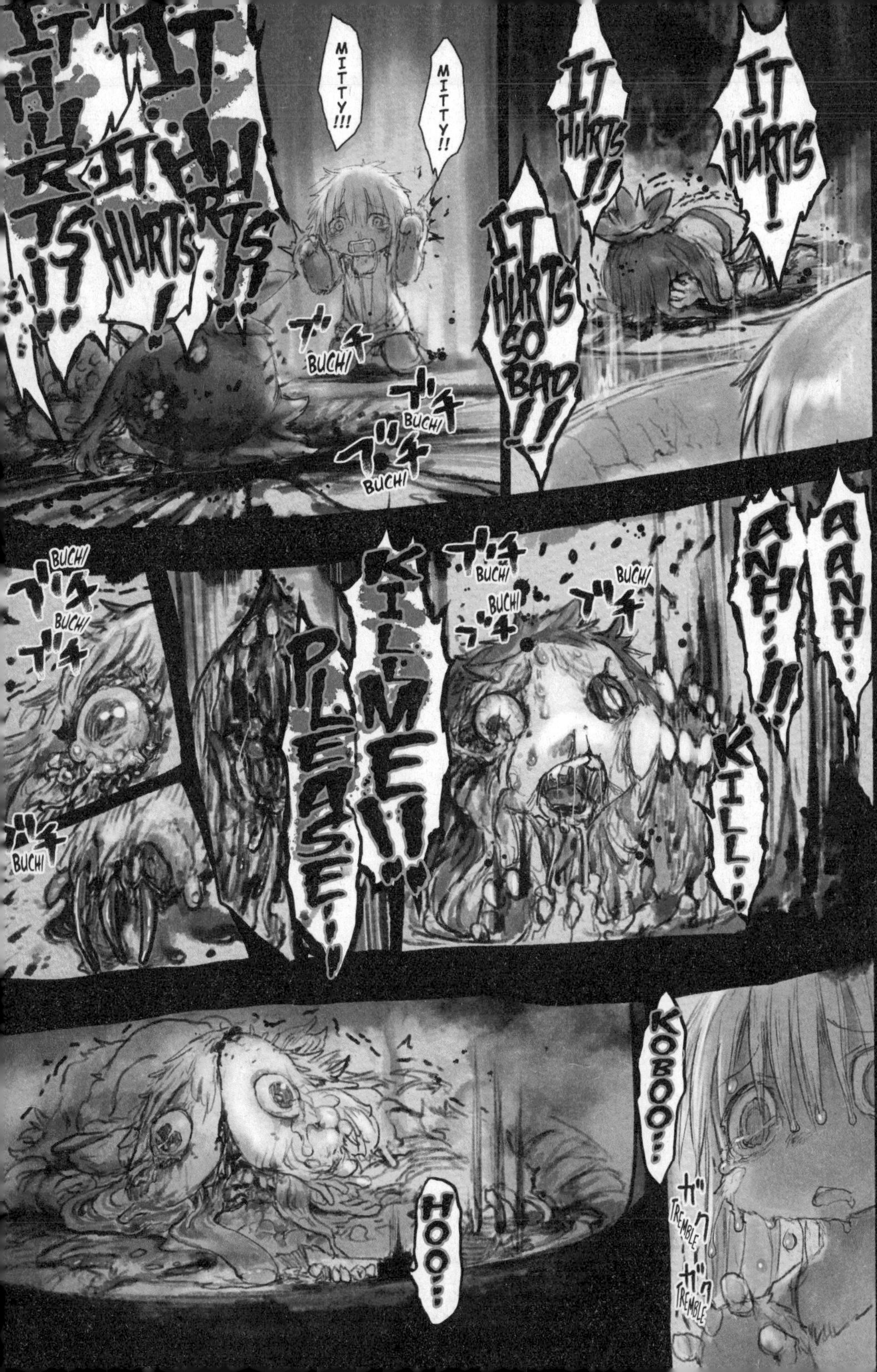
IT HURTS!
IT HURTS!!
IT HURTS SO BAD!!
MITTY!!
MITTY!!!
IT HURTS!!
IT HURTS!
IT HURTS!!
ブチ BUCHI
ブチ BUCHI
ブチ BUCHI
AANH...
ANH...!!
KILL...
ブチ BUCHI
ブチ BUCHI
ブチ BUCHI
KILL ME!!
PLEASE...
ブチ BUCHI
ブチ BUCHI
ブチ BUCHI
KOBOOO...
ガク TREMBLE
ガク TREMBLE
HOO...

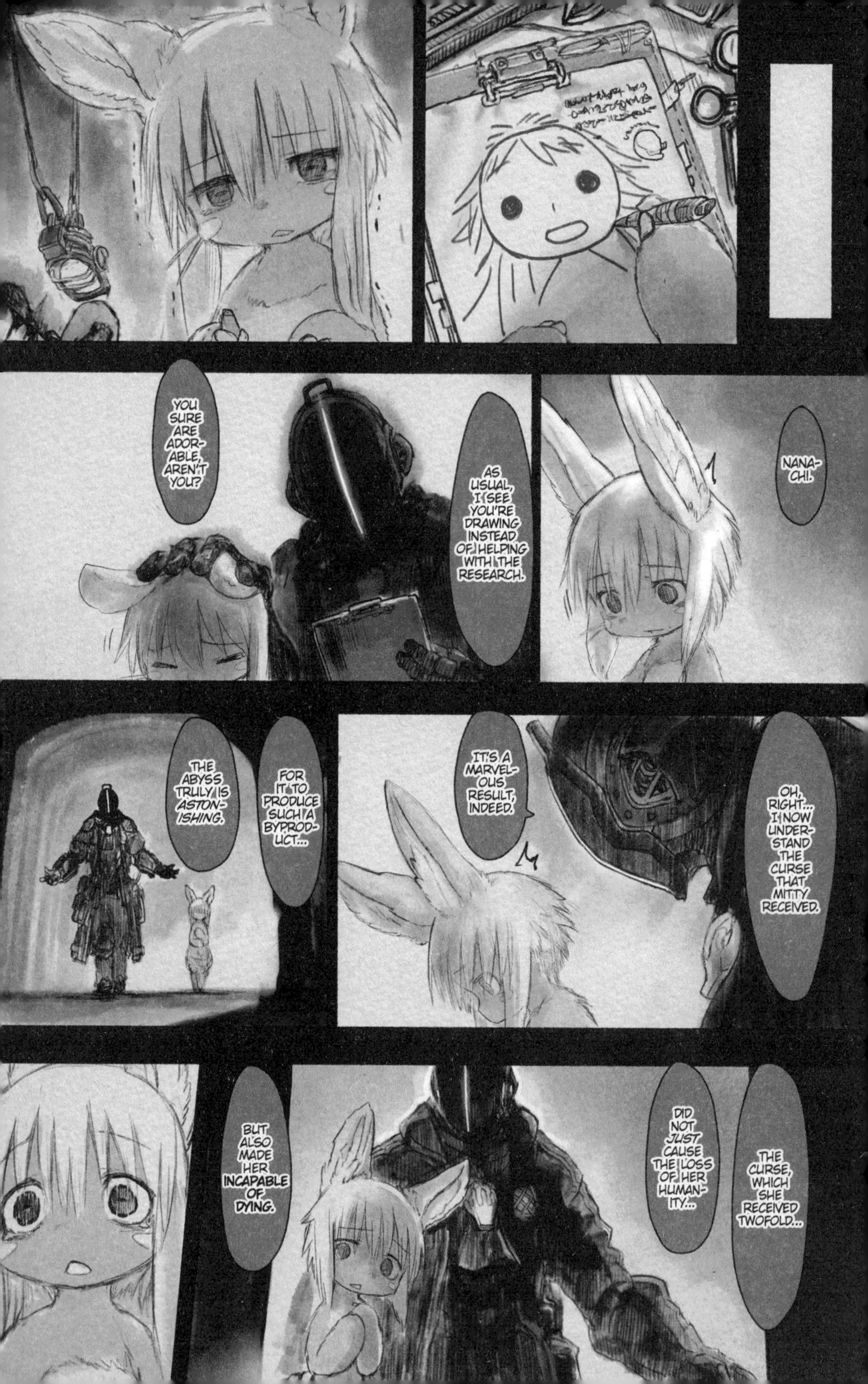
NANACHI.
AS USUAL, I SEE YOU'RE DRAWING INSTEAD OF HELPING WITH THE RESEARCH.
YOU SURE ARE ADORABLE, AREN'T YOU?
OH, RIGHT... I NOW UNDERSTAND THE CURSE THAT MITTY RECEIVED.
IT'S A MARVELOUS RESULT, INDEED.
FOR IT TO PRODUCE SUCH A BYPRODUCT...
THE ABYSS TRULY IS ASTONISHING.
THE CURSE, WHICH SHE RECEIVED TWOFOLD...
DID NOT JUST CAUSE THE LOSS OF HER HUMANITY...
BUT ALSO MADE HER INCAPABLE OF DYING.

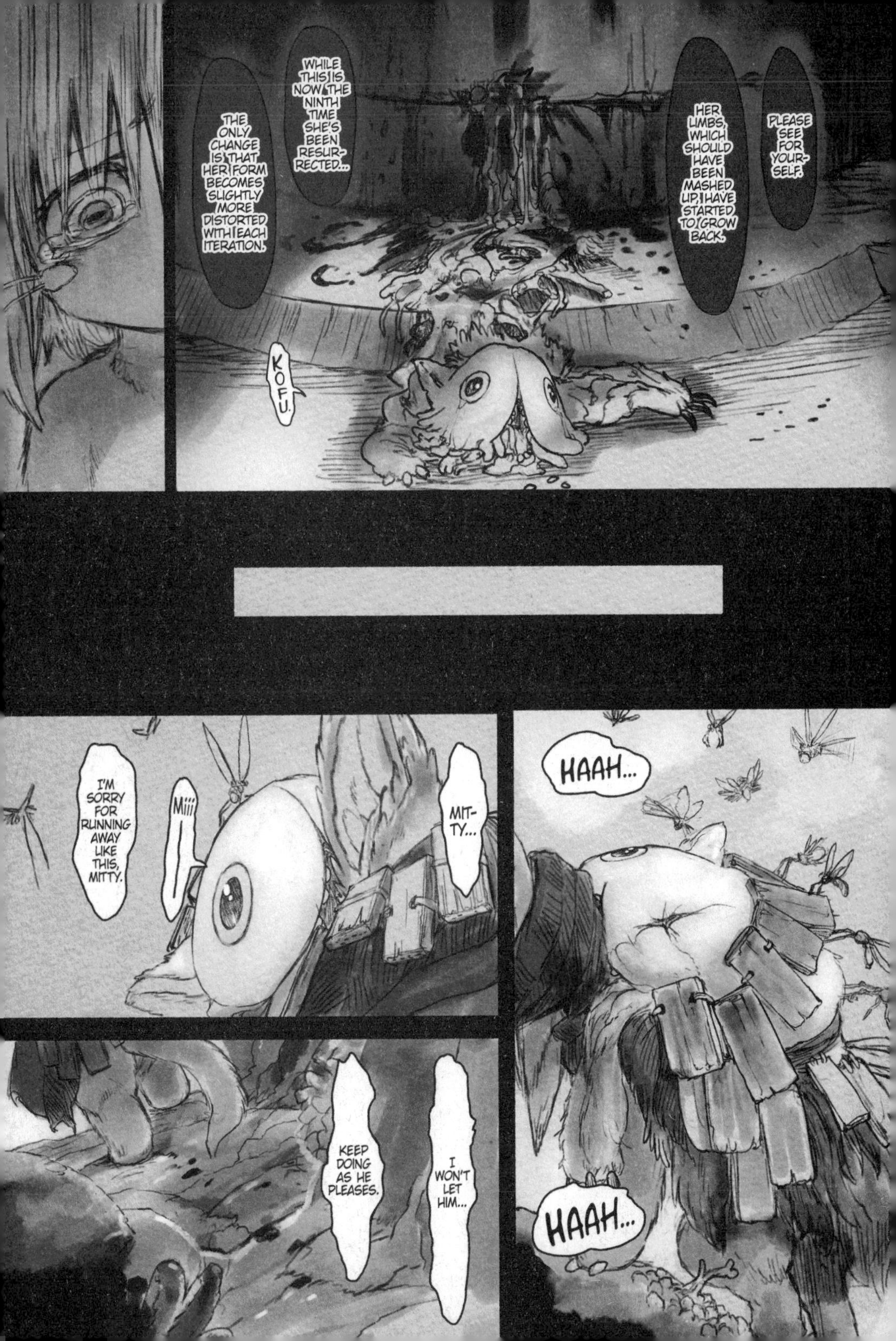
PLEASE SEE FOR YOURSELF.
HER LIMBS, WHICH SHOULD HAVE BEEN MASHED UP, HAVE STARTED TO GROW BACK.
WHILE THIS IS NOW THE NINTH TIME SHE'S BEEN RESURRECTED...
THE ONLY CHANGE IS THAT HER FORM BECOMES SLIGHTLY MORE DISTORTED WITH EACH ITERATION.
KOFU.
HAAH...
HAAH...
MITTY...
Miii
I'M SORRY FOR RUNNING AWAY LIKE THIS, MITTY.
I WON'T LET HIM...
KEEP DOING AS HE PLEASES.

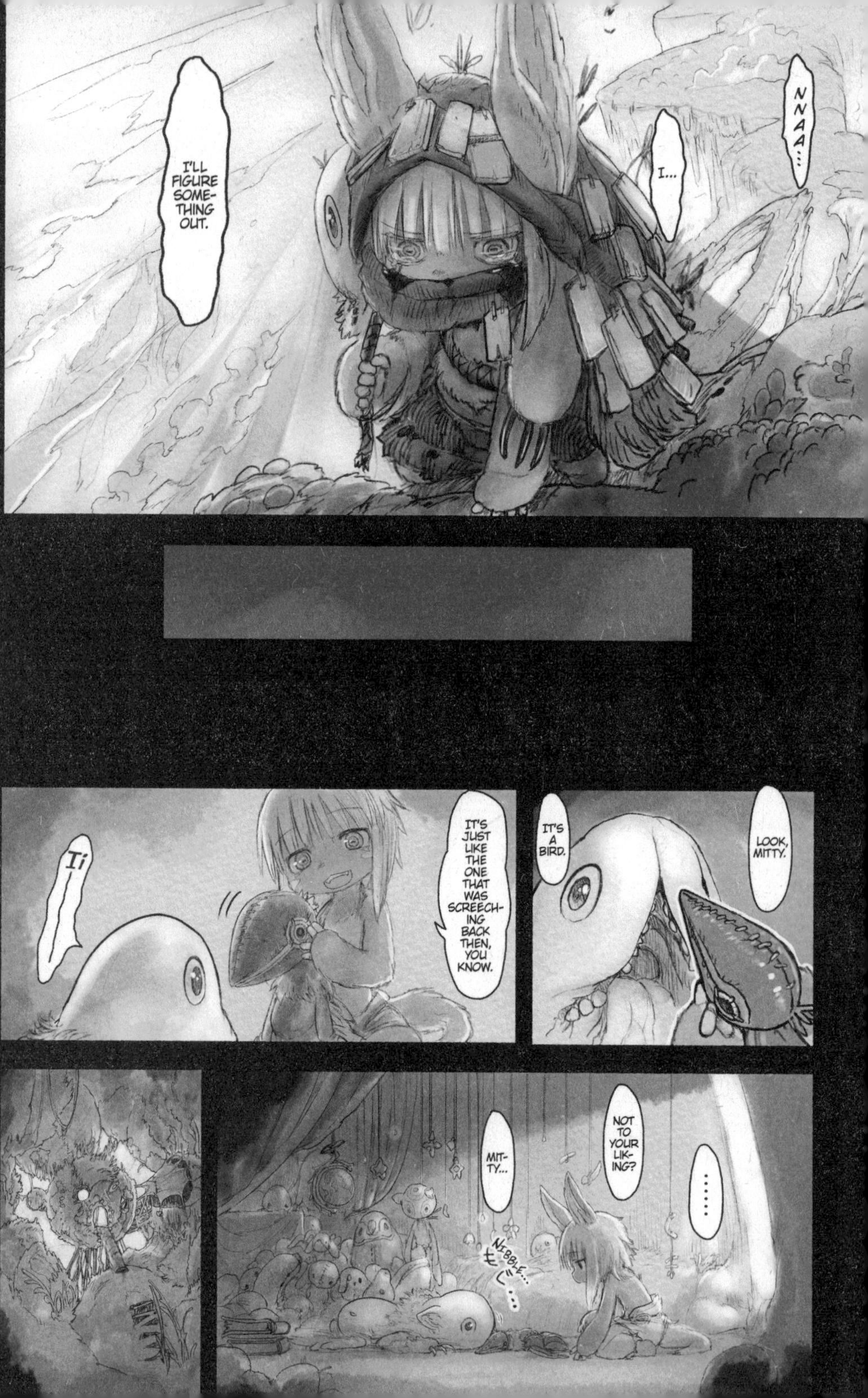
NNAA...
I...
I'LL FIGURE SOMETHING OUT.
LOOK, MITTY.
IT'S A BIRD.
IT'S JUST LIKE THE ONE THAT WAS SCREECHING BACK THEN, YOU KNOW.
Ii—
......
NOT TO YOUR LIKING?
MITTY...
NIBBLE...

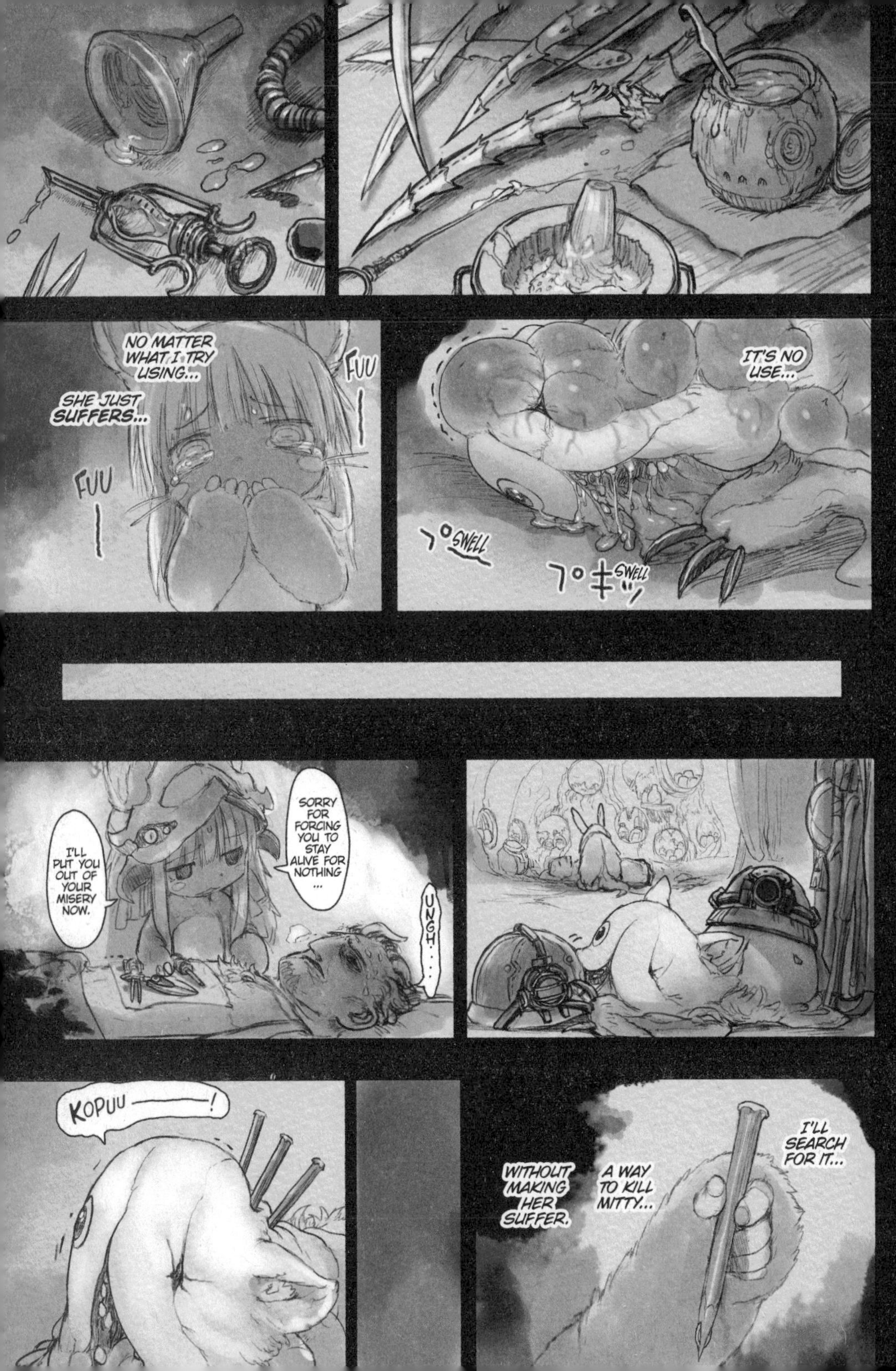
IT'S NO USE...
SWELL
SWELL
NO MATTER WHAT I TRY USING...
FUU
SHE JUST SUFFERS...
FUU
SORRY FOR FORCING YOU TO STAY ALIVE FOR NOTHING ...
UNGH...
I'LL PUT YOU OUT OF YOUR MISERY NOW.
I'LL SEARCH FOR IT...
A WAY TO KILL MITTY...
WITHOUT MAKING HER SUFFER.
KOPUU———!

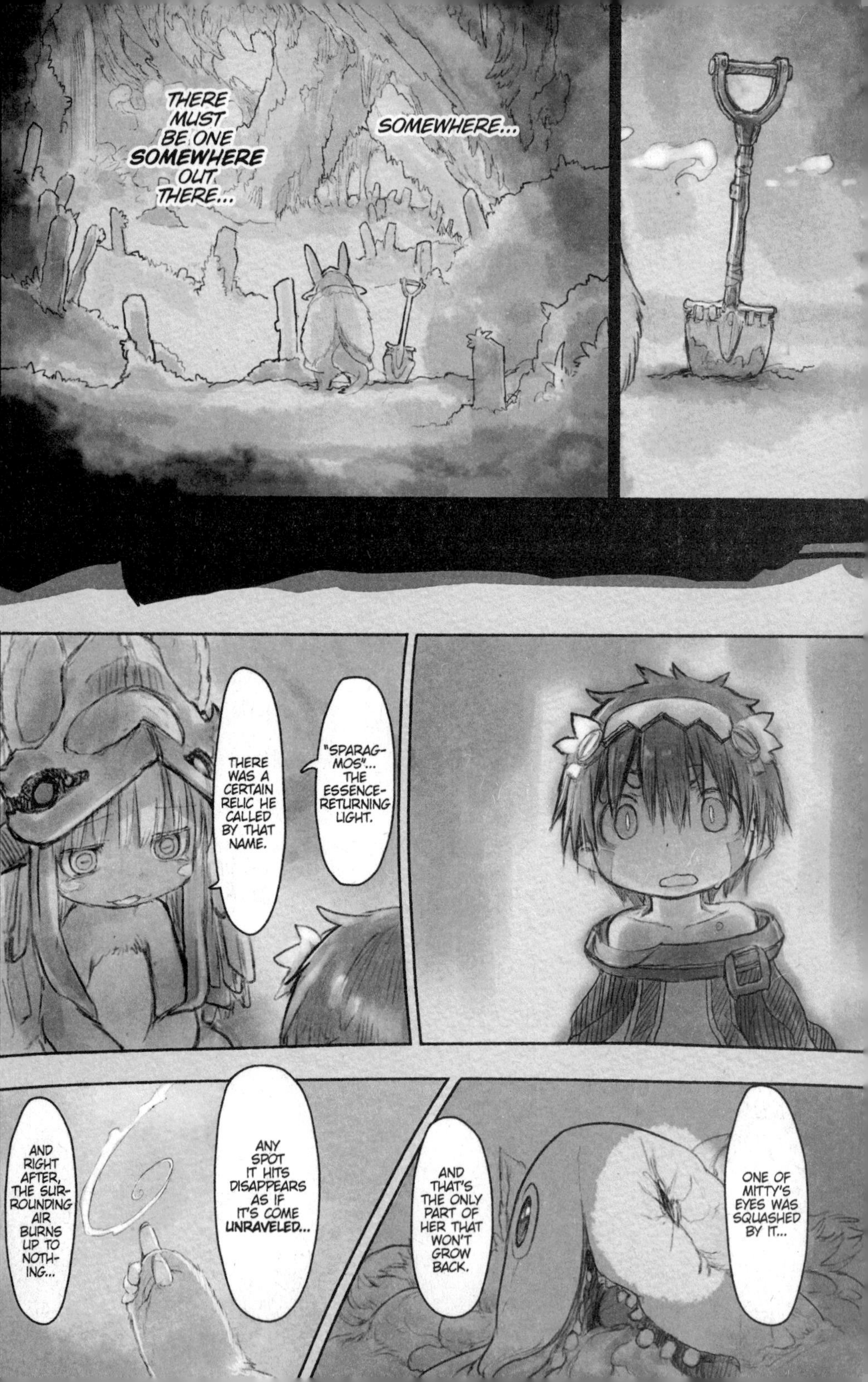
THERE MUST BE ONE **SOMEWHERE** OUT THERE...
SOMEWHERE...
"SPARAGMOS"... THE ESSENCE-RETURNING LIGHT.
THERE WAS A CERTAIN RELIC HE CALLED BY THAT NAME.
ONE OF MITTY'S EYES WAS SQUASHED BY IT...
AND THAT'S THE ONLY PART OF HER THAT WON'T GROW BACK.
ANY SPOT IT HITS DISAPPEARS AS IF IT'S COME **UNRAVELED**...
AND RIGHT AFTER, THE SUR-ROUNDING AIR BURNS UP TO NOTH-ING...

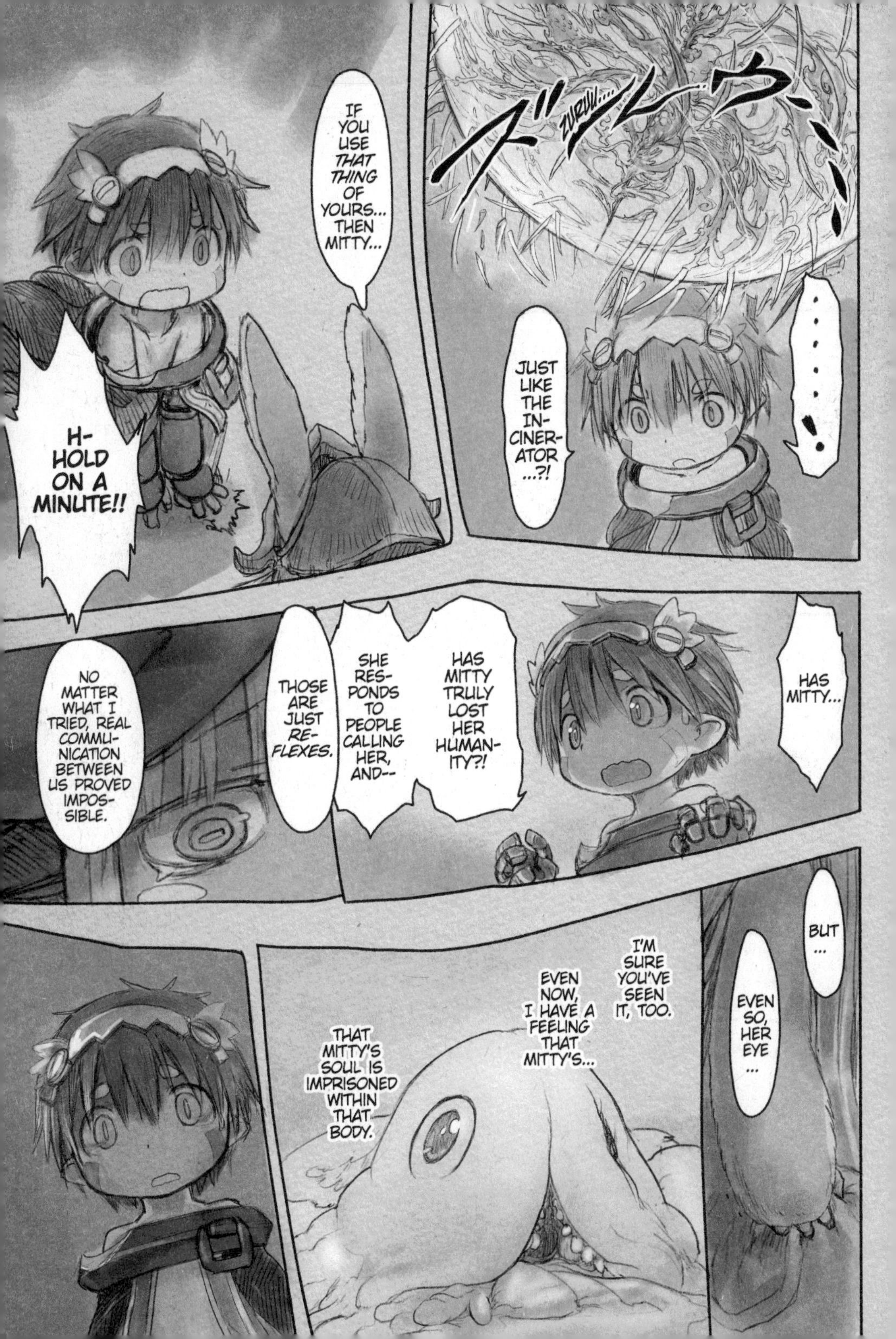
ZURUU...
...!
JUST LIKE THE IN-CINERATOR...?!
IF YOU USE *THAT THING* OF YOURS... THEN MITTY...
H-HOLD ON A MINUTE!!
HAS MITTY...
HAS MITTY TRULY LOST HER HUMANITY?!
SHE RESPONDS TO PEOPLE CALLING HER, AND--
THOSE ARE JUST *RE-FLEXES.*
NO MATTER WHAT I TRIED, REAL COMMUNICATION BETWEEN US PROVED IMPOSSIBLE.
BUT...
EVEN SO, HER EYE...
I'M SURE YOU'VE SEEN IT, TOO.
EVEN NOW, I HAVE A FEELING THAT MITTY'S...
THAT MITTY'S SOUL IS IMPRISONED WITHIN THAT BODY.

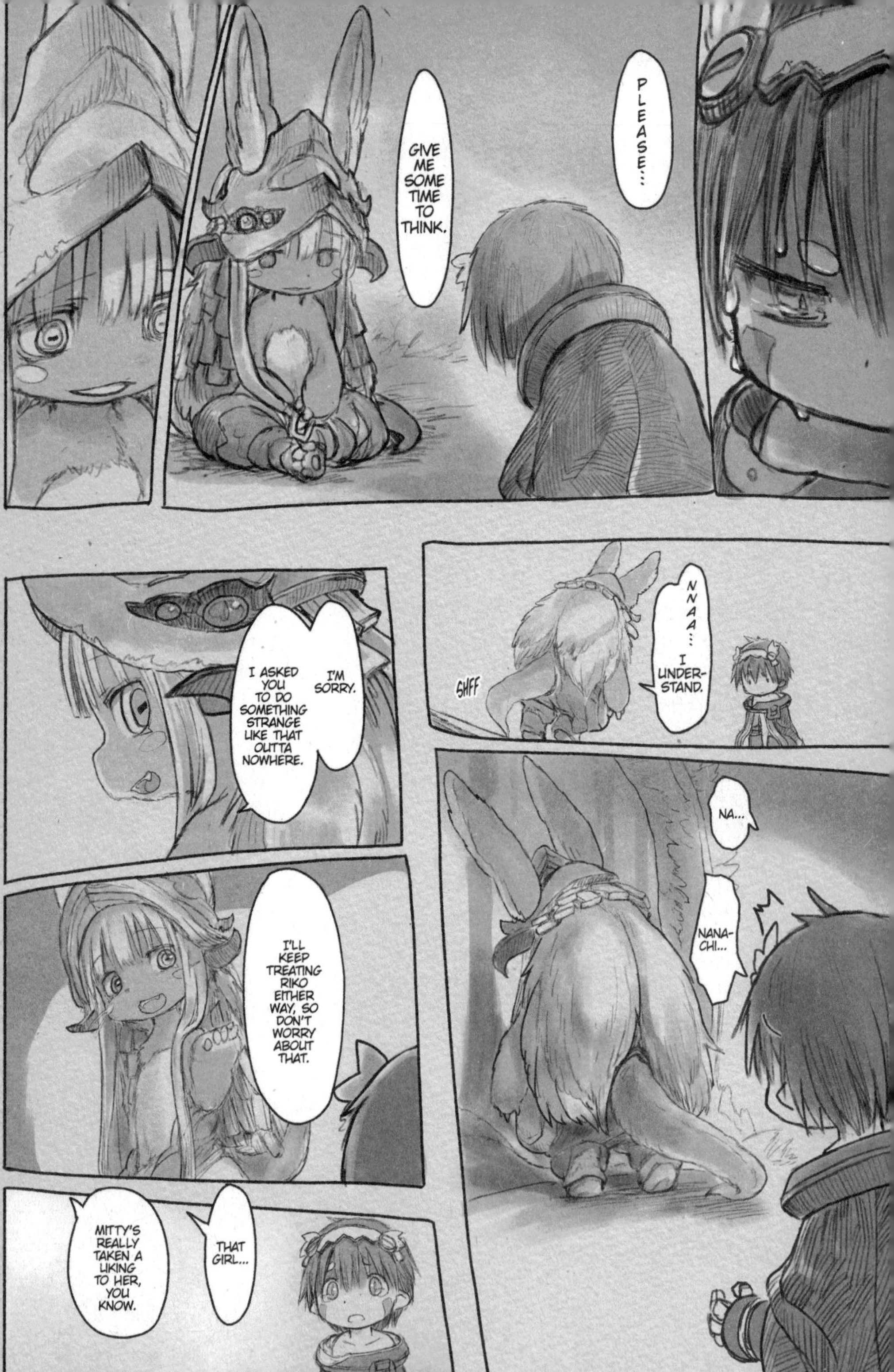
PLEASE...
GIVE ME SOME TIME TO THINK.
NNAA... I UNDERSTAND.
SHFF
I'M SORRY.
I ASKED YOU TO DO SOMETHING STRANGE LIKE THAT OUTTA NOWHERE.
I'LL KEEP TREATING RIKO EITHER WAY, SO DON'T WORRY ABOUT THAT.
THAT GIRL...
MITTY'S REALLY TAKEN A LIKING TO HER, YOU KNOW.
NA...
NANA-CHI...

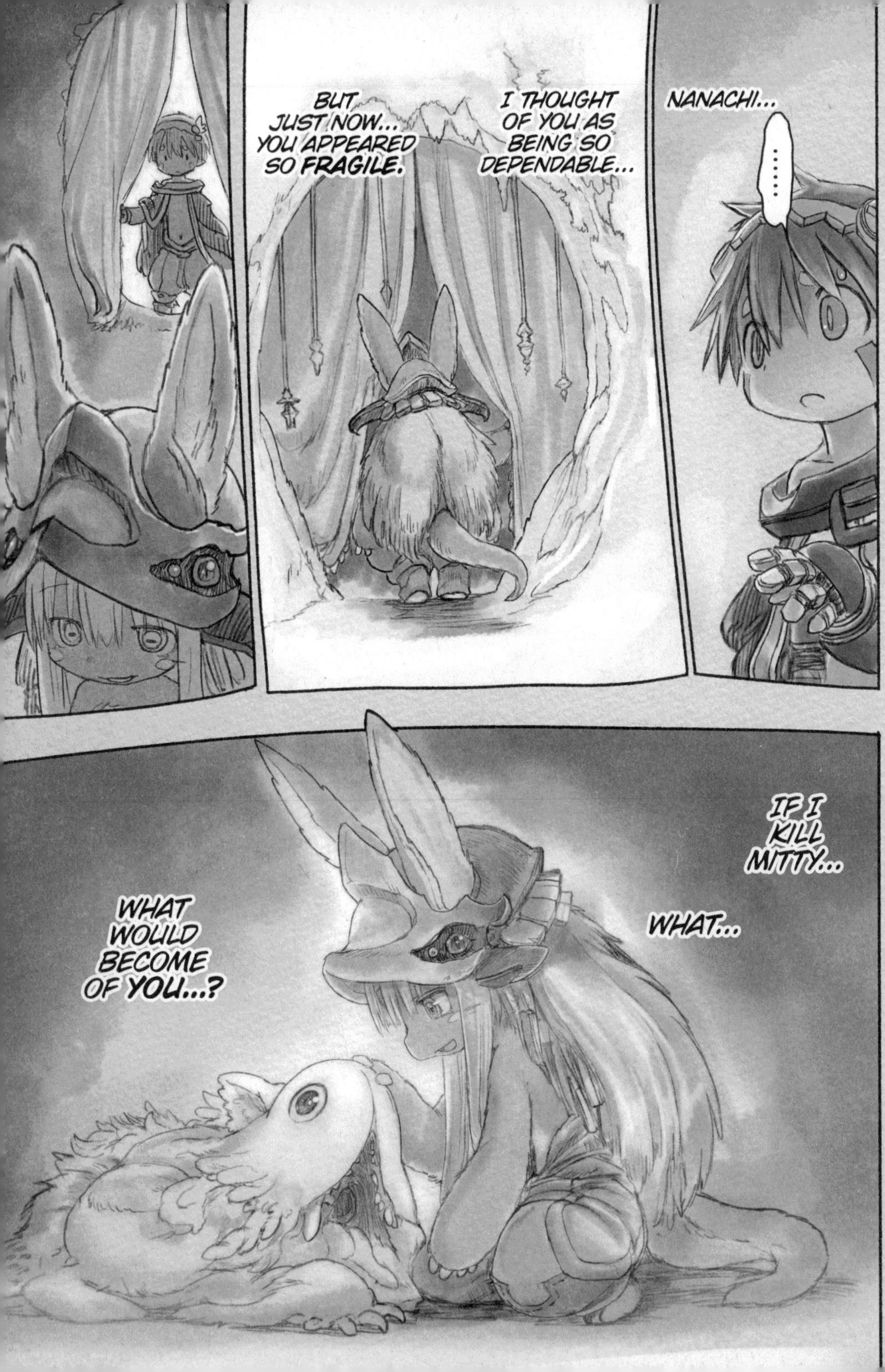
NANACHI...
......
I THOUGHT OF YOU AS BEING SO DEPENDABLE...
BUT JUST NOW... YOU APPEARED SO FRAGILE.
IF I KILL MITTY...
WHAT...
WHAT WOULD BECOME OF YOU...?

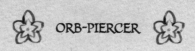 ORB-PIERCER

THIS LARGE PREDATOR INHABITS THE FLAT-CREEPER SPIKE STRETCH IN THE DEPTHS' FOURTH LAYER.

ALTHOUGH IT IS HERBIVOROUS AND EATS THINGS LIKE THE ALGAE GROWING ON THE FLAT-CREEPERS, IT IS EXTREMELY FEROCIOUS IN NATURE. THIS SINGLE SPECIMEN HAS ROBBED NO FEWER THAN A HUNDRED CAVE RAIDERS OF LIFE AND LIMB.

THE SPINES THAT COVER ITS BODY CONTAIN A LETHAL POISON. IN ADDITION, IT POSSESSES INTUITION SO SUPERB IT RESEMBLES PRECOGNITION. AN ORB-PIERCER ALSO HAS FEARSOME EXPLOSIVE POWER THAT REMAINS UNDIMINISHED EVEN WHEN STANDING IN THE WATER. ANY OF THESE ABILITIES IS ENOUGH TO INFLICT FATAL WOUNDS ON WHATEVER WILDLIFE CROSSES ITS PATH, SO IT WOULDN'T BE A MISTAKE TO SAY THIS CREATURE STANDS UNRIVALED IN THE DEPTHS' FOURTH LAYER.

ALTHOUGH THE FLAT-CREEPER SPIKE STRETCH IS A VITAL CAVE-RAIDING ROUTE, THE ORB-PIERCER HAS CLAIMED THE ENTIRE THOUSAND-METER DIAMETER OF IT AS ITS TERRITORY. WHEN PASSING THROUGH, EXERCISE THE UTMOST CAUTION AND PRAY TO THE NETHERWORLD FOR A SAFE CROSSING.

DANGER LEVEL: ★★★★★ (ABSURD)

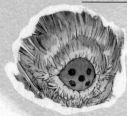

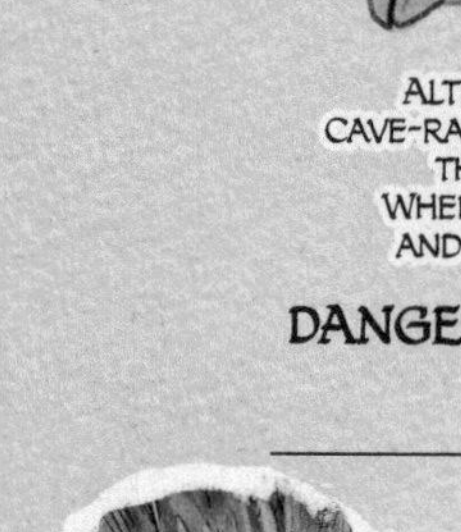

THE ANIMAL WAS ORIGINALLY CALLED A TOKAJISHI. HOWEVER, CAVE RAIDERS BEGAN TO CALL IT AN "ORB-PIERCER," AS IT SIMULTANEOUSLY LAYS WASTE TO BOTH TREASURES (SUCH AS ORB-LIKE JEWELS) AND LIVES (THE ORB-LIKE EYES CLOSE AS THE SOUL LEAVES THE BODY). THE NAME STUCK.

THOSE FIVE HOLES...THE FORCE-FIELD-SENSING ORGAN, IS ITS ONLY WEAKNESS. BUT YOU ESSENTIALLY HAVE NO CHANCE OF TOUCHING IT SINCE THE ORB-PIERCER CAN READ YOUR MOVEMENTS. UNCOUPLE YOUR ACTIONS FROM YOUR CONSCIOUS MIND AND ATTACK WHILE ITS GUARD IS DOWN.

POINTERS FROM NANACHI

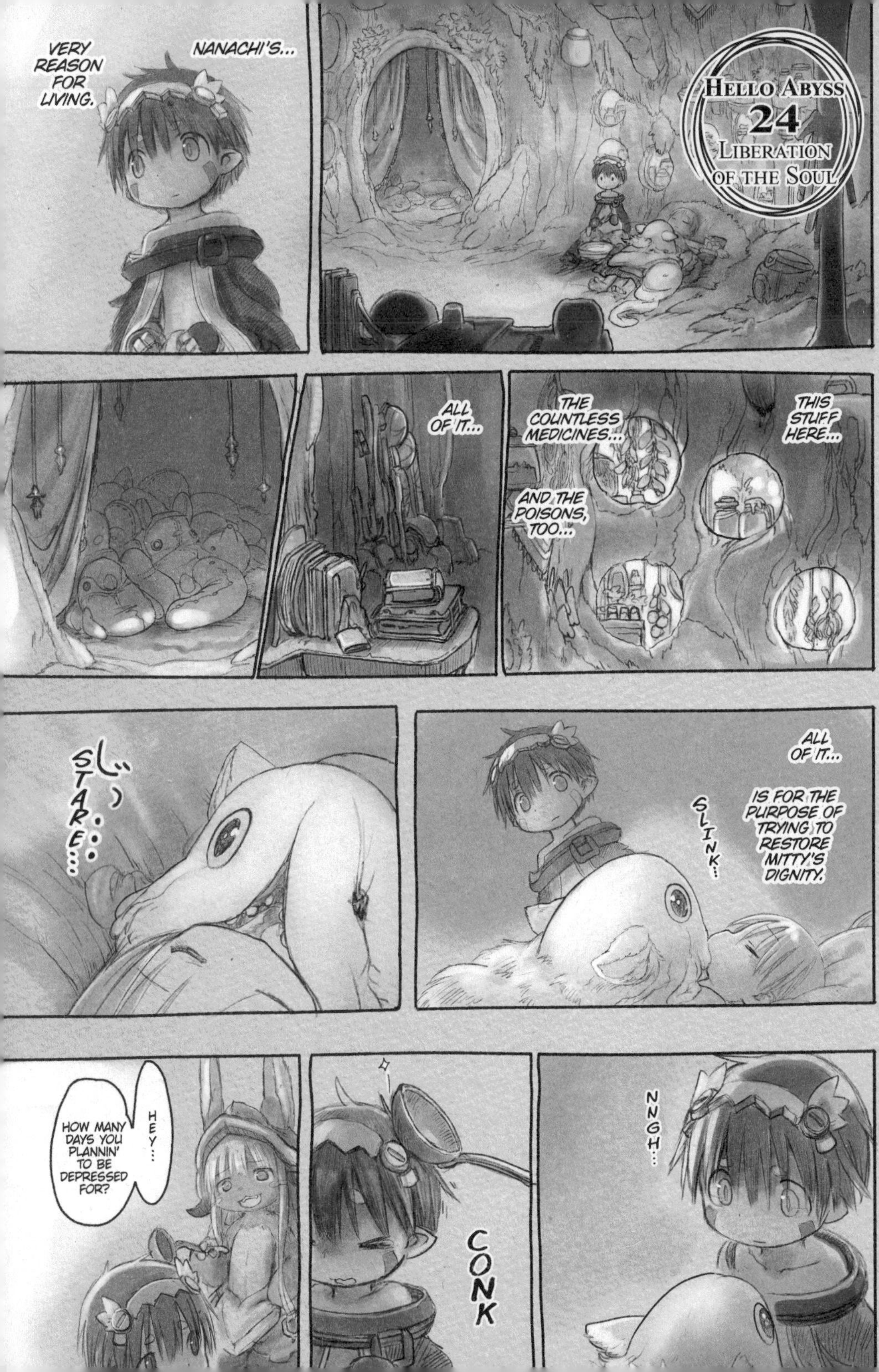
HELLO ABYSS
24
LIBERATION OF THE SOUL
NANACHI'S...
VERY REASON FOR LIVING.
THIS STUFF HERE...
THE COUNTLESS MEDICINES...
AND THE POISONS, TOO...
ALL OF IT...
ALL OF IT...
IS FOR THE PURPOSE OF TRYING TO RESTORE MITTY'S DIGNITY.
SLINK...
じっ
STARE...
NNGH...
CONK
HEY...
HOW MANY DAYS YOU PLANNIN' TO BE DEPRESSED FOR?

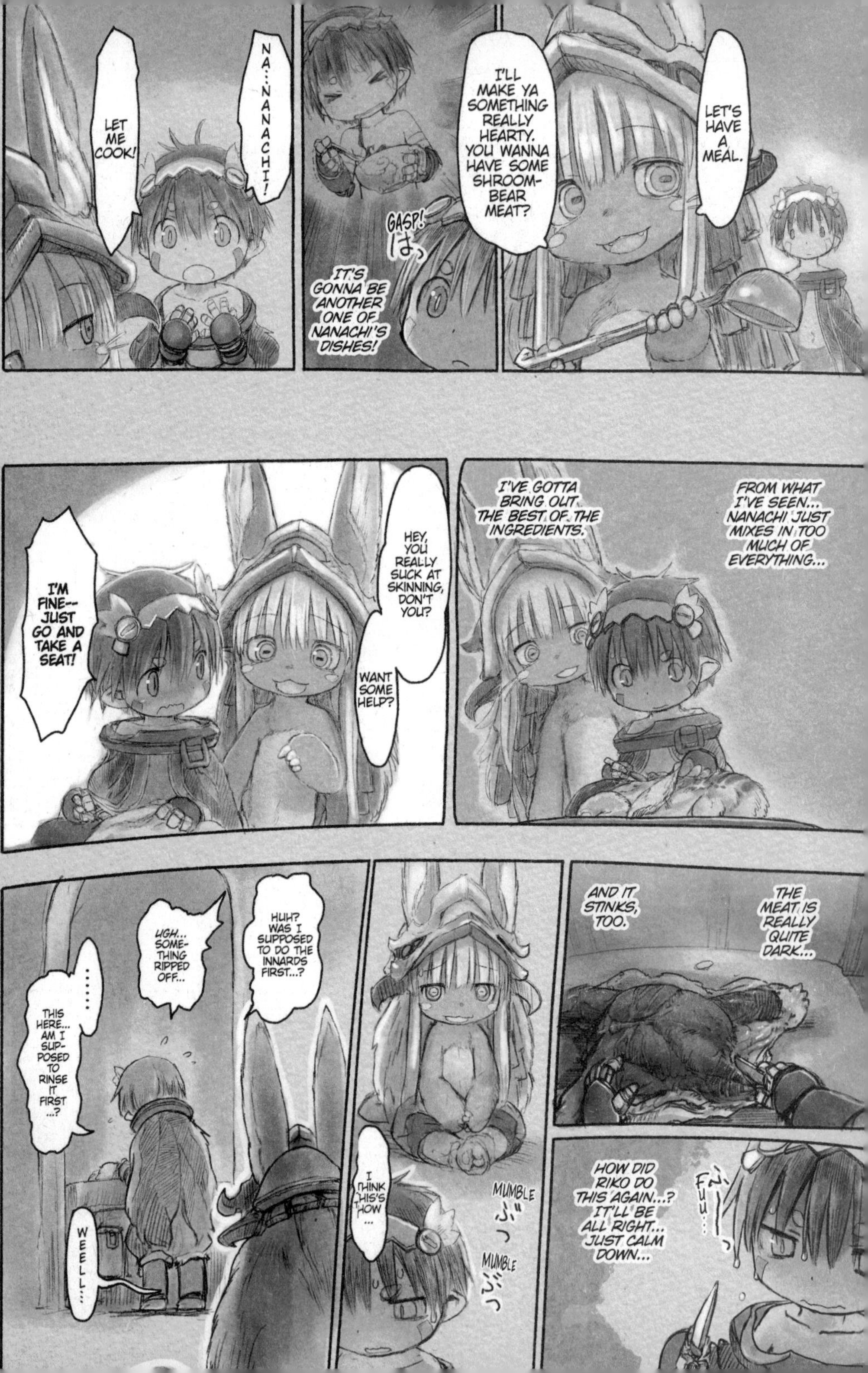

LET'S HAVE A MEAL.
I'LL MAKE YA SOMETHING REALLY HEARTY. YOU WANNA HAVE SOME SHROOM-BEAR MEAT?
GASP! は
IT'S GONNA BE ANOTHER ONE OF NANACHI'S DISHES!
NA...NANACHI!
LET ME COOK!
FROM WHAT I'VE SEEN... NANACHI JUST MIXES IN TOO MUCH OF EVERYTHING...
I'VE GOTTA BRING OUT THE BEST OF THE INGREDIENTS.
HEY, YOU REALLY SUCK AT SKINNING, DON'T YOU?
WANT SOME HELP?
I'M FINE-- JUST GO AND TAKE A SEAT!
THE MEAT IS REALLY QUITE DARK...
AND IT STINKS, TOO.
FUU...
HOW DID RIKO DO THIS AGAIN...? IT'LL BE ALL RIGHT... JUST CALM DOWN...
MUMBLE
MUMBLE
I THINK THIS'S HOW...
HUH? WAS I SUPPOSED TO DO THE INNARDS FIRST...?
UGH... SOMETHING RIPPED OFF...
......
THIS HERE... AM I SUPPOSED TO RINSE IT FIRST...?
WEELL...

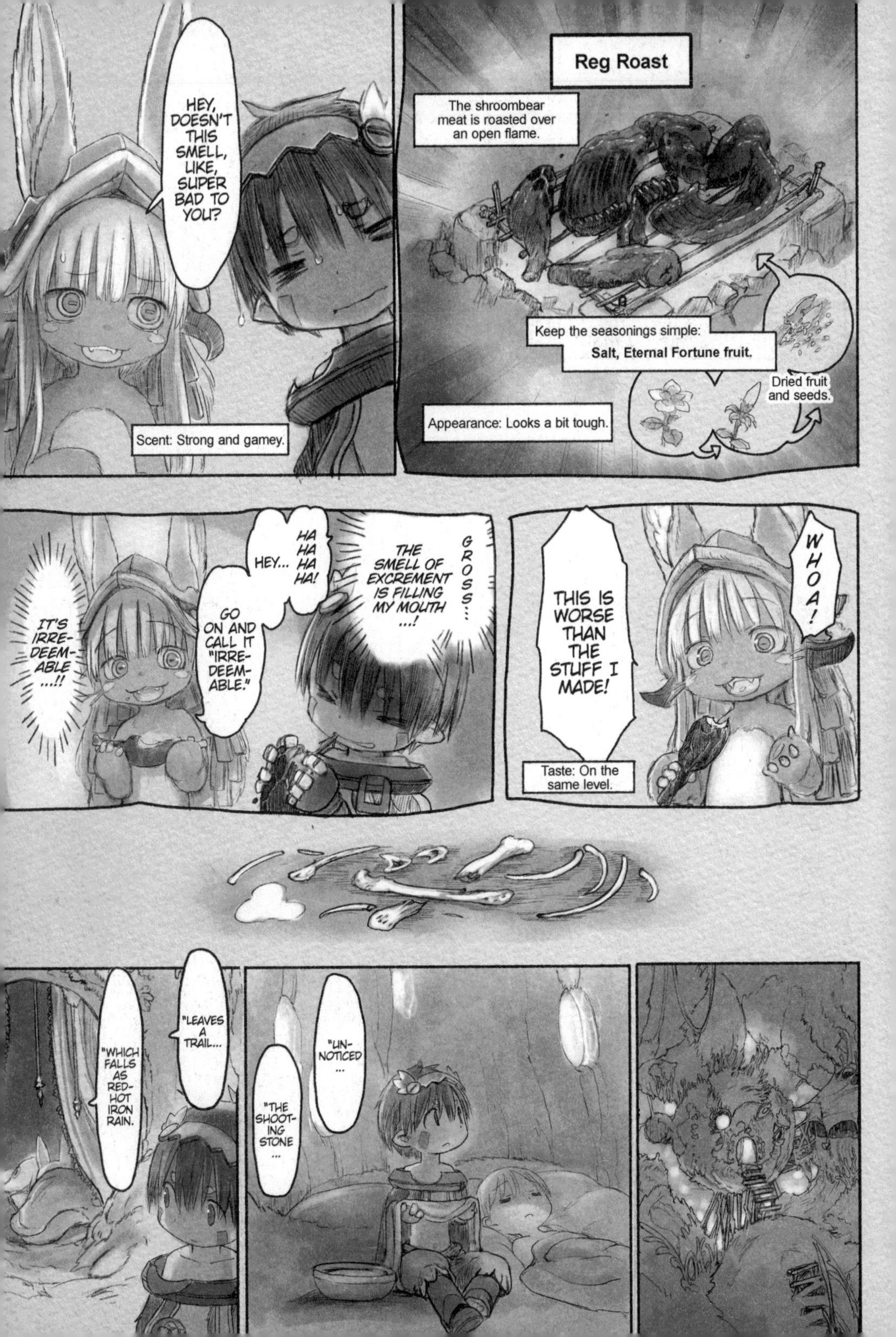
Reg Roast
The shroombear meat is roasted over an open flame.
Keep the seasonings simple:
Salt, Eternal Fortune fruit.
Dried fruit and seeds.
Appearance: Looks a bit tough.
HEY, DOESN'T THIS SMELL, LIKE, SUPER BAD TO YOU?
Scent: Strong and gamey.
WHOA!
THIS IS WORSE THAN THE STUFF I MADE!
Taste: On the same level.
GROSS...
THE SMELL OF EXCREMENT IS FILLING MY MOUTH...!
HA HA HA HA!
HEY...
GO ON AND CALL IT "IRREDEEMABLE."
IT'S IRREDEEMABLE...!!
"UNNOTICED...
"THE SHOOTING STONE...
"LEAVES A TRAIL...
"WHICH FALLS AS RED-HOT IRON RAIN.

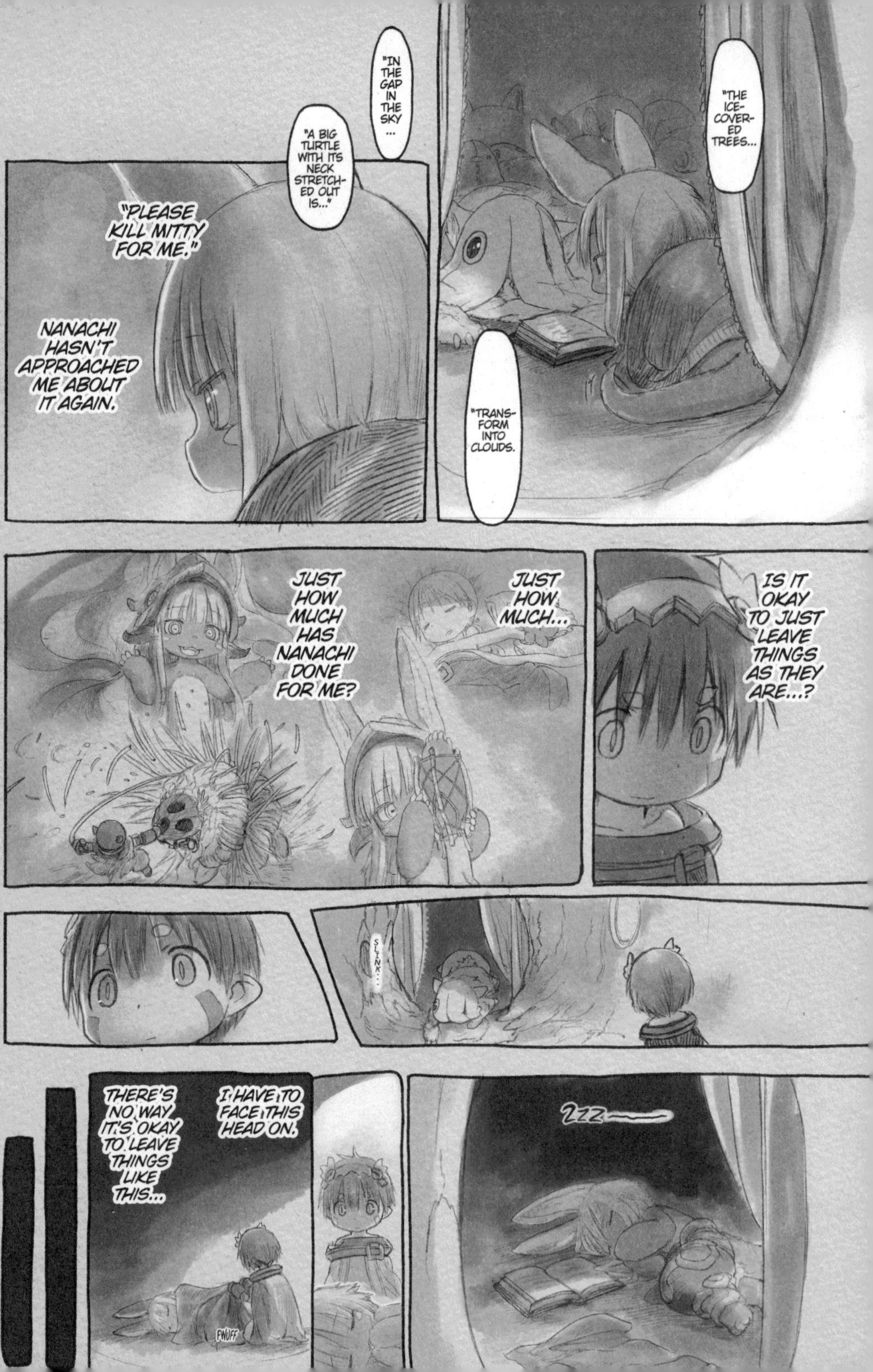
"THE ICE-COVERED TREES...
"IN THE GAP IN THE SKY...
"A BIG TURTLE WITH ITS NECK STRETCHED OUT IS..."
"TRANSFORM INTO CLOUDS.
"PLEASE KILL MITTY FOR ME."
NANACHI HASN'T APPROACHED ME ABOUT IT AGAIN.
IS IT OKAY TO JUST LEAVE THINGS AS THEY ARE...?
JUST HOW MUCH...
JUST HOW MUCH HAS NANACHI DONE FOR ME?
SLINK...
ZZZ——
I HAVE TO FACE THIS HEAD ON.
THERE'S NO WAY IT'S OKAY TO LEAVE THINGS LIKE THIS...
FWUFF

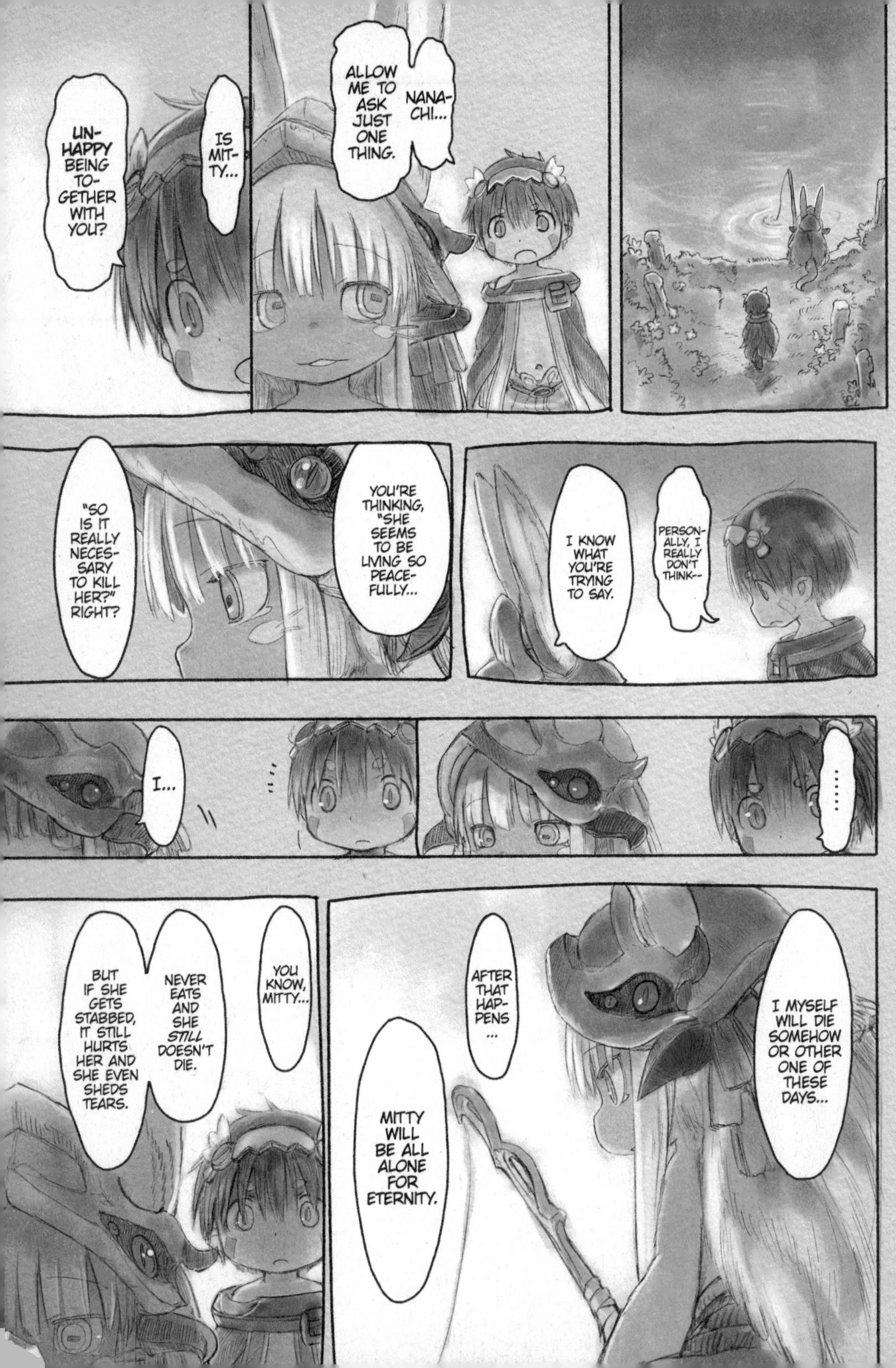
NANACHI...
ALLOW ME TO ASK JUST ONE THING.
IS MITTY...
UNHAPPY BEING TOGETHER WITH YOU?
PERSONALLY, I REALLY DON'T THINK--
I KNOW WHAT YOU'RE TRYING TO SAY.
YOU'RE THINKING, "SHE SEEMS TO BE LIVING SO PEACEFULLY...
"SO IS IT REALLY NECESSARY TO KILL HER?" RIGHT?
......
I...
I MYSELF WILL DIE SOMEHOW OR OTHER ONE OF THESE DAYS...
AFTER THAT HAPPENS...
MITTY WILL BE ALL ALONE FOR ETERNITY.
YOU KNOW, MITTY...
NEVER EATS AND SHE *STILL* DOESN'T DIE.
BUT IF SHE GETS STABBED, IT STILL HURTS HER AND SHE EVEN SHEDS TEARS.

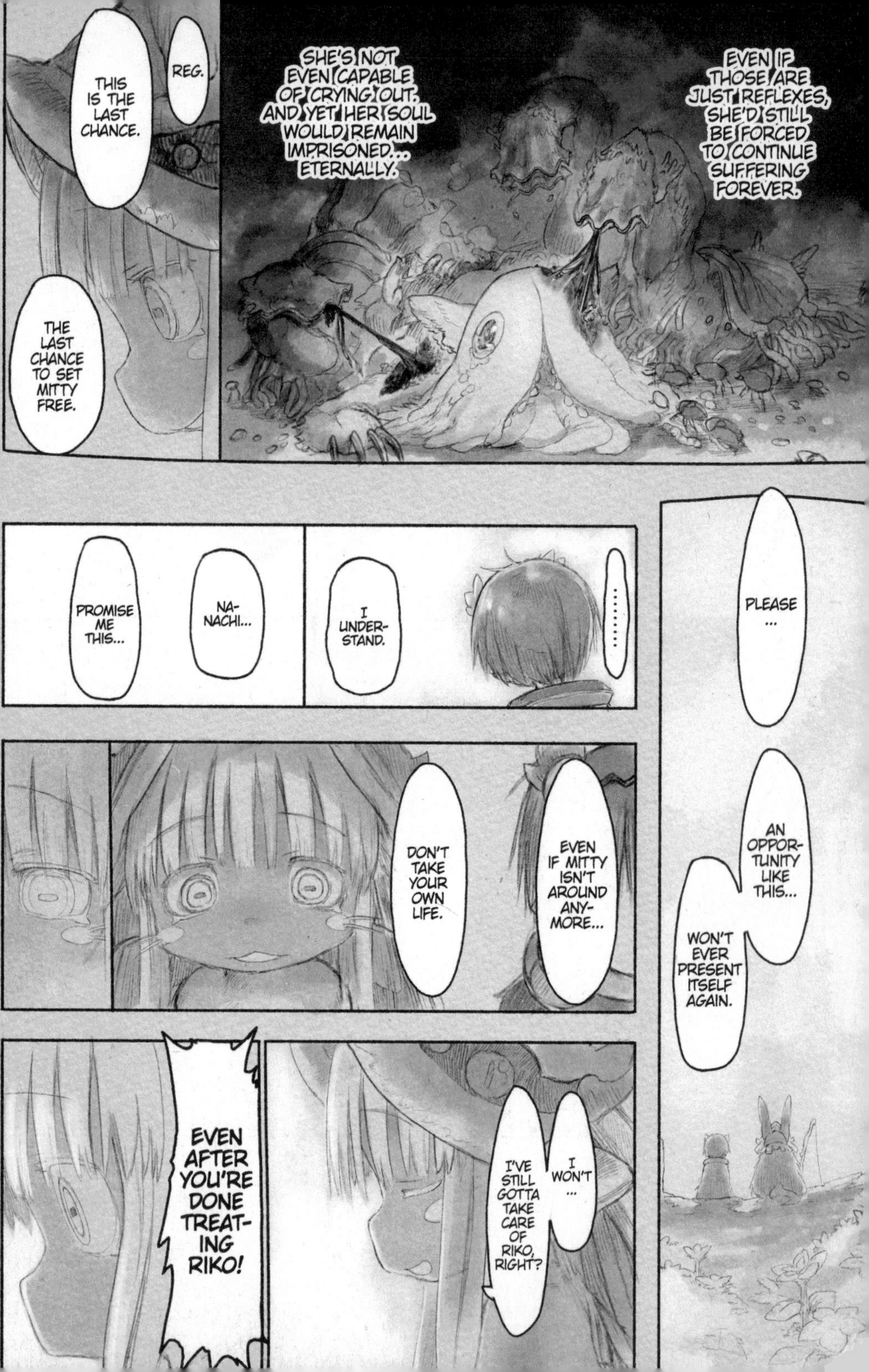
EVEN IF THOSE ARE JUST REFLEXES, SHE'D STILL BE FORCED TO CONTINUE SUFFERING FOREVER.
SHE'S NOT EVEN CAPABLE OF CRYING OUT. AND YET HER SOUL WOULD REMAIN IMPRISONED... ETERNALLY.
REG.
THIS IS THE LAST CHANCE.
THE LAST CHANCE TO SET MITTY FREE.
PLEASE...
AN OPPORTUNITY LIKE THIS...
WON'T EVER PRESENT ITSELF AGAIN.
......
I UNDERSTAND.
NA-NACHI...
PROMISE ME THIS...
EVEN IF MITTY ISN'T AROUND ANYMORE...
DON'T TAKE YOUR OWN LIFE.
I WON'T...
I'VE STILL GOTTA TAKE CARE OF RIKO, RIGHT?
EVEN AFTER YOU'RE DONE TREATING RIKO!

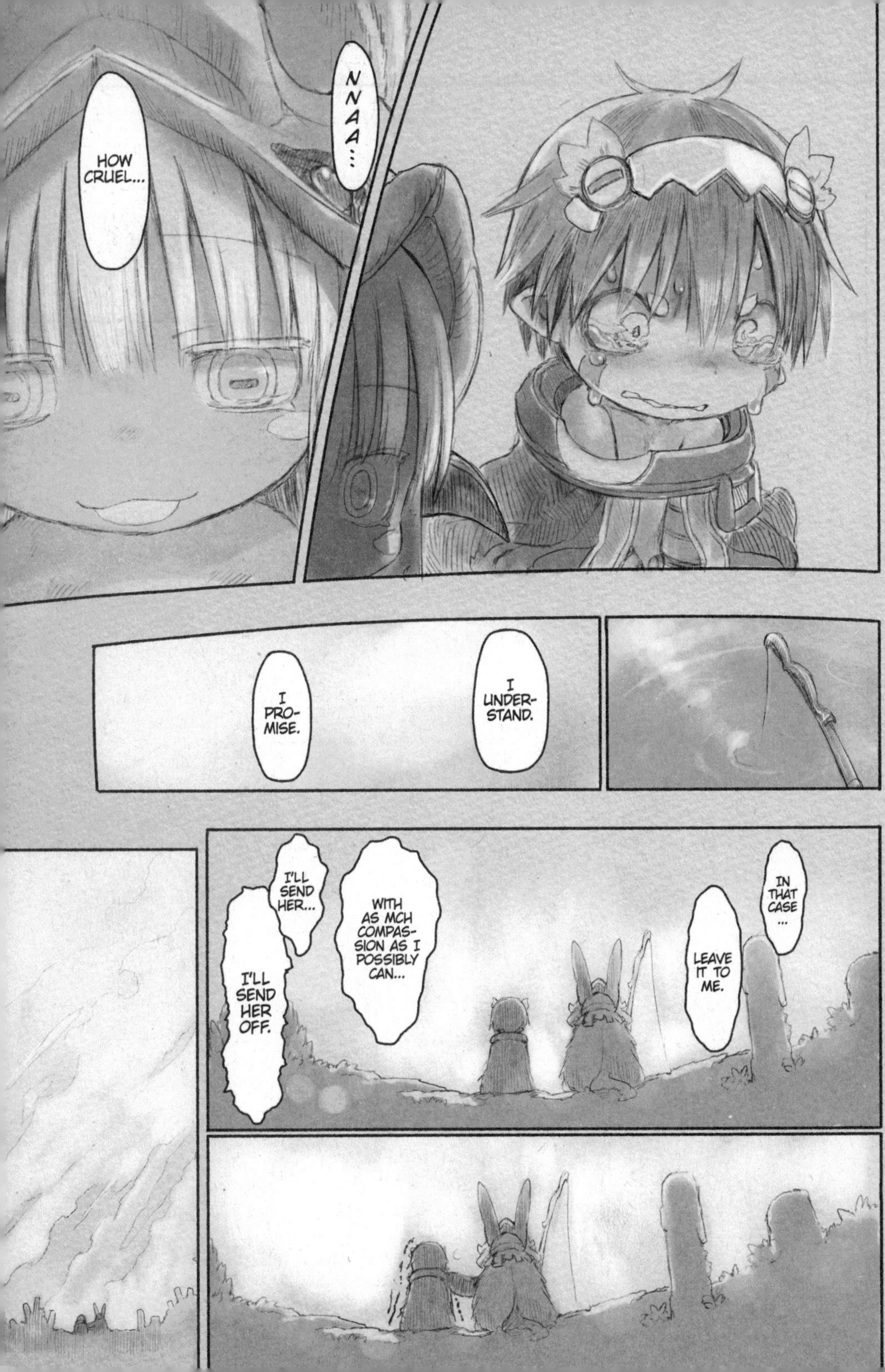
NNAA...
HOW CRUEL...
I UNDER-STAND.
I PRO-MISE.
IN THAT CASE ...
LEAVE IT TO ME.
WITH AS MCH COMPAS-SION AS I POSSIBLY CAN...
I'LL SEND HER...
I'LL SEND HER OFF.

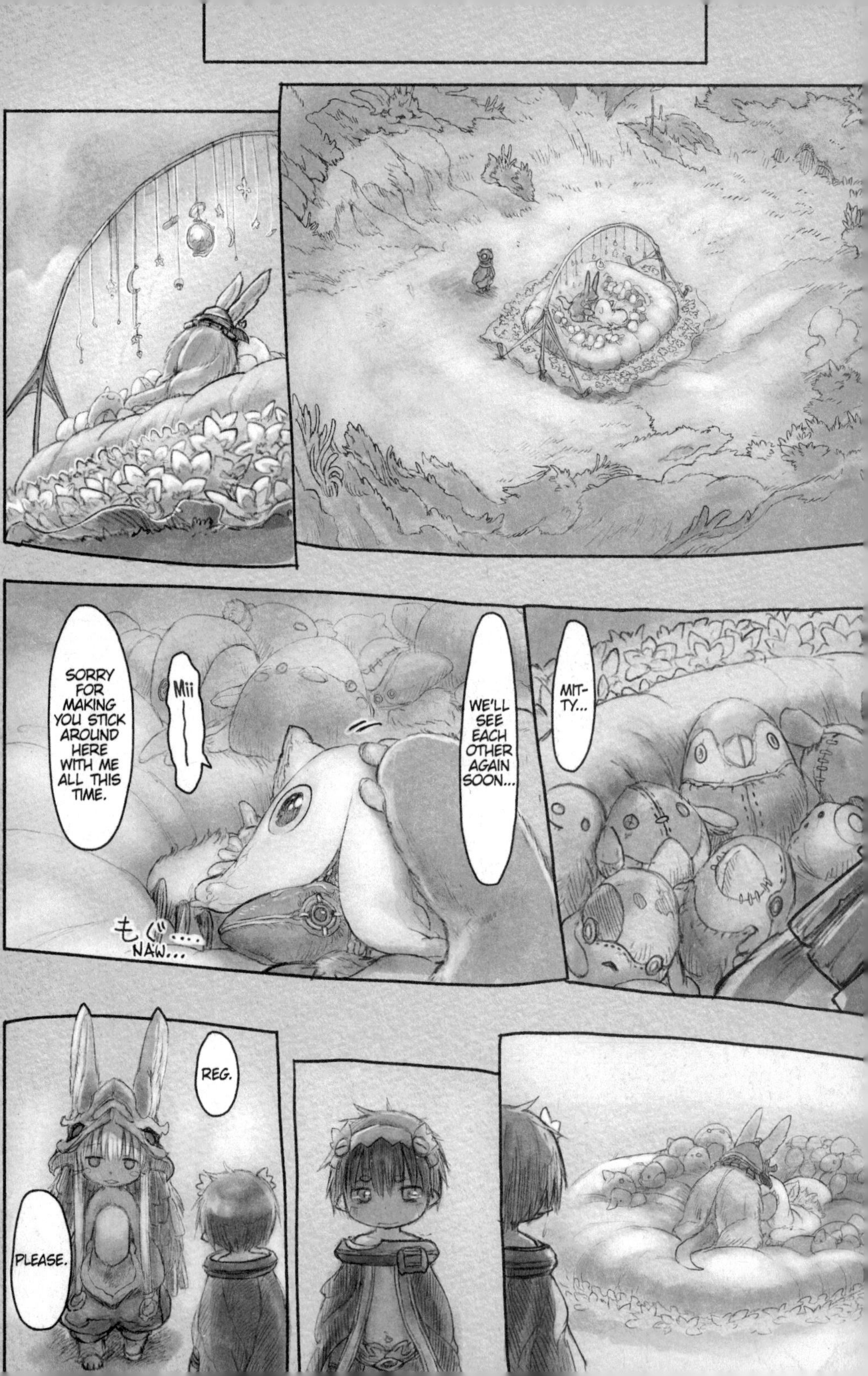
MIT-TY...
WE'LL SEE EACH OTHER AGAIN SOON...
Mii ―
SORRY FOR MAKING YOU STICK AROUND HERE WITH ME ALL THIS TIME.
もぐ…
NAW...
REG.
PLEASE.

CHAK っ

PLEASE MAY...

PLEASE...

Naa

NAW

NAW

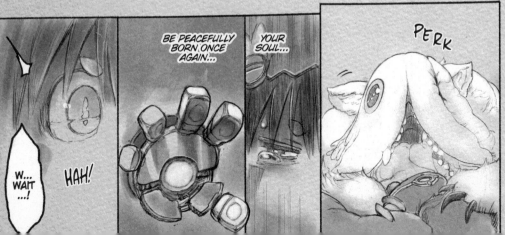

BE PEACEFULLY
BORN ONCE
AGAIN...

YOUR
SOUL...

PERK

W...
WAIT
...!

HAH!

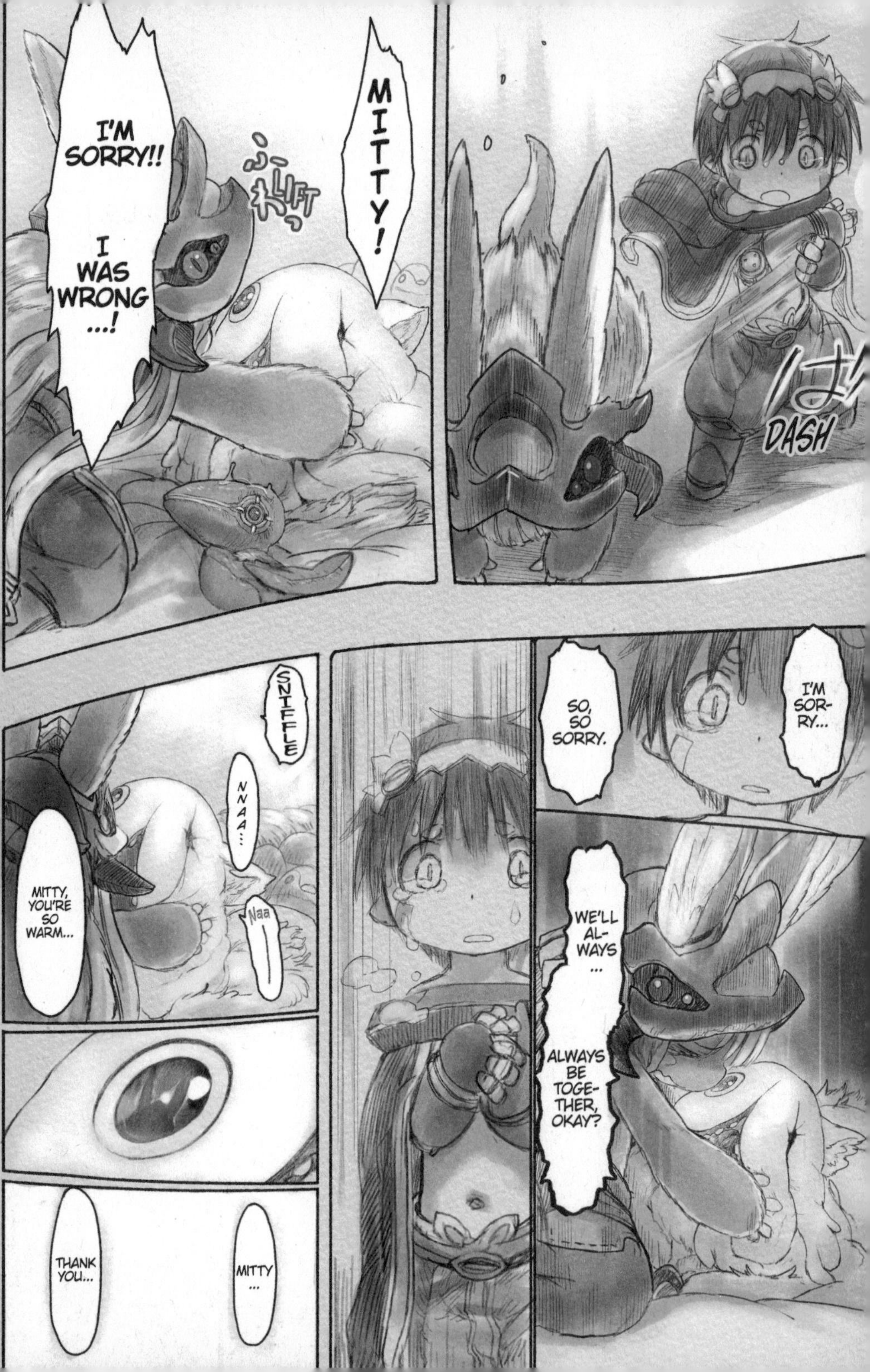
DASH
MITTY!
LIFT
I'M SORRY!!
I WAS WRONG...!
I'M SORRY...
SO, SO SORRY.
WE'LL ALWAYS...
ALWAYS BE TOGETHER, OKAY?
SNIFFLE
NNAAA...
MITTY, YOU'RE SO WARM...
Naa
MITTY...
THANK YOU...

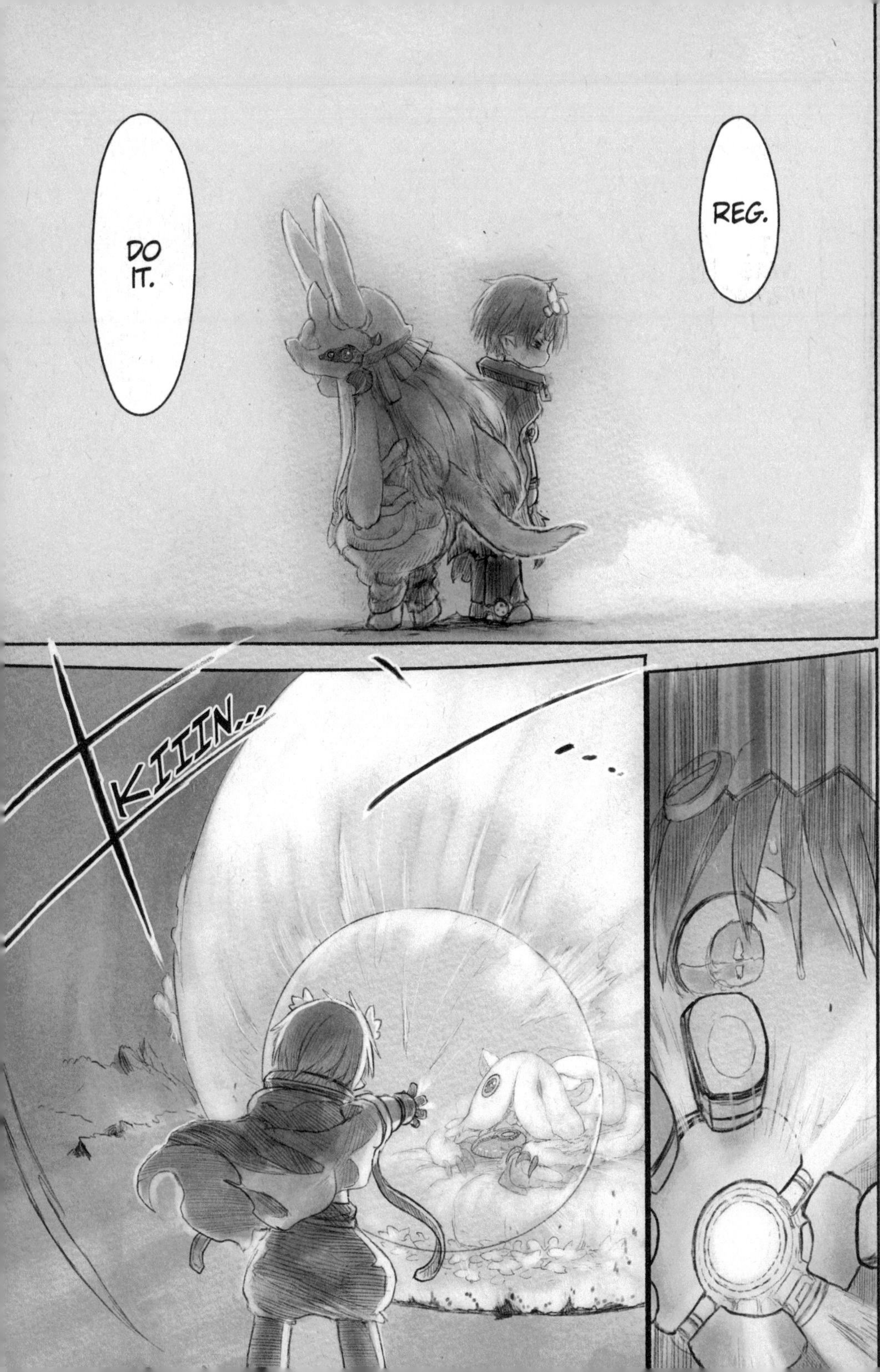
REG.
DO IT.
KIIIN...

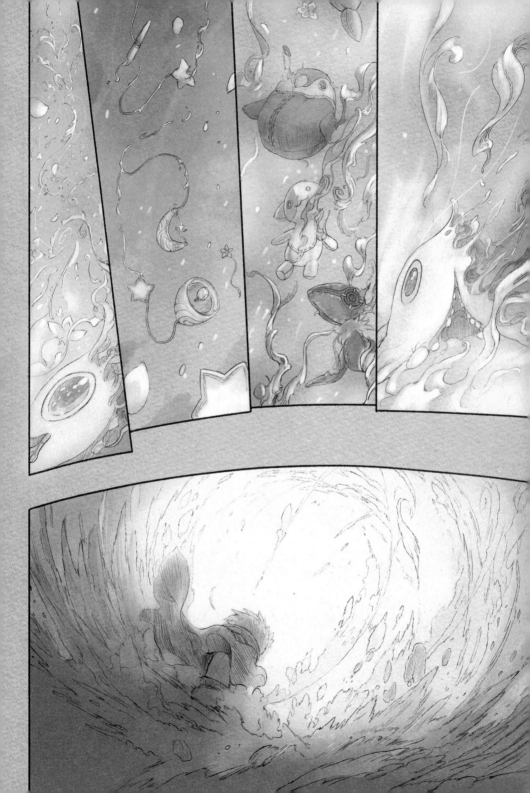

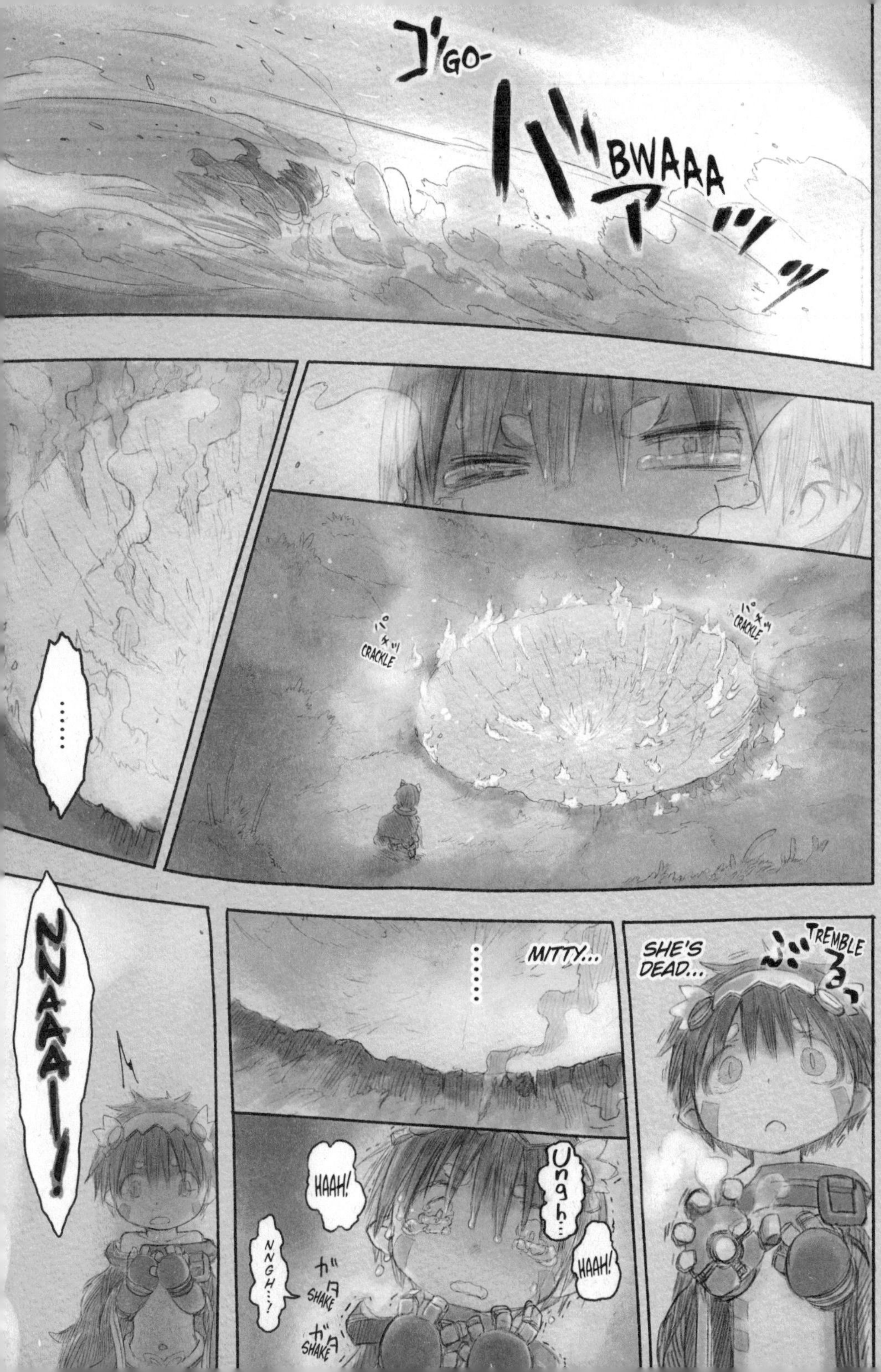
ゴ GO-
バァッ BWAAA
パチッ CRACKLE
パチッ CRACKLE
......
SHE'S DEAD...
ぶる TREMBLE
......
MITTY...
Ungh...
HAAH!
HAAH!
NNGH...?
ガタ SHAKE
ガタ SHAKE
NNAAA!!

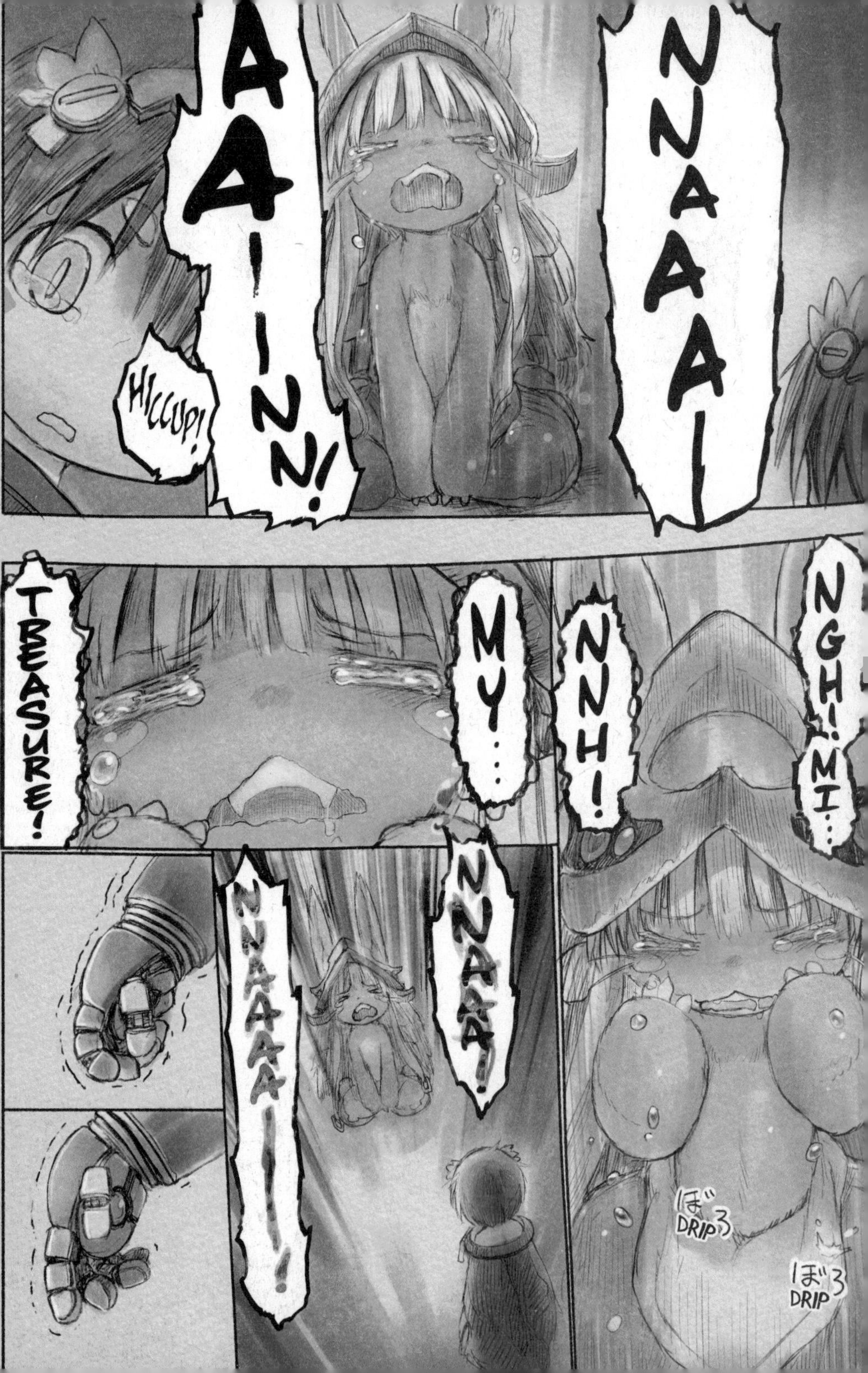
NNAAA—
AA-INN!
HICCUP!
NGH! MI...
NNH!
MY...
TREASURE!
ぼろ DRIP
ぼろ DRIP
NNAAA!
NNAAAAA—!

HUG
ST...
STOP IT...!
NNAAA--!!
HICCUP!
NNAA--!
HIC COUGH
NNAAA--N!
NNAA--ANN!
OH?
IT SEEMS HER SIGNATURE HAS DISAPPEARED.

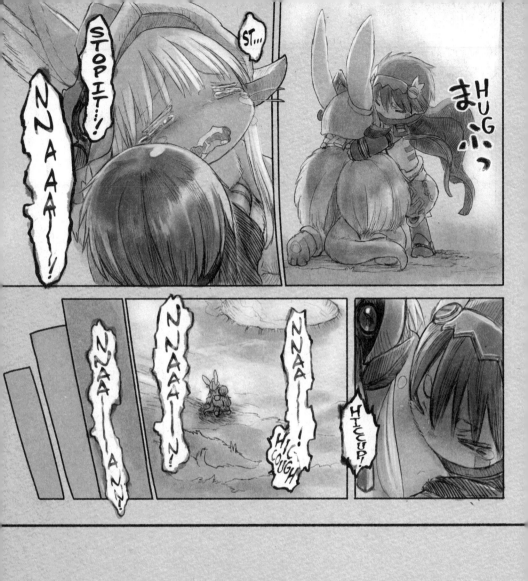

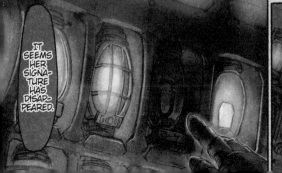

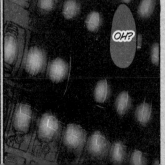

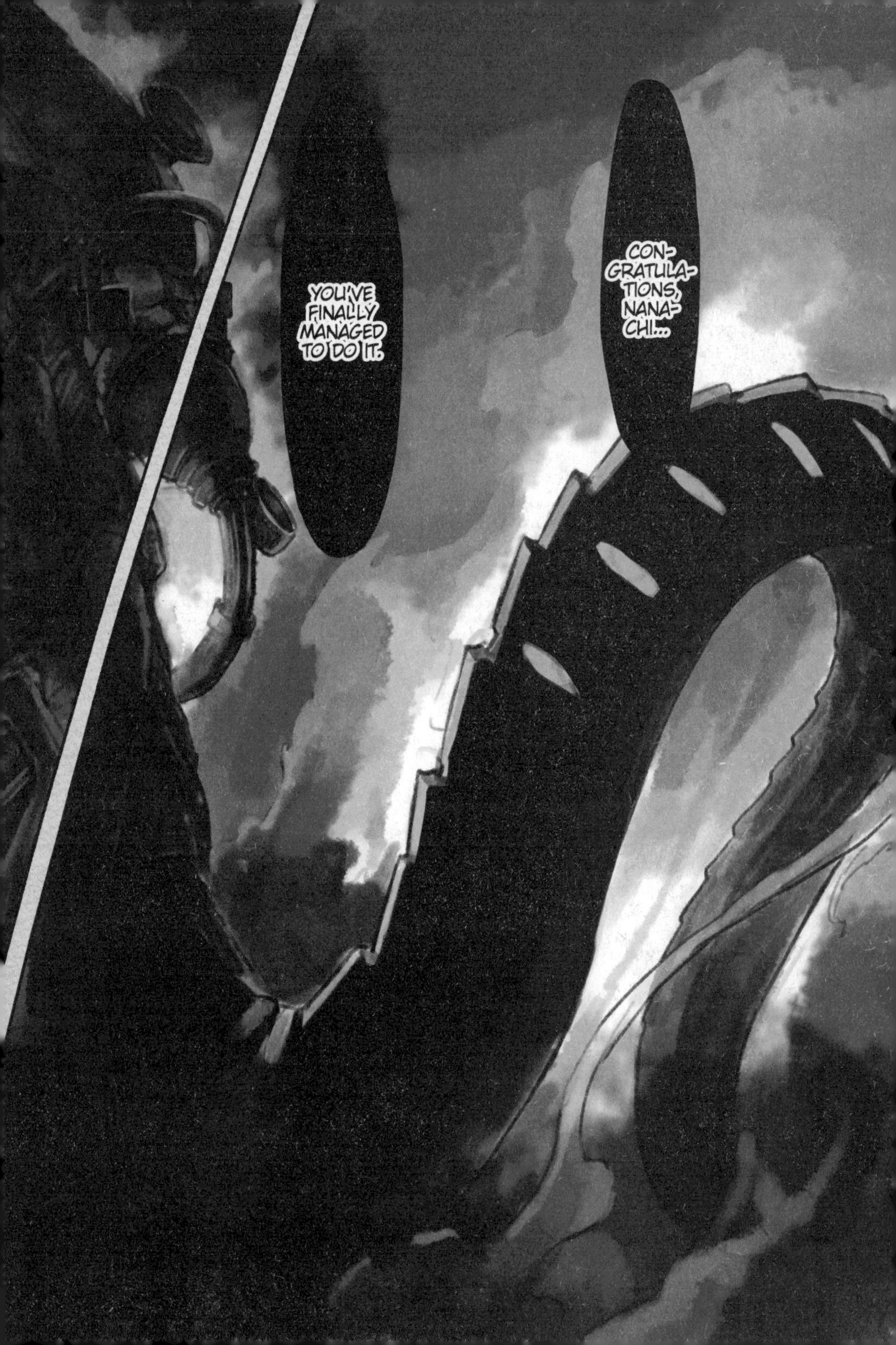
CON-GRATULA-TIONS, NANA-CHI...
YOU'VE FINALLY MANAGED TO DO IT.

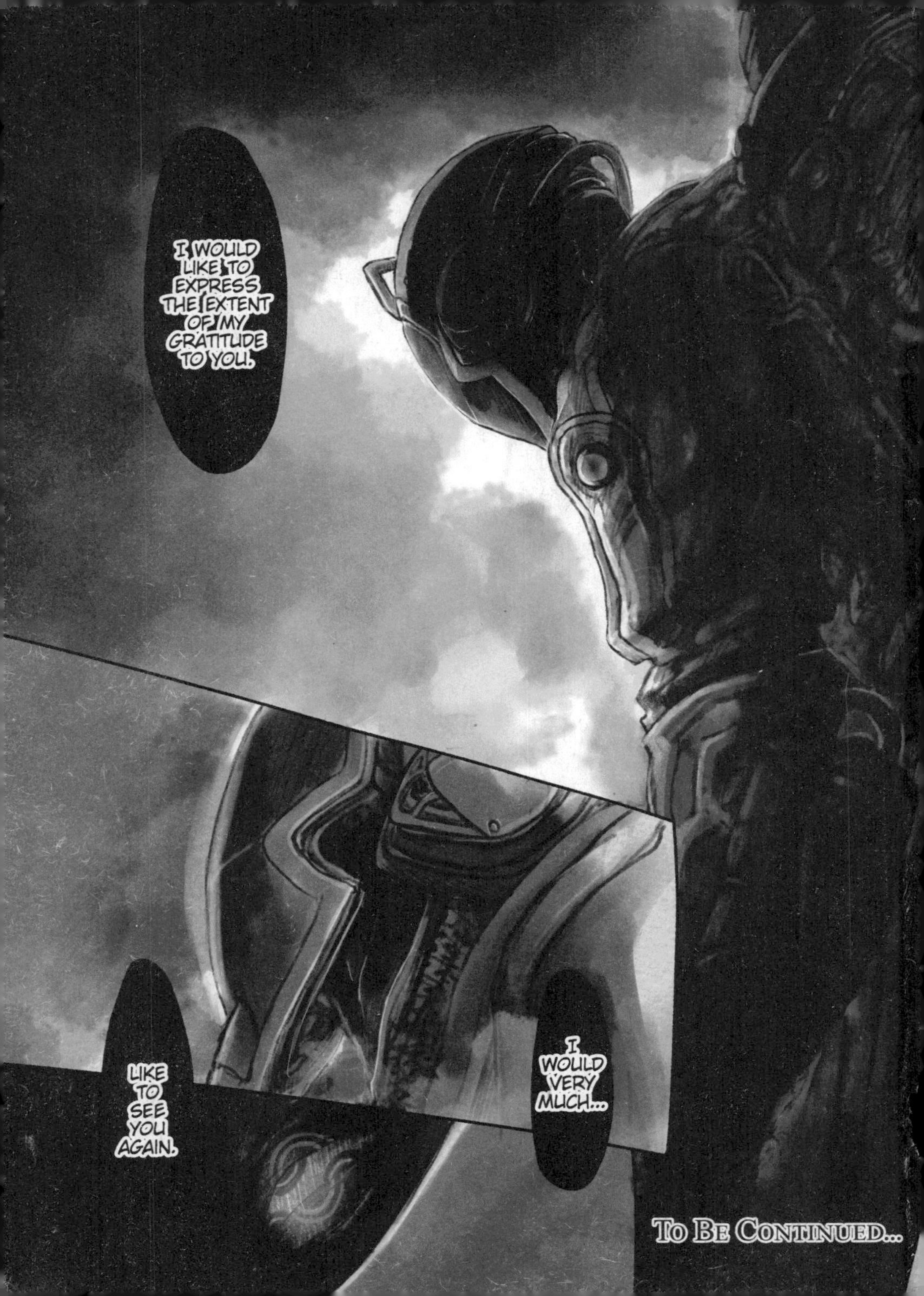
I WOULD LIKE TO EXPRESS THE EXTENT OF MY GRATITUDE TO YOU.
I WOULD VERY MUCH...
LIKE TO SEE YOU AGAIN.
TO BE CONTINUED...

SEVEN SEAS ENTERTAINMENT PRESENTS

MADE IN ABYSS

story and art by AKIHITO TSUKUSHI   VOLUME 3

TRANSLATION
Beni Axia Conrad

ADAPTATION
Jake Jung

LETTERING AND RETOUCH
James Gaubatz

LOGO DESIGN
Andrea Rodriguez

COVER DESIGN
Nicky Lim

PROOFREADER
Shanti Whitesides
Danielle King

EDITOR
Jenn Grunigen

PRODUCTION ASSISTANT
CK Russell

PRODUCTION MANAGER
Lissa Pattillo

EDITOR-IN-CHIEF
Adam Arnold

PUBLISHER
Jason DeAngelis

MADE IN ABYSS VOLUME 3
©Akihito Tsukushi/TAKE SHOBO
Originally published in Japan in 2015 by Takeshobo Co. LTD., Tokyo.
English translation rights arranged with Takeshobo Co. LTD., Tokyo,
through TOHAN CORPORATION, Tokyo.

Seven Seas books may be purchased in bulk for promotional, educational, or
business use. Please contact your local bookseller or the Macmillan Corporate
and Premium Sales Department at 1-800-221-7945, extension 5442, or by
e-mail at MacmillanSpecialMarkets@macmillan.com.

Seven Seas and the Seven Seas logo are trademarks of
Seven Seas Entertainment, LLC. All rights reserved.

ISBN: 978-1-626928-27-5

Printed in Canada

First Printing: July 2018

10 9 8 7 6 5 4 3 2 1

FOLLOW US ONLINE: *www.sevenseasentertainment.com*

READING DIRECTIONS

This book reads from *right to left*, Japanese style. If
this is your first time reading manga, you start
reading from the top right panel on each page and
take it from there. If you get lost, just follow the
numbered diagram here. It may seem backwards at
first, but you'll get the hang of it! Have fun!!

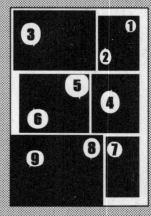